THE AGE OF KNOWLEDGE

Studies in Critical Social Sciences Book Series

Haymarket Books is proud to be working with Brill Academic Publishers (www. brill.nl) to republish the *Studies in Critical Social Sciences* book series in paperback editions. This peer-reviewed book series offers insights into our current reality by exploring the content and consequences of power relationships under capitalism, and by considering the spaces of opposition and resistance to these changes that have been defining our new age. Our full catalog of *SCSS* volumes can be viewed at www.haymarketbooks.org/category/scss-series.

THE AGE OF KNOWLEDGE

THE DYNAMICS OF UNIVERSITIES, KNOWLEDGE, AND SOCIETY

Edited by
JAMES DZISAH
HENRY ETZKOWITZ

Haymarket
Books
Chicago, IL

First published in 2012 by Brill Academic Publishers, The Netherlands.
© 2012 Koninklijke Brill NV, Leiden, The Netherlands

Published in paperback in 2013 by
Haymarket Books
P.O. Box 180165
Chicago, IL 60618
773-583-7884
www.haymarketbooks.org

ISBN: 978-1-60846-241-4

Trade distribution:
In the U.S. through Consortium Book Sales, www.cbsd.com
In the UK, Turnaround Publisher Services, www.turnaround-psl.com
In Australia, Palgrave Macmillan, www.palgravemacmillan.com.au
In all other countries by Publishers Group Worldwide, www.pgw.com

Cover design by Ragina Johnson.

This book was published with the generous support of Lannan Foundation
and the Wallace Global Fund.

Printed in Canada by union labor on recycled paper containing 100 percent
postconsumer waste in accordance with the guidelines of the Green Press Initiative,
www.greenpressinitiative.org.

10 9 8 7 6 5 4 3 2 1

Library of Congress Cataloging-in-Publication Data is available.

For
William K. Dzisah
Alex Etzkowitz
Justin Sedem Dzisah
Jayden Selasi Dzisah

CONTENTS

PART I

KNOWLEDGE, GLOBALIZATION AND IDENTITY

PART II

KNOWLEDGE INNOVATION, GOVERNANCE AND POLICY

PART III

UNIVERSITIES, INTERMEDIATE ACTORS AND THE KNOWLEDGE ECONOMY

LIST OF TABLES AND FIGURES

Tables

Figure

ACKNOWLEDGEMENTS

This book owes its existence to the foresight and encouragement of Professor David Fasenfest. He saw life beyond the margins of selected *special issue* articles we were putting together for the Journal of *Critical Sociology* which he edits. While the project has grown beyond its original scope, we remain ever grateful to David for those initial nudges. We are equally grateful for the opportunity to work with outstanding colleagues and contributors who pressed ahead in the midst of competing academic, personal and social life demands. The anonymous reviewers deserve great thanks for their diligence, time and critical comments.

Our deepest and sincere thanks go to our families and friends for keeping us grounded and focused on the task at hand so that we can get back to the 'normal' routines in which they are front and centre. We thank our respective institutions—Nipissing University and Human Sciences Advanced Research Institute at the Stanford University (H-STAR)—and colleagues for ensuring that we work within collegial and enabling environments. We wish to express our appreciation to Prof. Loet Leydesdorff, Prof. Jose Mello, Prof. Riccardo Viale, Dr. Marina Ranga, Dr. Marcelo Amaral, Dr. Chuyan Zhou, Dr. Devrim Göktepe-Hultén, Prof. Peter S. Li, Dr. Greg Brown, Dr. Trevor Smith, Dr. Amir Erfani, Dr. Ellie Berger, Dr. David Zarifa, Dr. Uldis Kundrats and Christina DeRoche for their friendship, support and collegiality. Warm regards to Nestor Hlynsky, G.B. Ashiagbor and George Gana.

NOTES ON CONTRIBUTORS

ZAHEER BABER is Professor of Sociology at the University of Toronto. He is the author of The Science of Empire (Albany: State University of New York Press, 1996), Secularism, Communalism and the Intellectuals (New Delhi: Three Essays, 2005) and the editor of CyberAsia (Leiden: Brill, 2006). Currently he is involved in research on the racialization of 'communal conflict in India' as well as the relationship between botanical gardens, the British Empire and the emergence of Botany as a science.

WILLIAM BOATENG is an Assistant Professor and Faculty Program Coordinator with the Department of Community Development and Health Sciences, the First Nations University of Canada, Northern Campus—Prince Albert. He holds a PhD in Sociology from the University of Saskatchewan, specializing in Sociology of Applied Knowledge and Health. His current areas of research interest include knowledge management in organizational decision-making. Recent publications in peer reviewed journals emanating from his studies include Knowledge Management in Evidence-Based Medical Practice: Does the Patient Matter? Knowledge Production in Contemporary African Society: Lessons for Universities; Knowledge Management Working Tool for Agricultural Extension Practice: The Case of Ghana; and Research Alternative for Nursing Practice: A Sociological Perspective.

CHOONLEE CHAI is Assistant Professor at the Red Deer College, Canada. His research and teaching revolves around issues of Science, Technology and Society.

HARLEY D. DICKINSON is a Professor and Vice-Dean, Social Sciences, College of Arts & Science, University of Saskatchewan. He has also served for five years as Head of the Department of Sociology, as well as several years as Director of the Social Research Unit. Dickinson completed his Ph.D. in Sociology at Lancaster University in the United Kingdom. He joined the University of Saskatchewan as an Assistant Professor of Sociology in 1983, granted tenure in 1985 and promoted to the rank of full professor in 1991.

JAMES DZISAH is an Assistant Professor of Sociology at Nipissing University. He was formerly an Assistant Professor of Sociology at the University of Saskatchewan and Research Associate in Innovation at the Newcastle University Business School, England. He is a member of the Editorial Board of *International Journal of Technology and Globalisation* and the Triple Helix International Scientific Committee. His main areas of research include: Science, Technology and Society, Triple Helix, Development and Policy.

PATIENCE ELABOR-IDEMUDIA is currently a Professor and Chair of Graduate Studies in the Department of Sociology at the University of Saskatchewan where she has been teaching and researching since 1995. Her research focused on Immigrant Women in Canada, Minorities in the Academy, Social Construction of Knowledge and Human Trafficking in Australia and West Africa. She served as the Chief Technical Adviser for the International Labor Organization's Special Action Programme to Combat Human Trafficking in West Africa from January 2005 to June 2006. She is the author of over 30 journal articles, monographs, book chapters, and technical reports among which are: "Immigrant Integration in Canada: Programs and Challenges"(2005), in Carl James (ed.), Possibilities and Limitations: Multicultural Policies and Programs in Canada. Halifax: Fernwood Books, pp. 58–74; "Participatory Research: A Tool in the Production of Knowledge in Development Discourse" (2002), in Kriemild Saunders (ed.) Feminist Post-Development Thought: Rethinking Modernity, Post-Colonialism and Representation. London: Zed Publishing, pp. 227–242; 2003. "Migration, Trafficking and the African Woman."Agenda: Empowering Women for Gender Equity. African Feminisms III. No 58, pp 101–116; and "Equity Issues in the Academy: An Afro-Canadian Woman's Perspective" (2001) The Journal of Negro Education: A Howard University Quarterly Review of Issues Incident to the Education of Black People. Black Women in the Academy: Challenges and Opportunities, 70(3):192–203.

HENRY ETZKOWITZ is a visiting Professor at the Human Sciences Advanced Research Institute, Stanford University. He was Professor and Chair of Management of Innovation, Creativity and Enterprise, and the Director of the Triple Helix Group Newcastle University Business School. He is the author of several books including *The Triple Helix: University-Industry-Government Innovation in Action* (Routledge

2008); a Member of the International Advisory Board, International Science Park Association and a Visiting Research Professor, Technology and Society Department, School of Engineering and Applied Sciences, State University of New York, Stony Brook and Chair of the Scientific Committee, Triple Helix International Conference Series.

DR. TOBY E. HUFF is a Research Associate at Harvard University in the Department of Astronomy and Chancellor Professor Emeritus in Policy Studies at UMass Dartmouth. He has lectured in Europe, Asia, and the Middle East and lived in Malaysia. He is the author of *The Rise of Early Modern Science: Islam, China and the West* (2nd ed. Cambridge 2003), and co-editor with Wolfgang Schluchter of *Max Weber and Islam* (Transaction Books, 1999). His most recent book is *Intellectual Curiosity and the Scientific Revolution. A Global Perspective* Cambridge University Press, (2010).

TARJA KNUUTTILA is a senior research associate in philosophy at the University of Helsinki. She holds MSc degrees in Economics and Business Administration from Helsinki School of Economics and an MA and PhD in Philosophy from University of Helsinki. Her research work revolves around Modeling and Scientific Representation, Methodology of economics, as well as the Commodification of Science. She has published in *Biology and Philosophy*; *Erkenntnis*; *Forum: Qualitative Social Research*; *Philosophy of Science*; *Semiotica*; *Studies in History and Philosophy of Science*; *Science Studies*; *Science, Technology and Human Values*, and in numerous edited books. She has co-authored a book in Finnish on the commercialization of science with a special focus on biotechnology and language technology (Miettinen, Reijo; Tuunainen Juha, Knuuttila, Tarja & Erika Mattila: *From science to product.* Helsinki: 2006).

MICHAEL W. KPESSA is a Research Fellow at the Institute of African Studies, University of Ghana. He holds a PhD in Political Science (Comparative Public Policy) from McMaster University, Canada. He was the Social Science and Humanities Research Council (SSHRC) of Canada Post Doctoral Fellow at Johnson-Shoyama Graduate School of Public Policy, University of Saskatchewan. His current research projects focus on institutional theory and development, participatory policy making, institutional change, pension reform, and the role of transnational actors in sub-Sahara Africa and beyond.

AMY SCOTT METCALFE is an Assistant Professor of Higher Education in the Department of Educational Studies at the University of British Columbia. She received her PhD from the centre for the study of higher education at the University of Arizona. The focus of her work is research policy, the theoretical basis of scholarship stems from critiques of capital formation in the public sphere, feminism and the sociology of science and organizations. Her recent publications have appeared in Higher Education, the Journal of Higher Education and the Canadian journal of Higher Education.

ZEEDA FATIMAH MOHAMAD is a lecturer with the Department of Science and Technology Studies, Faculty of Science, Universiti Malaya. She holds a BSc in Ecology from the Institute of Biological Sciences, Universiti Malaya, Malaysia; MSc in Environmental Management and Policy from IIIEE, Lund University, Sweden and MSc and PhD in Science & Technology Policy from SPRU, University of Sussex, United Kingdom. Her academic interests are in the Development of Science, Technology, Innovation, Environment, and Sustainable Development in Late-industrialising countries.

PETER W.B. PHILLIPS is a Professor at the Johnson-Shoyama Graduate School of Public Policy, and *Associate Member, Department of Bioresource, Policy, Business and Economics, University of Saskatchewan.* He holds a PhD from the London School of Economics. He spent 13 years in industry and government, mainly as an economist and policy advisor, and has since invested a matching 13 years at the University of Saskatchewan. Peter has been a member of four colleges or schools and four departments, and today combines his experiences in researching the interface between the state and the market. Peter is getting better at turning off his computer and escaping some weekends to sail in the summer (which has been doing since age 12) or downhill ski in the winter. He loves to sail Mirror Class boats, but is also certified to captain a yacht.

TERRY WOTHERSPOON is Professor and Head of Sociology at the University of Saskatchewan. He has also been designated Adjunct Professor at Xi'an Jiaotong University, China. He has degrees in Sociology and Education, and a Ph.D. in Sociology. In addition to several years of teaching experience at elementary, secondary and post-secondary levels, he has engaged in research and published widely on issues related to education, social policy, indigenous peoples, and social inequality in Canada. His research has been funded by agencies such as SSHRC, Saskatchewan Learning, the Laidlaw Foundation, and the Prairie Centre of Excellence for Research on Immigration and Integration. He is a recipient of the Canadian Education Association's Whitworth Award for Educational Research, while *The Sociology of Education in Canada: Critical Perspectives* was recognized with a book award from the Canadian Association for Foundations of Education. He currently serves as Chair of the Board of Governors of the Prairie Metropolis Centre, and is Managing Editor of the *Canadian Review of Sociology*. His latest book is. *The Sociology of Education in Canada: Critical Perspectives, 3rd edition*. Toronto: Oxford University Press (2009).

INTRODUCTION

THE DYNAMICS OF UNIVERSITIES, KNOWLEDGE AND SOCIETY

James Dzisah and Henry Etzkowitz

Transformations in the social organization of society are always diffi-cult to conjecture as the emerging configurations often contain seeds of 'creative reconstruction'. This explains why the word 'modern'—originally used in the late fifth century to denote Christian from the pagan and the Roman past (Habermas 1997)—continues to be useful in delineating the contours of contemporary society in spite of the relentless postmodern deconstructions. Consequently, while we labeled this collection *The Age of Knowledge*, we do so with the explicit understanding that it is often simple to magnify the reach and utility of knowledge irrespective of the often challenging and distinctive social, economic, cultural, political, and the gender-mediated contexts. Indeed, specifying the reach and magnitude of knowledge in contem-porary society, where knowledge is front and centre, is a very difficult and daunting task. In spite of this, the ongoing transformations in knowledge, universities, and society must be viewed as reflective of the much larger changes in the social structure. The fact that knowledge continues to be implicated in the habitual practices of the human social enterprise requires the consideration of factors far beyond their initial inclinations. This demands a critical examination of the, often hidden, social and materialistic contexts within which the emerging and evolv-ing transformations are implicated. This undertaking has become even more pressing as the process of globalization unleashed a new political economy of knowledge within which different institutions are considerably altering their place and identity.

Consequently, within the realm of higher education, universities have come under relentless pressure to change the way in which the business of tertiary education is conducted (Slaughter and Leslie 1997). The underlining push to reform according to some observers is indus-try induced (Axelrod 2002, Pelikan 1992, Slaughter and Leslie 1997,

Washburn 2005). Though Karl Marx has long identified the economic structure as the core foundation of the capitalist social structure, the increasing dependence of the economy and society on knowledge and information processing (Castells 1996) has deepened the reach of the economic sphere necessitating a significant institutional transformation in areas hitherto considered to be uncharted.

In fact, innovation which refers to the reconfiguration of elements into a more productive combination (Etzkowitz 2008), has taken on a broader meaning within the context of an economic structure predicated on knowledge. The implicit understanding inherent in this new transformation is that we are dealing with a new logic of 'innovation in innovation' based upon the restructuring and enhancement of the organizational arrangements and incentives that foster creativity. Based on these calculations, the university is increasingly being viewed as the institution capable of taking up, in addition to its traditional roles of knowledge production, preservation, and transmission, the task of socio-economic development and regional innovation. This ambitious mandate is derived from the growing awareness that productivity and global competitiveness are based on the constant production, mobilization and generation of both new and reformulated knowledge (Castells 1996).

However, there are disagreements as to the extent to which the rise of knowledge as the driver of the economy can be used as the basis to encourage cultural and institutional shifts in universities, and the larger society. In other words, is the rise of knowledge a pretext to overly generalize its transformative structures by selectively detailing, depending on peculiar interests, its pervasive influences in the larger domain of science, policy and gender? The debate is often fierce in the realm of science due to the impractical belief that "objectivity precluded particularism" (Merton 1973:270), making it essential that scientific knowledge claims be rooted in some impersonal and universalistic criteria. While the ideological self-conception of science helped in creating the public sphere for scientific research (Etzkowitz and Webster 1995), it will be naïve to construe science as a disinterested activity. As Michael Gibbons and his collaborators recently reminded us "Science does not stand outside of society dispensing its gifts of knowledge and wisdom; neither is it an autonomous enclave that is now being crushed under the weight of narrowly commercial or political interests" (1994:22).

Since, science has always been under the gaze of differing interests, it is not surprising that the displacement of the individual researcher by group research projects have led some scientists to focus on the organizational and economic aspects of their research (Etzkowitz and Webster 1995). This has, in the process, provided the impetus, along with funding agencies that offered diverse opportunities, for the institutionalization of polyvalent science (Etzkowitz and Viale 2010). In subsequent years, however, a variety of regional strategies evolved to promote knowledge-based economic growth with significant inputs from different levels of government, academia and industry. It is, therefore, not surprising that the rise into prominence of knowledge has triggered all sorts of banal, sincere and perfidious interests that the contributors, from varying standpoints, intend to unpack.

The book is divided into three broad parts. Part one is organized around six interrelated chapters focusing on such issues as knowledge, globalization, rationalization, gender and identity. The opening chapter by Henry Etzkowitz discusses the effects of the growing economic salience of science on scientific norms and academic practices. He offers an explanation as to why instead of defining entrepreneurial scientists as deviant, the social norms of science have rather changed to support entrepreneurship. As academic scientists take account of the economic value of research findings, the university moves into a more central institutional position in society as an equal partner with industry and government, in effort to promote technological innovation. Building on Etzkowitz's notion of the normative change and the birth of the triple helix, chapter two by Zaheer Baber sees Japan as a state grappling with the changing interplay between globalization of capital and scientific research. He argues that while the claims about the imminent disappearance of classical capitalism and the end of ideologies have been grossly overstated, there is no doubt that a major institutional reconfiguration of the institutional locus of knowledge production is underway.

Working within the broad scope of emerging relations of knowledge and its impact on higher education, Terry Wotherspoon explores, in chapter three, the interrelationships among two significant dimensions associated with changing postsecondary education. He draws attention to concepts that designate more general technological innovation and economic development processes, and dynamics of social inclusion and exclusion. He argues that the postsecondary expansion and parallel emphasis on science, innovation and creativity also carry with them tensions and contradictions. Keeping the focus within the knowledge production system, Toby Huff in chapter four, delves into the realm of higher education with a much more narrow focus-the crisis of universities. He linked this crisis to the ongoing deflections of the academic calling that emphasizes the need for professors to be fully conversant with contemporary, albeit make believe, popular culture. He draws attention to the implications that hundreds of research and consulting firms waiting to serve as hired guns for whatever political, commercial, regional, religious or ethnic interest have for academic and scientific knowledge.

In chapter five, Choonlee Chai moves the debate beyond analyzing universities to explore attempts to Islamize knowledge in Malaysia. For him, the constructivist debate about the nature of modern scientific knowledge has provided new impetus for those calling for cultural and religious involvement in the production of scientific knowledge. He argues that the context of the Islamization discourse is a response to the Weberian process of societal rationalization, with an increasing effort to seek the re-enchantment of the secular modern world. He sees the contradiction between the promotion of modern science in Malaysia on one hand, and the critique of it on the other as articulating the partial acceptance of the epistemological basis of modern science and the rejection of its ontological tenet. While arguing that success remains to be seen, he is of the view that Islamization of knowledge should be perceived as a creative effort of knowledge innovation in response to intense secularization.

Patience Elabor-Idemudia shifts gears, in chapter six, from the focus on the university system to the examination of the role played by gender in the various processes of negotiation of identity in globalized contexts. She contends that while globalization impacts our perception of gender identity and how knowledge about this is shaped by new ideologies, communication technologies, labor demands and the media, prior constructed gender roles continue to inform the perception of women and men in general. In the process, what has really changed is the fact that gender roles and identity have been reconstructed making traditional ideologies less apt in describing modern gender characterizations.

Part two of the book is organized around five interrelated chapters. The overriding focus here is on the larger context of knowledge innovation, governance and policy. The starting point is the discussion of the broader debate about the impact of knowledge in contemporary societies by Dzisah and Etzkowitz. They argue that there is an ongoing reconfiguration of organizational formats in different spheres necessitated by the need to place knowledge at the vanguard of economic activity. In a much broader context, these transformations are in their view, heralded by the dynamic investments in knowledge, innovation and creativity. They contend that the critical requirements for innovation and growth rest on finding an overriding policy niche that allows for the optimization of interactions among university, industry and government institutional spheres.

In chapter eight, Harley Dickinson takes up the emerging contexts of knowledge production. He argues that in the context of post-industrial knowledge societies, producing, transferring and using research knowledge and technology are interrelated processes that take place in loosely coupled networks of autonomous actors who have heterogeneous interests. He asserts that, in an age of knowledge, approaches that integrated both epistemic and socio-political boundary work are both timely and important. Pushing ahead with the notion of knowledge innovation and governance, chapter nine by Peter Phillips takes up the complexity and the governance challenge facing knowledge societies. He examines the fundamental challenges posed by the knowledge society, presents a conceptual framework for understanding the scope of governance of the system and offers some practical implications.

In chapter ten, Michael Kpessa keeps pace with preceding discussions on knowledge and its effect on contemporary institutions. He looks at the impact of the knowledge-based social order on public policy-making. He contends that the nascent transformations in knowledge have expanded the number of actors involved in policy decision-making, resulting in a shift in scholarly focus from policy-making to the context of ideas. In chapter eleven, William Boateng looks at the knowledge management practices at the macro level health-care decision-making in Canada. He argues that in any knowledge regime, strategies must be designed in a manner that enhances the goals and objectives of the organization. This he contends requires a critical examination of explicit and tacit knowledge forms, with emphasis placed on the dominant form of knowledge informing the decision-making processes.

The final part of the book is structured around four interconnected chapters. The overriding issue is the role of universities and other actors in the emerging knowledge economy. In chapter twelve, Amy Scott Metcalfe explores the notion of intermediating actors:

organizations that operate in the spaces between institutions of higher education, industrial firms, and government agencies. She argues that organizations situated in this interstitial space (between public and private entities) have been found to actively influence the formation of academy-industry-government relationships through the exchange of actors, resources, and commerce. James Dzisah discusses, in chapter thirteen, some of the ideals and contradictions embedded in the roles and functions of universities. He explores through survey data, the impact of industrial funding of academic research on scientists. He argues that while industrial funding is important in perception formation vis-à-vis knowledge capitalization, the growing notion that university-industry relations is harming the core functions of the university is, as articulated in some circles, too simplistic.

In chapter fourteen, Tarja Knuuttila traces the developmental trajectory of one research group, which operated at the University of Helsinki. She details the micro level practical management of academic spin-offs concentrating on the possibilities and problems that emerged, how the problems were solved, and which perspectives informed various academic and entrepreneurial actors. She contends that there are certain inherent ideals and norms that the university has come to embody that are not easily reconcilable with entrepreneurial principles. Yet, some of the problems faced by the research group could have been avoided had appropriate regulations and procedures, concerning the commercial activity in the universities, been put in place in the initial stages. Zeeda Mohamad explores, in chapter fifteen, the role of local universities in Malaysia and Singapore in the development of fuel cell technology. She argues that the extent of universities' contribution to the development of fuel cell technology is contingent upon four system level factors: the relationship of the research scope of universities to the broader dynamics of fuel cell technology, the influence of individuals with extensive expertise in the technology, the ability to engage with critical government and business actors, and the prevailing wider policy environment.

Bibliography

Axelrod, Paul. 2002. *Values in Conflict: The University, the Marketplace, and the Trials of Liberal Education*. Montreal and Kingston: McGill-Queens University Press.

Castells, Manuel. 1996. *The Rise of the Network Society*. Oxford: Blackwell.

Etzkowitz, Henry. 2008. *The Triple helix: University-Industry-Government Innovation in Action*. London and New York: Routledge.

Etzkowitz, Henry and Riccardo Viali. 2010. "Polyvalent Knowledge and the Entrepreneurial University: A Third Academic Revolution?" *Critical Sociology* 36(4):595–609.

Etzkowitz, Henry and Andrew Webster. 1995. "Science as Intellectual Property", in Sheila Jasanoff, Gerald Mankle, James Peterson and Trevor Pinch, eds., *Handbook of Science and Technology Studies*. London: Sage, pp. 480–505.

Gibbons, Michael, Camille Limoges, Helga Nowotny, Simon Schwartzman, Peter Scott, and Martin Trow. 1994. *The new production of knowledge*. London: Sage Publications.

Habermas, Jürgen. 1997. "Modernity an Unfinished Project," in d'Entrèves, Maurizio Passerin and Seyla Benhabib, eds., *Habermas and the Unfinished Project of Modernity: Critical Essays on The Philosophical Discourse of Modernity*. Boston, Mass: MIT Press, pp. 38–55.

Merton, Robert K. 1973. *The Sociology of Science: Theoretical and Empirical Investigations*. Chicago: University of Chicago Press.

Pelikan, Jaroslav. 1992. *The Idea of the University: A Re-examination*. New Haven: Yale University Press.

Slaughter, Sheila and Larry L. Leslie. 1997. *Academic Capitalism: Politics, Policies, and the Entrepreneurial University*. Baltimore and London: The Johns Hopkins University Press.

Washburn, Jennifer. 2005. University Inc: The Corporate Corruption of Higher Education. New York: Basic Books.

PART I

KNOWLEDGE, GLOBALIZATION AND IDENTITY

CHAPTER ONE

NORMATIVE CHANGE IN SCIENCE AND THE BIRTH OF THE TRIPLE HELIX[1]

Henry Etzkowitz

The university's unique status as a teaching, research and economic development enterprise, whose traditional and new roles reinforce each other, places it in a central position in the knowledge age. An entrepreneurial academic ethos that combines an interest in fundamental discovery with application is emerging as new and old academic missions persist in tension. Rather than being suborned to either industry or government, the university is emerging as an influential actor and equal partner in an innovation regime, the 'triple helix' of university-industry-government relations. The institutional spheres of science and the economy, which were hitherto relatively separate and distinct, have become inextricably intertwined.

Research results are routinely defined as 'intellectual property' and that property in knowledge is contested not only for its symbolic but also for its monetary value (Hagstrom 1965, Nelkin 1984, Samuelson 1987, Latour and Woolgar 1989, Florida and Kenney 1990). A relatively small number of professors, among them some of the most prestigious of academic scientists, have formed firms, both to commercialize and to support their research (Kenney 1986, Etzkowitz 1999). Most universities have established technology transfer offices and some have contracted corporations for research support in exchange for right of first refusal to license technology that is generated through these arrangements (Technology Access Report 1998).

This chapter discusses effects of the growing economic salience of science on scientific norms and academic practices. An explanation of why the social norms of science have changed to support entrepreneurship, instead of entrepreneurial scientists being defined as

[1] The Ethics and Values Studies Program, National Science Foundation, and the Andrew Mellon Foundation supported the research on which this article is based. Unless otherwise noted, quotations are drawn from the studies.

deviant, is offered. Academic scientists increasingly take account of the economic value of research findings as the university moves into a more central institutional position in society as an equal partner with industry and government in effort to promote technological innovation.

The Birth of the Triple Helix

Although some observers call for respect for a division of labor between academia and industry (Rosenberg and Nelson 1994), it is increasingly difficult to separate a series of cognitive and entrepreneurial activities that increasingly occur along a continuum rather than in dichotomous spheres. Thus, some university originated firms located in incubators appear as much, if not more, committed to research goals as to making money, despite the best efforts of incubator administrators to focus their attention on the latter. Conversely, some academics are so attentive to the commercial implications of findings produced in their research groups that they can attune their research program to produce results that will be amenable to commercialization even as they maintain their pursuit of fundamental research (Gold 1992).

If the disjuncture between theory and invention is accepted, the appearance of entrepreneurial scientists is an anomaly (Aitken 1976). Their research is typically at the frontiers of science and leads to theoretical and methodological advance as well as invention of devices. These activities involve sectors of the university, such as basic science departments, that heretofore in principle limited their involvement with industry. Thus, the phenomenon of academic scientists commercializing their research requires a new explanation. It must be one that goes beyond the availability of investment funds since earlier generations of scientists, such as Pasteur and the Curies, seldom took advantage of commercial opportunities (Etzkowitz 1983). The emergence of this new role calls for the construction of a framework that can account for a pluralistic universe of science and a differentiated normative structure among scientists. Such a model should account for the emergent role of the entrepreneurial scientist in the university as well as for industrial scientists who do not necessarily experience role strain in their research setting.

Resource dependency theory suggests that entrepreneurial academic behaviour can be explained by the fact that universities follow their interests and seek funds wherever they become available, government in the early post-war and industry, at present (Slaughter and Leslie 1999). The premise of this framework is that the seeker is subordinated to the funding source. A theoretical analogue, principal-agent theory, has also been applied to understand the so-called contract between government and academia in the early post-war (Guston 1999). However, if entrepreneurial scientists and entrepreneurial universities are now active and equal partners in their relations with industry and government, able to negotiate on an equal basis and maintain fundamental institutional interests such as the ability to publish, then the above explanations are partial, at best.

The first phase of entrepreneurial science is the internal development of academic research groups as "quasi-firms." The second phase refers to academic participation in the externalization and capitalization of knowledge in tangible products and distance learning courseware. As universities spin-off for-profit entities from their research and educational activities, and fund some of their own research, they shift their institutional focus from eleemosynary to self-generation. The ability to balance among multiple sources of support, including industry, state and local government and self-funding can be expected to increase the independence of the university.

During the 1980s as research results were scrutinized for commercial as well as theoretical relevance, the norm of 'communism' was modified to 'limited secrecy,' with research results kept under wraps until their economic value can be protected. Given the availability of university offices with legal staff or outside patent counsel this time lag need not be long. This shift in attitude and conduct among academic scientists with respect to the economic relevance of science contrasts with the traditional accommodation of industrial scientists. This difference may be explained by (1) the higher status of professors in the university than scientists in large corporate laboratories, (2) the transformation of the university into an economic actor and (3) the enhanced role of the university and some of its faculty in 'the new economy' (Sahlman 1999).

As the production of scientific knowledge has been transformed into an economic enterprise; the economy has also been transformed since it increasingly operates on an epistemological base (Machlup 1962). Intellectual property is becoming as important as financial capital as the basis of future economic growth, indicated by the inadequacy of traditional models of valuing firms primarily in terms of their tangible assets. Although the contemporary research university has not become a full-fledged commercial enterprise, it has taken on some of the entrepreneurial characteristics of a 'Silicon Valley' or 'Route 128' high technology firm even as such firms adopted some of the collegial forms and campus architecture of the university. The university's emergence as a participant in economic development has not only changed the nature of the relationship between industry and the university but also made the national university a significant regional actor (Goldhor and Lund 1993).

Academic research groups and science-based start-ups exist along a continuum, with attention to rewards of recognition and finance. Indeed companies developed on the basis of discoveries made at universities, tend to continue to publish the new findings based on their elaboration of the original discovery. Licensing, joint ventures, marketing and sales of products provide additional avenues for knowledge dissemination to broader areas of society, above and beyond the traditional means of academic dissemination. These commercial channels bring with them informal social relations that also provide pathways of dissemination (Saxenian 1994).

Organizational change within the university, and in its relation to industry and government, is accompanied by cognitive and behavioural effects. Indeed, the conduct of academic scientists has undergone a process of normative change, a reinterpretation and revision of unwritten rules since Robert K. Merton developed his classic formulation that, "the communism of the scientific ethos is incompatible with the definition of technology as 'private property' in a capitalistic economy" (1957[1942]: 338). A restructuring of the relationship between science and society has taken place as science has become a significant productive force in the economy. The transformation of science, from a weak and isolated to a major and central social institution, has affected the organizations in which science is conducted, the scientific role and the norms of science.

Norms are not invariant; they change over time, sometimes marked by controversy. Two norms of science, that is, "disinterestedness" and "communism" have been at least partially displaced by an institutional imperative to translate research into economic and social use. This chapter seeks to explain why normative change, rather than definition of deviance, accompanied the emergence of entrepreneurial science. If the advancement and capitalization of knowledge can be made compatible, this transformation does not necessarily represent loss or deformation of original academic purposes (Noble and Pfund 1980, Faulkner and Senker 1994).

To examine how the university's new and old roles (economic development, research and education) interact and conflict with each other, more than 150 in-depth interviews were conducted with academic entrepreneurs, other faculty members, and administrators. A sample of eight public and private universities, at the Carnegie I and II levels were selected to represent universities and departments with newly emerging and long standing connections to industry. The disciplines studied included: physics, chemistry, computer science, electrical engineering and biological sciences (Mitchell 1983). Following a pilot study of two disciplines (physics and biology) at two universities in the early 1980s, interviews were conducted in two waves, in the mid-1980s and mid-1990s.

The idea of free and open communication among scientists was espoused by most respondents but a significant minority adhered to 'limited secrecy' and was willing to hold back findings for a period of time in order to secure patent protection. A biologist who took this position called informing interested researchers without limit, 'a nineteenth century idea' and felt that it was necessary to protect one's research from competitors by, 'not providing key details'. On the other hand, all physicists and most biologists accepted that university scientists could properly undertake research whose goal is set by an external agency. Most biologists believed that it was possible to combine the pursuit of basic research with the objective of gaining financial rewards from one's research while the physicists divided evenly on this question.

Deviance or Normative Change?

In recent years, an increasing number of scientists and research organizations have sought to simultaneously advance and capitalize knowledge, calling their full adherence to the Mertonian norms of communality and disinterestedness into question. Communism implies that property rights in science are reduced to recognition of discoveries. Full and open communication represents the enactment of this norm; secrecy its antithesis. Disinterestedness denotes the institutional relationship of scientists to society, including a set of incentives to create knowledge for collegial approbation and public use in exchange for insulation from popular sentiment (Merton 1973[1942]). What happens when norms are flouted?

Deviance involves breaking a rule, leaving the rule intact, whereas when normative change occurs; the rule itself is transformed (Meier 1981, Marshall 1981). Under what conditions is normative change, rather than deviance likely to occur? When behaviour is inconsistent with norms, but is: (1) undertaken either by a large number of persons or by a few persons of high status; and (2) can be shown to be consistent with the values of a social system; it is unlikely to be successfully defined as deviant. Even scientific colleagues, who have no desire to become entrepreneurs themselves, seldom look upon their colleagues who do with disdain. The paucity of 'definition of deviance' can be explained by examining the position in the scientific world of many of the entrepreneurial scientists.

Entrepreneurial activities have been undertaken by leading scientists who are viewed as role models. For example, a molecular biologist at a leading research university viewed his colleagues at Harvard who have formed firms with admiration and wished to emulate them. However the willingness of a few 'low status' scientists to use findings for pecuniary advantage would likely have been taken as evidence of 'deviance.' If such normative infractions were negatively sanctioned they would likely have served to strengthen the old normative pattern.

For an increasing number of scientists, participating in the formation of a firm has come to be positively defined as a new badge of scientific achievement. Also, taking the path of firm formation does not necessarily mean abandoning the academy. Some, like Stanford University computer scientist, co-founder of Sun Microsystems and Netscape, Jim Clark, left the university and engaged in successive efforts at firm-formation. Others, like biologist Leroy Hood, combined firm formation with an academic career. However, the California Institute of Technology (Cal Tech) did not allow Hood to gain financially from his work in helping form Applied Biosystems in the early 1980s (Hood 1989). Hood eventually moved to a more compatible academic environment at the University of Washington where he organized a new department in bio-informatics as collaboration with Microsoft. Cal Tech, however, has since changed its policies and has become quite successful in promoting the entrepreneurial engagement that it had previously discouraged.

For an increasing number of scientists, especially in biotechnology and computer science, an association with a firm that they have helped start is no longer an unusual event, as it was in the late 1940s, when Carl Djerassi left an Assistant Professorship at Wayne State University in Detroit to become Research Director of Syntex, a start-up company in Mexico City. Building upon the firm's initial success in developing a novel method to synthesize progesterone as a feedstock to the chemical industry, Djerassi and his colleagues targeted artificial contraception as a product and research objective, contributing to the literature and carrying out product development simultaneously.

A two-way synergy between academia and industry was developed that de-emphasized barriers. Syntex's relationship with the chemistry department at the Autonomous National University of Mexico (UNAM), through joint research projects, supporting student fellowships and supplying research equipment facilitated the department's entry into the world scientific literature (Etzkowitz and Blum 1995). Djerassi's scientific achievements led to an offer of a position in the Stanford University's chemistry department. In 1960, Djerassi moved part of Syntax to Palo Alto and arranged with Stanford to continue as the firm's research director while building an academic research program. He participated in several firm formation efforts in the, 'industrial part of his day', combining scientific achievement with valorization of research in an academic environment that early supported this combination of dual goals (Djerassi 1992).

Some prominent scientists who initially questioned the trend toward academic entrepreneurialism have changed their views, either as opportunities became too tempting or as they realized the importance of industrial support to the future of academic research. Thus, Joshua Lederberg, an early critic of academic involvement in firm-formation eventually became a consultant to the Cetus Corporation (1996). Arthur Kornberg, another Nobel Laureate and self professed traditional academic, also found himself part of the 'golden helix', a biotechnology firm with academic connections (1995). Robert Pollack, an academic biologist who published *Academics in Pinstrips* in the early 1980s, decrying his colleagues 'corporate fling', revised his earlier views as his university generated significant research support from licensing intellectual property. Professor Pollack came to favour the university holding equity in firms formed from academia in order to move the university closer to self-supporting status (Pollack 1982 and 1999).

Many entrepreneurial scientists believe, even as critics define the same phenomena as self-justification, that they are in the cusp of a new relationship between science and business. In many entrepreneurial scientific ventures, in contrast to the subordinate position of scientists in corporate laboratories, scientists and business persons develop strategy together; mutually shaping the course and direction of the firm and share ownership and control.

Normative Change

Entrepreneurial scientists believe that they are acting in accord with scientific values and only a minority of their colleagues view them as deviant. Under such conditions the path is open to normative change. When behaviour conflicts with existing norms, but when deeper values remain stable, new norms can be identified with these values. Thus, 'capitalization of knowledge' is found to be in accord with the advancement of knowledge and the sale of intellectual property with the service mission of the university. Proponents of change such as university administrators often exploit the conflation of norms with values by redirecting debates over controversies from values (where there is usually great resistance to change) to particular cases in which a change can be shown to be advantageous. On the other hand, disputes such as the one over the introduction of the "Discovery Exchange" at the University of Colorado, Boulder, a new mechanism to capitalize intellectual property, can easily escalate into conflict over values. Nevertheless, at this university, and others where controversies have erupted over entrepreneurial science (for example, MIT in the early twentieth century), the overall trend is to acceptance within limiting conditions (Etzkowitz 2010).

Reinterpretation of formerly excluded behaviour often goes unnoticed when it is felt that values are not threatened, or is repressed when values are believed to be threatened but rule changers cannot psychically afford to admit to themselves their exercise in revision. Change in rules also takes place quietly when rule makers and enforcers do not wish to admit that a change is underway for fear of loss of authority, and when those subject to the change do not protest, for reasons of self interest or lack of interest. In the case of scientists operating under novel research conditions there may be two sets of relevant norms operating simultaneously, creating an inherently unstable situation.

Sociological ambivalence between dominant and subsidiary norms that exist in a state of tension with each other operates through normative sequencing, the shift from one set of norms to another (Merton 1973). For example, in a study of the Apollo moon scientists, Mertonian norms were found to be operative when scientists worked on well structured problems; while counter norms guided the study of ill structured problems (Mitroff 1974: 591).

Implicit in this formulation of norms and counter-norms is the existence of a mechanism for making the two sets of norms compatible with each other—the definition of a problem as structured or unstructured—thus, reducing or even eliminating the conflict between normative expectations. However, if an algorithm does not exist or cannot be invented to stabilize ambivalence, it may be resolved through reinterpretation or replacement.

Sociological consonance is the result of changes in the social structure that bring heretofore opposing normative expectations into a new complementary relationship with each other or replace one set by another. Such normative change is not merely an individual phenomenon but a social process in which a significant number of persons go through the same experience and express similar new conclusions. Entrepreneurship is made compatible with the conduct of basic research through a legitimating theme that integrates the two activities into a complementary relationship. For example, scientists often say that earnings from commercializing their research will be applied to furthering their basic research interests.

Reinterpretation takes place through an experience of realizing that what had previously seemed to be in conflict really was not. Thus, an initial reaction of a molecular biologist to the possibility of doing science for financial gain as well as the production of knowledge was, 'I never realized I had a trade', later followed by, 'I can do good science and make money'. This conversion experience suggests the transmutation of ambivalence—the opposition between two opposing principles, one primary, the other secondary, into consonance—reformulating apparently contradictory ideological elements into a consistent identity.

This transformation, with concomitant effect on norms, occurred initially in the industrial research laboratory and in recent decades has penetrated academia, as well. Norms are stable as long as they are effective and support efficient engagement in the world. When the environment changes, norms may no longer be effective, creating a

disjuncture between the workings of the organization and its environment. In the next sections I shall examine the institutional spheres of
industry and academia and specify the trajectories through which normative change in science takes place.

Normative Change in Industrial Science

One group of scientists, employees of corporate laboratories has long
been found not to only have a partial fit with Mertonian norms.
A body of research developed from the 1950s to the 1970s suggests a
variety of adaptations for industrial scientists including: (1) role strain
or transition to managerial norms; (2) a creative tension between
organizational and scientific norms; and (3) the existence of alternative
normative structures of science. Scientists in industry had been
expected to conform to corporate norms but academic science had
been held to be a world apart, with well defined boundaries between
science and society (Gieryn 1983). In reviewing fifty years of discussion of the norms of science, Joseph Ben-David has argued that the
different positions taken reflect the author's views on the major political issues of their era: democracy versus fascism in the 1930s and
the Vietnam War in the 1960s. The axis on which the debate turns is
the desired relationship of scientists to society, whether they should be
independent of or directed by political goals. Ben-David (1980) distinguished among different types of scientists in his review, holding that
propositions about autonomy referred primarily to academic scientists
in basic research disciplines.

Nevertheless, a central research question regarding scientists who
work in non-academic settings has been the degree to which Mertonian
norms conflict with organizational values (Marcson 1960, Kornhauser
1963, Glaser 1964, Cotgrove and Box 1970). Corporate norms such as
maximization of profit and acceptance of hierarchical authority have
been identified as incompatible with "communism" and "universalism." It was hypothesized that scientists who worked in industry would
either exist in a state of perpetual tension or departs from the scientific
role by accepting a management position. It was also suggested that a
scientist could achieve a limited successful adjustment to the industrial setting by bringing to bear an independent source of normative
authority, professionalism, and to resist organizational pressures. The
professional scientist accepts control over research problem choice but
retains control over the choice of techniques to perform the research
(Kornhauser 1963).

In general, however, it was expected that the industrial research laboratory would redirect scientists interested in esoteric research to more practical concerns. Managers noted, however, that many scientists resisted efforts at resocialization. For such scientists the norms of science were in conflict with corporate goals (Shephard 1956, Randall 1959, Burns and Stalker 1961) and such conflict, with its attendant role strain, was believed to result in a loss of productivity. An extensive literature was developed in which management was advised on techniques of replacing scientists' norms with organizational goals or accommodating some of their desire for autonomy (Bush and Battery 1945, American Management Association 1958, Orth 1959).

However, within a framework that postulated a single normative structure of science and a single normative structure in which technology could be most productively developed, there could be no satisfactory resolution of these conflicts. Of course, industrial scientists could resolve this role strain by replacing the value placed on autonomy with adherence to the organizational norms of their corporate employer. This role shift, while resolving the problem of role strain, is expected by other researchers to result in a loss of creativity (Pelz and Andrews 1976). This is where the dilemma of industrial science is: the very qualities of the scientists required in order to create innovations desired by the organization may be suppressed by it to promote smooth organizational functioning.

Yet, Pelz and Andrews (1976), in perhaps the most comprehensive study of the relationship between the productivity of scientists and research environments, found that the conditions for creativity differed somewhat from Marcson's expectations (1960). Whereas Marcson assumed that normative congruence would produce the best environment for creativity, Pelz and Andrews found, contrary to their expectation, that satisfaction with one's job—measured by the difference between desired levels and attained levels—was only moderately related to scientific productivity. To interpret this unexpected finding, Pelz and Andrews developed the concept of 'creative tension', a state of conflict between internal desires and external pressures. A curvilinear relationship between scientists' effectiveness and creative tension was postulated; effectiveness increased as tension increased up to some optimum 'moderate' level and then decreased again if tensions were too great. Pelz and Andrews treat all scientists (regardless of research setting) as a single group, that is, norms are presumed to be invariant.

However, in their study, Cotgrove and Box (1970) provide a key finding that indicates the existence of an alternative normative structure for some industrial scientists. A significant number of industrial scientists in their sample who lacked autonomy did not experience role strain. Moreover, no significant loss of productivity was noted among this group. Thus, Cotgrove and Box postulated 'the organizational scientist' who was willing to accept direction over both ends and means, over what research should be conducted as well as how the research should be conducted. Thus, a scientific role that operated without cognitive dissonance was postulated for the industrial arena. However, if the thesis of a self-regulating scientific community is pared down to its base in the university, the character of contemporary academic science becomes crucial to this thesis.

Transformation of the Academic-Industry Interface

Academic scientists have a long history of working with industry, having helped establish the early industrial research laboratories in the United States (Reich 1985). Until quite recently most university-industry connections separated academic and commercial practices. Limits were placed on how much time an academic could devote to outside concerns. A one fifth rule allowing one day per week became commonplace. Even as ongoing relationships, consulting arrangements were usually conducted apart from academic research, although based on the academic's expertise accumulated from campus based research. Consulting relationships typically involved brief visits to industrial sites or conduct of discrete projects on university premises.

A consequence of this separation was that it left control of commercial opportunities of academic research in the hands of industry whereas control over the direction of research and choice of research topics was left to academic scientists. Although regular payments were made to individual consultants, the large-scale transfer of funds from industry to the university was left up to the generosity of companies. The older forms of university-industry connections involved payment for services rendered, whether it was received directly in the form of consultation fees or indirectly as endowment gifts. Thus, the traffic between university and industry was policed so those boundaries were maintained even as exchanges took place through consultation and philanthropy.

From the early years of the research university in the late nineteenth century, university-industry relationships were largely established at the behest of industry to serve the needs of existing companies. Engineering schools reorganized themselves to serve the research needs and supply personnel for the growing science based electrical and chemical industries. The linkages included cooperative programs which sent students to industry for part of their training, university professors undertaking research at the request of industry and donations of money and equipment by industrial firms to support engineering education (Noble 1976). University-industry relationships declined in the 1930s due to the financial stringency of the depression and became relatively less important in the post war era with the growth in government funding of science.

The Dynamics of Entrepreneurial Science

A broad range of universities have taken on the tasks of economic development, at times due to external pressures, including funding constriction but also as the result of internal initiatives arising from the expansionary dynamic of scientific research. New forms of university-industry relationships involve the multiplication of resources through the university's and faculty members' participation in capital formation projects such as real estate development in science parks and formation of firms in incubator facilities. These also include academic scientist's involvement in firms e.g. through membership on advisory boards, boards of directors, stockholding in exchange for consultation services, assumption of managerial responsibilities and direct involvement in the formation of firms.

Relatively few open conflicts have erupted such as the one at Harvard in 1980 when the administration proposed that the university participate financially in a firm based on the research of one of its faculty members. Although controversy over the goals of the university abated when the plan was dropped, President Bok stated at the time that he would explore other means of involving Harvard in realizing financial gain from campus based research (Bok 1982, Culliton 1982). In 1988, when a joint venture involving the medical school was announced, the New York Times questioned whether traditional academic values were being abandoned, but there was no on-campus opposition as there had been eight years before. During the intervening period, similar proposals become accepted practice at other universities, as the University of Colorado and Columbia University accepted equity in faculty formed firms and Washington University, St. Louis and MIT took the role of venture capitalist.

One driving force behind normative change in academic science is industry's experience that although transfer of knowledge is, in principle, freely available through the literature but, in practice, closer relationships such as consultation and inserting industrial scientists into academic research groups is necessary to translate this knowledge into a usable form. A second factor is the perceived constriction in federal funds for academic research in recent years that has made support from industry significant, even in the form of marginal amounts to supplement short-falls in government research funds. Thirdly, increased international competition to US industry from the 1970s led to a 'hidden industrial policy' carried out by amendments to the patent law. The Bayh-Dole Act of 1980 assigned the intellectual property rights emanating from federally funded research to universities both as a requirement for receipt of such funds and as an incentive to earn funds by transferring technology to industry. The fourth factor is the 'inner dynamic' of academic science, the necessity to raise funds to support a research group.

Processes of Normative Change

As academic scientists make their claims for priority concomitant with the securing of intellectual property rights to their discoveries, the conditions for increased industrial connections are being created at a liberal arts research universities. These connections take place within limits that are designed to take account of the concerns of the liberal arts faculty but these restrictions gradually erode through the development of case law in the university's oversight committee. For example, a ban on exclusive licenses was changed to allow such licenses when companies could not otherwise be induced to participate in the transfer of technology.

Changes in university policy are institutionalized in the form of new administrative offices to carry out new tasks or the assignment of old offices to take on new functions. Thus, at MIT in 1940s when a contract office established in the 1920s to deal with industry was reassigned to monitor military contracts, it signified the advent of an era of extensive academic-government relations as other universities followed suit. The establishment of more than 250 university technology transfer offices during the past two decades exemplifies a similar transition in academic-industry relations. As linkage mechanisms are put in place, a two way flow overlays the traditional one-way flow of students to industry, with corporate procedures and personnel entering the university and academic modes and professors moving to industry.

Changes in Academic Policy and Practice

University administrations have put in place policies and programs to market the research of their faculty and adjust these policies to retain the loyalty of faculty. Faculty members in fields with commercial potential such as computer science take into account the university's patent and time policies in their decision to accept or retain positions. A number of universities have established committees, representing faculty and administrators, to respond to the problems and opportunities created by entrepreneurial science. Such committees are institutional mechanisms of normative change and constitute a strategic research site to examine how different viewpoints are expressed and mediated. Their task is to translate 'ambivalence' into 'confluence'. These committees are arenas in which representatives from different social locations in the university interact under conditions where they share a common charge to produce a position.

It is often believed that modest changes in university rules will allow commercial activities to be undertaken without endangering values. However, the process of conflict resolution in committees often leads, even those most highly opposed to normative change, to allow changes in rules to be made. Committee leaders produce rationalizations to show how old norms are not violated by new forms of behaviour, thus laying the foundations for normative change. Acceptance is gained through reinterpretation of values or through concessions to interests, for example, increased financial support for the humanities from revenues accruing to the university from industry. New forms of behaviour are then allowed, such as temporary withholding of research results as patents are sought, while traditional values are upheld. Some engineering faculty at Columbia were outraged at the attempt by the university to control their involvement with industry.

They argued that it would result in the creation of a new bureaucracy that would impede communication with industry.

Although no-one opposed sharing rewards with the university some were adamant about not being allowed to accept stock and make consulting arrangements at their discretion. These faculty members wished to maintain their status as independent entrepreneurs and not be superceded by the university as an entrepreneur. For example, a professor of Chemical Engineering characterized the new policy as both vague and restrictive. By giving the university control over patent rights it would create an inequity between copyright, left to the faculty and patents. He believed it would make the faculty into industrial laboratory employees and noted that "the university scientist, however, is unique among the members of the faculty. He raises the funds for his equipment, and from his research grants pays for the operation of his laboratories, the operation of the libraries and computers, and the stipends of his students. It is a gross exaggeration to imply that the university materially invests in the research of its faculty; the University operates its laboratories as profit centers."

They objected to the University getting involved in business while desiring to protect their right to do business under academic freedom. Other justifications included competitive pressures from other universities and industry, affecting Columbia's ability to attract faculty if their free access to consulting and other commercial arrangements were impeded. The University of Chicago expressed interest in having faculty enter into relations with industry including firm formation by faculty. Lacking actual cases at the time, the university committee discussed hypothetical instances of problems in industrial connections. Committee members expressed concerns over faculty allocation of time to external interests and loss of allegiance to the university. Nevertheless, the preponderant concern was to find ways to encourage such involvement in order to legitimate the university to the larger society on grounds of contributions to its economic development.[2]

Guidelines of conduct and organizational mechanisms to market patents were all oriented to encouraging faculty to become more aware

---

[2] The University of Chicago had a significant entrepreneurial success through its ARCH technology transfer and venture capital arm, organized in collaboration with Argonne National Laboratory (See Amy B. Candell and Adam B. Jaffee, "The regional economic impact of public research funding: A case of Massachusetts," in *Industrializing Knowledge* by Branscomb, Kodama and Florida 1999:510–530) and subsequently established an on-campus technology transfer office (Etzkowitz 2009).

of the potential economic value of their research where such interest was low. Alternatively, their purpose was to channel the translation of research into marketable products in ways acceptable to the university among faculty where interest in economic outcomes of research was high. These responses, indeed auger a shift in the direction of the research university, and its members, toward new normative patterns regarding the pecuniary content of knowledge. Whether built into organizational entities that handle the marketing of research, structured as guidelines for desired behaviour or felt as enticements from the outside world: a new normative structure is emerging in the research university. They are norms in the sense that they push behaviour in a clear direction with recognizable and consistent outcomes, enticing it where possible, coercing it where necessary.

As institutional spheres increasingly 'take the role of the other', universities that found firms and research-oriented firms operating as quasi-universities, holding seminars and sponsoring scientific meetings, overlap in their institutional functions. Attempts to fit new phenomena into existing categories and analyses only result in analytical confusion. For example, given the traditional separation between research and entrepreneurship, it is not surprising that 'Internet billionaires' did not invent the technology on which their fortunes are based. It is held that, "...many Internet pioneers were dyed in the wool academics [who]...wouldn't or couldn't shake off the values of academia" (The Economist 1999). However, many of these purported academics were actually employees of research firms such as Bolt, Beranek and Newman (BBN).

BBN was started by academic acoustical experts at MIT and provided a home for a "third shop" of artificial intelligence researchers who interacted with their peers at MIT and Harvard (Minsky 1987). Thus, some university professors became entrepreneurs and organizational innovators, synthesizing academic and business formats, often with government support. BBN, and its counterparts, represent one source of academic entrepreneurship, often based upon defense contracts that universities may not have wanted to assume directly (Vollmer 1962). BBN has since become part of GTE, a telephone company, which was then acquired by Bell Atlantic. Companies such as Applied Material Devices and Motorola have also developed increasingly sophisticated training programs, taking upon themselves some of the educational functions of the university.

Nevertheless, the university is unique in its integration of teaching and research, even as it takes on some business functions. The core competency of the university has expanded from the production and distribution of human capital and knowledge to the packaging and diffusion of intellectual property, increasingly by recombining and enhancing internal and external innovations (Sampat 1999). Indeed, corporations such as DuPont have donated intellectual property, unrelated to their core interests, to universities expecting that students and professors will be more effective than companies in taking it the next steps through development. As the corporation, the university and government, as loci of scientific research, have changed their practices; so has science itself been transformed.

Not surprisingly, as its economic consequences have become more widespread, science has gained greater attention from industry and government. As the center of significant research activity in the US, the university has become the focus of policies and programs to encourage technological innovation and reindustrialization. Government has invented new cooperative mechanisms (e.g. Industry, University Research Centers (IUCRC's) and Cooperative Research and Development Agreements (CRADA's) and provided 'public venture capital' to translate academic research into economic activity, and industry problems into academic research (Johnston and Edwards 1987, Etzkowitz et al. 2000).

Conclusion

The transformation of the institutional spheres of academia, industry and government, and their interrelations, increasingly shape the dynamics of innovation at the multi-national, national and regional levels (Etzkowitz and Leydesdorff 1997, Etzkowitz 2008). As these spheres interact more intensively, the social location of scientific research and the way research is put to use are also affected. Hybrid organizations such as co-operative research centers, strategic alliances and incubator facilities have been created at the interface of academia, industry and government to stimulate innovation.

Norms should be viewed as part of the process of social change as well as a source of stability for social order. Norms delineate how an institution works at the same time as they say how it should work. Thus, a norm is inherently value relevant since it incorporates an ethical standard as well as an empirical descriptor. Since a norm is both an 'is' and an 'ought' it has been presumed to be a relatively stable entity since even when it is disobeyed and the 'is' does not completely hold;

the 'ought' is still believed to be valid. Normative disobedience has been conceptualized as deviance and when negative sanctions are imposed it is viewed as a reinforcement of the norm in question. However, it must also be asked under what conditions is the 'ought' of a norm subject to change and how can normative change be explained.

Long term organizational change, such as the development of academic research that have many of the characteristics of a small business—save the profit motive—helps create the conditions under normative change takes place. Whereas financial success is a common goal in American society, the norms of science traditionally oriented scientists toward recognition from peers as a substitute for personal wealth. Yet the increasing financial resources required for the conduct of research inevitably led scientists to pay more attention to the tasks of fund raising and success at these tasks increasingly became a prerequisite for the ability to achieve success in research. This experience helps explain why many academic scientists who formed firms felt that there was relatively little difference between their activities that were nominally inside and outside of the university. In both instances, they were acting as entrepreneurs.

Nevertheless, even when funds were raised to support an academic research group and not for personal profit, the research/finance linkage introduced a collectivist ethic of capital accumulation into science in contrast to the individualistic ethic of the larger society. Nevertheless, for some scientists it was but a short step to embracing the individualistic ethic as well. Many had never rejected this ethic, in any case, but merely put it aside as simply not relevant given their choice of careers. Having already secured recognition from peers for their research, once the possibility of attaining individual personal wealth through scientific achievement appeared they willingly accepted it.

Following upon the first 'academic revolution', the assumption of a research mission in the late nineteen and early twentieth century, a 'second academic revolution' is underway as universities take up the task of economic development (Jencks and Riesman 1968). During the first academic revolution, the theoretical and specialized outlook of the graduate schools was conveyed throughout the academic institutional order (Storrs 1953, Geiger 1999:63). In the course of the second academic revolution, the valorization of research is integrated with scientific discovery, returning science to its original seventeenth century format prior to the appearance of an ideology of basic research in the mid-nineteenth century (Merton 1938, Kevles 1978). Just as a research ethos was universalized throughout the academic sphere, so is a concern with maximizing the economic uses of research that was formerly the province of a specialized academic sector—the land grant schools (Veysey 1965).

Nevertheless, industrial research funding and receipts from licensing of intellectual property rights are small in absolute terms in comparison to government funding sources that have become traditional, with their controversial origins forgotten by succeeding academic generations (Genuth 1987). Nevertheless, a secular trend can be projected of an academic system, closely involved with industry as well as government. During the 1980s industry funding of academic research rose from about four percent to seven percent and, by the end of the 1990s to about 10 percent. Much of this increase was concentrated in few fields with strongly perceived industrial relevance, such as, biotechnology and civil engineering. University research centers closely tied to industry increased nearly two-and-half times during the 1980s. The number of patents awarded to US universities tripled between 1984 and 1994 (Zusman 1999). While still small in scale, if not in scope, a new academic model is emerging from its chrysalis.

Bibliography

Aitken, Hugh. 1976. *Syntony and Spark: The Origins of Radio*. New York: Wiley.

Ben-David, Joseph. 1980. "The Ethos of Science: The Last Half-Century" in *Silver Jubilee Symposium*, Volume I. Canberra: Australian Academy of Sciences.

Bok, Derek. 1982. *Beyond the Ivory Tower: Social Responsibilities of the Modern University*. Cambridge: Harvard University Press.

Bush, George P. and Lowell H. Battery, eds. 1953. *Scientific Research: Its Administration and Organization)*. Washington D.C.: American University Press.

Burns, Tom and Gibson M. Stalker. *The Management of Innovation*. London: Tavistock.

Cotgrove, Stephen and Steven Box. 1971. *Science, Industry and Society*. London: Allen and Unwin.

Culliton, Barbara. 1982 "The Academic Industrial Complex." *Science* 216(4549): 960–962.

Diamond, Arthur. 1996. "The Economics of Science," *Knowledge Technology and Policy* 9(2–3): 6–49.

Djerassi, Carl. 1992. *The Pill, Pygmy Chimps and Degas Horse*. New York: Basic Books.

Etzkowitz, Henry. 2010. "A company of their own: entrepreneurial scientists and the capitalization of knowledge," in, Riccardo Viale and Henry Etzkowitz, eds., *The Capitalization of Knowledge: A Triple Helix of University-Industry-Government*. Cheltenham: Edward Elgar, pp. 201–217.

Etzkowitz, Henry. 2009. Interview with Director of Technology Transfer, University of Chicago.

Etzkowitz, Henry.2008. *The Triple Helix: University-Industry-Government Innovation In Action* London: Routledge.

Etzkowitz, Henry. 2002. *MIT and the Rise of Entrepreneurial Science*. London: Routledge.

Etzkowitz, Henry.1999. "The Evolution of Entrepreneurial Science," in Lewis Branscomb, Fumio Kodama, Richard Florida, eds., *Industrializing Knowledge*. Cambridge: MIT Press, pp. 203–233.

Etzkowitz, Henry.1983. "Entrepreneurial Scientists and Entrepreneurial Universities in American Academic Science." *Minerva* 21(2–3): 198–233.

Etzkowitz, Henry, Magnus Gulbrandsen and Janet Levitt. 2000. *Public Venture Capital: Government Funding Sources for Technology Entrepreneurs*. New York: Harcourt.

Etzkowitz, Henry and Loet Leydesdorff, eds. 1997. *The University in the Global Knowledge Economy*. London: Cassell.

Etzkowitz, Henry and Elsa Blum. 1995. "Entrepreneurial Science in Mexico as a Development Strategy," in Terry Shinn, Jack Spaapen and Venni Krishna, eds., *Science and Technology in a Developing World*. Dordrecht: Kluwer.

Faulkner, Wendy and Jacqueline Senker. 1995. *Knowledge Frontiers; Public Sector Research and Industrial Innovation in Biotechnology, Engineering Ceramics and Parallel Computing*. Oxford: Oxford University Press.

Florida, Richard and Martin Kenney. 1990. *The Breakthrough Illusion: Corporate America's Failure to Move From Innovation to Mass Production*. New York: Basic Books.

Geiger, Roger. 1986. *To Advance Knowledge: The Growth of American Research Universities, 1900–1940*. New York: Oxford University Press.

Geiger, Roger. 1999. "The Ten Generations of American Higher Education", in Philip Altbach, Robert Berdahl, and Patricia Gumport, eds., *American Higher Education in the Twenty-first Century*. Baltimore: Johns Hopkins University Press, pp. 38–70.

Glaser, Barney. 1964. *Organizational Scientists*. Indianapolis: Bobbs Merill.

Genuth, Joel. 1987. "Groping Toward Science Policy in the United States in the 1930's" *Minerva* 25(3):238–268.

Gieryn, Thomas. 1983. "Boundary Work and the Demarcation of Science from Non-Science: Strains and Interests in the Professional Ideologies of Scientists" *American Sociological Review* 48: 781–95.

Gold, Lawrence. 1992. "Molecular, Cellular and Developmental Biology Department, University of Colorado, Boulder". Interview with the author.

Goldhor, Richard and Robert T. Lund. 1983. "University-to-Industry Advanced Technology Transfer: A Case Study." *Research Policy* 12(3):121–152.

Gouldner, Alvin. 1976. *The Dialectic of Ideology and Technology: The Origins, Grammar and Future of Ideology.* New York: Seabury.

Guston, David. 1999. *Between Politics and Science: Assuring the Productivity and Integrity of Research.* Cambridge: Cambridge University Press.

Hagstrom, Warren. 1965. *The Scientific Community.* New York: basic Books.

Hood, Leroy. 1989. Interview with author.

Hill, Karl, ed. 1963. *The Management of Scientists.* Boston: Beacon Press.

Johnston, Robert F. and Christopher G. Edwards, 1987. *Entrepreneurial Science.* Westport: Quorum.

Kaplan, Norman. 1965. "Professional Scientists in Industry: An Essay Review" *Social Problems* 13 (1):88–97.

Kenney, Martin. 1986. *Biotechnology.* New Haven: Yale University Press.

Kevles, Daniel. 1978. *The Physicists: The History of a Scientific Community in Modern America.* New York: Knopf.

Kornberg, Arthur. 1995. *The Golden Helix: Inside Biotech Ventures.* Mill Valley CA: University Science Books.

Kornhauser, William. 1959. *Scientists in Industry.* Berkeley: University of California.

Knorr-Cetina, Karin. 1980. *The Manufacture of Knowledge: An Essay on the Constructivist and Contextual Nature of Science.* Oxford: Pergamon.

Latour, Bruno and Steve Woolgar. 1979. *Laboratory Life.* Beverly Hills: Sage.

Lederberg, Joshua. 1996. Interview with the author.

Marshall, Gordon. 1981. "Accounting for Deviance." *International Journal of Sociology and Social Policy* 1(1): 17–48.

McDonald, Kim. 1982. "'Commercialization' of University Research is Decried." *The Chronicle of Higher* Education January 13.

McDonald, Kim. 1982. "Universities Urged to Bar Secrecy in Pacts with Private Industry." *Chronicle of Higher Education* April 7.

Marcson, Simon. 1960. *The Scientist in American Industry.* New York: Harper.

Machlup, Fritz. 1962. *The Production and Distribution of Knowledge in the United States.* Princeton: Princeton University Press.

Mannheim, Karl. 1936. *Ideology and Utopia*. New York: Harvest Books.

Meier, Robert. 1981. "Norms and the Study of Deviance: A Proposed Research Strategy." *Deviant Behavior* 3:1–25.

Merton, Robert. K. 1970 [1938]. *Science, Technology and Society in Seventeenth-Century England*. New York: Harper & Row.

Merton, Robert. K. 1957. *Social Theory and Social Structure*. New York: Free Press.

Merton, Robert. K. 1973[1942]. *The Sociology of Science*. Chicago: University of Chicago Press.

Merton, Robert. K. 1990 "Personal Communication to the author".

Minsky, Marvin. 1987. Department of Electrical Engineering and Computer Science, Interview with the author, Cambridge MA.

Mitchell, Clyde. 1983 "Case and Situation Analysis" *Sociological Review* 31 (2): 187–211.

Mitroff, Ian. 1974. "Norms and Counter-Norms in a Select Group of the Apollo Moon Scientists: A Case Study of the Ambivalence of Scientists" *American Sociological Review* 39:579–595.

National Science Foundation. 1999. Science Indicators www.nsf.gov.

Nelkin, Dorothy. 1984. *Science as Intellectual Property*. New York: Macmillan.

Noble, David. 1987. *America by Design*. New York: Knopf.

Noble, David and Nancy Pfund. 1980. "The Plastic Tower: Business Goes Back To College." *The Nation*. September 20.

Orth, Charles 1959 "The Optimum Climate for Industrial Research" Harvard Business Review. Vol. 47: 55–64.

Pelz, Donald and Frank Andrews. 1976. *Scientists in Organizations*. Ann Arbor: Institute of Social Research.

Pollack, Robert. 1982. Interview with the author.

Pollack, Robert, 1999, Personal Communication to the author. December.

Reich, Leonard. 1985. *The Making of American Industrial Research*. Cambridge: Cambridge University Press.

Sampat, Bhavat. 1999. "The Research Corporation" Presentation to the "Interfaces Seminar" Columbia University, December.

Rosenberg, Nathan and Richard Nelson. 1994. "American Universities and Technical Advance in Industry". *Research Policy* 23(3): 323–348.

Sahlman, William 1999. "The New Economy Is Stronger Than You Think." *Harvard Business Review* 77(6):99–106.

Saxenian, AnnaLee. 1994. *Regional Advantage: Culture and Competition in Silicon Valley and Route 128*. Cambridge: Harvard University Press.

Samuelson, Pamela. 1987. "Innovation and Competition: Conflicts over Intellectual Property Rights in New Technologies" *Science, Technology and Human Values* 11(1):6–21.

Slaughter, Shelia and Larry Leslie.1997. *Academic Capitalism*. Baltimore: Johns Hopkins University Press.

Stehr, Nico. 1976. "The Ethos of Science Revisited: Social and Cognitive Norms." *Sociological Inquiry* 48(3–4): 173–196.

Storr, Richard J. 1953. *The Beginnings of Graduate Education in America*. Chicago: University of Chicago Press.

The Economist. 1999. "Lost in Cyberspace" December 18, 1999 Vol. 353 No. 8150, pp. 78.

Toren, Nina. 1983. "The Scientific Ethos Debate: A Meta-Theoretical View." *Social Science Medicine* 17(2):1665–1672.

Veysey, Laurence. 1965. *The Emergence of the American University*. Chicago: University of Chicago Press.

Vollmer, Howard. 1962. *A Preliminary investigation and Analysis of the Role of Scientists in Research Organizations*. Menlo Park: Stanford Research Institute.

Zusman, Ami. 1999. "Issues Facing Higher Education in the Twenty-first Century," in Philip Altbach, Robert Berdahl and Patricia Gumport, eds., *American Higher Education in the Twenty-first Century*. Baltimore: Johns Hopkins University Press, pp. 109–150.

CHAPTER TWO

GLOBALIZATION AND SCIENTIFIC RESEARCH IN JAPAN

Zaheer Baber

Globalization or the Logic of Late Capitalism

Globalization, driven by the structural logic of late capitalism with all its inequities has unleashed dramatic transformations in every sphere of life even as these very transformations fuel the very processes that are transforming them. The broad outlines of this dynamic were captured way back in 1848 by Marx and Engels's remarkably prescient observation that the need of a "constantly expanding market for its products chases the bourgeoisie over the whole surface of the globe. It must nestle everywhere, settle everywhere, establish connections everywhere....as in material, so also in intellectual production" (Marx and Engels 1848 cited in Sayer 1989:106). As David Harvey (1990) and Frederic Jameson (1991) among others have convincingly demonstrated, it is impossible to get a handle on globalization as a process without reference to the logic of late capitalism. There is however, no shortage of academic as well as non-academic tomes where the discussion of globalization proceeds without any attempt to contextualize within the larger dynamics of global capitalism. And when global capitalism is acknowledged, it is usually with the aim of asserting that it has been transcended and replaced by globalization.

The deployment of the concept of "post-industrial society" represents one such prominent attempt to circumvent the structural reality of global capitalism. Coined by Daniel Bell (1973) and Clark Kerr (1983) proponents of the concept of "post-industrial society" argue that the production, commodification and consumption of knowledge, ideas, images and icons represents a fundamental break from the dynamics of classical capitalism. Their argument is that labor and capital as the essential ingredients of capitalism have been either supplanted or are well on their way to being superseded by knowledge, information and symbols as the main ingredients in the creation of value. As Daniel Bell (1980: 506) pointed out, "knowledge not labor is the source of value". There is indeed no doubt that increasingly knowledge and ideas as commodities constitute the key ingredients for the creation of value under global capitalism. At the same time however, as scholars such as David Harvey (1990), Frederic Jameson (1991), Sunder Rajan (2006), Aneesh (2006), Waldby and Mitchell (2007) have convincingly demonstrated, the idea that in a presumably "post-industrial" society, the conflict between labor and capital has been transcended amounts to nothing more than wishful thinking.

Proponents of "post-industrialism" who point to the relative decline of traditional manufacturing and the dramatic rise of the services sector in the global North ignore the fact of the relocation of industry to the global South. The fact that the traditional manufacturing sector appears to have shrunk in the advanced capitalist economies can partly be explained by the fact of the globalization of both capital and labor. The phenomenal growth of information and communication technologies as well as transportation systems has obviously enhanced the dramatic mobility of capital. The mobility of labor evident in "voluntary" and forced migrations around the world has also contributed dramatically to the process of globalization. The process of globalization itself has contributed to the hybridization of economic and social life, and its consequences for the texture of social life will no doubt continue to be profound and in many ways unpredictable. In addition to enhancing the mobility of capital and labor, globalization is also contributing to the reconstitution of scientific and technological research even as the pace and trajectory of globalization itself is profoundly influenced by new scientific and technological developments.

In many ways, directly and indirectly, the reconstitution of a complex globalized world is dramatically reconfiguring science, technology and the cultures of research. The phenomenal growth of biotechnology, nanotechnology, material science etc. are indeed driven by formal scientific knowledge systems, but these are also fields that are responding to global reconfiguration of markets in food, communication technologies etc. (Rajan 2006, Aneesh 2006). There seems to be little doubt that continued growth of transdisciplinary fields such as nanotechnology, superconductivity and artificial intelligence will only enhance this trend. As Immanuel Wallerstein (1991) has pointed out, the gradual dissolution of disciplinary boundaries that were drawn up during the nineteenth and sustained during the long, violent twentieth century is now quite evident in most universities and research institutions. It would indeed be surprising if the transgression of traditional disciplinary boundaries by the new forms of scientific knowledge were not accompanied by a corresponding restructuring of institutional sites where they were incubated and produced. After all, the university as a distinctive institutional site for the production and certification of expert knowledge was simultaneously a product and producer of modernity. The same is the case with the other two institutional components of the triple helix: the nation-state and industrial houses with their own research laboratories (Etzkowitz and Leydesdorff 1997).

The rationalization and standardization of products through the rise of industry and of people through the coercive, disciplinary institutions and practices of both the state and universities were integral component of the production of modernity. Institutions such as the Royal Society in England and many other associations in Italy were instrumental, albeit after protracted struggles, in carving out separate, autonomous spaces for the practice of science. It was in the nineteenth century, beginning in colonial India (Huff 2003, Visvanathan 1984, Baber 1996) that engineering training was incorporated into universities—a move that signaled the transformation of craft practices into formal academic disciplines and ultimately led to the application of scientific principles to the practice of engineering. If the emergence and consolidation of modernity led to the rise of distinctive institutions like the university, the state and industry, the movement towards transdisciplinary knowledge production currently underway is now contributing to a re-configuration of those very institutions that originally made formally demarcated disciplines possible (Etzkowitz and Leydesdorff 1997).

To make sense of these rapid institutional changes unfolding, a number of models and metaphors are available. Gibbons et al. (1994) in *The New Production of Knowledge* discuss the transition from Mode 1 to Mode 2 type of knowledge production. Mode 1 refers to the classical and idealized Newtonian model where the location of production of knowledge is institutionally demarcated from the site of application. Mode 2 on the other hand refers to knowledge production carried out in the context of application and is characterized by transdisciplinarity, heterogeneity and organizational transience. Along roughly the same lines, the "triple helix" model offered by Etzkowitz and Leydesdorff (1997) emphasizes the decline of the linear conception of basic and applied research where theoretical and practical issues are tackled in separate institutional sphere, namely the university and industry. The model, extending the metaphoric representation of the double helix of

the DNA, anticipates the increasing growth of a spiral model of innovation where the theoretical and practical questions are interrelated,
cross over the boundaries or occur at the interstices of what until
recently were rigidly demarcated institutional spheres. Universities,
states and industries that were differentiated from each other as a condition for the constitution of modernity are now intersecting with each
other to create unique institutional configurations. Thus, universities
are taking on the characteristics of firms, many firms are beginning to
resemble universities, and many states function as private corporations. These developments are partly driven by the commodification
of scientific knowledge, even as they reflexively contribute further to
that process.

The Commodification of Scientific Knowledge

Neither the conversion of scientific knowledge nor the emergence of
the entrepreneurial university is entirely new. After all, MIT pioneered
the infusion of science-based engineering into industry in the mid-
nineteenth century and an institutional arrangement that was the
model for Stanford in the post-war era (Etzkowitz 2002, Guston and
Kenniston 1994). What has changed however is the sheer scale of the
commodification of scientific knowledge that is pushing the formation
of strategic alliances and new institutional configurations. Following
Etzkowitz and Webster (1995: 480–505), the commodification of scientific knowledge or its conception as intellectual property itself is
driven by a number of factors: the rise of technologies based on generic
forms of knowledge that underpin a diverse range of industrial sectors
without being unique to any one sector; the gradual blurring of boundaries between basic and applied research, particularly evident in the
field of biotechnology. As a consequence of this blurring of boundaries
that were not too distinct to begin with, universities emerge as significant sites for pre-competitive research due to their institutional cultural capacity for focusing on generic principles and models that can
be adapted for specific technical systems (Mukerji 1989).

Driven by the emergence of post-Fordist production systems, industrial research houses increasingly underemphasize specialized research
that can have generic applications and closer commercial links with
specialized research in universities have been one of the solutions to
this problem. The universities themselves have experienced an erosion

of the grants economy and being in a position of holding and exploiting patents, they have sought to expand their linkages with industry and to establish themselves as commercial enterprises; in settings such as the United States, where national planning for science and technology has been absent, the state has used linkages between universities and industry as a surrogate for industrial policy (Etzkowitz and Webster 1995: 480–505).

There are of course other important factors that have contributed to the emergence of the triple helix, but the increasing transformation of scientific knowledge into capital and property constitutes one of the key driving forces. In view of these far reaching changes that promise to dramatically restructure the nature and location of scientific research, against the backdrop of globalization, the specific configuration of social factors that are at work in the constitution of the triple helix in Japan are examined in this paper. The specific focus of this paper is on the mix of historical, global and local social factors that have contributed to the detailed configuration of the triple helix of the state, university and industry in Japan.

The Triple Helix in Japan: Historical and Contemporary Transformations

The truism that under globalization no country is an island rings particularly true for Japan comprised as it is, entirely of islands with no physical connections to any mainland. Although for long periods in history, Japan was indeed relatively isolated from the rest of the world, it wasn't obviously as isolated as its myths of origins imply. Japan's colonization of Korea and parts of China predate its occupation of many parts of Southeast Asia and its involvement in the Second World War. Even during the periods of relative isolation, there were always linguistic, religious and architectural exchanges between Japan and its neighbours, particularly China and Korea. Even though like any other nation under globalization, Japan is not an island, when it comes to scientific research, until recently, Japanese universities constituted veritable islands in their own societies. As a consequence of the war, when some universities constituted sites for research and production of armaments by private corporations, until the 1990s Japanese universities did not engage in direct collaborative research with industry. To be sure, as Diana Hicks (1993) has rightly pointed out, informal collaboration always existed, but until recently the situation was quite different when one compares Japanese universities with American institutions such as MIT and Stanford.

Until the mid-1990s Japanese university scientists worked in an institutional environment and culture that was shaped by restrictive governmental regulations that prohibited research collaborations with industry. On their part, university scientists radicalized by the anti-Vietnam war movement, did not want to have anything to do with private corporations. Even though dramatic changes have been underway due to the implementation of the "incorporation law" introduced in 2004, scientific and technological research continues to be influenced by a specific organizational structure and culture that has been in place for a long time. This organization structure is the *koza* system comprising of units that include a professor, an associate professor, two assistants and a couple of technical assistants, all employed directly by the Ministry of Education. The university scientists together with the research support staff have the status of civil servants that implicates them in a specific institutional relationship with the state. Although this organizational structure system ensures the freedom and autonomy of each research unit or *koza* in terms of research, it also gravitates against co-operation between different units. It is not that such co-operation is impossible or that it never happens.

However the general trend is toward competitive autonomy that serves research in certain fields better than others. With the emergence of complex, transdisciplinary fields in which isolated expertise in a particular discipline is not enough, the institutional bottleneck generated by this organizational form becomes apparent. Fields that cannot survive without equipment and instruments that are costly are at a particular disadvantage. Thus when it comes to the crucial issue of the purchase of expensive equipment, different *kozas* cannot pool their resources together as there is no real mechanism for such co-operation. Until recently, this problem was complicated further by the unequal distribution of funds to all *koza* within a faculty and by the relatively low level of technical support for university research. In response to the bottlenecks induced by the *koza* system prevalent in the universities, a number of research institutes independent of the traditional faculties have sought to create post-*koza* academic environments. A number of university based research institutes have begun to function completely outside the *koza* framework, but a substantial proportion of research is still conducted in the traditional departments and faculties (Sigurdson 1995: 72–80, Traweek 1992).

The transformation of the existing organizational structure has continued dramatically, and much of this change has been triggered off by globalization driven by late capitalism. Until the 1990s, when Japanese corporations needed the expertise of university scientists, they were forced to collaborate with mostly American universities. Indeed, the MIT Tokyo Office to facilitate precisely such collaborations has been in existence for a fairly long time. As for university scientists, those who were looking for collaborating with industrial corporations had found it easier to work in foreign, mostly American universities or corporations. With the consolidation of global capitalism and the onset of neo-liberalism during the Reagan era, the structural pressures for institutional change and realignments were felt everywhere, including of course, Japan. Indeed Japan was frequently singled out by some American lawmakers and accused of getting a "free ride" for allegedly relying on the results of American research to build its economy. The pressure on the Japanese government from its corporations and university scientists who wanted to engage in direct collaboration with each other, had been building up for a long time.

The autonomous and island-like existence of the Japanese universities enforced by post-War legislation began to erode not just due to globalization but also because of specific local and scientific factors as discussed below. Responding to the global and local changes, the Japanese University Council in 1991 instituted self-monitoring and self-evaluation exercises in an attempt to enforce quality controls (Mok 2006). This initiative was followed up by the Science and Technology Basic Law announced in 1995, and the First Basic Science and Technology Plan (1996–2000). Among other things, this plan dramatically increased the science and technology budget and made it legal for universities to collaborate with industry while simultaneously enhancing the links between the universities and the state. This Japanese equivalent of the Bayh-Dole Act or "the Law on Promoting Technology Transfer from Universities to Industry" (TLO) was passed in 1998. The passage of this law has led to the formation of over two dozen Technology Licensing Organizations or TLO's (Kitagawa 2006:10–12, Kitagawa 2009).

In 2001, the powerful Ministry of Economy, Trade and Industry or METI (formerly MITI or the Ministry of International Trade and Industry) proposed a dramatic shift in industrial policy that would fundamentally affect the organizational and research culture of Japanese universities. Known as the 'Hirunama Plan', this state-led initiative specifically focused on "venture businesses born in universities"

(Kitagawa 2006:11). During the same year, specifically, in June 2001, the 'Toyama Plan' titled *Basic Principles for Structural Reforms of Universities* was formally released by MEST or the Ministry of Education, Culture, Sports, Science and Technology. Just a year later, the *Basic Law* on *Intellectual Property* was passed in 2002. Following closely on the heels of these initiatives that unfolded in a short space of time, the plan finally paved new ground rules for the dramatic transformation of the structure, funding and the relationship of the universities with industry and the state. What came to be known as the "The Incorporatisation Law" (*kokuritsu daigaku hojin*) was subsequently passed by the House of Representatives and enacted as law in April 2004 (Kitagawa 2006: 13). With the passage of this law, the national universities that were until now funded and controlled by the state were converted into corporations or more specifically, National University Corporations.

As summarized by Kitagawa (2006:13–14) a number of transformations that represent a clear break from the past, followed. First, the responsibility for recruiting faculty and staff was transferred from the government to the newly formed National University Corporations or NUC's. Secondly, the NUC's were granted fiscal autonomy from the state–all assets and financial obligations were transferred from the government to the universities. Finally, new management and quality evaluations structures emerged at the apex of which were the presidents of the NUC's as the heads of the corporations. When compared to the existing institutional arrangement under which higher education and research had been pursued until 2004, these measures triggered off quite dramatic institutional changes and reconfigurations in their wake (Tabata 2005, Yamamoto 2004, Kitagawa 2009, Mok 2006). Given the enormity of changes underway, it is hardly surprising that these initiatives have evoked some very sharp responses that need to be taken into account (Tabata 2005, Ozawa and Nakayama 2009, Iwasaki 2009).

In addition to globalization, there is another major factor at work. Scientific and technological research in Japanese universities is not supported by the military. The situation in the United States is quite the opposite, with many research universities receiving extensive funding for basic research from the department of defense. For example, the mega Human Genome project was funded largely by the Departments of Energy and Defense. At one level, such funding opportunities are not available to Japanese academic researchers. At another level,

however, the university community, radicalized by the anti-war movement of the 1960s coming after the general post-war academic culture has generated a general hostility toward research funds from
non-academic sources that could compromise the relative independence of universities. Partly because of the declining funding situation,
this hostility toward private funds is no longer that strong, and this
situation is pushing leading Japanese universities towards collaborative research with the private sector.

The funding situation is critical. Of the total R&D, private industry
accounts for about 70 percent of the expenditure, the state is responsible for about 20 percent and the contribution for university research
comes to about 10 percent (Low 1997:132–33). In a period where scientific research requires enormous amounts of funds, most universities are feeling the crunch. However, whether the corporatization of
Japanese universities will actually enable to them to generate the much
needed funds or not is not yet clear (Yamamoto 2004). Finally, the
push towards the so-called knowledge based economies has led to the
realization that the R&D establishments of most companies need basic
science skills that are not too specialized and rigid. This is particularly
the case with a number of trans-disciplinary fields where university
researchers are better placed than their counterparts in private
corporations.

The combination of all these factors is leading to significant changes
in the mode of scientific knowledge production in Japan (Goto et al.
1998, Goto 1998). The gradual erosion of the *koza* system, the emergence of university-industry joint research centres in the national universities, and the creation of the Tsukuba city and the Kansai region as
well as other science cities and parks is gradually eroding what one
respondent referred to as the "very rigid walls and boundaries" that
until relatively recently separated university and corporate research
institutions. In addition to the emergence of the university based
research centers that enter into alliance with industry, a number of
new institutional configurations are emerging in Tsukuba Science City,
80 miles north of Tokyo.

Hybrid Institutional Configurations in Japan: TARA, TRC and RCAST

One example of the initiative coming from the university comes in
the form of TARA or the Tsukuba Advanced Research Alliance that

represents one of the many hybrid institutions cropping up. Although a part of Tsukuba University, TARA provides the institutional setting for bringing researchers from the university, industry and state laboratories to work together on specific projects. Having won extensive backing from the Ministry of Education, TARA represents a post-Fordist research culture that seeks to replace rigid and rule-bound departments with "research aspects". The only reason for the existence of "research aspects" is a specific collaborative project on which teams comprising of researchers from Tsukuba University, private industry and state laboratories work together. The initial life of a particular "research aspect" is three years, after which it can be renewed. In effect TARA as an institution is attempting to create a hybrid institutional setting for research that is organizationally and institutionally different from the three existing forms: the university, the private company and state labs. TARA is funded by the Ministry of Education, other government agencies and private industry.

The second such hybrid institution that does not exist anymore but provides lessons for understanding the emerging alliances was the Tsukuba Research Consortium (TRC). Located in the heart of Tsukuba Science City, the TRC was a private sector initiative that sought to simulate all the social, cultural and structural aspects of a university campus. Researchers working on transdisciplinary projects were housed together, shared seminars, played together and used the library together. The focus was on eroding, even if for a short while, the boundaries created by affiliation to particular companies, by creating an environment where the idealized goals of sharing knowledge and information, as opposed to jealously guarding them from competitors, was emphasized. In other words, TRC sought to develop and sustain the distinctive "norms of science" as enunciated by Robert Merton (1973) that are presumably not to be found in the research labs of private companies.

The gradual erosion of the *koza* system and the appearance of hybrid institutions such as TARA and TRC represent a step in the evolution of knowledge production from Mode 1 to Mode 2. These institutions, together with many other new cross disciplinary institutions such as the RCAST (Research Centre for Advanced Science and Technology) at the University of Tokyo, signal not just the transition to Mode 2 of knowledge production but also the consolidation of the triple helix in a setting where the three institutions have been more separated from each other than most other societies. There is no doubt that the breaking down of traditional disciplinary boundaries that were drawn up in the nineteenth century is leading to a corresponding blurring of boundaries between institutions that have so far been relatively rigid. Although the claims about the imminent disappearance of classical capitalism and the end of ideologies have been grossly overstated, there is no doubt that a major institutional reconfiguration of the institutional locus of knowledge production is underway. The landscape of scientific research is being altered in a dramatic fashion, an alteration whose actual long-term consequences are hard to predict.

Tensions in the Transformation of the Norms of Science

In the case of Japan, the dramatic institutional changes are gradually modifying the norms of scientific research as enunciated by Robert Merton. In his original formulation, Merton (1973) had stipulated four major norms of science that were crucial for the growth of science. These include "communalism," "disinterestedness", "organized skepticism" and "universalism". As many commentators have pointed out, these norms are no doubt idealized representations of the professional ideologies that serve to demarcate science from the rest of society, and to resist encroachment from the non-scientific sectors of society. This ideological self-conception of science was particularly useful for the creation of a public sphere for scientific research or a space that successfully resisted the power of religious and state authorities, even while science contributed enormously to the consolidation of the modern nation-state. Thus, even before the emergence of the triple helix, the pursuit of science was never as totally a disinterested activity as its ideological representations would have one believe. Academic scientific research was always influenced in subtle and not so subtle ways by a variety of agendas and factors typically conceived to be outside of the sphere of science (Etzkowitz and Webster 1995).

However, with the emergence of institutional alliances and configuration such as the "triple helix", the professional norms of academic scientists that have generated resistance against directly transforming research into monetary value is being eroded. Academic scientists who are marketing their research are increasingly no longer seen as deviants who are flouting the basic norms of science even though many of them are still very ambivalent of their changing institutional location.

Some recent studies of long-term university-industry collaborations in Britain seem to indicate that scientists no longer see these tie-ups as problematic and most do disagree with the idea that private corporations will totally dictate research agendas that used to be independent (Webster 1994). The authors of a recent study concluded that, although scientific research has largely become project science, big science or commercial science, it has not led professionals to hand over the definition and direction of their fields of research to external forces (Slaughter and Rhoades 1990: 358).

One of the issues brought up by these studies is the idea that some private companies are seeking alliances with industry precisely because academic scientists have cultivated not just some skills but also norms of research that cannot be duplicated in industrial laboratory settings. The argument here is that since university scientists are not their direct competitors, it is not rational for them to try and totally subvert an established non-commercial research culture that provides advantages for tackling certain kinds of questions that cannot be addressed in non-academic settings. Academic scientists on the other hand feel they have to create alliances outside of academia, while trying very hard to maintain a degree of control and autonomy over their research agendas and actual research.

Finally, states are under increasing pressure to stimulate economic growth, and given the fact an increasing proportion of at least some economies will continue to be influenced by the conversion of scientific knowledge into capital, they are institutionally pressured to restructure universities and to some extent industries. Whether scientific research will be increasing directly controlled and dominated by private corporations; whether reconfigured universities will redefine existing professional ideologies and continue to defend institutional spaces for the relative autonomy of scientific research is hard to predict. Either way, although the predicted demise of capitalism due to the emergence of knowledge societies is little more than ideological hyperbole, it is imperative to grasp the general contours of the structural forces that are dramatically re-structuring institutions inherited from an earlier era.

In the final analysis, globalization constitutes the major structural factor that is contributing to the transformation of the mode and culture of scientific and technological research in Japan. During the period when Japanese corporations could not create linkages and alliances with Japanese universities, the remarkable efflorescence of information and communication technologies that have fuelled glo-balization enabled these corporations to create and consolidate ties with American universities. Specifically, the increased use of the inter-net in scientific and technological research enabled creation of link-ages and communities that were no longer confined by the boundaries of a particular institution or even a particular nation-state. Simultane-ously the emergence of transdisciplinary fields such as nanotechnol-ogy, superconductivity and artificial intelligence would not have been possible without extensive collaborative research that cut through many spatial boundaries, local and global.

The development of these fields, made possible to some extent by globalization, has necessitated a re-thinking of the organization of research in Japanese universities, an arrangement that was not meant for tackling such complex issues. The creation of new institutional alliances between corporate and university researchers in Japan are driven, at least in part, by the forces of globalization that are trans-forming entire fields of inquiry as well as the culture of research. The creation of these new alliances has been facilitated by the abolition in 1989 of a law that prohibited these ties. Finally, some American jour-nalists and policy-makers had accused Japan of taking a free-ride and not contributing enough to the global pool of basic scientific research. As Low, Nakayama and Yoshioka (1999) point out, these accusations do not necessarily accord with the empirical reality and they simplify the complex social processes involved in the transfer of technology.

Not surprisingly, such accusations have appeared each time American officials have negotiated with Japan over trade. Such percep-tions have contributed to the re-organization of existing institutions of scientific and technological research and the creations of new ones such as Tsukuba Advanced Research Alliance with the goal of creating institutional linkages between industries and universities under the auspices of MITI which is now METI and the Ministry of Education, Culture and Sports, or MEXT. Most of these transformations in Japan were carried out under the ex-Prime Minister Koizumi Junichiro who had initiated the privatization of a number of public sector enter-prises. Despite the dramatic change in the government in Japan, it is very unlikely that the new Prime Minister Kan Naoto representing a left of the centre party will, given the global forces at work, reverse the conservative policies of the LPD that had a monopoly on power for half a century. As Mok (2006) indicated, the universities are caught in a delicate balancing act. On the one hand, they are promised institutional autonomy by that state while on the other hand, this autonomy is circumvented by powerful forces of late capitalist globalization as well as local factors. How this balancing act will play itself out in the future, is not at all clear. What is clear however is that, universities have no choice but to deal with the transformations unleashed by globalization.

Bibliography

Aneesh, A. 2006. *Virtual Migration: The Programming of Globalization*. Durham: Duke University Press.

Baber, Zaheer. 1996. *The Science of Empire: Scientific Knowledge, Civilization and Colonial Rule in India*. Albany: State University of New York Press.

Bell, Daniel. 1973. *The Coming of Postindustrial Society*. New York: Basic Books.

Bell, Daniel. 1980. "The Social Framework of the Information Society," in Tom Forester, ed., *The Microelectronics Revolution*. Oxford: Basil Blackwell, pp. 500–549.

Etzkowitz, Henry. 2002. *MIT and the Rise of Entrepreneurial Science*. London and New York: Routledge.

Etzkowitz, Henry and Andrew Webster. 1995. "Science as Intellectual Property", in Sheila Jasanoff, Gerald Mankle, James Peterson and Trevor Pinch, eds., *Handbook of Science and Technology Studies*. London: Sage, pp. 480–505.

Etzkowitz, Henry and Loet Leydesdorff, eds. 1997. *Universities and the Global Knowledge Economy: A Triple Helix of University-Industry-Government Relations* London: Pinter.

Gibbons, Michael, Camille Limoges, Helga Nowotny, Simon Schwartzman, Peter Scott and Martin Trow.1994. *The New Production of Knowledge: The Dynamics of Science and Research in Contemporary Societies*. London: Sage Publications.

Goto, Kunio, David V. Gibson, Heidi Lopez-Cepero and Graham Stewart, eds.1998. *The Science City in a Global Context*. Austin, TX: IC2 Institute.

Goto, Kunio. 1998. "The Privatization of Science and Technology: The Public-Private Relationship in Perspective", in Goto, Kunio, David V. Gibson, Heidi Lopez-Cepero and Graham Stewart, eds. *The Science City in a Global Context* Austin, Texas: IC2 Institute, pp. 205–210.

Guston, David and Kenneth Kenniston, eds. 1994. *The Fragile Contract: University Science and the Federal Government*. Cambridge, MA: MIT Press.

Harvey, David. 1990. *The Condition of Postmodernity* Oxford: Blackwell.

Hicks, Diana. 1993. "University-industry research links in Japan." *Policy Sciences* 26: 361–395.

Huff, Toby E. 2003. *The Rise of Early Modern Science*. Cambridge: Cambridge University Press.

Iwasaki, Minoru. 2009. "The Deception of the Idea of Self-Responsibility and Individualization: Neo-Liberal Rhetoric as Revealed in the Corporatization of Japan's National Universities." *Inter-Asia Cultural Studies* 10(2):248–259.

Jameson, Frederic. 1991. *Postmodernism or the Cultural Logic of Late Capitalism*. New York: Verso.

Kawamoto, Tetsuko. 1998. "Partnership among the Public, Academic, and Private Sectors in Tsukuba", in Goto, Kunio, David V. Gibson, Heidi Lopez-Cepero and Graham Stewart, eds. *The Science City in a Global Context* Austin, Texas: IC2 Institute, pp. 55–60.

Kerr, Clark. 1983. *The Future of Industrial Societies: Convergence or Continuing Diversity?* Cambridge, MA: Harvard University Press.

Kitagawa, Fumi. 2009. "Universities-Industry Links and Regional Development in Japan", *Science, Technology and Society* 14(1):1–33.

Kitagawa, Fumi. 2006. "New Science and Technology Policies and Re-Positioning of Universities in the Changing National Innovation System: A View from Japan", *European University Institute, Florence* Working Paper No. 2006/09.

Low, Morris. 1997. "Japan: From Technology to Science Policy" in Henry Etzkowitz and Loet Leydesdorff, eds. *Universities and the Global Knowledge Economy: A Triple Helix of University-Industry-Government Relations* London: Pinter, pp. 132–140.

Low, Morris, Shigeru Nakayama and Hitoshi Yoshioka. 1999. *Science, Technology and Society in Contemporary Japan*. Cambridge: Cambridge University Press.

Merton, Robert. 1973. *Sociology of Science* Chicago: University of Chicago Press.

Mok, Ka Ho. 2006. *Education Reform and Education Policy in East Asia*. London: Routledge.

Mukerji, Chandra. 1989. *A Fragile Power: Scientists and the State*. Princeton, NJ: Princeton University Press.

Ozawa, Hiroaki and Izumi Nakayama. 2009. "Domination by Money Power: One Year after the Corporatization of National Universities." *Inter-Asia Cultural Studies*, 10(2):181–190.

Sayer, Derek, ed. 1989. *Readings from Karl Marx*. London: Routledge.

Sigurdson, Jon. 1995. *Science and Technology in Japan* London: Cartermill.

Sunder Rajan, Kaushik. 2006. *Biocapital: The Constitution of Postgenomic Life*. Durham: Duke University Press.

Rhoades, Gary and Sheila Slaughter. 1997. "Academic Capitalism, Managed Professionals, and Supply-Side Higher Education." *Social Text 51* 15(2): 9–38.

Tabata, Hirokumi. 2005. "The Incorporation and Economic Structural Reform of Japan's National Universities." *Social Science Japan Journal* 8(1):91–102.

Traweek, Sharon. 1992. *Beamtimes and Lifetimes: The Life of High Energy Physicists*. Cambridge, MA: Harvard University Press.

Visvanathan, Shiv. 1984. *Organizing for Science* Delhi: Oxford University Press.

Waldby, Catherine and Robert Mitchell. 2006. *Tissue Economies: Blood, Organs and Cell Lines in Late Capitalism*. Durham: Duke University Press.

Wallerstein, Immanuel. 1991. *Unthinking Social Science: The Limits of Nineteenth Century Paradigms*. Cambridge: Cambridge University Press.

Webster, Andrew. 1994. "University-Corporate Ties and the Construction of Research Agendas", *Sociology* 28(1):123–142.

Yamamoto, Kiyoshi. 2004. "Corporatization of National University in Japan: Governance or Rhetoric for Downsizing?" *Financial Accountability and Management*, 20(2):153–181.

CHAPTER THREE

TRIPLE HELIX OR TRIPLE JEOPARDY?
UNIVERSITIES AND THE SOCIAL RELATIONS OF KNOWLEDGE

Terry Wotherspoon

Nearly four decades ago, researchers promoting the advancement of what they termed (overly) optimistically a "new sociology of education" advocated the need to "make" rather than "take" educational problems as laid out by those with specific interests or in positions of influence (Young 1971). Educational analysis and the conditions and contexts which researchers were attempting to understand have changed significantly in many respects since that time, but the insight remains crucial for researchers seeking to balance critical inquiry with research that speaks to important public issues. These considerations are especially pertinent to an understanding of social relationships in and around contemporary universities. Social and economic transformations in which capacities related to knowledge and information figure prominently have been accompanied by massive expansion of postsecondary education on a global scale. For universities, which until relatively recently enjoyed a status that was somewhat hallowed but typically outside the realms of experience for all but select groups of social participants, there are unprecedented opportunities but also unfamiliar challenges and risks.

Notions that a strong postsecondary education sector is a hallmark of progressive enlightened societies may be relatively uncontested, but there is considerably less consensus about what roles universities should play with regard to various social, economic, cultural, and political functions, and how these roles are to be activated. In the process, as they position themselves (and are positioned by external agents) to take advantage of the benefits promised by knowledge-based economies and learning societies, universities must contend simultaneously with pressures posed by rising expectations, unaccustomed forms of scrutiny, and more mundane concerns like how to sustain adequate financial resources, attract and retain highly qualified researchers and students, maintain the value of the credentials they offer in relation to other institutions and alternative learning sites, and justify their social and economic relevance to constituencies that are increasingly more diverse and concerned about differing types of accountabilities. Understanding of how universities are being repositioned and with what consequences for the development of knowledge-based societies is often blurred or complicated by debates and discourses that are typically fragmented across numerous disciplinary perspectives and focal points.

This chapter explores interrelationships among two significant dimensions associated with changing postsecondary landscapes. While the paper's title is somewhat misleading, it draws attention to concepts that designate more general processes that represent, respectively, technological innovation and economic development. The contextual usage applied here includes in part intertwining relations among universities, governments and industries and dynamics of social inclusion and exclusion. This again, extends to explicating prospects for knowledge-based societies to reproduce or transform articulations among class, race, gender and other pervasive forms of social inequality. Both discourses include possibilities to understand how universities and knowledge are constituted by and embedded within complex social relationships rather than being simply paraded as abstract, formal or corporate entities.

As postsecondary education comes to be linked with economic productivity, especially insofar as education's importance is determined more by the productive role of knowledge in a new economy than by its value as a social service or public good, the social relations of knowledge production and knowledge workers take shape through novel as well as longstanding dynamics of social inclusion and exclusion. Postsecondary expansion and parallel emphasis on science, innovation and creativity are accompanied by democratic and meritocratic prospects to broaden societies' knowledge-generating capacities, but these processes also carry with them tensions and contradictions.

Thus, both within and across national, regional and institutional contexts, broadly convergent pathways also yield a disparate range of patterns of differentiation, hierarchy and inequality. As they are drawn more completely into knowledge-based economic development, universities risk reinforcing selective processes and inefficiencies that lie at the heart of new economies, particularly in their constrained ability to recognize, draw from, and utilize a full range of knowledge and human capacities.

The Changing Role of Universities in the Knowledge Economy

Universities, like other major social institutions, are undergoing significant transformations in the context of intersecting processes of globalization, technological innovation, and changing organizational dynamics. With relatively few exceptions, governments across the globe have adopted policies to promote massive expansion of higher education to foster innovation and increase the supply of knowledge workers required for competitive performance in a globalizing economy. Enrolment in tertiary education programs worldwide increased from slightly below 30 million in 1970 to over 152 million in 2007; expressed as a proportion of those who were within five years of formal secondary school-leaving age at each respective time, tertiary participation rose from nine percent in 1970 to 26 percent in 2007 (UNESCO 2009: 14). Although rates vary by nation and region, over three-quarters (between 77 and 79 percent) of all those enrolled in tertiary education are in university or equivalent programs eligible for qualification for university degrees (UNESCO 2009: 136–7). By 2006, university credentials had been attained by nearly 20 percent of the population ages 25 to 64, and one-quarter of those in the 25 to 34 year age cohort, in OECD nations, though rates in comparison nations like Brazil and Indonesia were well below ten percent (OECD 2009: Table 1.3a).

In concert with the movement of knowledge relations from the shadows to the centre of contemporary social and economic activities, universities come to take on a more prominent role in advancing regional, national and global agendas for change, fuelled by both stated and tacit expectations that education and training investments will yield high returns in the form of a highly skilled workforce and innovative ideas, production capacities, and working relationships. These transition processes have profound consequences for universities and the institutional environments within which they operate, reflected in frequent contestation over the nature and orientations of the changing postsecondary landscape. A growing array of discourses appearing variously in managerial, critical and postmodernist accounts suggests the destabilization and repositioning of the academy is of sufficient magnitude as to be designated an "academic revolution" or "third generation" of universities led by "new paradigms of knowledge production," sometimes depicted as the corporate or entrepreneurial university, in the process breaking down boundaries and dismantling or at least moving beyond the ivory tower (Clark 1998, Etzkowitz 2004, Moravec 2008, Wissema 2009).

Amidst conceptual variations and differing conclusions about the pace and significance of change, there is general agreement that these transformations are accelerated by a convergence of an impetus towards greater degrees of external orientation on the part of universities with growing levels of scrutiny over university activities and overtures to engage universities from outside agencies. These relationships are typically understood with reference to a 'third mission' that takes universities beyond their core historical mandates of teaching and research, compelling researchers and their scholarly activities to become more fully immersed in relations with external communities and partners. Posed in knowledge terms, the role of knowledge translation is layered upon activities related to knowledge dissemination and knowledge production, respectively.

There is nothing strikingly new in these mandated activities (typical standards for faculty promotion and tenure in many universities, for instance, have long included assessment in categories of research, teaching, and professional service or outreach). What has changed are the ways in which these activities are intertwined and differentially nurtured and evaluated. New hierarchies and divisions of labor, often accompanied by tensions within and across institutional settings, arise alongside disparities in access to fiscal, social and political resources. Thus, a seemingly benign or welcome emphasis on making research useful through outreach and engagement, when characterized as holding universities accountable for their longstanding commitment to service to the community, also invites new scrutiny and controversy whether posed in terms of relatively neutral (but often contested) relationships with community partners and government and regional agencies or opening additional controversies and inequities as these arrangements proceed from university-business or corporate partnerships to more clearly delineated steps along market-driven pathways (Laredo 2007).

The often asymmetrical relationship that emerges between discourses and practices as universities position themselves to deliver third mission mandates is illustrative in these regards. Conceptions of the third mission range widely from narrowly defined commercial activities to broadly-framed social and economic outreach. Deem (2008), reviewing analyses of recent university transformations, observes substantial discrepancies in how researchers and policy-makers understand these changes and the motivations behind them. In the meantime, regardless of how mandates are framed, the conjuncture of various factors, including declining or targeted fiscal support from governments, the selection of narrowly defined performance indicators by institutions themselves, overtures from industry, and dedication of university priorities and resources to revenue generating activities, has tended to concentrate third mission-related practice on research output that can be licensed, patented or employed in commercial applications that will yield the highest fiscal returns. The massive scale of investment required to establish and mobilize many innovation-related activities often requires comprehensive social and economic policy interventions that include redistribution of resources from other fundamental needs within and across nations (Brown et al. 2001, Hale 2002, Stehr 1996: 17, Pierson 2001). Even Peter Drucker (1994: 2–3), a leading proponent of the advancement of knowledge societies, recognized the potentially serious policy consequences that could follow growing status and income gaps between a relatively small "leading class" of knowledge workers and the majority of highly productive workers in other economic sectors.

These trends, whether mobilized by direct investment or steering (such as state funding for research infrastructure or initiatives intended to increase the supply of graduates in science and technology fields) or through more indirect circuits, are nonetheless general tendencies rather than uniform or unidirectional in nature. Policies and practices related to innovation and higher education are influenced by numerous variables (see, e.g., Brown at al. 2001: 52–55). Along with national and regional variances in relation to economic factors like fiscal capacity, industrial structures, and labor market priorities, diverse political alignments and policy structures contribute to the coexistence, in one direction, of an impetus to develop a pattern of "global universities" and, in another, a proliferation of alternative models of university development. Integrated national innovation strategies may be facilitated by conditions in which states or core industries are strong, highly concentrated, or linked institutionally with other key sectors, as in corporatism.

In other cases, however, uneven institutional arrangements may reflect lesser ability to coordinate innovation strategies and partnerships or circumstances that contribute to 'loose coupling' of policy and practice. In Canada, for instance, where education is an area of provincial jurisdiction but the federal government also plays a role in postsecondary training and research through various funding programs and activities in related areas of jurisdiction, proposals from a few of the largest universities to consolidate national research and development spending in those institutions periodically generate extensive controversy (see, e.g., Engelhart 2009). In short, the overall university landscape increases in complexity as institutions and nations grapple with common challenges and logics that are crosscut with a series of diverse political economic circumstances and capacities to take decisive action in any particular direction.

Knowledge, Knowledge Workers and Knowledge Economies

Efforts to understand how universities become variously positioned to address issues associated with knowledge-based economies are frequently compounded by the imprecise ways in which knowledge and knowledge work are typically defined and measured. Knowledge work is normally defined with reference to one or more of three core elements: (i) non-manual work in which core tasks involve the development, transfer or application of knowledge; (ii) high levels of education and specialized skills dependent, in large part, upon formal credentials and training; and (iii) immersion in a high technology environment. The precise reference points for these terms tend to vary widely (Powell and Snellman 2004, Guile 2006), and are associated with diverse orientations that offer competing assessments of the role and extent of knowledge work in the global economy. The predominant assessment of knowledge work and the expansion of the knowledge economy, popularized through the work of Bell (1973) and Drucker (1993), is relatively optimistic and consensus-based. The development of human capital in conjunction with innovations in technology and the spread of information systems are seen to make it possible for nearly all workers to benefit from newly defined roles as knowledge workers (Brown et al. 2003).

In the most common expressions, knowledge workers are defined as those with highly specialized forms of training and advanced credentials, so that frequently the number or proportions of persons with university degrees stand as a proxy for the scale of knowledge workers within a given population (Brinkley et al. 2009: 13–14). Viewed this way, the expansion of university spaces and graduates is taken as a progressive development. By contrast, a range of alternative conclusions emerge from analyses that frame knowledge work in narrower terms that take into account variations in fields of specialization or the degree of fit as competencies and credentials are translated into practice within distinct occupational settings. There is a fundamental dilemma in much of this analysis. If the equation of higher education or training with knowledge work is made too loosely, there is no accounting for the kinds of work that people actually do after gaining formal qualification (most typically expressed as the problem of overeducation). If the delineation is too specific, there is a risk of simultaneously undermining assessments about the general value of education and credentials to human development and ignoring evidence that most graduates continue to gain qualifications in areas outside the sciences, technologies, and other fields most commonly defined in relation to knowledge work.

These contrasting foci broadly parallel debates between proponents of human capital theories, which pose investment in education and training as a core driver of economic expansion and innovation, and those who see in the phenomenon of credentialism a loose and imprecise relationship among education, training and practical applications of knowledge. Human capital orientations are given credence with the linkages between aggressive university expansion and innovation-driven economic growth, underscoring as well the dangers of not investing heavily in universities' capacities to foster research and development. Credentialist approaches, drawing upon more skeptical Weberian orientations to how various forms of certification are constructed and assessed, emphasize more fully the contradictions between formal credentials and the actual content associated with them.

Substantial empirical investigation has led to widely varied conclusions about where the balance of evidence lies, demonstrating nonetheless that each of the relevant phenomena—educational expansion, credentials, specializations, and jobs—is highly diversified and complex in itself as well as the interactions with one another (Bills 2003, Brown 2001). Knowledge-based social and economic developments tend to be less rational and efficient than typically intended and depicted, at least in a formal sense. Processes related to innovation are likely to be indeterminate or somewhat "sloppy" insofar as they depend upon degrees of freedom to allow for inquiry, creativity, and serendipity. Many hybrid arrangements to facilitate knowledge transfer do not work out as intended, while other opportunities are lost because they receive insufficient attention or resources.

These contradictions are evident in the social relations associated with knowledge work. The production of knowledge workers involves the development of formal credentials and human capacities to levels well beyond what is actually required or likely to be applied in employment settings. High levels of unemployment or underemployment among recent university graduates have drawn attention the need to integrate an understanding of processes related to demand as well as supply of labor power development and mobilization. In one of the most systematic accounts of these relationships, Livingstone (2004: 200–201) locates within the dynamics of advanced capitalism the tendency simultaneously to produce large proportions of highly qualified workers whose skills and capacities exceed those required to perform their jobs while leaving some sectors reliant on workers whose credentials are below job requirements.

Educational qualifications and requirements are continuously ratcheted up through competitive pressures produced in the context of innovation, accelerated productivity and positioning to gain access to desirable types of employees and employment prospects. Bourdieu's (1984; 1988) analysis of higher education as a field structured in relation to power dynamics highlights how various position-taking strategies undertaken by agents within and outside educational settings have increased the stakes associated with particular kinds of credentials. Several scholars, drawing attention to shifting alignments among training, knowledge and jobs in different national contexts, have employed this framework to demonstrate that, despite some predictability, formally rational decisions by individuals and organizations to invest in education often yield considerable volatility, uncertainty and inequality (Andres and Adamuti-Trache 2007, Margison 2008, Naidoo 2004). Dynamic labor markets and job requirements are also represented in education, training and employment discourses. Increased reference to concepts related to employability or "core" skills denotes the process by which a wide range of transferable knowledge replaces the eroding correspondence between many specific forms of jobs and training. The realm of "useful" knowledge changes quickly as ideas, techniques and capacities are rapidly discarded to make way for new forms. At the same time, individuals and family members look to an ever-increasing array of differentiated education and training options to gain competitive positioning for valued credentials and employment prospects.

Intersecting with these shifting work relations is a series of tensions and contradictions associated with questions about what counts, and is validated and valued, as knowledge. The advent of knowledge-based economies suggests the potential for comprehensive means by which different forms of knowledge and skill can be widely introduced, assessed, accepted, and dispersed across populations. The extent to which the stock of advanced bodies of knowledge (as well as more questionable bits of information) has increased and become incorporated into the lives of substantial segments of the population with the expansion of information and communications technologies, the expansion of formal education, and everyday demands in homes, workplaces and other social sites has become almost overwhelming.

In the process, the social relations associated with knowledge acquisition and use, along with the capacity to define and recognize socially or economically valued knowledge, tend to be highly exclusionary and hierarchical. There is a premium especially for those kinds of knowledge determined to be higher-end scientific and technical in nature, and especially knowledge that is transferrable for commercial applications. Knowledge, in other words, especially when transformed into commodified forms itself, refers primarily to formulations that are valued for their utility in the creation, production and distribution of other marketable commodities. The knowledge and capacities associated with tasks and activities central to the lives of large segments of the population, by contract, are considerably less likely to be validated and valued. Alternative knowledge systems, such as local and indigenous knowledge, tend to be validated only to the extent that they can be appropriated or stand as barriers to scientific and commercial activities. At the same time, claims made by specific cultural groups or communities seeking recognition for their own distinct knowledge forms and cultural traditions may give rise to increasing skepticism about the extent to which technical knowledge actually stands up to the standards expected of it, as signified by postmodern critiques of science and the gap between politics and science in relation to climate change and other pressing issues.

These challenges become more significant insofar as core knowledge relations focused on the development and transfer of technical rational and scientific knowledge themselves tend to be highly exclusionary. Innovation is mostly conducted among a small segment of "insider" participants in universities, private firms, and government agencies who have access to the kinds of resources, knowledge and networks highly valued in innovation processes (Strathdee 2006: 153, Etzkowitz and Leydesdorff 1997). Innovation driven by commodity production is more likely to be knowledge-intensive and capital-intensive than labor-intensive. Instead of improving job prospects, many of the most successful industries and firms in the new economy have grown rapidly with small numbers of specialized employees or high demands for relatively low-skill, low waged production and service workers (Brown and Lauder 2006: 31–32).

The contradictory relationships associated with the application of knowledge work have significant implications for universities as sites within and around which much of the production of knowledge workers and what counts as knowledge occurs. Sustained challenges around boundaries that differentiate universities from other institutional and functional sites are subject to contention externally as well as from within.

Universities and Knowledge Relations

Increased alignment of university mandates with economic relations defined in terms of the advancement of knowledge-based growth has intensified several long-standing tensions within universities while also producing new ones. Although there is some symmetry in the way in which these dynamics are experienced regardless of national or institutional context, considerable variation from one context to another is evident in the specific characteristics of change, the strategies adopted to foster or accommodate change, and the impact of these changes on particular groups. Three sets of relationships—the increasing diversity of post-secondary education providers, the division of labor within universities, and social differentiation in university access, participation and outcomes—illustrate this growing diversity.

It is important first to acknowledge more general policy and fiscal considerations within which the repositioning of postsecondary education and the promotion of innovation and knowledge work are occurring. Governments, even in many nations strongly committed to state investment in higher education and innovation agendas, are being severely tested in their willingness and ability to reconcile massive enrolment growth and rising costs in core expenditure categories with competing political and economic demands associated with other sectors such as health care as well as market stimulation. Consequently, while overall levels of spending on tertiary education have remained relatively stable in most nations they have not kept pace with growth in key areas of activity, with government shares of overall postsecondary expenditure in decline. Among OECD countries, for example, spending on tertiary education institutions as a proportion of GDP increased or remained the same between 1991 and 2006 in all but three member nations, during which time public expenditures on tertiary education increased modestly from 2.8 percent to 3.1 percent of total public expenditures (OECD 1998, 2009).

Nonetheless, spending has not kept pace with increases in enrolment and other postsecondary activities. Data presented by Tilak (2008: 457) reveal that per student public expenditures on higher education, expressed as a proportion of GDP per capita, declined between 24 and 62 percent in all regions for which figures are available, including high and upper middle income nations, between 1991 and 2006. Consequently, the share of educational costs borne by individuals (mostly tuition increases) and other private funding sources (both directly and indirectly) has grown steadily. In nations like India, where tertiary education until the end of the twentieth century was almost entirely funded by public sources, private spending reached 14 percent by 2004, while across OECD nations, the private share of funding for tertiary education institutions grew from about 22.2 percent in 2000 to 27.2 percent by 2006 (UNESCO 2007, OECD 2009).

These trends point to a high degree of affinity between discourses related to the third mission of universities (especially those related to commercialization and related themes) and postsecondary fiscal policies. State funding remains prevalent in most nations (proportions of private funding for tertiary education exceed public levels in only a few nations, although these include the United States, Korea, Japan, Chile, and Australia), but governments are refocusing their efforts, pursuing more strategic investments in universities and other postsecondary education and sometimes encouraging institutions to generate private funding (Altbach et al. 2009: 79ff.). In addition to internal policy factors, international agents like the World Bank and domestic lobby groups are exerting pressure on states to abandon some areas of postsecondary activity while moving to more direct intervention, in the form of targeting institutional and research spending on designated program areas, as well as indirect funding, such as scholarships, tax benefits, and vouchers for students in selected program areas (Salmi and Hauptman 2006).

As observed in the previous section, Bourdieu (1984, 1988) characterizes the field of higher education as a set of arrangements in which hierarchically organized agents (including institutions of higher education, researchers, and other participants) are engaged in strategic actions to gain access to desired resources and positions. Recent analysis suggests that alongside reproduction of longstanding inequalities there has emerged prolific growth of new institutional forms and arrangements as industry, states, and other participants erode the relative autonomy the field has traditionally maintained (Marginson 2008, Maton 2005, Naidoo 2004). Targeted initiatives undertaken by institutions to position themselves in order to optimize their access to state research funds, private sector resources, and tuition from high demand areas has produced what Sörlin (2007) terms a process of 'competitive differentiation.' Across institutions, a few core elite or global universities have undertaken (often with state direction or support from other key partners) to differentiate themselves from general research universities, those with graduate programs, and others that focus their missions primarily on activities related to undergraduate teaching or training. Within institutions, the focus on 'third mission' activities has an uneven impact as divisions of labor and allocation of resources privilege some program areas or sectors over others. While this often occurs within a single campus site, differentiation is also apparent in the growing trend to focus different types of activity coordinated electronically or through the establishment of new campuses in diverse locales.

These issues are not entirely new insofar as there have been longstanding differences across institutions, disciplines or departments with respect to their relative degree of emphasis and ability to support research and teaching-related activities, but they are being intensified and stretched in directions that are not always compatible with one another. High degrees of investment in research infrastructure and expert faculty or research personnel in defined areas of strength (predominantly in areas related to physical and material sciences, new technologies and bio-resources, medicine and health care) often coexist with the concentration of high levels of teaching responsibility in areas in which tuition revenues can be optimized by accommodating expanded student demand in low cost programs (including many social sciences and humanities) or those charging premium tuition

rates (as in the case of many business and professional degree or certification programs). In the process, institutions or units are differentially poised to benefit from these emerging practices and relationships
as participants with the capacity to generate new revenue streams and
resources from innovations and strategic partnerships (related especially to the production of patents and commodified knowledge) are
distinguished from others for which the emphasis on external partnerships and engagement is layered on top of additional demands to
increase student numbers and research productivity despite limited
prospects for new resources.

As observed in the previous section, many of these initiatives are
contested and do not necessarily unfold as planned. While institutional differentiation and hybridization may be seen as positive
advancements by proponents of educational marketization, higher
education institutions risk in the process the loss of integrity and
claims to the kinds of legitimacy on which their relatively privileged
status and authority is grounded. As Tilak (2008: 462) emphasizes,
"higher education is not a business commodity that can be subject to
liberalization, privatization and commercialization and be bought and
sold in markets. Higher education is related to the national culture and
the values of a society. It protects culture, intellectual independence
and the values of a civilized society. Higher education institutions act
as bastions of rich traditional values, at the same time as providing the
setting for a new kind of social imagination and experience." Even if
considered only with respect to narrower economic functions, universities, as they come to be drawn into the nexus of commercial and
policy activities, risk the loss of their authority to arbitrate among various truth claims which serves as the impetus for many of these relationships to be pursued by industry and state interests in the first place
(McSherry 2001: 64, Blackmore 2001: 353).

Accompanying tendencies in the direction of greater institutional
differentiation and hierarchical organization are patterns of inequality
within key groups of participants, including students and faculty. As in
the institutional case, some of these patterns are not new but their
impact is likely to be profound. In the case of faculty, for whom merit
has for several decades played at least some role in decisions over
career advancement and recognition, especially as long as there has
been a small but reliable pool of candidates with doctoral degrees, strategic investment in selected priority or commercially viable areas by
universities, governments and partners has rapidly expanded the range

of career trajectories and prospects for inequality among them. While these distinctions are most evident in the parallel development of casualized and typically lower-cost labor pool for term lecturers or research associates in sharp contrast with a cadre of elite faculty who occupy the most prestigious and highly resourced chairs, the disparities come to be more widely evident across the spectrum of faculty-related positions as differential resource allocations sharpen to favour selected priority areas. Even in cases in which meritocratic or collegial decision-making processes remain vital, there can be significant tensions when internal capacities (such as the need to provide laboratory space, hiring commitments, or continuing operating costs) are skewed by policy or commercial factors accountable to agencies outside the institution. There is evidence that faculty workloads have tended to intensify overall, sometimes through the concentration of activities in particular areas and in other cases through taking on higher loads across a full range of duties, but also with differential access to the kinds of resources and support to sustain this activity across institutions and disciplines (Milem et al. 2000, Dehli and Taylor 2006).

Similar patterns are evident among students. Globally, and within most national contexts, the expansion of university spaces has created unprecedented opportunities for students from diverse backgrounds, especially those historically underrepresented in higher education. This is most notable in the case of gender, with women's enrollment and graduation rates increasing steadily since the initial phase of rapid postsecondary expansion in the 1960s and 1970s. Exploding enrollments in universities and other postsecondary institutions have subsequently absorbed and been further fuelled by increasing participation rates by students from lower socioeconomic classes, racial and ethnic minority populations, rural regions, adult learners, and those in various disability categories. These growth rates, and the ability to foster wider social inclusion, have been impressive, but they are far from overcoming longstanding patterns of inequality.

University participation rates have tended to be highest, and increased most rapidly, among the wealthiest regions, and for middle and upper income groups within national and regional populations. Overall post-secondary enrolment rates have increased the most over the past decade in regions with initially high enrolment rates, primarily in Europe and North America, as well as rapidly developing nations like China and India, while remaining low across most of sub-Saharan

Africa, south and west Asia and Arab States, and Latin America (Altbach et al. 2009: 38). Even within highly industrialized nations such as those in the OECD in which educational expansion has fostered wider enrolment among diverse social groups, gaps in participation rates have not disappeared because more privileged groups have pushed their participation even higher (Shavit et al. 2007). Several factors in addition to or compounded by socioeconomic inequalities also affect chances for and types of postsecondary participation. For some of these, like disability status and rural-urban differences, innovation and policy choices can sometimes foster greater inclusion (by offering supportive technologies or distance and web-based learning options, for example) while simultaneously posing new barriers such as clustering viable or accessible program options in a small number of urban sites (OECD 2006: 42, Santiago et al. 2008b: 31–34).

Similarly, with respect to racial and ethnic minority populations and immigration status, changing policy and institutional environments that have contributed to enhanced participation by many subgroups have not been sufficient to eradicate enduring participation gaps. In some cases, as with indigenous populations in Australia, Canada and the United States, and ethnic minorities in numerous less developed nations, these patterns are consistent across national contexts. In other instances, as in the case of particular immigrant groups and categories, there are considerable variations across context, populations and related dimensions (Altbach et al. 2009, Encel 2000, Wotherspoon 2009).

Fewer comprehensive data sources are available once the focus shifts from overall participation in higher education to the characteristics of students in specific program types. Nonetheless, there are clear patterns of differentiation, as evident especially in pronounced inequalities among diverse population groups according to type of institution. The largest increases in postsecondary participation rates among minority populations has occurred typically within non-degree granting institutions and programs, and at the university level in less prestigious institutions and lower-cost programs. In the United States, for example, considerable attention has been paid to the over-representation of African-American students in community colleges and state universities, and their under-representation in elite universities (Rowley 2004).

There are further selective mechanisms that influence who gains entry into and success in core fields relevant to knowledge-based economic activity or which groups have access to credentials that are valued most highly for innovation-related jobs. While global competition for the most talented prospects has contributed to high concentrations of international students in prestigious doctoral engineering and science programs, for instance, there is also widespread concern about the impact the flow of highly skilled workers has for educational and labor market development in both home and receiving nations. The dramatic expansion of university graduates in China, for instance, has been tempered somewhat recently by high unemployment rates, prompting at the same time a demand for foreign credentials especially by those best situated to afford tuition and relocation costs. In India, China, many African nations, and other parts of the world, rapid and often poorly regulated university expansion has left large numbers of graduates, including those in knowledge-sector fields like engineering, with qualifications that are not recognized by employers or that do not cover the kinds of knowledge that employers require for adequate job performance (Altbach 2009: 12, World Bank 2008).

The primary conclusions conveyed through an extensive, and growing, body of literature is the continuing reproduction of educational inequality not just at any single point along the way, but via a cumulative process in which patterns of early advantage or disadvantage are strong predictors of subsequent relative educational success. Within a tremendous array of specific possible trajectories, there emerges a general pathway in which economic status, often intersecting with other socio-cultural resources, affects the prospects for and time required to complete basic education, which in turn affect levels of qualification and entry to postsecondary education, as well further differentiation according to such factors as selection of institutional type, institution, program, and field of study, exit or successful credential completion, prospects for postgraduate education, adult and continuing education, and employment circumstances. In a recent comparative review of participation in adult education and training, Desjardins, Rubenson and Milana (2006: 110–111) observe, despite some variations within and across national contexts, "a cycle of intergenerational reproduction of inequalities that are strongly linked to lifelong learning processes" in which the lowest participation rates are experienced by "those who are women, older, come from poor socio-economic backgrounds, are less-educated, less-skilled, are in low-skill jobs or are unemployed, and/or are immigrants."

Innovation, Exclusion and Higher Education

The field of higher education, and the role and nature of universities within it, is changing rapidly, even if not as nimbly as some proponents would advocate and too quickly or in the wrong directions as viewed from other vantage points. Postsecondary education systems, regardless of national and regional contexts, are following broadly similar pathways as they engage with numerous common influences, challenges, pressures, and constraints. However, there is little consensus as to whether or to what degree these movements represent path dependence or convergence towards a distinctly new, global model of higher education. What has emerged is an amalgam, not always evenly balanced or harmonious, produced by various intersections among conventional arrangements, founded upon such principles as collegiality, merit and university autonomy, with initiatives to increase the pool of highly skilled workers and increase participation across population groups, which in turn are not necessarily compatible with objectives to advance a knowledge-based society built upon the kinds of innovation that requires rapid and relatively seamless diffusion of applied knowledge (Altbach 1998: 217, Beerkens 2008).

Policies and activities that are carefully coordinated or steered in predetermined directions coexist, often uneasily, with differentiated and individualized strategies and actions. As Deem (2008: 21) observes in her overview of a broad spectrum of university transformations, "what we now understand a university to be is enormously complex and varies both across and within countries, irrespective of the attempts of the World Bank, the OECD, and the European Union, to encourage common processes" of reform in postsecondary education. There is considerable distance to cover if universities are to fulfill expectations related to mandates related either to social inclusion or innovation, even when questions as to the extent to which these are compatible with one another, or the relative merits and risks of pursuing one or the other of these, are put aside.

Bibliography

Altbach, G. Philip. 1998. *Comparative Higher Education: Knowledge, the University, and Development*. London: Ablex Publishing Corporation.

Altbach, G. Philip. 2009. "One-third of the globe: The future of higher education in China and India." *Prospects* 39 (1): 11–31.

Altbach, Philip G., Liz Reisberg and Laura E. Rumbley. 2009. *Trends in Global Higher Education: Tracking and Academic Revolution. A Report Prepared for the UNESCO 2009 World Conference on Higher Education.* Paris: United Nations Educational, Scientific and Cultural Organization.

Beerkens, Eric. 2008. "University Policies for the Knowledge Society: Global Standardization, Local Reinvention." *Perspectives on Global Development and Technology* 7(1): 15–38.

Bell, Daniel. 1973. *The Coming of Post-Industrial Society: A Venture in Social Forecasting.* New York: Basic Books.

Bills, David B. 2001. "Credentials, Signals, and Science: Explaining the Relationships Between Schooling and Job Assignment." *Review of Educational Research* 73(4):441–469.

Blackmore, Jill. 2001. "Universities in Crisis? Knowledge Economies, Emancipatory Pedagogies, and the Critical Intellectual." *Educational Theory* 51(3):353–371.

Bourdieu, Pierre. 1984. *Distinction: A Social Critique of the Judgement of Taste,* translated by Richard Nice. Cambridge, MA: Harvard University Press.

Bourdieu, Pierre. 1988. *Homo Academicus.* Cambridge: Polity Press.

Brinkley, Ian, Rebecca Fauth, Michelle Mahdon, and Sotiria Theodoropoulou. 2009. *Knowledge Workers and Knowledge Work - A Knowledge Economy Programme Report.* London: The Work Foundation. Accessed Nov. 27, 2009 from http://www.theworkfoundation.com/assets/docs/publications/213_know_work_survey170309.pdf.

Brown, David K. 2001. "The Social Sources of Educational Credentialism: Status Cultures, Labor Markets, and Organizations." *Sociology of Education* 74 (Extra Issue), 19–34.

Brown, Phillp, Andy Green, and Hugh Lauder. 2001. *High Skills: Globalization, Competitiveness, and Skill Formation.* Oxford: Oxford University Press.

Brown, Phillip, Anthony Hesketh, and Sara Williams. 2003."Employability in a Knowledge-driven Economy." *Journal of Education and Work* 16 (2):107–126.

Brown, Phillip and Hugh Lauder. 2006. "Globalisation, Knowledge and the Myth of the Magnet Economy." *Globalisation, Societies and Education* 4(1):25–57.

Clark, Burton. 2001. "The Entrepreneurial University: New Foundations for Collegiality, Autonomy, and Achievement." *Higher Education Management* 13(2): 9–24.

Deem, Rosemary. 2008. "Producing and Re/producting the Global University in the 21st Century: Researcher Perspectives and Policy Consequences," *Higher Education Policy* 21(4):439–456.

Desjardins, Richard, Kjell Rubenson, and Marcella Milana. 2006. *Unequal chances to participate in adult learning: international perspectives.* Paris: UNESCO International Institute for Educational Planning.

Drucker, Peter F. 1993. *Post-Capitalist Society*. New York: HarperCollins.

Drucker, Peter F. 1994. *Knowledge Work and Knowledge Society: The Social Transformations of this Century*. Cambridge, MA: The 1994 Edwin L. Godkin Lecture, John F. Kennedy School of Government, Harvard University.

Encel, John Daniel. 2000. *Indigenous Participation in Higher Education*. Higher Education Division Occasional Paper Series, Department of Education Training and Youth Affairs (May). Canberra: Australian Government Publishing Service.

Englehart, Katie. 2009. "Reality check for a big Idea: What the provinces think of the Big Five's revolutionary ideas for university reform." *Maclean's* 122(36): 64–65.

Etzkowitz, Henry. 2004. "The evolution of the entrepreneurial university." *International Journal of Technology and Globalisation* 1 (1): 65–77.

Etzkowitz, Henry and Loet Leydesdorff, eds. 1997. *Universities and the Global Knowledge Economy: A Triple Helix of University-Industry-Government Relations*. London: Pinter.

Guile, David. 2006. "What Is Distinctive About the Knowledge Economy? Implications for Education," in Hugh Lauder, Phillip Brown, Jo-Anne Dillabough, and A.H. Halsey, eds., *Education, Globalization & Social Change*. Oxford: Oxford University Press, 355–366.

Hale, Geoffrey E. 2002. "Innovation and Inclusion: Budgetary Policy, the Skills Agenda, and the Politics of the New Economy," in G. Bruce Doern, ed., *How Ottawa Spends 2002–03: The Security Aftermath and National Priorities*. Don Mills, ON: Oxford University Press, 20–47.

Laredo, Philippe. 2007. "Revisiting the Third Mission of Universities: Toward a Renewed Categorization of University Activities?" *Higher Education Policy* 20 (4):441–456.

Livingstone, David W. 2004. *The Education-Jobs Gap: Underemployment or Economic Democracy?* Aurora, ON: Garamond.

Marginson, Simon. 2008. "Global field and global imagining: Bourdieu and worldwide higher education." *British Journal of Sociology of Education* 29 (3):303–315.

Maton, Karl. 2004. "A question of autonomy: Bourdieu's field approach and higher education policy." *Journal of Education Policy* 20(6):687–704.

McSherry, Corryne. 2001. *Who Owns Academic Work?: Battling for Control of Intellectual Property*. Cambridge, MA; Harvard University Press.

Milem, Jeffrey F., Joseph B. Berger and Eric L. Dey. 2000. "Faculty Time Allocation: A Study of Change over Twenty Years," *The Journal of Higher Education* 71 (4):454–475.

Moravec, John W. 2008. "A new paradigm of knowledge production in higher education." *On the Horizon* 16(3):123–136.

Naidoo, Rajani. 2004. "Fields and institutional strategy: Bourdieu on the relationship between higher education, inequality and society." *British Journal of Sociology of Education* 25(4): 457–471.

Organization for Economic Co-operation and Development (OECD). 1998. *Education at a Glance 1998: OECD Indicators.* Paris: Organization for Economic Co-operation and Development.

Organization for Economic Co-operation and Development (OECD). 2006. *Education Policy Analysis: Focus on Higher Education – 2005–2006 Edition.* Paris: Organization for Economic Co-operation and Development.

Organization for Economic Co-operation and Development (OECD). 2009. *Education at a Glance 2009: OECD Indicators.* Paris: Organization for Economic Co-operation and Development.

Pierson, Paul, ed. 2001. *The New Politics of the Welfare State.* Oxford: Oxford University Press.

Powell, Walter W. and Kaisa Snellman. 2004. "The Knowledge Economy." *Annual Review of Sociology* 30:199–220.

Rowley, Larry L. 2004. "Dissecting the Anatomy of African-American Inequality: The Impact of Racial Stigma and Social Origins on Group Status and College Achievement," *Educational Researcher* 33 (15):15–20.

Salmi, Jamil and Arthur M. Hauptman. 2006. *Innovation in Tertiary Education Financing: A Comparative Evaluation of Allocation Mechanisms.* Education Working Paper Series of the World Bank Number 4 (September). Washington, DC: The World Bank.

Santiago, Paulo, Karina Tremblay, Ester Baori, and Elena Arnal. 2008. *Tertiary Education for the knowledge Society. Volume 2: Special Features: Equity, Innovation, Labor Market, Internationalization.* Paris: OECD Publishing.

Shavit, Yossi, Richard Arum, and Adam Gamoran, editors. 2007. *Stratification in Higher Education: A Higher Study.* Palo Alto, CA: Stanford University Press.

Sörlin, Sverker. 2007. "Funding Diversity: Performance-based funding regimes as bases of differentiation in Higher Education Systems," *Higher Education Policy* 20 (4):413–440.

Stehr, Nico. 1996. *Knowledge as a Capacity for Action.* Ottawa: Statistics Canada, Science and Technology Redesign Research Paper.

Strathdee, Rob. 2005. "Globalization, Innovation, and the Declining Significance of Qualifications Led Social and Economic Change," *Journal of Educational Policy* 20 (4): 437–456.

Tilak, Jandhyala B.G. 2008. "Higher education: a public good or a commodity for trade? Commitment to higher education or commitment of higher education to trade," *Prospects* 38(4):449–466.

United Nations Educational, Scientific and Cultural Organization (UNESCO). 2006 "Education Statistics," UNESCO Institute for Statistics, updated December 11, http://stats.uis.unesco.org/TableViewer/tableView.aspx. Last visited September 30, 2010.

United Nations Educational, Scientific and Cultural Organization (UNESCO). 2007. *What do societies invest in education? Public versus private spending.* Montreal: UNESCO Institute for Statistics, Factsheet 07/04, October.

United Nations Educational, Scientific and Cultural Organization (UNESCO). 2009. *Global Education Digest 2009: Comparing Education Statistics Across the World.* Montreal: UNESCO Institute for Statistics.

Wissema, J.G. Hans. 2009. *Towards the Third Generation University: Managing the University in Transition.* Cheltenham, UK: Edward Elgar.

Wotherspoon, Terry. 2009. *The Sociology of Education in Canada: Critical Perspectives,* third edition. Don Mills, ON: Oxford University Press.

Young, Michael F.D. 1971. *Knowledge and Control: New Directions for the Sociology of Education.* London: Collier-McMillan.

CHAPTER FOUR

THE BIG SHIFT: SCIENCE AND THE UNIVERSITIES IN CRISIS*

Toby E. Huff

As we complete the first decade of the twenty-first century there is a profound sense of a shift in the nature of higher education, the role of research and the ties between universities and industry. Some have suggested that we are experiencing deep *structural* changes in the academy and society (Etzkowitz 2002, Calhoun 2006, Mowery et al. 2004, Washburn 2005). Some would even say that the shift marks an epic alteration of the traditional Western conception of disinterested scientific inquiry as well as the nature and priorities of the university.

Only brief reflection on the origins and development of the university as an autonomous zone of free inquiry protected from the incursions of religious and political censors is necessary to reveal its unique foundations (Huff 2003: chapter 4; Grant 1996). For Western universities are unique cultural creations that emerged only in the West in the twelfth and thirteenth centuries. They emerged as *legally autonomous entities* because they were *corporations*, that is, legal entities that enjoyed a bundle of rights, such as the right to make their own rules and regulations, to buy and sell property, to sue and be sued, and to self-govern themselves on the basis of majority rule following the Roman legal maxim, "what concerns all should be considered and decided by all" (Berman 1987: 221; Post 1964: chapter 4). It was the existence of this bundle of corporate rights that enabled the European universities to ensconce the naturalistic writings of Aristotle at the center of the curriculum which created a disinterested agenda of scientific inquiry that was meant to explore all the realms of human existence. Scholars of that age were continuously debating such things as whether there might be multiple worlds, whether the earth is the center

---

* This is a revised and expanded version of an essay that appeared in *Society* (2006)43 (4): 30–34.

of the universe, whether every cause has an effect, whether a vacuum could exist, whether objects could move instantaneously, and so on (Grant 1994: "Catalogue of Questions," 681–741). They also studied the nature of the animal kingdom, biological questions, conducted anatomical dissections, and much more. Clearly there were no commercial interests capable of directing research or rewarding scholars for their new ideas.

Conversely, the Islamic colleges, the *madrasas* of the time, were dedicated to religious studies, to memorizing and explicating the *Quran*, the sayings of the Prophet Mohammad, and related religious topics, especially Islamic law (Huff 2003: 147–58). This was in keeping with their mission as pious endowments, places of study devoted to the conservation and spread of the Islamic faith. Consequently, the naturalistic agenda of Aristotle was excluded and human dissection was forbidden by sacred law.

Likewise, in China, none of the academies or other places of learning had anything approaching legal autonomy, nor were scholars independent of the Chinese bureaucracy able to establish themselves or a curriculum based on disinterested scientific inquiry. Instead, learning was geared to the passing of triennial examinations focused on Confucian values, moral questions, history, and elements of statecraft. Only rarely were limited aspects of scientific inquiry considered (Elman 2000).

In short, Western universities dedicated to disinterested inquiry protected from outside incursions were culturally unique in world historical development. Hence the contemporary shift whereby capitalistic interests shift the motives and rewards for inquiry within universities represents an unparalleled historical shift. Of course, anyone reviewing the history of academic research can find intimations of university-industry collaboration in the nineteenth and early twentieth century, but the scale and force of corporate capitalism has never before been so pervasive. The corporate status that colleges and universities have enjoyed for centuries has now been met by the overpowering demands of global capitalism. These institutions are now threatened by a set of powerful forces greater than any experienced earlier in human history. It is not at all clear that the university culture of independent inquiry can withstand these new forces. What is clear is that in addition to the difficulties and transformations now enveloping higher education, there has been diminished state funding and yet a proliferation of programs coupled with new demands for student-oriented consumer services, all of which contribute to a crisis of legitimacy that goes to the heart of the academic enterprise.

The Ethos of Science vs. Bayh–Dole

The shift of academic commitments toward the adoption of industrial values of commercial gain has been a long time in the making. Observers who viewed these developments up close early in the twentieth century often expressed concern that the pursuit of commercial gain by university faculty could have long run negative effects on academic values. The Bayh-Dole Act of 1980 that legitimized the licensing and patenting of research results produced by federal funding is thus the capstone of this long drift toward a conception of intellectual ideas, including scientific results as "property." Once the conception was widely accepted that "intellectual property" includes virtually everything dealt with in university settings, along with the notion that the "knowledge economy" is fueled by this intellectual "capital," the gold rush was on. Of course, the engineering and other professional schools within the academy were at the forefront of these developments designed to turn scientific results into "technology transfers."

With the recent collapse of the global financial system in 2008, new questions are being raised about the culpability of the economics profession as a contributor to the newly "engineered" financial assets that turned toxic, causing among other factors, the markets to shut down and billions of dollars of assets to be destroyed (Ferguson 2010, Krugman 2009, Cassidy 2010). The Columbia economist and former Associate of the Federal Open Market Committee of the Federal Reserve Frederic Mishkin authored a study on "The Financial Stability of Iceland" in 2006 for which he was paid $124,000 by the Icelandic Chamber of Commerce. His analysis assured readers that prudential supervision of Iceland's banks and markets was in place and there was nothing to worry about. This was shortly before the banks failed and Iceland became the first European country to go bankrupt in the new century (Ferguson 2010, www.economicdisasterarea.com/index.php/features/mishkins-iceland-fail-video/). A large portion of business school faculty and economics professors at elite universities serve on corporate boards making hundreds of thousands of dollars for their services. The recent financial crisis suggests that they were a little less than diligent in their duties on those boards.

Just how radical the shift in conceptions of scientific research from public interest goals towards *intellectual property rights* can be seen by recalling the classic statement of the *ethos of science* by Robert Merton. Writing in 1942, Merton argued that the ethos of science was composed of such values as *universalism, organized skepticism, disinterestedness*, and the *communal sharing* of scientific results. This latter value assumes that scientific knowledge belongs to the scientific community as a whole. The scientist has no claim to his or her *intellectual property* but is limited to the public recognition of his work, and the esteem that that recognition conveys. Merton was aware that during the war effort of the Second World War scientists were urged to become entrepreneurs and promoters of economic enterprises. Yet he maintained that the scientific ethos was in conflict with the idea of technology as *private property* that was coming into vogue. More than a decade later, in a paper on the importance of priority in scientific discovery, Merton argued that once a scientist has announced his discovery, he has no property rights to his discovery, that his only reward is the recognition by others that he brought a new scientific result into being.

All of this now seems distant and quaint. The Bayh-Dole Act of 1980 grants explicit permission for universities to take out patents and licenses to safeguard the discoveries of their faculty members who make intellectual advances using federal money. When the bill was being drawn up, Senator Long of Louisiana thought that this represented a form of illegitimate privatization of tax payer-generated resources. But the bill gained approval. The profit motive entered in by granting, in principle, equal shares of patent and license fees to the university, to the faculty member's department, and to the originating researcher. Given such a calculus of incentives, universities and faculty members are encouraged to go into the intellectual property business. Quite recently the head of Harvard University's sponsored research office announced a major campaign to "commercialize" as much of its intellectual property as possible, hoping to become "the most effective technology-transfer program in the country" (Boston Globe, Nov 9, 2005).

The growing library of books and reports on the consequences of this major shift reveals the extent to which this has resulted in large jumps in university based commercial activities, in the rise of a variety of conflicts of interest, an increase in secrecy surrounding scientific results, the employment of "ghostwriters" for articles to be "placed" in scientific journals, the false reporting of scientific data in cases of prescription medicine, and a number of other maladies.

As state support for universities has declined very significantly during the last quarter of a century or more, it is easy to see how attractive this potential new source of revenue would become. Consequently virtually all major universities across the country jumped to create new Offices of Technology Transfer, each of which could become members of the newly created *Association of University Technology Managers* (AUTM). There are now well over 1300 such members. The purpose of all these offices is clearly to commercialize as much intellectual property as possible generated by their individual faculty members.

With the publication of Jennifer Washburn's *University Inc* (2005), the composite picture of negative consequences for traditional academic values, has become far more visible. Her diligent compilation of cases of conflicts of interests, faulty contracts, unreported deaths in drug trials and other medical applications, faculty dismissals because of whistle blowing about such misbehaviour, biased reports churned out by university-based policy groups, along with negative consequences for undergraduate teaching, seem to envelop a large portion of the top ranked research universities across the country.

Derek Bok, a former president of Harvard, was well aware of these trends and their negative consequences. In his book, *Universities in the Marketplace* (Bok 2003), he noted that "universities may not yet be willing to trade all of their academic values for money, but they have proceeded much further down that road than they are generally willing to acknowledge." Washburn is surely right to subtitle her book, "the Corporate Corruption of Higher Education." Given the new economic incentives dangling before academics everywhere, it is not surprising that, as Calhoun (2006) notes, the critical voices of academe have remained silent, ignoring the problem.

The Media-Technology Complex

What then are the stakes in this great gamble that hopes to trade academic values for monetary remuneration? The first thing that has to be said is that American universities and their faculties, more so than European, are actors engaged in the prevailing culture of American society. The more they engage in that culture, accepting the extra academic rewards of that participation, the more they become co-opted

and identified with that culture. It is apparent that contemporary
American culture is increasingly mesmerized by the mass media,
entertainment, and the sensibilities of television and Hollywood
imagery. As a long-term user of computers and related technology
I appreciate the virtues of it, but we should not overlook the way this
new technology dominates expectations for faculty and students, and
even more, how content is repackaged to meet computer styles and
limits, not human cognitive needs. The fact is that educational interests
are entirely secondary to the design, selling, and stylized-use of most
of this technology.

Apart from the unvarnished need and desire to lead an affluent life,
academics find that they must adopt all the latest glitz and entertainment devices marketed by Hollywood and the ubiquitous software
(and hardware) manufacturers. Fast action, PowerPoint presentations
(poorly constructed), "jump cuts" in video shots lasting less than five
seconds (a "long" scene), and special effects such as flashing lights,
inevitably become the style expected by students socialized by the new
visual media. What this does to attention spans hardly needs discussion. Movie and documentary producers are more than happy to supply faculty members with class room material while students are hard
pressed to discern the difference between fiction and analysis. This is
compounded by the existence of the Blogosphere where self-appointed
bloggers are enabled to operate free from filters (competent adult editors), further confounding serious analysis.

All of these deflections of the academic calling need to be added
to the crisis of universities. Of course, all those who think that professors should be "cool" and fully conversant with contemporary (make
believe) popular culture, will applaud these developments. My concern, however, is with the implications for academic and scientific
knowledge more broadly. It is well known that hundreds, probably
thousands, of research and consulting firms are out there waiting to
serve as hired guns for whatever political, commercial, regional, religious or ethnic interest that may want the favour of a "study" of its
latest endeavour. Washington, D.C. has its own version of think tanks
to which one may apply for arguable defense of any trend of thought.
Those who think that "we make our own reality" have only to supply
the money to get such firms to supply the desired outcome. Given this
cultural climate, the need for authentic analysis jumps out. How can
any public health or safety issue be resolved without such unbiased and
scientific analysis? It is widely perceived that the safety and efficiency

reports of major drug companies are not to be believed, and for good reasons. And so it goes for environmental, energy, tobacco, media and many others sectors where commercial interests have produced as much confusion as possible with the hope that no objective conclusion can be reached.

All sorts of conflicts of interests between established powers and academic thinkers have existed since the advent of universities in the West. In our distant past scholars and scientists attached to universities were thought to provide something like objective and scientifically corroborated knowledge. But with the new gold rush to capitalize on intellectual capital, seemingly produced under the old rules, this aura of objectivity and authenticity is rapidly declining. In fairness, I do believe that public authorities and leaders of business and industry still look to academic researchers for objective analysis. But this is probably not true for that segment of the medical academy that has been besmirched by ghostwritten articles, incomplete data reporting, and biased opinions given for monetary considerations. It remains to be seen how much longer universities do retain the public trust.

With the new rules provided by the Bayh-Dole Act, all sorts of previously unimaginable conflicts of interest have arisen for academic researchers. Some of the most dramatic and egregious cases come from biological research in which the principal investigator is an academic, but who also runs a start-up firm seeking to commercialize his or her findings (Krimsky 2003). If a graduate student happens to be working on a problem related to the professor/entrepreneur's work, and she makes a breakthrough, she could easily find, as Washburn reports in her book, that the student's results suddenly appear as part of the promotional material of the professor/entrepreneur's new company, without her acknowledgement. Of course this is unethical, but the new dispensation makes this kind of conflict routine and unavoidable. Projecting this kind of conflict across all the disciplines of the academy that may lay claim to some marketable product, the situation is horrifying. And when the rewards are boldly monetary rather than honorific, no holds can be bared. If that old-fashioned notion of the life of the mind still hides somewhere in the academy, the defenders of it will have to muster far more courage, not to mention resources, than ever before to reclaim it. As Derek Bok observed with regard to the loss of objective standing by the academy due to its trading of essential values for monetary considerations, restoring such values will be "all but impossible."

There is an equally serious problem that concerns the *scientific commons*, the pool of scientific knowledge that ought to be freely available to all those who can find ways to use it. By many accounts this pool is dwindling, which means that fewer and fewer elements of that common stock of knowledge are available, either directly or through second party licensing agreements. When universities make exclusive licensing contracts with commercial interests, the results of scientific discoveries, as well and the procedures used to get the results, may be placed exclusively in the hands of one large commercial interest—despite the general assumption that university scientists should make their results available to the general public, especially if they were produced using federal dollars.

The embarrassing case of the Aids/HIV treatment known as d4T and marketed as *Zerit* developed at Yale stands out among others (Washburn 2005:166ff). Professor William Prusoff had discovered the effectiveness of d4T against HIV (in the mid 1980s) and assigned the patent to Yale, which in turn gave an exclusive license to the drug company Bristol-Myers Squibb. In the 1990s Yale made several hundred million dollars on the license. In the year 2000 a movement emerged in South Africa to make the drug available at prices affordable by South Africans, something Bristol-Myers Squibb declined to do. When it was discovered that the drug had been invented by a Yale professor and that Yale owned the original patent, it became an embarrassment to Yale, which said that it was powerless to break a contract with the drug company. But shortly thereafter (March 2001) Bristol-Meyers announced a drastic reduction in costs for the drug in South Africa.

A similar case concerns the drug *Ziagen*, developed by faculty at the University of Michigan. It too was exclusively licensed to another drug company, Glaxo Wellcome (later GlaxoSmithKline), and withheld from affordable pricing in developing countries (Washburn 2005:166). The pending crisis of science and universities seems real enough. From tsunamis, earthquakes, hurricanes, wars, global warming, and global epidemics, blunt realities have a way of breaking into the pursuit of our natural desires, now so fully shaped by image makers.

What Can Be Done?

The conceit that something *can* be done is part of American national character. But sociological trends, as the French sociologist Emile

Durkheim noted, are facts. They are forces of nature that have to play themselves out. One has only to look at crime statistics from 1960 to the end of the twentieth century to see how the trend rose inexorably and very gently subsided, however modestly, in the mid nineteen nineties. The current crisis of universities, as I have suggested, is much broader than the universities themselves. It is part of a cultural wave rooted in economic interests, an attempted solution to the competitive threat coming from other countries experienced in the 1970s, and the trends of our media and technology-driven culture that has other priorities. It is not mainly a shortage of money, just as there is no shortage of food; there is just a maldistribution of the resources. It is widely noted that CEO's today are paid at a rate hundreds of time higher than the wages of average workers. One wonders what that tidy sum of excessive income would amount to if added up.

A number of scholars have attempted to put forth suggestions that would remedy and deflect the market forces that have been unleashed on the university. Jennifer Washburn (2005: 228–41) reviewed these and put forth her own list. They consist of four steps:

1. the creation of independent third-party licensing bodies... that would assume control over university technology transfer and commercialization activities nationwide;
2. an amendment to the Bayh-Dole Act clarifying that the true intent of the legislation is to provide more widespread use of taxpayer-financed research, not to maximize short-term profits;
3. new requirements that all federally funded university scholars must comply with strict conflict-of-interest laws;
4. the creation of a new federal agency to administer and monitor industry-sponsored clinical drug trials submitted to the Food and Drug Administration.

These are sensible recommendations that I would applaud, however, resistance to some of them can be expected. The requirement of third-party licensing is nicely spelled out by Washburn. It turns out that a precedent for third party licensing to facility technology transfer goes all the way back to 1912. It was then that a Berkeley professor, Frederick Cottrell, set up the *Research Corporation* for this purpose. The idea was to keep universities and their officials out of conflicts that have now become so commonplace. Washburn proposes that a nation-wide network of such nonprofit "technology-transfer hubs" be established in each of the regions of the country. Each of these *academic technology-transfer agencies* (ATTAs) would be well staffed to handle all the third-party licensing and patenting required to take the inventions and discoveries from the university to the private sector in the service of the public. She would also include a prohibition preventing a university from taking an equity or other financial position in the spin-off companies. This provision will, I expect, be rejected by many university officials.

Nevertheless, her plan would allocate the revenues from the ATTAs to defray the costs of the originating researcher, while granting equal shares of all remaining profits to the investigator, the federal government, and to the investigator's university. The federal portion would be reinvested in new peer-reviewed research grants. The conflict of interest provision outlined by Washburn would also entail a prohibition against any researcher (or family member) taking an equity or other financial position in any company that her research would effect by her results. This would be the case where federal grant money was used to support the research. This provision seems to be eminently sensible.

A further reform suggested by Washburn would prohibit the *commingling* of federal and industrial research funds. This is a bold suggestion that reverses the received wisdom of the last quarter of a century, or more. It was then thought that to require *matching funds* from industry and federal (or other university funding) was a clever way to leverage larger pots of research funds. However, Washburn notes that large and experienced commercial firms often give supporting research funds to universities in order to gain access to pioneering researchers with cutting edge technologies and bright post-docs who have already embarked upon promising paths of research. By such a commingling maneuver corporations get access to far more resources and potential discoveries than they would ever think of initially funding. When such matched funding results in non-disclosure contracts for the participating faculty, and when other kinds of exclusive rights are granted to the commercial sponsors, the public interest is seriously compromised.

If these reforms could be introduced, it would serve in a measure to turn the clock back to a less conflictual situation. Whatever the long-term outcome will be regarding the search within universities to capture the commercial value of their intellectual capital, it is wise to heed the conclusion of Walter Powell and associates (Powell et al. 2007: 240) who studied the issue of selling private rights to public knowledge.

The future prospects of commercialized intellectual capital depend upon "the capacity of research universities to generate public science," yet at the same time, "corporations will never finance the university's primary mission of teaching and research." With declining state revenues for universities and their research imperative, the dangers of encroaching capitalism are likely to be more serious and indeed, more powerful than either religion or politics in deflecting scientific aims.

Bibliography

Barrow, Clyde. 2010. "The Rationality Crisis in U.S. Higher Education." *New Political Science* 3 (2): 317–44.

Berman, Harold. 1987. *Law and Revolution. The Formation of the Western Legal Tradition*. Cambridge, Ma: Harvard University Press.

Bok, Derek. 2003. *Universities in the Marketplace. The Commercialization of Higher Education*. Princeton: Princeton University Press.

Calhoun, Craig. 2006. "Is the University in Crisis?" *Society* 43(4):8–21.

Cassidy, John. 2010. "Letter from Chicago, 'After the Blowup.'" *The New Yorker,* January 11, pp. 28ff.

Elman, Benjamin. 2004. *A Cultural History of the Civil Examinations in Late Imperial China*. Berkeley: University of California Press.

Etzkowitz, Henry. 2002. *MIT and the Rise of the Entrepreneurial University*. London: Routledge.

Ferguson, Charles. 2010. "Inside Job." A Documentary Film on the Financial Crash of 2008.

Grant, Edward. 1994. *Planets, Stars, & Orbs. The Medieval Cosmos, 1200–1687*. New York: Cambridge University Press.

Grant, Edward. 1996. *The Foundations of Modern Science in the Middle Ages*. New York: Cambridge University Press.

Huff, Toby E. 2003. *The Rise of Early Modern Science: Islam, China and the West*. 2nd edition. New York: Cambridge University Press.

Krimsky, Sheldon. 2003. *Science in the Private Interest. Has the Lure of Profits Corrupted Biomedical Research?* Lanham, Md: Rowman & Littlefield.

Krugman, Paul. 2009. "How Did Economists Get it So Wrong?" *New York Times Magazine,* September 2.

McSherry, Corynne. 201. *Who Owns Academic Work? Battling for Control of Intellectual Property*. Cambridge, Ma; Harvard University Press.

Mowery, David C., Richard R. Nelson, Bhaven N. Sampat, Arvids A. Ziedonis. 2004. *Ivory Tower and Industrial Innovation. University-Industry Technology Transfer Before and After the Bayh-Dole Act*. Stanford: Stanford University Press.

Powell, Walter W., Jason Owen-Smith and Jeannette A. Colyvas. 2007. "Innovation and Emulation: Lessons from American Universities in Selling Private Rights to Public Knowledge," *Minerva* 45: 121–42.

Washburn, Jennifer. 2005. *University, Inc.: The Corporate Corruption of Higher Education*. New York: Basic Books.

CHAPTER FIVE

SOCIETAL RATIONALIZATION: CULTURAL INNOVATION AND KNOWLEDGE ISLAMIZATION IN MALAYSIA

Choonlee Chai

The significant entry of modern science into Malaysia happened mainly during the British colonial period. But the rapid and wide-ranging development of modern science and technology in Malaysia occurred after Malaysia's independence. Emulating the developmental model of Western countries and Japan, the Malaysian government made industrialization a major strategy of nation building. In fact, one of the nine challenges of the Vision 2020, launched by former Prime Minister Mahathir Mohamad in 1990, was to make Malaysia 'a scientific and progressive society...that is not only a consumer of technology but also a contributor to the scientific and technological civilization of the future' (Mahathir Mohamad 1991). While the progress of the vision was hampered first by the 1997 financial crisis, and more recently by the global economic downturn, development of science and technology remains central to the agenda of national development.

In light of this, the chapter seeks to clarify the place of modern science within the context of attempts of knowledge innovation through Islamization. The basis of the project of Islamization of scientific knowledge is outlined using Weber's theory of societal rationalization, which could be used to interpret the effort of knowledge Islamization as a response to the disenchantment brought about by knowledge of modern science. The fact that knowledge Islamization can be attempted, in and out of itself, is a testament to the openness of modern science that at once embodies its power and limit as an objective and universal knowledge. The contradiction in the promotion of modern science by Islamists on one hand, and the critique of it on the other, is understood as occurring at different levels of modern science. It speaks to the partial acceptance of the epistemological basis of modern science and the total rejection of its ontological tenet by Islamists in Malaysia.

This allows for the fervent promotion of modern science without ceding to its implicit secular demand. The Islamization of knowledge can thus be perceived as a creative effort of knowledge innovation in response to intense secularization. The success of this, however, remains to be seen.

Malaysia as a Developing Islamic Nation

Like many developing and developed nations, religious legitimacy remains important to the majority of the population. This is especially so in Malaysia given the fact that Islamic identity is a national identity and Islamic legitimacy is central to political legitimacy. Consequently, political contest and discourse in Malaysia is tightly intertwined with religious discourse, and national policy developments often have to accommodate Islamic religious sensitivity. By and large, this is not, difficult to achieve given the rich universal values encoded in Islam. However, similar to the controversy surrounding the teaching of evolution and creationist theories in United States (Moore 1993, Fuller 2006, Kitcher 2007), some quarters of Malay Muslim intellectuals in Malaysia harbour strong misgivings about the teaching of modern science in its current form, which delinks modern science, or modernity in general, from religion (Mohd Hazim 2004). What is unique in Malaysia, however, is that unlike Western societies where secularism has come to be accepted as the dominant ideology, the learning and practice of modern science in Malaysia happens in a society that still largely defines itself as a religious society through Islamic identity. What does this mean to the everyday practice of science? And how is the tension between the interpretation of modern science and Islamic religion being managed? How can we understand the urge to Islamize Western features of modern development, including the Islamization of knowledge and science? These are some of the questions that are often obscured, yet analysis is crucial as Malaysian leaders seek to chart a path of Islamic modernity that embraces the material success of Western modernity yet denies its secular tenet.

Theories of Science and Society

The development of modern science can be viewed from a variety of perspectives. In general, these perspectives can be subsumed under two broad themes—one conceives science as an agent that is capable of independent influence over society; the other sees science as yet another avenue and instrument of human influence and domination. The former perspective, sometimes called scientific determinism (Schroeder 2007), emphasizes the influence of science on society especially in terms of the shaping of worldview, morality, and attitude of individuals. One way this perspective is articulated is to view modern science as possessing a cultural authority that increasingly challenges, displaces, and substitutes traditional and religious authorities.

As a cultural authority, modern science is conceived to be capable of bestowing legitimacy and validity to human deeds and words. It changes perceptions, imparts universal values, builds social movements, shapes political culture, and fashions worldwide standardization (Drori et al. 2003). In this perspective, modern science, like religion, is considered to be laden with its own beliefs, values, rituals, and most importantly, a cosmology that is as comprehensive as that provided by any religion. In present day modern societies, scientific cosmology is said to have substantially replaced a religious worldview in helping us to make sense of the natural world. The scientific cosmology—dubbed "sacred canopy"—is based on two assumptions: first, that nature is orderly, and second, that nature's order is intelligible (Drori et al. 2003: 30). Within this scientized picture of the world, science is believed to be able to unravel orders, and to remedy disorders. Modern science thus commands an overarching authority to define problems and prescribe solutions. The ascendancy of the environmental movement in recent decades, for instance, from this perspective, is construed as a result of scientific diagnosis of environmental problems. In other words, science helps to shape and position social actors, that is, individuals and organizations, within a scientized setting that is understood through a scientific lens.

Contrary to scientific determinism, social constructivists understand modern science as part and parcel of the instruments of national development and domination. The constructivists analyze modern science chiefly as a social institution governed by different layers of social interactions and relations (Aronowitz 1988). From this viewpoint, modern science and technology are relatively passive and susceptible to social, economic, and political conditioning. Scientific authority, especially in relation to its image of objectivity, is a valuable asset that can be deployed to support or defeat competing social agendas. Often, this authority of science is expropriated by the state, with the tacit consent of scientists who rely on the state for research funding, to give an aura of objectivity and provide legitimacy to state rule (Mukerji 1989). When a scientist disagrees with the state over policy issues, it is not uncommon that the scientist is isolated and his/her personal authority put into question in order to keep scientific objectivity on the side of the state. This, for example, was what transpired as Robert Oppenheimer openly challenged the United States government on the necessity of H-bombs as part of the United States' defense strategy (Thorpe 2002).

In its extreme form, constructivists contend that even the cognitive content of scientific knowledge is socially conditioned (Barnes 1977, Mulkay 1979). For instance, mathematics, which is one of the most logic-driven subjects, is argued to have been influenced by social interests (MacKenzie 1978). Scientific knowledge, instead of representing an objective reality, is said to be a social construct; there is "nothing in the physical world which uniquely determines the conclusions of [the scientific] community" (Mulkay 1979: 61) and social factors are not "contaminants but constitutive of the very idea of scientific knowledge" (Shapin 1995: 297). Some critics view the analyses of constructivists as being redundant and a retreat in knowledge production (Gieryn 1982). The constructivist discourses of scientific knowledge are often conducted using Kuhn's analysis of scientific revolutions as evidential support, much to Kuhn's dismay (Baber 2000). The debate between objectivists and constructivists at the end culminated in the "Science Wars" in the 1990s (Segerstråle 2000), with supporters of physical and social scientists in both camps acrimoniously engaged, intersected with the "Sokal hoax" which cast a shadow over the stringency of the academic field of cultural studies (Editors of Lingua Franca 2000). The "Science Wars" subsided as the twentieth century drew to an end (Baber 1998), and some of the major proponents of social constructivism found their ideas had been overstated by others (Latour 2004).

Scholars of the sociology of science and scientific knowledge span the relativist and objectivist spectrum. In between the extreme poles of objectivist and relativist views of science, there is a range of positions that in general are recognized as "moderate constructivist." The moderate constructivist conceives science and society as engaging in a co-constructive process. Modern society and scientific knowledge, in this view, is a product of interaction and negotiation between the two. The outcome of scientific knowledge and modern society is determined by the tenacity of the internal logic of scientific knowledge and the obstinacy of societal influence. In general, however, it is true that the priority of scientific research is driven by social, economic and political needs; much of the scientific knowledge taught in schools nevertheless is grounded in a concrete understanding of nature. Moderate constructivists in general agree that there exists a common and stringent standard of scientific practice that is used to determine the validity of scientific claims. However, as new understanding and knowledge emerge, valid claims of today may become false claims of yesterday. Like a map, scientific knowledge represents certain aspects of natural realities that can be exploited. Thus, as our understanding of a place changes, we redraw the map. In other words, scientific knowledge provides an objective depiction of nature within the limit of tentative shared understanding, which can be subject to refutation and renewal (Kitcher 2001, Gieryn 1999).

Science, Modernity and Societal Rationalization

One of the chief impacts of modern science on society is societal rationalization. According to Max Weber (1948: 139–40), the advent of modern science gives birth to a worldview that has shaped the progress of Western societies in a unique and irreversible way. Modern scientific exposition of nature as a mechanistic construct that is devoid of divinity empties nature of its mystical content and directly challenges traditional and religious accounts of nature. By removing divinity, and other supernatural forces, from the account of natural occurrences, a scientific worldview also robs nature of perennial meanings and purposes that come with traditional and religious expositions of nature. As science progresses and society modernizes in a secular direction, human undertakings and decision-making are increasingly conducted in relation to the effectiveness and efficiency of means rather than meanings of those undertakings in the scheme of nature. In order to maximize efficiency, chance occurrences and random actions are suppressed, and individuals are subjected to more rigid though less violent social control. Consequently, Weber views modern society as evolving into an "iron cage" in which individual freedom is curbed, and social and political legitimacy is increasingly subject to means-end justification (Weber 1930: 181–2).

The concern that modern society is evolving into an "iron cage" and betraying the promise of human emancipation is central to the debate on modernity. As modern society increasingly emphasizes social order, stability, cohesion, and the continuity of economic prosperity, knowledge of science, both social and physical, is used to solicit and enforce conformity, engendering a disciplinary society in which individuals are subject to increasing surveillance and self-discipline (Foucault 1995). In most cases scientific knowledge in modern societies is perceived to be in service of modern states that enjoy a monopoly of violence over their subjects. As a result, science, and more fundamentally reason, is perceived to have become an instrument of domination, and a target of intellectual critique (Horkheimer 1947, Horkheimer and Adorno 1972). The critique of reason, science, and modernity culminates into a broad intellectual movement that can be subsumed under the banner of postmodernism. On different fronts, postmodern theorists deconstruct the stability and unified view of nature, and the validity and universality of scientific knowledge. Often, this leads to a relativist stand on knowledge and moral principles (Rosenau 1992).

The critique of modernity draws diverse reactions from academics. Some relish the deconstruction of the myth and fallacy of modern science or more generally modernity (Clifford 1988, Haraway 1989), while others abhor its lack of coherence and consistencies (Gross and Levitt 1994). Jürgen Habermas, an ardent defender of modernity, concurs with Weber's insight on the increasing domination of instrumental rationality, in his *Theory of Communicative Action* (1984), but is less ambivalent in arguing that the one-sided rationalization can be corrected by the withdrawal of instrumental rationality from certain life spheres. Habermas divides social spheres into *System* and *Lifeworld*. The System, mainly in the realm of politics and economy, is a life sphere that is ruled by means-end instrumental rationality. In a modern society, the *System* is the domain of material production and reproduction. It provides for the material needs of humankind. The *Lifeworld*, alternatively, is a life sphere where meanings are defined, values are inculcated, and decisions are achieved consensually among members of society. In the *Lifeworld*, the cultural traditions of a society are reproduced. The *System* operates according to instrumental rationality while the *Lifeworld* functions according to communicative rationality. In his analysis, Habermas suggests that the problem of modernity is a consequence of the colonization of the *Lifeworld* by the *System*, or the application of instrumental rationality in the *Lifeworld*, in place of communicative rationality. Accordingly, the solution to the malaise of modernity (Taylor 1991) does not lie with the desertion of reason, but the withdrawal of instrumental rationality from, and the reinstatement of consensual-based communicative rationality to the *Lifeworld*. In this respect, modernity is still an "unfinished project" that must be given a longer lease of life (Habermas 1997).

Initial Modern Societal Rationalization in Malaysia

Societal rationalization is an ongoing process. However, with the advent of modern science, the process is intensified. In the context of Malaysia, this happened during the British colonial period. The British did not only introduce modern science but also brought along modern administration, education, health, and judiciary systems. The introduction of modern science and social institutions was mainly to facilitate colonial economic extraction. The scientific knowledge transmitted, for instance, was largely modern medical and public health knowledge that was essential to the survival of expatriates and the health of tin mining and rubber plantation laborers. It is in this context that Arnold attributes the introduction of modern medical services to British India as a part of "the accountancy of [the British] empire" (Arnold 1988: 16). According to Mohd Hazim (2007), the rationalization that happened during the British colonial period was mainly instrumental in nature. Unlike modern Europe where societal rationalization involved intense rationalization of the religious realm (Weber 1930), rationalization in Malaysia during the British colonial period took place mainly in areas that were closely related to bureaucratic administration, education and public health.

In fact, there was an agreement between Malay rulers and British colonialists that the latter would not interfere with the religious and cultural affairs of the Malays but would leave them with the Malay rulers who were the political leaders of Malaya prior to British colonization (Khoo 1974). The consequence of this arrangement was a process of societal rationalization in Malaysia that was distinctive from the West and underpinned chiefly by instrumental rationality, with traditional and religious values and beliefs largely remaining untouched, without concurrent rationalization, as all other areas of society underwent intense instrumental rationalization (Mohd Hazim 2007). However, given the force of instrumental rationalization in all other realms of society, it was unclear if religious and traditional practices and beliefs of the indigenous population could be upheld without succumbing to the domination of instrumental rationalization, much like what has happened in the West. More importantly, with the introduction of modern science by the British, substantive rationality located in religious and traditional beliefs would increasingly be challenged by modern science which served as an alternative "sacred canopy" and provided a comprehensive alternative worldview that could be substituted for a religious worldview (Drori et al. 2003).

In other words, despite the non-interference policy in traditional and religious matters, the British colonial administration, through the introduction of modern science and the production of modern knowledge about Malaya would, in effect, inevitability alter the understanding, values, and worldview of the indigenous population. The production of British colonial knowledge was part of the strategy of the management of native society to serve the interests of British colonists. It at once provided colonial administrators with an ontological safety in an alien environment while informing them of the measures of imperial administration. The census, geographical survey, and the collection of a plethora of statistical data were efforts to organize, categorize, code, archive, disseminate, and eventually reproduce knowledge about British colonies that served both to assure colonial administrators of the place they ruled and of the way to rule (Cohn 1996). The constructed knowledge was then internalized by the indigenous population and permanently altered their way of understanding, consciousness, and culture (Pannu 2009).

It is in this context that the issue of cultural authenticity, including knowledge formation, arises. To what extent modernization can be achieved with substantial input, and retention, of local and traditional knowledge and practice remains a central issue in many developing countries, including Malaysia (Mohd Hazim 2003). More significantly, without undergoing a process of cultural and religious rationalization like the West, there is not the process of accommodation in Malaysia towards the encroachment of instrumental rationality on traditional and religious values as experienced by European societies (Mohd Hazim 2007). The quest for Islamization in Malaysia may then be construed as a belated awakening and an effort to answer the challenge presented by the domination of instrumental rationality that comes with modernization.

Apart from being a process that constantly seeks to improve efficiency, societal rationalization is also a process of differentiation. The non-interference policy on tradition and religion, as such, can be perceived as part of the rationalization process where Islamic religion is being differentiated from politics, or in Shamsul's word, the "disembedding" of Islam from politics (Shamsul 2005). Through indirect rule, the British practically stripped traditional Malay rulers of their political power and confined their rule to only matters pertaining to Malay culture and Islamic religion. The British manoeuvre gave a result that was not entirely dissimilar to the separation of church and state in Europe. The strategy would lead to a response by Malaysian leaders to re-embed Islam into politics after Malaysia gained independence.

The colonial rule left behind major political, economic, financial, and social institutions, transforming Malaysia from a feudal society to a modern society in the Western form. However, there remained significant differences between European and Malaysian modernity. As argued by Mohd Hazim (2007), there was no equivalent process of value rationalization in the West that has happened in Malaysia. This leaves the contestation between science and religious interpretations of human destiny untouched and unresolved. While this provides the opportunity to define a distinctive, i.e. non-secular, form of modernity in Malaysia, the shape and outcome of this distinctive form of Malaysian modernity remains uncertain. More often than not, the effort to define a non-secular form of Malaysian modernity is construed as part of the larger worldwide Muslim response to the rise and domination of the West that has its roots stretched further back in history and covering a wider range of societies.

Early Response to the Rise of Modern Science and Western Civilization

The introduction of modern medical knowledge, to Malaya by British colonialists did not encounter significant opposition. In areas where religious and traditional sensitivities were involved, community leaders or village 'headmen' were often enlisted to bridge the trust between the indigenous population and the modern medicine and medical practices introduced by the British (Chai 2008: 74–77). In addition, the circumscription of the power of traditional rulers to only Islamic religion and traditional Malay culture left to the colonial administrators the full authority over the introduction of various modern institutions, one of which was modern science and technology. However, the encounter between modern science and traditional knowledge was not without hesitation and reflection on the part of the intellectuals of the indigenous community. Often, the debate is subsumed under the larger issue of modernization of which modern science is only one of its key components. Central to the debate of modernization is the issue of national identity: that is, to what extent can a country aspiring to modernize achieve this goal without sacrificing traditional values and identity, and/or without being westernized? In areas where Western influence is perceived to have taken root, the call to purify indigenous culture through de-Westernization is often heard (Syed Muhammad Naquib al-Attas 1978). .

Like other major non-Western civilizations, how to respond to the rise of Western civilization amid the stagnation, even decline, of Islamic civilization has been the pre-occupation of Islamic communities around the world since the modern era after the eighteenth century. This prompted various Islamic reformist movements that seek through reflection and action to retain the glory of Islamic civilization (Azizan Baharuddin 1994). In Malaysia, a key indigenous intellectual reaction to Western influence happened in the early twentieth century when there were significant divisions between the traditional elite and a group of younger generation Malays. This younger generation of Malays, the *Kaum Muda* as they were called, were mainly trained and influenced by religious teachings in Egypt. In one of their earliest periodicals, *Al-Imam*, they proposed a revamping of the education system to include the teaching of English and modern science, but at the same time stressed the return to the true teaching of Islam that purportedly was in line with the quest for modernity. They encouraged *ijtihad* (informed independent investigation) and rejected *taklid buta* (blind acceptance of intermediate authority). Inadvertently, their ideas challenged the traditional aristocrats and village religious leaders and their activities were not well-received by the authorities (Roff 1962). Their critical role was later superseded by the emerging categories of locally and overseas trained Malays who were equally enthusiastic for ethnically-based Malay nationalism (Roff 1967).

Crises of Modernity

After independence from the British, Malaysia continues to undergo intense modernization and social change. This is reflected not only in the mushrooming of modern physical infrastructures and rising living standards, but also in social and cultural dislocations similar to what Durkheim (1984) characterized as social anomie. The emergence of child abuse, youth crime, drug addiction, and a display of "aimlessness" among the youth (Ariffin 1995), though it reflects very much our new conception of knowledge, deviance and illness (Foucault 1971), nevertheless points to a changing social reality that needs to be addressed in order to maintain social stability. Social ills aside and as a society modernizes, one cannot forget the specter of the iron cage envisaged by Weber. The decline of meaning and substantive values provoked a response from religious institutions, since it is in religion that many of our social values are seated.

In fact, one of the key issues in contemporary Malaysian society is the Islamic revivalism of the 1980s (Nagata 1984, Zainah Anwar 1987, Muzaffar 1987, Hussin Mutalib 1993). Today Islam has become an indispensable source of political legitimacy in Malaysia, and both ruling and opposition parties try to out-Islamize each other (Liow 2004, Stark 2003). While the Islamic resurgence is partly inspired and encouraged by the Iranian revolution, its manifestation in Malaysia is often perceived as a disguised class struggle, where religion is said to be used as a rallying point by disadvantaged social groups to express their discontent over their condition of marginalization (Kessler 1978). Amid the tide of globalization, Islamic resurgence in Malaysia is also understood as a response to a crisis of identity in the face of inter-ethnic competition and the homogenization effect of the process of globalization (Nagata 1984, Muzaffar 1987). In the 1990s, there was also a segment of Malay intellectuals who earnestly engaged in the debate about the nature of scientific knowledge and sought to Islamize it. According to Abaza (2002), a key actor within this movement in both Malaysia and Egypt, had close relationships to political leaders who sought to increase their Islamic credibility.

Apart from Islamic resurgence, there is also a call for a revival of Malay tradition. This call comes mostly from the middle class Malay who, while experiencing and enjoying the fruits of modernity, nevertheless are apprehensive of their waning cultural identity. According to Kessler (1992:144–7), the quest to preserve traditional culture in turn is tightly enmeshed with the need of the 'New Economic Policy' to define who the Malay are. As a result, the yearning for tradition is said to be closely tied to economic considerations. In fact, the regeneration of tradition, such as the construction and display of elegant traditional Malay houses at tourist spots, often overshadows the disturbing reality

of lower income citizens who continue to dwell in dilapidated traditional Malay houses as the pace of modernization quickens (Goh
2001). The revival of tradition in a sense can be said to be more an
"invention" in the face of rapid social change than a representation of
a social and historical reality and ethnic identity (Hobsbawm and
Ranger 1983).

The recent waves of Islamization in Malaysia, however, cannot be
conceived solely as a continuation of the Islamic reformist reaction to
Western progress in the late 18th and early 19th centuries. At the close
of twentieth century, part of the socioeconomic and physical landscapes of Malaysia had been transformed. In fact, by the end of twentieth century, Malaysia had achieved substantial economic and material
developments and was perceived in some circles as the fifth members
of the so-called "Asian Tigers"—a name denoting the four newly industrialized countries: South Korea, Taiwan, Singapore, and Hong Kong—
in Asia (Jomo et al. 1995). In other words, the current spate of
Islamization is occurring amid rapid industrialization and modernization that has uplifted the standard of living for a substantial proportion
of Malaysians and is approaching Western standards.

One key difference between current Islamic reformists and early
twentieth century reformists lies in the attitude towards Western
modernity. Unlike current reformists, the earlier reformists viewed the
West as a model of development to be emulated. The more recent reaction, however, has adopted a more critical view of Western modernization; the latter itself is undergoing internal critique by Western
intellectuals. Still, the call to Islamize is not a call to reject modernization but a quest to reform the Western form of modernization. In fact,
the discourse on Islamization of knowledge does not shy away from
the content of intellectual discourse in the West, and the call to Islamize
scientific knowledge borrows readily the constructivist contention of
scientific knowledge in the second half of the twentieth century.

There have been substantial analyses done on the Islamic revivalism
in the second half of the twentieth century (Nagata 1984, Muzaffar
1987, Zainah Anwar 1987, Hussin Mutalib 1993). Most scholars understand the recent waves of Islamization from the perspectives of political economy and identity contests. While these views have a strong
empirical basis they nevertheless do not address the importance of
religion and tradition as perennial sources of meaning. The fact that
religious interests cut across diverse social classes, among the rich and
the poor, points to a different dimension that religion and tradition

may offer. It is here that Weber's theory of societal rationalization may shed some light on the process of Islamization in Malaysia. According to Weber, modernization goes hand in hand with secularization. The disenchantment of the world and the decline of substantive rationality will eventually give rise to the domination of instrumental rationality. The disenchantment of the world causes the loss of purpose and meaning, or the "eclipse of the sacred" in industrial society (Acquaviva 1979). Can we then conceive the resurgence or revivalism of religious interests in Malaysia as a search for meaning in the face of rapid modernization and erosion of tradition as Malaysian society undergoes the process of modernization and industrialization?

Scientific Knowledge as a Site of Re-enchantment

One area where the critique of Western modernity manifests itself is in the discourse of modern science, especially in relation to the misuse of science and the abuse of reason (Horkheimer 1947, Bauman 1989). The constructivist critique of modern science adds to the distrust over the claim of scientific objectivity, and provides an opportunity for the reconstruction of scientific knowledge at different localities. This coupled with the postcolonial discourse of nationalism in developing countries gives rise to the quest for indigenous or national identity in the realm of modern science that is distinct from the West. For instance, in India, the pursuit of "Hindu science" is earnest and contentious, and closely aligned with the postcolonial discourse of reclaiming national pride and identity (Nanda 2003). In Malaysia, there has also been an effort by a group of Malay Muslim intellectuals to engage in the debate of Islamization of scientific knowledge (Mohd Hazim 2004).

The intensification of Islamization in the late twentieth century in Malaysia was meant to construct a modernity that was distinct from the West and rooted in Islamic values. The content, tone and the urge for Islamic reform in the early and late twentieth century has significantly different emphasis. The earlier call happened at a period of Western rise and extolled the values of the modern West, while the late-century call cautions against Westernization, especially the disapproval of Western secularism. There are many reasons behind the reservation toward a Western model of modernization in the late twentieth century. One of the reasons is the lack of trust in the promotion of modernity by the West. The key to the disaffection of the West lies with the lack of social and economic progress in many developing countries and Islamic societies in the twentieth century despite the adoption of the developmental model and aids of the West. In fact, some countries are said to be "under-developed" (Frank 1967) and remain subordinated to the West (Wallerstein 1974). The success of East Asian economies, however, gives hope that the emulation of Western success in industrialization and modernization (Amsden 2001) remains feasible. The Japanese ability to blend Western modernity with the preservation of traditional culture (Bellah 2003) has added to the belief in the compatibility between Western development and Eastern culture. Yet, reservation still remains over the secular tendency of Western modernity, and in Muslim societies in general, the aspiration is to have a modernity that brings about material success without sacrificing the sacred or in the words of Tibi (1995), semi-modernity rather than a full-fledged Western modernity.

In Malaysia, the adoption of a Western model of development by and large has been successful although the tension between a secular modernity and religious obligation remains, and continues to serve as a point of contention and possible innovation. As a society with Islam as one of its key identities, a major concern about modernization in a Western mould is the rejection of the public role of religion, which in Malaysia, if not addressed, will ultimately challenge the legitimacy of the Islamic identity of the nation. To confront and reform Western modernity often means to tackle the secular outlook of Western modernity. And the root of secularization is in the teaching of modern science that has over the last few centuries substituted a religious worldview with a scientific worldview which is equally comprehensive. To arrest the secular trend in the West often means to arrest the secular interpretation of modern scientific knowledge.

In a Weberian interpretation, the exposition of modern science leads to an understanding of nature that is devoid of divine quality. Nature operates solely on the basis of mechanical laws that do not require an immediate role of the divine. This also implies emptying meanings associated with divinity, especially in relation to the place and purpose of the human species in the universe. The anxiety over the loss of the sacred and its meaning is vivid in the critique of information technology in Hairudin Harun's *Malay Cosmology in the Era of Information Technology* (2001). Hairudin Harun's critique is an example in which the trepidation over the rise of the soulless "Turing Man" is central. It is an attempt by the author to discern the epistemological basis behind such a technology and its possible impact on the mental makeup of the Malays. The main concern lies with the demise of transcendental and religious belief such as the denial of spiritual existence in the modern conception of man.

In line with social constructivism, Hairudin Harun (2001) suggests that the design of information technology is closely shaped by human values and beliefs. Technology as a human creation is said to reflect more human mind than technical necessity. The advent of information technology, as such, is only another manifestation of rationalist Western culture. The creation of computer technology that is able to mimic the human mind and interact with human beings hence suggests a cosmology that perceives human beings as machines without spirits. They are merely mechanistic entities. It is clear that the author seeks to remind his readers that technological progress interferes not just with our physical existence but also our spiritual well-being.

The same concern is raised by Daud and Zain (1999). While the discourse in the Islamization of knowledge is partly contributed by the rise of the sociology of knowledge in the West, as evidenced by the authors' constant reference to the "Kuhnian revolution," the sociology of knowledge possibly provides a channel to reflect upon a concern that has long been seated in the psyche of the modern man. As a nation where religion plays an important role in everyday life, it is only natural that any hint of obsolescence of religion is disquieting. The concern over the decline of the sacred is not unique to Muslim communities. Indeed, in all three monotheistic religions, the central critique of the modern West by a section of followers, sometimes exaggerated as fundamentalists, is the decoupling of modern science from religion (Mendelsohn 1993). In their view, nature is part of the creation of God, and as a result, it is difficult to conceive of a scientific understanding of nature which denies the existence of God. In fact, scientific interpretation should be guided by religious understanding, and scientific knowledge cannot be viewed as an independent branch of knowledge, which has no relation to knowledge of the divine.

Another response to the disenchantment of modern society can be seen in re-mystification. If we are to subject ourselves to Weber's thesis of societal rationalization, mystical practices should subside and eventually vanish. This, however, is not the case. In the case of Malaysia, amid euphoric economic success, the practice of the occult remains prevalent, even among those who are at the upper echelon of

the political structure (Malaysiakini, May 2, 2006, http://www
.malaysiakini.com/news/50470). Hairudin Harun accords this phenomenon to a search for spiritual meaning amid an increasingly
rationalized society. It is a quest for a more "holistic" existence that
fulfills both material and spiritual needs. The continuity of mysticism
is certainly not unique to Malaysia. An earlier study in Bali reveals the
same phenomenon (Boon 1979), where the author comes to the same
conclusion that the process of societal rationalization and modernization had prompted efforts to re-enchant or re-mystify the world instead
of demystification. In fact, this did not happen only in Islamic societies
like Malaysia, it occurred also in Western societies. As argued by
Tiryakian (1992), exoticism in the West is a form of "re-enchantment"
and the quest for a collective consciousness, whether in the French
Revolution or more recent social movements are different forms of
"dedifferentiation." Both forces of re-enchantment and dedifferentiation are directed at the disenchanting tendency of modernity.

It is in this light that Islamic banking in Malaysia is said to be an
effort to "re-embed" religious values into the instrumentalized modern
system of capitalism (Schrader 2000). There is no doubt that Islamic
principles are more closely observed in Islamic banking. They are, in
fact, said to have helped to mitigate the impact of the currency crisis in
1997 due to their lesser involvement in high risk investment (Shamsul
1999). However, doubts remain regarding whether the Islamic Bank is
not the same as other commercial banks in terms of the practice of
usury, which is prohibited by Islam (Yaakob 2004). Although no interest giving is involved, the Islamic Bank nevertheless shares its profits
at a competitive rate that closely matches other commercial banks.
As such, it is said to practice quasi-interest. Still, it attracts a substantial
number of customers, Muslims and non-Muslims, and is a credible
alternative to the more conventional commercial banking system. As a
symbol of Islamic practice, it has certainly served the purpose of
bestowing religious meaning upon the otherwise mechanistic system
of capitalist economy.

The current quest for Islamic reform, as a result, must also be understood as a reaction against the inadequacies of the project of modernity in Western societies. The quest for Islamization is not a mission to
denounce modernity. Instead, it seeks to reap the fruit of modernity
without repeating the perceived shortcomings of Western secularization. In this sense, it engages in the reflection of modernity much
like the ongoing reflection occurring in the West (Fuller 2006: 153,

Ali Hassan 2006) except that the return of a larger public role of religion in society is less likely option in the West.

Dialogue with or a Challenge to Western Hegemony?

The discourse on the Islamization of knowledge is also used by certain Muslim intellectuals as an avenue to challenge Western hegemony. Rooted in this perception is the understanding that knowledge is contextual and not neutral, and dominant Western knowledge, including modern scientific knowledge, is perceived to be engaging in "epistemological imperialism" (Sardar 1985: 85). The outcome is the suppression if not the elimination of non-Western knowledge, which has led to the oppression of non-Western societies. In order to regain an Islamic "way of life" in accordance with Islamic teaching, it is essential to Islamize Western knowledge, which is regarded as secular knowledge devoid of divine quality. As a result, "de-westernization" of knowledge means the reintroduction of the divine into the corpus of modern knowledge, and achieves the Islamic dream of semi-modernity—a modernity that embraces the material success of the West yet rejects its secular tenet (Tibi 1995).

While the struggle to make Islamic identity distinct from Western tradition is an overt objective of the Islamization of knowledge, the discourse has a greater relevance than merely being a reaction to Western hegemony. As argued by Ali Hassan Zaidi (2006), the project of the Islamization of knowledge may also be conceived as an effort to engage in a dialogue with Western civilization. In this view, Islamization of knowledge is a response to the malaises of modernity (Taylor 1991), especially in relation to the loss of meaning due to the disenchantment of the world. Viewed in this light, the Islamization of knowledge is said to be an effort to address this particular dilemma of modernity and re-enchant the modern knowledge of science.

Conclusion

Why is the attempt of cultural and religious interpretation possible in modern science? And what does it say about modern science? These questions lead us back to the earlier analysis of the nature of scientific knowledge—whether it is objective or it can be socially conditioned. Proponents of knowledge Islamization in Malaysia hold the latter view, that is, scientific knowledge is not entirely based on the external material world but also the cultural interpretation of the material world. As a result, different religious and cultural traditions may arrive at a different interpretation and understanding of modern science. As there remain gaps in modern scientific knowledge, such as the continuous contention regarding the *Theory of Evolution*, there will always be room for non-scientific explanations of natural phenomena, although one may also remain an atheist, or agnostic. Moreover, since modern science can only adjudicate true and false knowledge, but not right and wrong conduct, there will continue to be areas where scientific authority ceases to function, and alternative authorities, such as religious authority, prevails. The lack of ultimate closure in modern science, both in terms of knowledge claims and moral judgment provides room for the re-enchantment of modern society despite the fact that inconclusiveness of knowledge is expected of, and is not necessarily an issue in, science.

A consequence of the openness of scientific knowledge—openness in terms of the lack of closure in many fresh as well as old theoretical debates—allows for the practice of modern science on different levels. At the practical level, knowledge of modern science continues to be deployed to build modern physical infrastructures in Malaysia; on the other hand, one does not need to subscribe to the 'Theory of Evolution' without jeopardizing the practice of modern science in other areas. In other words, one can choose to delink from, or to stay in connection with, the divine while learning and practicing the same modern science. The choice leads to different worldviews about the human place in the universe without the need to question the validity of majority aspects of modern science.

This allows for the pursuit of different modernities under the same cover of modern science. One way to look at this is to conceive modernity, which is undergirded by modern science, as comprised of two dimensions—institutional and cultural (Tibi 1995: 3). Viewed in this framework, Malaysia has adopted the institutional dimension of modernity wholeheartedly, but is still in the process of negotiating the cultural dimension. While playing catch-up to the West in the institutional dimension of science, Malaysia is also actively pursuing the cultural dimension of modernity in the mould of Islam (Kessler 1994). The Islamization efforts, including Islamization of scientific knowledge by a small number of Malay Muslim intellectuals, are examples of the endeavour to define a modernity that is institutionally similar but culturally distinct from the West. It is indeed an attempt of knowledge and cultural innovation, the outcome of which remains to be seen.

Bibliography

Abaza, Mona. 2002. "Two Intellectuals: The Malaysian S.N. Al-Attas and the Egyptian Mohammed 'Immara, and the Islamization of Knowledge Debate." *Asian Journal of Social Science* 30 (2): 354–383.

Acquaviva, S. Samele. 1979. *The Elipse of the Holy in Industrial Society*. Oxford: Blackwell.

Ali Hassan Zaidi. 2006. "Muslim Reconstruction of Knowledge and the Re-enchantment of Modernity." *Theory, Culture & Society* 23(5): 69–91.

Amsden, Alice. 2001. *The Rise of "The Rest": Challenges to the West from Late-Industrializing Economies*. New York: Oxford University Press.

Ariffin, Jamilah. 1995. "At the Crossroads of Rapid Development: Malaysian Society and Anomie." *International Journal of Sociology and Social Policy* 15: 343–371.

Aronowitz, Stanley. 1988. *Science as Power: Discourse and Ideology in Modern Society*. Minneapolis: University of Minnesota Press.

Arnold, David, ed. 1988. *Imperial Medicine and Indigenous Societies*. Manchester: Manchester University Press.

Azizan, Baharuddin. 1994. "Muslims' Encounter with Modern Western Thought–The Reformists' Experience." *Sarjana* Special Issue: 99–116.

Baber, Zaheer. 1998. "Science and Technology Studies after the 'Science Wars.'" *Asian Journal of Social Science* 26(1): 113–120.

Baber, Zaheer. 2000. "An Ambiguous Legacy: The Social Construction of the Kuhnian Revolution and Its Consequences for the Sociology of Science." *Bulletin of Science, Technology & Society* 20 (2): 139–155.

Barnes, Barry. 1977. *Interests and the Growth of Knowledge*. London: Routledge and K. Paul.

Bauman, Zygmunt. 1989. *Modernity and the Holocaust*. Ithaca, New York: Cornell University Press.

Bellah, Robert Neelly. 2003. *Imagining Japan: the Japanese Tradition and its Modern Interpretation*. Berkeley; Los Angeles: University of California Press.

Chai, Choon-Lee. 2008. *Science and Modernity: Modern Medical Knowledge and Societal Rationalization in Malaysia*. Unpublished Ph.D. Dissertation, Department of Sociology, University of Saskatchewan.

Clifford, James. 1988. *The Predicament of Culture: Twentieth-century Ethnography, Literature, and Art*. Cambridge, Mass.: Harvard University Press.

Cohn, S. Bernard. 1996. *Colonialism and Its Forms of Knowledge: the British in India* Princeton, N.J: Princeton University Press.

Daud, Wan Ramli bin Wan, and Shaharir in Mohamad Zain. 1999. "*PeMalaysian dan PengIslaman Ilmu Sains dan Teknologi Dalam Konteks Dasar Sains Negara*" (Malaynisation and Islamization of Science and Technology in the Context of National Science Policy). *Kesturi* 9 (1): 1–32.

Drori, S. Gili, John W. Meyer, Francisco O. Ramirez and Evan Schofer. 2003. *Science in the Modern World Polity: Institutionalization and Globalization*. California: Stanford University Press.

Durkheim, Emile. 1984[1933]. *The Division of Labor in Society*. New York: Free Press.

Editors of *Lingua Franca*, eds. 2000. *The Sokal Hoax: the Sham that Shook the Academy*. Lincoln: University of Nebraska Press.

Foucault, Michel. 1971. *Madness and Civilization: a History of Insanity in the Age of Reason*. London: Tavistock Publications.

Foucault, Michel. 1995. *Discipline and Punish: the Birth of the Prison*. New York: Vintage Books.

Frank, Andre Gunder. 1967. *Capitalism and Underdevelopment in Latin America: Historical Studies of Chile and Brazil*. New York: Monthly Review Press.

Fuller, Steve. 2006. "Intelligent Design Theory: A Site for Contemporary Sociology of Knowledge." *Canadian Journal of Sociology* 31 (3): 277–289.

Gieryn, F. Thomas. 1982. "Relativist/Constructivist Programmes in the Sociology of Science: Redundance and Retreat." *Social Studies of Science* 12(2): 279–297.

Gieryn, Thomas F. 1999. *Cultural Boundaries of Science: Credibility on the Line*. Chicago: University of Chicago Press.

Goh, Beng Lan. 2001. "Stability in Flux: The Ambivalence of State, Ethnicity and Class in the Forging of Modern Urban Malaysia." *Comparative Urban & Community Research* 7: 51–96.

Gross, Paul R., and Norman Levitt. 1994. *Higher Superstition: the Academic Left and its Quarrels with Science*. Baltimore: Johns Hopkins University Press.

Habermas, Jürgen. 1984. *The theory of Communicative Action*. Boston: Beacon Press.

Habermas, Jürgen. 1997. "Modernity: an Unfinished Project", in Maurizio Passerin d'Entrèves and Seyla Benhabib, eds., *Habermas and the Unfinished Project of Modernity: Critical Essays on the Philosophical Discourse of Modernity*. Cambridge, Massachusetts: The MIT Press, pp. 38–55.

Hairudin Harun. 2001. *Kosmologi Melayu Dalam Era Teknologi Maklumat* (Malay Cosmology in the Age of Information Technology). Kuala Lumpur: Dewan Bahasa & Pustaka.

Haraway, Donna Jeanne. 1989. *Primate Visions: Gender, Race, and Nature in the World of Modern Science*. New York: Routledge.

Hobsbawm, Eric and Terence Ranger, eds. 1983. *The Invention of Tradition*. Cambridge: Cambridge University Press.

Horkheimer, Max. 1947. *Eclipse of Reason*. New York: Oxford University Press.

Horkheimer, Max, and Theodor W. Adorno. 1972. *Dialectic of Enlightenment*. Translated by John Cumming. New York: Herder and Herder.

Hussin Mutalib. 1993. *Islam in Malaysia: from Revivalism to Islamic State?* Singapore: Singapore University Press.

Jomo, K. Sundaram, Boo Teik Khoo and Yii Tan Chang. 1995. *Vision, Policy and Governance in Malaysia*. Occasional Paper No. 10, Private Sector Development Department, World Bank.

Kessler, Clive S. 1978. *Islam and Politics in a Malay State, Kelantan, 1838–1969*. Ithaca, New York: Cornell University Press.

Kessler, Clive S. 1992. "Archaism and Modernity: Contemporary Malay Political Culture", in Joel S. Kahn, and Francis Loh Kok Wah, eds., *Fragmented Vision: Culture and Politics in Contemporary Malaysia*. Honolulu: University of Hawaii Press, pp.133–157.

Kessler, Clive S. 1994. "'Secularization' in Malaysia? Some Further Remarks." *Sarjana* Special Issue: 309–317.

Khoo, Kay Kim. 1974. "The Pangkor Engagement of 1874." *Journal of the Malaysian Branch of the Royal Asiatic Society* 47(1): 1–87.

Kitcher, Philip. 2001. *Science, Truth, and Democracy*. New York: Oxford University Press.

Khoo, Kay Kim. 2007. *Living with Darwin: Evolution, Design, and the Future of Faith*. New York: Oxford University Press.

Latour, Bruno. 2004. "Why Has Critique Run Out of Steam? From Matters of Fact to Matters of Concern." *Critical Inquiry* 30 (2): 225–248.

Liow, Joseph ChinYong. 2004. "Political Islam in Malaysia: Problematising Discourse and Practice in the UMNO-PAS 'Islamization Race.'" *Commonwealth and Comparative Politics* 42(2): 184–205.

MacKenzie, Donald. 1978. "Statistical Theory and Social Interests: A Case Study." *Social Studies of Science* 8: 35–83.

Mahathir Mohamad. 1991. *Malaysia: the Way Forward*. Kuala Lumpur: Malaysian Business Council.

Mendelsohn, Everett. 1993. "Religious Fundamentalism and the Sciences", in Martin E. Marty & R. Scott Appleby, eds., *Fundamentalisms and Society*. Chicago: University of Chicago Press, pp. 23–41.

Mohd Hazim, Shah. 2003. "Science, Technology, Modernity and the Question of Cultural Authenticity." *Malaysian Journal of Science and Technology Studies* 1: 117–153.

Mohd Hazim, Shah. 2004. "A Tale of Two Scenarios in the Development of Science and Technology in Malaysia", in Mohd Hazim Shah and Phua Kai Lit, eds., *Public Policy, Culture and Globalization in Malaysia*. Selangor, Malaysia: Malaysian Social Science Association, pp. 59–84.

Mohd Hazim, Shah. 2007. "Historicising Rationality: The Transmission of Rationality and Science to the Malay States under British Rule." *Asian Journal of Social Science* 35(2): 216–241.

Moore, James. 1993. "The Creationist Cosmos of Protestant Fundamentalism", in Martin E. Marty & R. Scott Appleby, eds., *Fundamentalisms and Society*. Chicago: University of Chicago Press, pp. 42–72.

Mukerji, Chandra. 1989. *A Fragile Power: Scientists and the State*. Princeton, New Jersey: Princeton University Press.

Mulkay, Michael. 1979. *Science and the Sociology of Knowledge*. London: George Allen & Unwin.

Muzaffar, Chandra. 1987. *Islamic Resurgence in Malaysia*. Petaling Jaya, Malaysia: Fajar Bakti.

Nagata, Judith A. 1984. *The Reflowering of Malaysian Islam: Modern Religious Radicals and their Roots*. Vancouver: University of British Columbia Press.

Nanda, Meera. 2003. *Prophets Facing Backward: Postmodern Critiques of Science and Hindu Nationalism in India*. New Jersey: Rutgers University Press.

Pannu, Paul. 2009. "The Production and Transmission of Knowledge in Colonial Malaya." *Asian Journal of Social Science* 37(3): 427–451.

Roff, William R. 1962. "Kaum Muda–Kaum Tua: Innovation and Reaction Amongst the Malays, 1900–1941", in K. G. Tregonning, ed., *Papers on Malayan History*. Singapore: Journal of South-East Asian History.

Roff, William R. 1967. *The origins of Malay nationalism*. Singapore: University of Malaya Press.

Rosenau, Pauline Marie. 1992. *Post-modernism and the Social Sciences: Insights, Inroads, and Intrusions*. Princeton, N.J.: Princeton University Press.

Sardar, Ziauddin. 1985. *Islamic Futures: The Shape of Ideas to Come*. New York: Mansell Publication Company.

Schrader, Heiko. 2000. "Modernisation between Economic Requirements and Religious Law: Islamic Banking in Malaysia." *Internationales Asienforum* 1–2: 39–56.

Schroeder, Ralph. 2007. *Rethinking Science, Technology, and Social Change*. California: Standford University Press.

Segerstråle, Ullica, ed. 2000. *Beyond the Science Wars: the Missing Discourse about Science and Society*. Albany: State University of New York Press.

Shamsul, Amri Baharuddin. 1999. "Consuming Islam and Containing the Crisis: Religion, Ethnicity, and the Economy in Malaysia", in Mason C. Hoadley, ed., *Southeast Asian-Centred Economies or Economics?* Copenhagen, Denmark: Nordic Institute of Asian Studies (NIAS).

Shamsul, Amri Baharuddin. 2005. "Making Sense of the Plural-Religious Past and the Modern-Secular Present of the Islamic Malay World and Malaysia." *Asian Journal of Social Science* 33(3): 449–472.

Shapin, Steven. 1995. "Here and Everywhere: Sociology of Scientific Knowledge." *Annual Review of Sociology* 21: 289–321.

Stark, Jan. 2003. "The Islamic Debate in Malaysia: the Unfinished Project." *South East Asia Research* 11(2): 173–201.

Syed, Muhammad Naquib al-Attas. 1978. *Islam and Secularism.* Kuala Lumpur: Muslim Youth Movement of Malaysia (ABIM).

Taylor, Charles. 1991. *The Malaise of Modernity.* Concord, Ontario: Anansi.

Thorpe, Charles. 2002. "Disciplining Experts: Scientific Authority and Liberal Democracy in the Oppenheimer Case." *Social Studies of Science* 32, no. 4: 525–562.

Tibi, Bassam. 1995. "Culture and Knowledge: The Politics of Islamization of Knowledge as a Postmodern Project? The Fundamentalist Claim to De-Westernization." *Theory, Culture & Society* 12(1): 1–24.

Tiryakian, A. Edward. 1992. "Dialectics of Modernity: Reenchantment and Dedifferentiation as Counterprocesses", in Hans Haferkamp, and Neil J. Smelser, eds., *Social Change and Modernity.* Berkeley: University of California Press, pp. 78–94.

Wallerstein, Immanuel Maurice. 1974. *The Modern World-System.* New York: Academic Press.

Weber, Max. 1930. *The Protestant Ethic and the Spirit of Capitalism.* London: Allen & Unwin.

Weber, Max. 1948. "Science as Vocation", in H. H. Gerth, and C. Wright Mills, eds., *From Max Weber: Essays in Sociology.* New York: Routledge.

Yaakop, Rosli. 2004. "Is Islamic banking Truly Islamic?" *Malaysiakini*, June 14, 2004. http://malaysiakini.com/opinionsfeatures/200406140041700.php

Zainah, Anwar. 1987. *Islamic Revivalism in Malaysia: Dakwah among the Students.* Selangor, Malaysia: Pelanduk Publications.

CHAPTER SIX

GENDER AND IDENTITY IN A GLOBALIZED WORLD

Patience Elabor-Idemudia

In the contemporary age of globalization necessitated by the ever-increasing flows of people, goods, ideas, and images the blending of cultures and lifestyles has been enhanced leading in most instances to the formation of 'hyphenated' social and personal identities and communities. The resulting freewheeling diasporic communities entail clear and unequivocal advantages to being able to operate in increasingly knowledge-based but multiple cultural codes, traverse cultural spaces and identities in post-national citizenship (Suarez-Orozco 2001). Identity, thus, becomes the distinguishing feature characterizing individuals. Some of its features may be visible (e.g. gender, race, age, etc.), psychological (e.g. personality), social (e.g. class), social roles (e.g. parents, academic) or invisible (e.g. sexual orientation) (Mullaly 2010:75). In this chapter, the visible characteristic of identity specifically gender identity is interrogated to explore the underlining shifts in perception as a result of globalization and heightened migration.

In view of the changing nature of culture over time and space, the chapter examines how globalization impacts our perception of gender identity and how knowledge about gender identity has been shaped by new ideologies, communication technologies, labor demands and the media. It is argued that while prior constructed gender roles continue to inform the perception of women and men in general, gender roles and identity have been reconstructed making traditional ideologies less apt in describing modern gender roles. For instance, contemporary women are increasingly highly educated, are acquiring skills and knowledge needed to survive in a complex world; have gained large entrances into the labor force, and are migrating independently because of their roles as heads of households and care providers for their families.

The chapter interrogates the conditions in which particular 'cultures', 'identity' or 'knowledge' about men and women have and continue to undergo constant negotiations, dissonant exchanges, and operations of power that engrave particular differences and underwrite pedagogies on gender and identity in an increasingly knowledge-based societies.

Globalization, Transnationalism and Identity

As the process of globalization is characterized by mass mobilization and increases in migratory trends, transnationalism involving cross border activities has become one of the integral phenomenon impacting people's lives and identities. Originally coined during the second half of the twentieth century by scholars working within the broader field of 'International Economics', to describe flows of capital and labor across national borders, transnationalism has come to be applied to the study of international migration and ethnic diaspora and found to be useful in exploring such issues as immigrant economic integration, identity, citizenship, and cultural retention. The term, and its usage, embraces a variety of multifaceted social relations that are both embedded in and transcend two or more nation-states, cross-cutting socio-political, territorial, and cultural borders.

There are those who conceive of transnationalism as something to celebrate, as an expression of subversive popular resistance from below (Guarnizo and Smith 1998) as depicted by the notion of cultural hybridity, multi-positional identities, and transnational businesses engaged in by ordinary people to escape domination by capital and the state. The fact remains, however, that transnationalism as a process affects power relations, constructions of cultural identity, economic interactions and more generally, social organization at the level of the locality. The enduring asymmetries of domination, inequalities, class conflicts and even unequal development in which transnational practices and processes are embedded, are often left unanalyzed. The specific case of gender identity, its construction and how the notion of diaspora is used as a theoretical concept to challenge its fixed understandings needs interrogating within the broader context of what is being called a knowledge society.

Identity is generally defined as involving a process organized around the concept of self, that is, the ideas and feelings we have about ourselves that are derived from various sources (based on what Horton Cooley (1927) calls the looking-glass self. Under globalization, the concept of identity becomes subjected to multiple interpretations resulting in significant shifts in its theorizing as people find themselves in multiple locations in their lifetime. Those who belong to different groups and spaces begin to define themselves in terms of multiple affiliations without necessarily placing their belongings in a hierarchical order (Fleras and Elliot 2008:348). Many authors such as Featherstone (1995), Jameson (1998), and Gergen (1991) claim that the notion of the 'core of self' loses it significance, giving way to new definitions of identity that are conceptualized as fluid, incoherent, constantly in flux and changing. In the context of globalization, Henry and Tator (1991:99) see identity as "dynamic, historically situated and involving process that is always changing to fit moods or personality changes".

This implies that identity can no more be fixed. This, thus, contradicts the way it was perceived before the debates on globalization became widespread. Identity as a social construct has not only been made complex but the vagaries of globalization and the rise of knowledge as the organizing principle of contemporary society. Indeed as emphasized by Hall (1999), because identities and expressions vary far more than the prescriptive roles to which we are presumably assigned, any attempt to problematize or analyze the dynamic nature of identity and its construct as gendered is fraught with potential difficulties.

The Social Construction of Gender Identity

The definition of gender identity is one of those instances in which we can best recognize the ambivalence of the process of individualization. On the one hand, to the extent that traditional characterizations of gender have been de-institutionalized, contemporary individuals enjoy more flexibility to develop individual ways of realizing gender identity. At the same time, however, it seems as if the traditional references once available in the social sphere are now being replaced by references provided by the media. It must be noted that, at the individual level, we find that neither social structure nor media-culture has the last word in matters of defining one's identity. After all, human beings are not merely the result of the intersection of social structures; they have minds and bodies of their own. They also develop a variety of relationships whose impact on the definition of their identity does not simply derive either from social structure or media-culture.

Consequently, Gilbert (2008) defines gender identity as encompassing a person's internal psychological self-concept of being either male or female or possibly a combination of both. Part of one's gender identity involves the incorporation of roles that are arbitrarily imposed from without rather than developing from within. Its social construction is based on sex considered to be an important determinant of a system of attitudes, behaviours, and values that are distinctive for men and women—motivated by the production of social representations different from each other—from which a social stratification is put into place. This partly explains why women live at a disadvantage in the face of men, that is to say, where men exercise their influence (or dominance) over women. Although, according to Bourdieu (2001: 114),

> the order of things is not a natural order that nothing can be done about as there exists instead a mental construction, a vision of the world where men satisfy their network of domination. A vision that women themselves and those victimized have assumed while unconsciously accepting their inferiority.

The formation of gender identity and specifically, female gender identity is an extremely complex entity and tends to engulf the totality of the personal and occupational lives of individuals. In most societies in the world, the accepted cultural perspective on gender identity views women and men as naturally and unequivocally defined categories. However, Kimmel (2011) sees women and men as distinct social groups constituted in concrete, historically changing and generally unequal social relationships. Gender identity is thus constituted by the product and the producer (Combs et al. 1979), the object and the subject (James 1946), the actor and the author (Herman et al. 1992), the 'I' and the 'Me' (Mead 1934). Dominelli (2002) argues that fragmentation in identity creates various sets of binary oppositions that, in turn, sets up a 'we-they' division between and among those individuals not possessing the characteristics considered to be of value or desirable (e.g. affluence, maleness, whiteness) who become socially excluded and subjected to discrimination, marginalization and/or exploitation. This binary, by extension, encompasses contemporary debates about ideals and contradictions of academia, and knowledge capitalization (see Dzisah, chapter thirteen, this volume), and the accompanying tensions and contradictions embedded in contemporary postsecondary expansion and parallel emphasis on science, innovation and creativity (see Wotherspoon, chapter three, this volume).

Postmodernists see identity as fragmented and split between our conscious and unconscious selves and continually in the process of being constructed due to the politicization of differences among various characteristics that privilege the attributes of some groups at the expense of others. This is the case with gender identity whose discourse positions all people as either men or women—with the categories relational. Judith Butler (1990), a leading post-structuralist argues that although many feminists reject the idea that 'biology is destiny', they have developed accounts of patriarchal culture that assume that masculine and feminine gender identities are inevitable. She posits that gender is an act that is performatively constituted by the very 'expressions' that are said to be its results. Gender, therefore, is "what you do" at particular times rather than a universal "who you are" (Butler 1990:25). It must be noted that gender identity formation entails a process of learning about cultural norms, values and mores that always constitute a strain on the individual because they are operationally informed by stereotypes and assumptions that are often psychologically dysfunctional for the individual (Pleck 1981). As such, a key theme in gender identity is the way in which other differences (race, class, ethnicity, sexuality, age, and region) inform, shape and modify its definition.

Gender and Migration

Globalization and migration have become almost synonymous as connections have become just a mouse click away, and over 170 million people are on the move at any time. Statistics reveal that more women are on the move today in search of work than ever before in view of on-going economic crisis, wars and unrest, unemployment, poverty, violence against women, and the need for economic survival. Women's identities are thus changing although still dominantly constructed in terms of their familial and care-giving roles. This is because portion of the literature emphasizes the role of the household in decision-making processes that leads to female migration, but does not do so in the case of male migration—thus, disregarding or underestimating women's personal agency, on the one hand, and the role of family and household on men's migratory decisions, on the other. This has led to a dangerous idealization, and even naturalization, of the family that tends to be portrayed as a harmonious and homogeneous unit where men and women naturally perform their socially assigned roles, and in the process obscures the power imbalances and conflicts of interest that may underlie the decision-making dynamics.

The term 'feminization of migration' has been adopted in describing women's migratory trends since the 1990s and involves the fact that more women are migrating independently in search of jobs in addition to 'family reunification'. Thus, while we continue to highlight the primacy of knowledge in contemporary social organization, the fact remains, however, that a good number of the female migrants are of low socio-economic status, from racial and ethnic minorities and generally perceived as a people with limsited knowledge or inferior formal education (Elabor-Idemudia 2002, Ng 1988). Even so, most of the women migrate in order to take up employment for the generation of much- needed income. Deepening poverty is a major contributing factor informing the decision to migrate as government programs fall short in making a significant impact in reducing poverty.

Additionally, the adverse impact of globalization and its attendant neoliberal economics has further impoverished the poor by favouring religious and cultural practices that perpetuate patriarchal structures and socio-economic dominance of women and children in the name of free enterprise. These factors push women to look for work outside their home communities, in urban areas and subsequently in international settings where they end up doing the most available job—domestic work.

The most notable feature of female migration is the extent to which it is founded upon the continued reproduction and exploitation of gender inequalities by global capitalism. For the most part, female labor migrants perform "women's work" as nannies, maids and sex workers—the worst possible occupational niches in terms of remuneration, working conditions, legal protections and social recognition. In this way, gender identity acts as a basic organizing principle of labor markets in destination countries, reproducing and reinforcing pre-existing gender patterns that oppress women. It is not just that women perform these jobs, but women of particular race, class, ethnicity and/ or nationality do so. That is, gender cross-cuts with other forms of oppression to facilitate the economic exploitation of women migrants and their relegation to a servile (maids) and/or despised (sex workers) status. It has been argued that the state plays a major role in determining the patterns of international female migration as emigration policies treat men and women differently (Oishi 2002). Some countries do not restrict male migration but do restrict and or even ban female migration. The regulatory frameworks of destination countries (and to a lesser extent, of source countries) also play an important role in channeling migration, not only by directly or indirectly promoting the immigration of particular groups according to the requirements of their labour markets, but also through laws and policies that restrict labour mobility, deny or complicate migrant's access to legal status, and restrict their access to basic social and labour rights.

Moreover, there tends to be a portrayal of migrant women as constantly self-sacrificing for the well-being of their families and their related idealization as reliable remitters, better managers of remittances, more credit-worthy investors. This not only feeds on gendered construction of women, but leads to their instrumentalization by community development interventions that are often built around women's role as remitters or as remittance managers (UN-INSTRAW 2007). In this context, and given the conceptual and empirical complexities involved in evaluating the gender impacts of migration, praising the empowerment potential of migration for women may turn out to be both unwarranted and premature. This is evidenced by the fact that where women are socially located in the society, with respect to gender, race, ethnicity and class profoundly influences their identities and experiences, opportunities and outcomes. For migrant women especially those of colour who are incredibly isolated in unfamiliar environments with no safe place or even home to go to, they confront loss of traditional support of extended family, friends, and advisers from their home countries of origin. This compounds their isolation, weighs heavily on them and increases their vulnerability to exploitation.

Diverse studies using different measures and samples converge and confirm that racialized women of colour confront both systematic and systemic discrimination especially as migrant workers (Satzewich 2000). Not only do such women earn less, they often find themselves in occupations that are dangerous or unprotected. In my study of African migrant women in the Netherlands, the women interviewed revealed their maltreatment by their employers who did not even make efforts to know their real names. Although exploitation as cheap sources of labour applies to men and women, it is only women who are deliberately imported for gender-specific jobs pertaining to child-rearing, domestic labour and even the sex trade (Macklin 1999). As the dawn of knowledge society beckons, there is no real transformation in gender division of labour, as female domestic migrants, together with sex-trade workers, according to the United Nations, continue to be the most widely exploited and abused of all migrant workers.

As already alluded to, during my research study of African migrant women in the Netherlands in 2005 while on an International Labour

Organization (ILO) research mission, I had the opportunity to meet, observe and hold interviews with 15 African immigrants in Bijlmer, a community of over 50,000 African migrants in Amsterdam. The subjects of the study were mostly West Africans from Ghana, Nigeria, Sierra Leone, and Cameroun with irregular statuses in the Netherlands. The research aimed to determine the experiences of Africans who migrated independently or had been trafficked to Europe for 'employment' with the hope of ensuring the economic survival of family members back home and, to explore how gender and irregular status mediated their experiences and integration, or lack thereof. The study revealed that the 15 irregular African migrants were between 18 to 35 years old and with educational background ranging from high school to university degree holders. They were all of low-income family background and had experienced poverty ranging from mild to extreme as a result of extended periods of unemployment in their countries of origin.

In addition, they all had aged parents and siblings who were dependent on them. Three men interviewed had wives and children back home and had lost their jobs for over a year before migrating illegally to the Netherlands. All the fifteen migrants interviewed indicated that they were forced under prevailing conditions of poverty to leave their home countries with the belief that jobs awaited them in the Netherlands. The women migrants said that they had been led by traffickers to believe that they would work as domestics and childcare providers upon arrival in the Amsterdam but were instead sold into the sex trade industry at the end of their arduous journey. One of the respondents had this to say:

> I was working as a receptionist in a local company where I met a man (one of the company's clients) who told me that he had a recruitment agency for positions in the Netherlands and that he could assist me in getting a job overseas. Considering that I was desperate for a better job to enable me meet with my family responsibilities, I accepted the man's offer. He was very convincing as he provided me with relevant forms and invited me for an interview where I met several other young women seeking employment abroad. Five of us were recruited and "sponsored" with what turned out to be fake document to the Netherland to discover that we had been trafficked. We were soon sold into the sex trade industry where I "worked" for the man until I was interrogated by the law enforcement agents nine months after my arrival. Although I gave the bulk of my wages to my "employer", I was still able to send some money home to my family for their subsistence (Respondent 1).

The African migrants' length of stay in the Netherlands was found to range from three years for the longest and eight months for the shortest. In terms of their experiences, they were all awaiting the outcomes of their trials (as they could either be deported or allowed to stay on humanitarian grounds, depending on their testimony against and arrest of their traffickers) and were living in fear of re-arrests and deportation. All the male migrants indicated that they had come legally to the Netherlands but had overstayed their legal permit. They had applied for asylum but had been rejected.

As 'illegal' migrants, they revealed that were vulnerable to exploitation as they constituted rejected asylum seekers among whom 26,000 had already been evicted and deported from the asylum centres where they were initially housed. What was most revealing was their claim that the 'illegal' migrants from Eastern Europe were given the opportunity to relocate to other parts of Europe while most of the illegal African migrants were deported to their countries of origin. As indicated by an interviewee,

> the law enforcement agents treat us like criminals while treating our white counterparts with respect. They extend privileges like different curfew hours to the white illegal migrants and allow them more freedom of movements. We have to report to the police station or the social workers everyday and we have not been able to find any decent work despite possessing temporary work permit. We are very broke and do not have money to purchase even the most basic requirement. But for the pastor who has been kind to us by supplying some of our needs, we would have gone crazy (Respondent 2).

Some of the illegal migrant who were awaiting the outcomes of their court cases under 'B9' immigration law received no government assistance and could only find 'black market jobs' in the construction, transport or flower industries, sometimes for extremely low wages with no access to medical care in case of workplace accidents. Most of the interviewed migrants said that they lived under the hospitality of an African church clergy or church members.

The migrants also revealed that there were no special shelters for victims of trafficking in the Netherlands. Shelters for battered women could each only accept two to three victims of trafficking due to limited resources. For men, the only shelters available were those for the homeless. The African community provided temporary shelter, counseling and vocational training to African girls rescued from pimps. Eight apartments and one emergency centre set up through churches and community efforts were operational in Bijlmer. Finally, it was revealed that the community was working with various groups in Africa in planning to set up educational centres in Lagos (Nigeria) and Accra (Ghana) for those who wished to return.

The migrants' narratives regarding their experiences on the 'black market' or under-the-table jobs were heart-wrenching. The male migrants spoke of their experiences of working in 'black market jobs' after being hired and taken to remote sites outside the city to grow flowers. They reported working for 12–14 hours daily without breaks for little or no pay and were offered a single room with only a chair and no bed to sleep on. The men took turns sleeping in sitting positions on the chair for three hours at a time. When one's time was up, the next person would ask the occupant to vacate the chair for him to take his turn. There were no mattresses or sleeping mats offered and the floor of the room was too rugged to sleep on. They endured this uncomfortable situation for several weeks, until government raids put the employers out of business. The employers would then relocate and set up shop elsewhere with the process starting all over. Incomes generated from such jobs by the migrant workers were halved with a part remitted to countries of origin to meet the needs of dependent family members who were left behind. As to the reason why they did not voluntarily return to their home countries, the migrants indicated that they preferred to remain in Amsterdam to seek amnesty rather than return to nothing back home.

The highlighted case-study provides some indications that identity is a factor that mediates the experiences of the African migrants. Identity is taken to relate to the position that an individual may be embedded in, interpreted as belonging to and negotiated with (Hall 1990, Gergen 1991, Søndergaard 2005). For example, an African woman in Amsterdam may negotiate transverse ways of making 'Africanness', 'blackness', 'citizenship' and 'nationality'. The different use of additive and transversal intersectionality constitutes a matter of operating within categories or identities. In view of the intersections of the various forms of illegal status of the immigrants, it is no wonder that the issue of identity and to some extent, gender and class are shrouded in grey areas. While the immigrants identified themselves as hybrids of countries of origin and destination, government officials perceive them differently as illegal aliens. With no clear sense of identity, the issue of belonging and integration becomes secondary.

The ingredients for developing a sense of belonging are missing for the immigrants in this study. Such ingredients include membership, rights and duties (as in the case of citizenship) or forms of identification with groups which the African migrants were not entitled because of their irregular status.

The fact that migrants captured as illegal by government agents are incarcerated and subsequently repatriated is indicative of a shift in government (Dutch) policy from welfare state to a penal state (Schinkel 2009). The materialistic base of the incarceration of the irregular migrants is the detention center and its superstructure is made up of procedures. Incarcerated immigrants await either repatriation or release from detentions into 'illegality' and the immediate risk of being reincarcerated. Their identity as irregular immigrants coupled with their race and gender resulted in their constant harassment by authorities. The totality of their personhood was thus reduced to the instrumental label of illegal aliens who were constantly harassed and on the run from law enforcement agencies.

Conclusion: Stating the Obvious

Globalization has been shown to entail a universalistic trend and a time-space compression of lived experience that have permeating effects on building relationships between and among various locales. It is thus the leading factor contributing to the decentralizing and dislocation of identities because mass communication (a characteristic of globalization) has exacerbated the pace of development of relationships in various spheres of life with the individual becoming more involved in the process of mutuality of the world. Such an individual becomes submerged in a number of various dialogues and debates that expose him or her to the widest opinions and viewpoints that are mostly contradictory and reconcilable. This has a direct impact on the individual's identity in the form of multiple sources of pervasive influence. With the increase in the number of groups originating from various cultural background, carrying various values and articulating diverse norms, and possessing different abilities concerning decoding of the message one is trying to convey as a constructive part of his/her identity, identity becomes more vulnerable to the influence of external forces and more difficult to affirm.

The position of nation-state or a region in such identity construction network especially gender identity becomes the dominant force shaping socio-economic outcomes, such as labour conditions (Bonacich et al. 1994) or structure of inequality (Castells 1997, Sassen 1999, 1990). The result is the formation of a 'global culture' due to the rapid growth of mass media penetration and cheap high-speed communication that promotes homogenizing cultural construction of freely choosing, pleasure-seeking individual consumers around the globe. Castells (1997) and Gereffi (1994), for instance, argue that transnational corporations increasingly organize (their production within such a context) global commodity chains across a variety of social and institutional settings. The success of these chains rely heavily on the exploitation of women's labour in view of their vulnerability due to poverty, their inferior status in the society, their limited power to negotiate and their lack of alternative. Castells further posits that our world and our lives are being shaped by the conflicting trends of globalization and identity. He sees hope in the primary opposition to the power of globalization that lies in "the widespread surge of powerful expressions of collective identity that challenge globalization…on behalf of cultural singularity and people's control over their lives and environment" (Castells 1997: 2).

Thus, far from being the fragile flower that globalization tramples, identity has potential in becoming synonymous with the upsurging 'power' of local cultures that offer, albeit multi-form, disorganized and sometimes politically reactionary, 'resistance' to the centrifugal force of capitalist globalization. This more robust view of the 'power of identity' is one to which anyone surveying the dramatic rise of social movements based around identity positions (gender, sexuality, religion, ethnicity, nationality) might easily subscribe. In that case, the impact of globalization consequently becomes more plausibly, a matter of the interplay of an institutional-technological impetus towards globality with counterposed 'localizing' forces. Gender under globalization can thus be viewed as a system of both classification and identity and a structure of power relations. West and Zimmerman (2008: 92) call gender a 'managed property' that is contrived with respect to how others judge and respond to us in particular ways. Gender becomes perceived as "something one does not something one has, a relationship not a thing and like all relationships, and something we are active in its construction" (West and Zimmerman 2008: 92). They go on to say that gender is the activity of managing situated conduct in light of normative conception of attitudes and activities appropriate for one's sex category" (West and Zimmerman 2008:93). This was evident in the case study of African migrants presented in this chapter.

The social construction of men and women in gendered ways can be seen as impacting on their roles in their society. Findings from my case study indicate that the dualism in perception of feminine and masculine gender identities situate women as sex workers and domestic servants and males as construction and factory workers. Although shifts have occurred in the traditional perception of gender from an achieved status constructed through psychological, cultural and social means to one that embodies "a complex of socially guided perceptual, interactional and micropolitical activities that cast particular pursuits as expressions of masculine and feminine 'natures'" (West and Zimmerman 2000:133), social inequality between women and men continues to persist. Masculine and feminine gender roles and status in global contexts are yet to experience major shifts in the way that they are perceived and valued. Such roles still tend to be essentialized, and viewed as fixed and never changing especially for women. Gender identity thus serves as a powerful ideological device that produces, reproduces and legitimizes choices and limits that are predicated on sex category.

The fact is that under globalization, women have become increasingly significant as national and international migrants, with the complex relationship between migration and human development operating in gender-differentiated ways. Even though we now live in an increasingly knowledge-based society, the modern individual is still confronted with the titanic task of defining his or her personal identity through the development of a more or less original lifestyle. This is also the case in considering the processes leading to the definition of gender and identity in a globalized world. Therefore, there is need for significant and valuable shifts in gender and identity construction in view of Judith Butler's (1990:25) claim that "there is not gender identity behind the expressions of gender...identity is performatively constituted by the very expressions that are said to be its results". According to view, our "performances" are driven by discourses of power that shape the limits and possibilities of the construction of our identities (Ravelli and Weber 2010). Gender is but one of these performances.

Bibliography

Bonacich, Edna, Lucie Cheng, Norma Chinchilla, Nora Hamilton, and Paul Ong. 1994. *Global Production: The Apparel Industry in the Pacific Rim*. Philadelphia, PA: Temple University Press.

Bourdieu, Pierre. 2001. *Masculine Domination*. Stanford, Calif.: Stanford University Press.

Butler, Judith. 1990. *Gender Trouble*. New York: Routledge.

Castells, Manuel. 1997. *The Power of Identity*. Oxford: Blackwell.

Combs, Arthur W., Donald L. Avila and William W. Purkey. 1979. "Self-concept: Product and producer of experience", in D.P. Elkins, ed., *Self-concept sourcebook: Ideas and activities for building self-esteem*. New York: Growth Associates, pp. 77–93.

Cooley, Charles Horton. 1902. *Human Nature and the Social Order*. New York: C. Scribner's Sons.

Dominelli, Lena. 2002. *Anti-oppressive Social Work Theory and Practice*. Basingstoke, UK: Palgrave MacMillan.

Elabor-Idemudia, Patience. 2002. "Participatory Research: A Tool in the Production of Knowledge in Development Discourse," in Kriemild Saunders, ed., Feminist Post Development Thought: Rethinking Modernity, Post-Colonialism and Representation. London: Zed Publishing, pp. 227–242.

Featherstone, Mike. 1995. *Undoing Culture: Globalization and Identity*. London, Thousand Oaks, New Delhi: Sage Publications.

Fleras, Augie. 2010. *Unequal Relations: an Introduction to Race, Ethnic and Aboriginal Dynamics in Canada* (6th edition). Toronto, ON: Pearson Canada

Jean Leonard Elliot. 2008. *Unequal Relations: an Introduction to Race, Ethnic and Aboriginal Dynamics in Canada*, 5th edition. Toronto, ON: Prentice Hall.

Foucault, Michel. 1980. *Power/Knowledge: Selected interviews and other writings, 1972–1977*. Brighton, England: Harvester Press.

Gereffi, Gary (1994). "The Organization of Buyer-Driven Global Commodity Chains: How U.S. Retailers Shape Overseas Production Networks," in G. Gereffi and M. Korzeniewicz, eds., *Commodity Chains and Global Capitalism*. Westport, CT: Praeger, pp. 95–122.

Gergen, Kenneth. 1991. *The Saturated Self: Dilemmas of Identity in Contemporary Life*. New York:Basic Books.

Guarnizo, Luis E. and Michael P. Smith. 1998. "The locations of transnationalism," in Michael P. Smith and Luis E. Guarnizo, eds., *Transnationalism From Below* (Vol. 6, Comparative Urban and Community Research) Transaction: New Brunswick, NJ, pp. 3–34.

Hall, Stuart, David Held, Don Hubert and Kenneth Thompson, eds.1996. *Modernity: An Introduction to Modern Societies*. New York: Basil Blackwell.

Hall, Stuart. 1990. "Cultural Identity and Diaspora," in Jonathan Rutherford, ed., *Identity, Community, Culture, Difference*. London: Lawrence and Wishart, pp.222–237.

Henry, Frances and Carol Tator. 1991. *Multicultural Education: Translating Policy into Practice*. Ottawa: Multiculturalism Canada.

Herman, Hubert J.M., H.J.G. Kempen, and R.J.P. Van Loon. 1992. "The Dialogical self: Beyond individualism and rationalism." *American Psychologist* 47:23–33.

James, William. 1946[1890]. Precis de Psychologic [Handbook of Psychology]. Paris: Librairie Marcel Riviera.

Jameson, Frederic. 1998. "Globalization as a Philosophical Issue", in Fredric Jameson and Masao Miyoshi, eds., *The Culture of Globalization*. Durham and London: Duke University Press, pp. 54–77.

Kimmel, Michael S. 2011. *The Gendered Society*, 4th Ed. New York: Oxford University Press.

Mead, George Herbert. 1934. *Mind, Self and Society from the Standpoint of a Social Behaviorist*. Chicago: University of Chicago Press.

Macklin, Ruth. 1999. *Against Relativism: Cultural Diversity and the Search for Ethical Universals in Medicine*. Oxford: Oxford University Press.

Mullaly, Bob. 2010. *Challenging Oppression and Confronting Privilege*. (2nd Edition). Don Mills, ON: Oxford University Press.

Ng, Roxana. 1988. *The Politics of Community Services: Immigrant Women, Class and State*. Toronto: Garamond Press.

Oishi, Shigehiro. 2002. "Experiencing and Remembering of Well-Being: A Cross-Cultural Analysis". *Personality and Social Psychology Bulletin*, 28, pp. 1398–1406.

Pleck, Joseph H. 1981. *The myth of masculinity*. Cambridge: MIT.

Ravelli, Bruce and Michelle Webber. 2010. *Exploring Sociology: a Canadian Perspective*. Toronto, ON: Pearson

Sassen, Saskia. 1999. *Globalization and Its Discontents: Essays on the New Mobility of People and Money*. New York: The New Press.

Sassen, Saskia. 1990. "Economic Restructuring and the American City". *Annual Review of Sociology* 16: 465–490

Satzewich, Vic. 2000. Whiteness Limited: Racialization and the Social Construction of "Peripheral Europeans". *Histoire Sociale/Social History* 32 (66): 271–90.

Schinkel, Willem. 2009. "'Illegal Aliens' and the State, or: Bare Bodies vs. the Zombie. *International Sociology* 21(6):779–806.

Søndergaard, Dorte Marie. 2005. Making Sense of Gender, Age, Power and Disciplinary Position: Intersecting Discourses in the Academy. *Feminism & Psychology* 15 (2):191–210.

Søndergaard, Dorte Marie. 1996. *Tegnet på kroppen* (The Sign on the Body). Copenhagen: Museum Tusculanum.

Suarez-Orozco, Carola and Marcelo Suarez-Orozco. 2001. *Children of Immigration*. Cambridge, MA: Harvard University Press.

UN- INSTRAW (2007). Gender, Remittances and Development: Feminization of Migration. Working Paper 1. United Nations International Research and Training Institute for the Advancement of Women. Cesar Nicolas Penson 102-A, Santo Domingo.

West, Candace and Don H. Zimmerman. 2008. "Doing Gender," in Michael S. Kimmel, Amy Aronson and Amy Kaler, eds., *The Gendered society Reader*. Don Mills, ON: Oxford University Press, pp. 90–105.

West, Candace and Don H. Zimmerman. 1987. "Doing Gender". *Gender and Society* 1: 125–151.

PART II

KNOWLEDGE INNOVATION, GOVERNANCE AND POLICY

CHAPTER SEVEN

THE TRIPLE HELIX OF KNOWLEDGE[1]

James Dzisah and Henry Etzkowitz

The process of globalization has created new challenges for many societies and induces contrasting emotions across varying domains. In fact, it is not only countries and societies that are confronted by the challenges of globalization, institutions of knowledge such as universities that were until recently seen as idyllic islands, have now become theatres within which the globalization battle is routinely fought. Beyond their constant supply of human capital, universities have become more integral to the permutations and calculations of global capitalism. It is, therefore, not surprising that the so-called 'globalization thesis,' take pains to draw attention to the "instrumentalization of the university as it embraces market values and information technology" (Delanty 2001*a*:150). The increasing awareness is derived from the realization that the dynamics and parameters of a knowledge-based society, operates according to a different set of matrix with a growing institutional role taking among knowledge producers (Etzkowitz 2008). In this operational theatre, productivity and competitiveness are said to be based on the constant production, mobilization and generation of both new and reconfigured knowledge (Castells 1996).

However, since knowledge has always been implicated in the fundamental intricacies of daily social life (Znaniecki 1940), it is germane that contemporary alterations be placed within appropriate historical context. In feudal society, the lore of tradition, the taken for granted relationships of superiors and inferiors and the obligations owed to each other, was the most important knowledge. The inherent understanding derived from this early comprehension, particularly the perceived independence of knowledge from the social order, to a degree

[1] This chapter draws on our article "Who influences whom? The Transformation of University-Industry-Government Relations" that appeared in a special issue of *Critical Sociology* 36(4):491–501. The authors are grateful to SAGE (the publisher) for permission to substantially revise the piece for inclusion in this book.

motivated some Enlightenment thinkers to look for the necessary but intrinsic metaphysical codes, which they believed once decoded, would unshackle people from the manacles of tradition (Delanty 2001b:134). In line with this evolutionary foundation, the social organization of industrial society was theorized as rooted on the erudition of bureaucracy, the understanding of the basis of willingness to accept orders from above, and the capacity of management to give relevant instructions (Weber 1947, Etzkowitz and Dzisah 2010).

In fact, in the spirit of the Enlightenment, the emancipatory potential of knowledge, and the whole modernity project, was rooted in the idea that the power of knowledge resided in its capacity to offer a unifying narrative. The hope was that through a new kind of politically-motivated design, the core of a new society was not only possible but practically within reach (Delanty 2001b). However, as detailed by Jean-Francois Lyotard (1984), this meta-narrative is not only deceptive, but has itself been rendered irrelevant by the emerging postmodern turn. In spite of this, knowledge-laden terminologies—knowledge/knowledgeable society (Lane 1966, Drucker 1969, Stehr 1994), post-industrial society (Touraine 1971, Bell 1973), and post-capitalist society (Drucker 1993)—have not only continue to dot the academic landscape, but serve to detail its centrality and constitutive parameters (Bell 1973, Castells 1996, Delanty 2001b, Drucker 1993, Florida 1995, Nonaka 1991, Nonaka and Takeuchi 1995, Stehr 1994, Slaughter and Leslie 1997). The realization is that economies around the world are increasingly becoming intertwined, necessitating a new form of relationship between economy, state and society (Castells 2000).

Consequently, we argue that there is an ongoing reconfiguration of organizational formats in different institutional spheres necessitated by the need to place knowledge at the core of economic activity. In the realm of the university, these nascent transformations are quickening the move from narrowly confined disciplinary interactions to an entrepreneurial dynamics derived from the permeability of institutional boundaries. In a much broader context, the move is heralded by the dynamic investments in knowledge infrastructure and processes essential for innovation and growth. While these investments are critical in generating the necessary resources of the knowledge-based economy: knowledge, innovation and creativity, a sufficient policy niche capable of optimizing the interaction among university, industry and government as relatively independent, yet inter-dependent institutional spheres is indispensable.

Institutional Transformations

There are several intimations and counsels within classical social science relating to institutional differentiation and the inherent structural imbalances between political and economic structures (Polanyi 2001). By analyzing the separation of a capitalistic economy from the feudal social relations of medieval society, Karl Marx had laid the groundwork for a theory of differentiated social spheres (Etzkowitz 2008). Recognizing the role of technology in the capitalist quest for appropriating production relations, Marx posited science as a source of the future economy, utilizing William Henry Perkins research on *dyestuffs* in England that was developed into an industry in Germany (Marx 1973). For Weber (1947), three independent dimensions— economics, politics and status-belief in the reality of social differences based on any criteria, co-exist in a relationship of mutual causation. Political power generates economic wealth and the ability to live off politics; while ideas may be translated into economic and political power (Etzkowitz 2008, Etzkowitz and Dzisah 2010). Ethical ideas associated with the Calvinist discourse of '*predestination*' was an ideological impetus that aided the material and institutional conditions of various kinds in providing the so-called '*spirit of capitalism*' that in addition, to accumulation of technological forces unleashed the rapid development of economic activity in the West (Weber 1958).

The issue of differentiation raised by Marx was taken up and developed from the systems theory standpoint by Niklas Luhmann (1982 and 1996), who argued that forms of differentiation determine the degree of complexity that a society can attain. However, moving beyond systems theorizing, organizational behaviour theorists focus on the relations of interactions within specific inter-organizational fields. This move enables them to capture the way and manner in which interactions between two organizations are affected by the network within which they find themselves (Warren 1967, Simpson and Gulley 1962). This analysis is derived from Karl Mannheim's (1951) elaboration of the concept of 'field structure' as indicative of a situation in which various parties interact in ways, which not only influence their mutual clout but often exceeding the borders of structured institutional and organizational channels. The 'field' idea was further explored by Pierre Bourdieu (1984 and 1990) in unraveling how power relations are employed and deployed in the 'habitus' of the academic 'field'.

In spite of the insightful theoretical and empirical excursions, much of the emphases in institutional theorizing have been on the construction and convergent change processes (Oliver 1992, Scott 2001). Institutional perspectives suggest that institutional logics defined the norms, values, and beliefs that structure the cognition of actors in organizations and provide a collective understanding of how strategic interests and decisions are formulated (Friedland and Alford 1991, DiMaggio 1997, Jackall 1988). While attention has, in recent times, shifted to the consideration of the trend of deinstitutionalization—the processes by which institutions weaken and disappear (Scott 2001: 182). This process can be placed within the broader context of institutional change since the "weakening and disappearance of one set of beliefs and practices is likely to be associated with the arrival of new beliefs and practices" (Scott 2001:184). Consequently, three major sources of demand on institutionalized norms or practices—functional, political, and social sources—may invariably be tied to those originating from the perceived usefulness associated with institutionalized practices.

While these pressures are seen as related to broader environmental changes due to the intensified competition for resources (Dacin et al. 2002), a distinction is usually made in the institutional theory literature between old and new institutionalism. The old institutionalism denotes influence, coalitions, competing values, power and informal structures, while the new type is more concerned with legitimacy, the embeddedness of organizational fields, the centrality of classification, routines, scripts and scheme (Selznick 1948 and 1996, Powell and DiMaggio 1991). The growing convergence is an indication that the dynamics of global transformations are stimulating firms of different capacities to rethink their competitiveness. Research has shown that the intensification of actions consolidated in inter-organizational partnerships are impacting the formation of favourable environments necessary in sustaining companies (Ghisi and Martinelli 2006). There are, of course, differences in the ways inter-institutional linkages are forged but in an increasingly knowledge-based society, institutions including many universities are connected by common issues revolving around innovation and sound financial competitiveness (Ghisi and Martinelli 2006).

It is not surprising that within the last two decades there have been a remarkable increase in academic scholarship on university technology transfer and its effects, both positive and negative (Greenberg

2007, Siegel, Waldman and Link 2003; Thursby and Thursby 2002, Washburn 2005). As a close observer describes it, "it is hard to point to a robust regional economy that is not in some sense anchored by a major research university or two" (Schmidt 2002: 26). However, university's early foray into the economic sphere was based on sporadic requests from industry to serve the needs of existing companies. Engineering schools reorganized themselves to serve the research needs of growing science-based electrical and chemical industries and to supply them with personnel (Wise 1980). The institutional interactions included cooperative programs that sent students to industry for part of their training, university professors undertaking research at the request of industry, and donations of money and equipment by industrial firms to support engineering education (Noble 1976). These interactions, however, declined in the 1930s because of the depression, elevating foundations as important sources of sponsored research.

Around similar time frame, however, new series of relationship formats were being created at the Massachusetts Institute of Technology (MIT), such as, the faculty-formed firm, an explicit role for the university in shaping regional economic development, the interdisciplinary centre, and the invention of the venture capital firm (Etzkowitz 2002). The older forms of university-industry connections involved payment for services rendered, whether it was received directly in the form of consultation fees or indirectly as endowment gifts. The new formats of university-industry relationships are built upon the development of scientific-research capabilities and the creation of a series of boundary-spawning mechanisms like technology-transfer offices and spinoff firms. This institutional transformation is reflected in the enactment of the Bayh-Dole Act of 1980, which transferred ownership of intellectual property emanating from government-sponsored research to universities on the condition that they take steps to promote their utilization. Similar new legal frameworks followed in other countries, often supported by funding programs, to legitimate and foster the transformation of the university into a critical economic actor.

Consequently, ccontemporary university-industry relations arose from two distinct sources and an emerging third hybrid stream: basic research interests funded by research councils and similar bodies, industrial projects for which academic input is solicited and in a creative fusion, and a joint formulation of research programs with conjoint basic and applied goals and multiple funding sources. Basic research increasingly takes place in research groups that function as 'quasi-firms' that have many of the attributes of a private corporation except for the profit motive (Etzkowitz 2003). The university's increasing involvement in science, however, engendered a more organized approach to managing research and its practical consequences. For instance, when researchers at the University of Toronto invented an insulin treatment for diabetes in 1922, the university found that it had to patent and license the technology in order to protect itself from potentially unethical manufacturers (Bliss 2007).

In fact, as the university realizes the potential economic gains, early strains were lessened by generous leave policies followed by the development of centres with translational research capabilities and training programs to sensitize researchers to intellectual property issues. While expectations of deleterious effects on research have been disconfirmed, critics are still wary (Mowery et al. 2004). In spite of this, the capitalization of knowledge has replaced disinterestedness as a norm of science. This new norm has arisen from the practices of industrial science and the emergence of an entrepreneurial dynamic within the university. It stems also from the changes in the rules for disposition of intellectual property arising from government funded research and from direct industrial policies (Etzkowitz 2002). As a result, the experimental relations initiated by the growing science-based electrical and chemical industries with universities to serve their research needs and to supply them with personnel (Wise 1980), in the early nineteenth century, have now reached a transformative stage where we begin to see significant institutional reconfiguration.

Universities and the Knowledge Economy

The global 'knowledge-based' economy emerged in the last years of the twentieth century (Castells 2000:135) marking a break in continuity with earlier periods (David and Foray 2002). In the realm of production and services, it is an economy that is based on "knowledge-intensive activities that contribute to an accelerated pace of technological and scientific advance as well as equally rapid obsolescence" (Powell and Snellman 2004:201). The nub of this transformation is traceable to the accelerating and often unprecedented speed, at which knowledge is created, accumulated and depreciated (David and Foray 2002). The critical mechanism of a knowledge economy include a "greater reliance on intellectual capabilities rather than on physical inputs or natural resources, combined with efforts to integrate improvements in every stage of the production process, from the R&D lab to the factory floor to the interface with customers" (Powell and Snellman 2004:201). Most of these changes are the results of the growing proportion of investments in the production and dissemination of knowledge and sustenance of the physical state of human capital (Abramovitz and David 1996, David and Foray 2002).

This development is not an isolated occurrence because in an increasingly knowledge-based society, novel and diverse 'innovators' are appearing in unexpected situations, making users the unlikely origin ators and sources of innovation (von Hippel 1988). In the process, non-traditional knowledge brokers have become more visible in the relentlessly evolving 'epistemic community' (Haas 1992). In fact, the growth of science-based technology, from the seventeenth century, intersecting with the emergence of independent institutional spheres in the eighteenth century founded a new dynamics of innovation. These two dimensions came together in the creation of the Research University in the nineteenth century, incorporating experimental science. The teaching laboratory was invented, scaling up the integration of research and teaching, including research with practical implications, as the university gained autonomy from other social spheres (Rossiter 1975). These twin developments foretold the transition from a society based on vertical stratification in the pre-modern era to one increasingly based on horizontal relationships among inter-related institutional spheres (Etzkowitz and Dzisah 2010).

A parallel renovation along the lines of the changes that took place during the transition to industrial society where larger emphasis, in the production process was placed on achieving flexibility in management, decentralization and networking of firms played a role. This has since emerged on the university scene as well. However, the consequent decline of middle management ranks, assisted by the proliferation of information technology, superseded earlier analysis that failed to detect the effects of computerization (Castells 2000, Etzkowitz and Dzisah 2010). The foundation of new health and computer technology related domains gave rise to a new ground for the legitimation of science as the source of high technology until the late nineteenth century split between pure and applied science. This cultural divide is disappearing under pressure from scarcity of resources and convergence, ushering in the need not only to address areas of fundamental science but to equally take steps to meet concerns about environmental sustainability and robust economic growth (Etzkowitz and Dzisah 2010).

The vertical hierarchies of the pre-industrial and industrial eras, the first based on tradition, the second on expertise, are gradually superseded in the transition from an industrial to a knowledge-based society (Etzkowitz 2008). A new political economy of knowledge, is unfolding in which the often unequal relationship between university and industry is receding, giving the holder of knowledge, packaged in the form of intellectual property, significant say in setting the terms of its utilization. As David Fasenfest (2010:484) incisively detailed, "we are on the doorstep of a new transformation in knowledge production through changes in funding, research and innovation". Since the origins of modern science, scientists interwove research and practice with fundamental investigation and consultation largely without worry (Brown 1989). The late nineteenth century movement to create "pure science" in an Ivory Tower university, propelled in the US by fears that private benefactors might influence the object of their donation and in Germany by parallel concerns over state control, created an ideological divide between university and industry.

However, the increased relevance of science to future economic development means that funds for research must now be distributed to all areas of the country. All regions want a share of research funding because they are now aware that it is the basis of future economic growth. That is why the peer-review system breaks down with funding in the United States increasingly being made on other bases of direct Congressional appropriations for research centres at local universities. These practical political considerations have been raised to an explicit policy level in Europe where goals of achieving cohesion and rectifying regional imbalances are built into the European Union's Framework Programs for technological and economic development. In fact, the traditional legitimation for support of science still holds, the cultural justification of support for science as an end in itself, and the support for defense and health research remain a strong stimulus to research funding. The future legitimation of scientific research that will keep funding at a high level is that it is the basis of economic growth.

The idea that culture, including science, could be transformed into capital became apparent when it was seen to generate a stream of income. While some scientists, like Pasteur, expected their ideas to have industrial applications even though they were not personally interested in capturing financial rewards, it came as a surprise to others to find out that their ideas had become the basis of entire industries. For example, sociologist Robert K. Merton, who invented the 'focus group' interviewing technique during the 1940s, was astonished to learn, years later, that a research method that he had played a part in developing during World War II to analyze interaction among residents of a New York city housing project with different ethnic and racial backgrounds had become the basis of a multi-million dollar advertising and political industry during the post-war (Etzkowitz and Dzisah 2010). As a result, the renewed tendencies toward secrecy, which Merton acknowledged existed even in late seventeenth century has expanded into all segments of the university. There is the high probability that these normative changes would become normalized. As Merton pointed out "not alone in what Henry Etzkowitz has described as 'entrepreneurial science' will, if extended and prolonged, introduce major change in the institutional and cognitive workings of science" (Merton 1996: 335-336).

The Academic Transition

The first academic revolution emerged through the introduction of science into the academy in the mid-nineteenth century. Research conducted as part of the PhD training process spread throughout the university as the pre-eminent knowledge creation model. Useful knowledge was sometimes created as a by-product of research and this phenomenon has become increasingly important in recent decades with the decline of industrial society. The university moved from an ancillary to a primary social institution, with concomitant effects on industry and government. In fact, as functions shift from periphery to the core, organizational boundaries are being redrawn. For example, university's new role in socio-economic development was initially enacted by ancillary administrative offices but has gradually become internalized into faculty and student roles. As this process takes place new legitimating themes are created to justify and smooth the transition. For instance, it was argued that research enhanced rather than detracted from the traditional teaching mission of the university during the first academic revolution. Scientific research, as late as the mid-nineteenth century, either outside of or on the periphery of the university is now an essential part of the university's core and one of the reasons for its very existence.

This repositioning of the university represents a major shift from its original medieval function as a preserver and transmitter of knowledge rather than as an inventor of new knowledge. Since a knowledge-based society is more complex and combines elements of prior production modes on a global scale (Castells 1996), there arose the need for an independent yet interdependent institutional framework of university, industry and government linkages to model this global infrastructure. A triple helix regime typically begins as university, industry and government enter into a reciprocal relationship in which each attempts to enhance the performance of the other. Most of these initiatives take place at the regional level to address problems in industrial clusters, gaps in academic development and lack of governing authority. The first step usually involves collaboration among universities, firms and governments in a project to enhance a local cluster or create a science and technology hub. Lack of fit between academic capabilities and firm needs is a typical issue in such arrangements. To address such problems each triple helix partner takes the role and the view of the other (Etzkowitz 2008).

Unlike earlier forms of collaboration, the contemporary structure involves the participation of academic scientists in firm formation through the utilization of their academic research. The university takes on an entrepreneurial role, developing some business capacities even as firms increase their academic capabilities, including the ability to share knowledge with each other. In fact, the message of the triple helix model is not that universities become firms or governments become businesses but that each of the institutional actors adopts elements, capabilities and perspectives of the other while maintaining their primary roles and distinct identities. Each institutional sphere is thus more likely to become a creative source of innovation and to support the emergence of creativity that arises in other spirals. A reorganization of institutional relationships from opposed starting points in statist and laissez faire societies takes place with differentiation as the primary process in the former and integration, in the latter (Etzkowitz et al. 2007).

In the process, university-industry relations have been transformed from arms-length relationships between two distinct entities with different purposes to interaction among overlapping institutional spheres. Government, at various levels, increasingly encourages university-industry interactions in order to foster public economic goals such as job creation and economic growth, and culminating in the transformation of university-industry relations into university-industry-government relations, simply referred to as the 'triple helix' (Etzkowitz and Leydesdorff 1997). The norm of capitalization has been embedded in organizations such as technology transfer offices and the requirements of government granting programs to show broader impacts from research. As a result, the 'cogitization' of capital is displacing 'rule of thumb' and other tacit methods of investment decision-making (Etzkowitz 2002).

In reality, the methods and principles of organizing and producing knowledge have also changed. Professor Henry Rowland of Johns Hopkins University, as President of the American Association for the Advancement of Science, posited a sphere of science that would be beyond the control of economic interests. If external interests intervened in the university, it would harm the conduct of science. Therefore, it was best that even philanthropists keep hands off. When universities were a weak institutional sphere, an ivory tower model, emphasizing isolation and de-emphasizing practical concerns, served to protect academic freedom. The autonomy of science was strengthened by Robert K. Merton's (1973) theory of the normative structure of science. This sociological theory of science as a self-organized and self-regulating social process defended the free space of science against attack by Nazi proponents of racialist ideas as science and from Lysenko's attempt to control biology in the former Soviet Union.

The independence of science was further strengthened by Vannevar Bush's (1945) *Science: The Endless Frontier* report as the supply of practical results from science during World War II constituted a *de facto* justification. Of course, fears persist from an earlier era when universities were relatively weak secondary institutions, that too much institutionalization of commercial activities at universities and political intervention may influence the scientists in the wrong way, for example, redirecting attention from fundamental research. However, the epiphany experienced by basic researchers during the 2nd World War, that involvement with practical projects, in this case wartime weapons research, could lead to new theoretical insights, have become widespread, leading in the post-war to the acceptance of government funding of research by the academic community. Indeed, such funding, feared before the war as inevitably leading to government domination of academia is now considered a bulwark against industrial control. As this takes place, there is a shift from single and double helices to university-industry government joint projects like the land grant universities in the US, the centres of excellence program in Canada, the research schools program in Sweden, and the incubator movement in Brazil (Etzkowitz and Dzisah 2010).

Conflicts of interest are part of this nascent transformation. As indicated by the move from old to new institutionalism, conflicts of interest that were once central are now regarded as peripheral

(Scott and Meyer 1991; Powell and DiMaggio 1991). Indeed, Georg Simmel (1950) had long intimated that social triads provided more quality, dynamics and stability than other types of social relationships (Krackhardt 1999:184). This is because in a standard dyadic arrangement, conflicts escalate, and positions may be hardened but the "appearance of the third party indicates a transition, conciliation, and abandonment of absolute contrast" (Simmel 1950:145). Even if a third party does not act decisively in resolving a conflict between two parties, the mere presence can ameliorate dissension. Consequently, the emergence of conflict over missions is an indicator that transition from one academic mode of production to another is underway (Etzkowitz 2008). This transition is exemplified by Harvard College founded in 1636 as a teaching college focused on liberal education in preparation for later professional training and careers. This academic type predominated until the early nineteenth century.

While most of these schools have moved on, (like Harvard, Yale and Columbia) to become Research Universities, the teaching college lives on as a recognized unit either within universities, like the College of the University of Chicago, or as independent schools, such as, Amherst, Bryn Mawr and Pomona Colleges. Nevertheless, even the smallest liberal arts college has typically added graduate training in some specialized field of interest, like music at tiny Marlboro in Vermont, making it difficult to find a pure type in practice. Tightly focused engineering (polytechnic) schools on particular topics, West Point (military), and Rensselear Polytechnic Institute (civil engineering-canals), founded from the early nineteenth century were the next innovation. Again, most of these schools have also moved on to broader formats but West Point and its sister school; Annapolis and Air Force Academy remain tightly focused (Etzkowitz and Dzisah 2010).

The next and related type is the "land grant" university, an early nineteenth century innovation. Beginning with the founding of the University of Connecticut in 1816, the focus was initially on research in an agricultural experiment station, founded at the behest of 'scientific farmers' to do research on their behalf. They next pressed for training for their children. To economize, the research unit and a college emphasizing practical topics were joined together, with the same persons as professors, responsible for both teaching and research. An interface group of agricultural extension officers undertook what we would now call technology transfer, operating according to an interactive model, bringing the farmers problems to the researchers and translating the solutions back to the farmers (Rossiter 1975).

This academic model was generalized to all states by the Morill Act of 1861, the Bayh Dole Act of its era in taking a "bottom-up" innovation and making it the basis of a national system (Nevins 1962). MIT, founded in 1862 extended this model, unifying teaching and research on practical problems, to industry while adding additional elements: a focus on technologically oriented basic research, to infuse industry with new ideas; including liberal arts elements from the classical teaching college into the education of engineering students to give them a broader perspective, orienting them to higher management leadership roles; and a focus on regional economic development (Etzkowitz and Dzisah 2010). Spin-off firms in the late nineteen and early twentieth century were an unexpected consequence of this model, especially when new research with practical outcomes did not fit existing firms, or led to development of instrumentation that could be marketed both to academia and industry, and organized consulting practices that served a particular industry or industry in general.

Conclusion

A transformation in the scientific role reflected a change in the role of knowledge in the political economy. While experimental science provided the instrumentation that allowed ocean commerce to be carried on in a secure fashion, professional science and the discoveries that were scaled up provided the basis for the chemical and dye industries. Academic revolutions presage a broader social revolution, with increasing number of social structures, including the rise of think-tanks and consulting firms as adjuncts to government, but based on academic models. The functional differentiation of institutions in the early modern era is being displaced by integration and hybridization of functions in the post-modern era. Although this process originated from a different starting point among institutional spheres, a converging, albeit, secular triple helix format is discernible.

Triple helix regimes have enhanced ability to create new knowledge-based enterprises. A knowledge-based strategy, utilizing information technology tools and bio-nanotechnology capabilities are capable of speeding up the rates of social change. As the university becomes ever more central to the innovation process, it complements the industrial enterprise as a source of new economic activity. Government and international agencies can promote the growth of entrepreneurial universities with a broad inter-disciplinary scope and mission, and support the birth of an entrepreneurial scientist who integrates knowledge and innovation. Thus, rather than the university being subsumed by the economy and policy, new arrangements are put in place alongside old formats in creating a complex interplay among organizations and roles with ensuing conflicts and confluences of interest. As the university takes on industrial roles, industry takes on some of the values of the university, sharing as well as protecting knowledge. Governments assume a new role in innovation by encouraging university-industry interactions of various kinds.

As new institutional infrastructures, which combine inputs from diverse sources emerged as critical innovation actors, interactions based on 'double helix' arrangements require an independent arbiter along Simmelian triad formats, in this instance triple helix institutional actors to solve problems and meet emerging needs. Consequently, the institutional reconfiguration of organizational formats has, in the process, revealed the next great transformation as dependent upon an independent but interactive triple helix.

Bibliography

Abramovitz, Moses and Paul A. David. 1996. "Technological change and the rise of intangible investments. The U.S. economy's growth-path in the twentieth century." In *Employment and Growth in the Knowledge-Based Economy*. Paris: OECD, pp. 35–60.

Bell, Daniel. 1973. *The Coming of Post-Industrial Society*. Heinemann: London.

Bourdieu, Pierre. 1984. *Homo Academicus*. Cambridge: Polity Press.

Bourdieu, Pierre. 1990. *In Other Worlds: Essays Toward a Reflexive Sociology*. Cambridge: Polity Press.

Bliss, Michael. 2007. *The Discovery of Insulin*. Chicago: University of Chicago Press.

Brown, M. Chandos. 1989. *Benjamin Silliman: A Life in the Young Republic*. Princeton: Princeton University Press.

Bush, Vannevar. 1945. *Science: The Endless Frontier*. Washington, DC: US Government Printing Office.

Castells, Manuel. 1996. *The Rise of the Network Society*. Oxford: Blackwell.

Castells, Manuel. 2000. *The Rise of Network Society* (2nd edition). Malden, MA: Blackwell.

Dacin, M. Tina, Jerry Goodstein, and Richard Scott. 2002. "Institutional Theory and Institutional Change: Introduction to the Special Research Forum." *The Academy of Management Journal* 45 (1):43–56.

David, A. Paul and Dominique Foray. 2002. "An introduction to the economy of the knowledge society." *International Social Science Journal* 171:9–23.

Delanty, Gerard. 2001a. "The University in the Knowledge Society." *Organization* 8(2):149–153.

Delanty, Gerard. 2001b. *Challenging Knowledge: The University in the Knowledge Society*. Ballmoor, Buckingham: Open University Press.

DiMaggio, Paul.1997. "Culture and Cognition." *Annual Review of Sociology* 23:263–287.

Drucker, Peter. 1993. *The Post-Capitalist Society*. Oxford: Butterworth-Heinemann.

Dzisah, James and Henry Etzkowitz. 2008. "Triple helix circulation: the heart of innovation and development." *International Journal of Technology Management and Sustainable Development* 7(2):101–115.

Etzkowitz, Henry. 2008. *The Triple Helix: University-Industry-Government Innovation in Action*. Routledge: London.

Etzkowitz, Henry. 2003. "Research groups as 'quasi-firms': the invention of the entrepreneurial university." *Research Policy* 32(1):109–121.

Etzkowitz, Henry. 2002. *MIT and the Rise of Entrepreneurial Science*. London and New York: Routledge.

Etzkowitz, Henry and James Dzisah. 2010. "Who influences whom? The Transformation of University-Industry-Government Relations." *Critical Sociology* 36(4):491–501.

Etzkowitz, Henry, James Dzisah, Marina Ranga and Chuyan Zhou. 2007. "The Triple Helix Model for Innovation: The University-industry-government interaction." *Asia Pacific Tech Monitor* 24(1)14–23.

Etzkowitz, Henry and Loet Leydesdorff.1997. *Universities in the Global Knowledge Economy: A Triple Helix of Academic-Industry-Government Relations*. London: Cassell.

Fasenfest, David. 2010. "A Political Economy of Knowledge Production." *Critical Sociology* 36(4):483–487.

Friedland, Roger and Robert Alford. 1991. "Bringing Society Back In: Symbols, Practices and Institutional Contradictions", in Walter W. Powell and Paul DiMaggio, eds., *The New Institutionalism in Organizational Analysis*. Chicago: University of Chicago Press, pp. 223–262.

Florida, Richard. 1995. "Toward the learning region." *Futures* 27 (5):527–536.

Ghisi, A. Flavia and Dante P. Martinelli. 2006. "Systemic View of Interorganizational Relationships: An Analysis of Business networks." *Systemic Practice and Action Research* 19: 461–473.

Gibbons, Michael, Camille Limoges, Helga Nowotny, Simon Schwartzman, Peter Scott and Martin Trow.1994. *The New Production of Knowledge.* London: Sage Publications.

Greenberg, S. Daniel. 2007. *Science for Sale: The Perils, Rewards, and Delusions of Campus Capitalism.* Chicago: The University of Chicago Press.

Haas, M. Peter. 1992. "Epistemic Communities and International Policy Coordination: An Introduction." *International Organization* 46(1): 377–404.

Jackall, Robert. 1988. *Moral mazes: The world of corporate managers.* New York: Oxford University Press.

Krackhardt, David. 1999. "The ties that torture: Simmelian tie analysis in organizations." *Research in the Sociology of Organizations* 6:183–210.

Lane, E. Robert. 1966. "The decline of politics and ideology in a knowledgeable society." *American Sociological Review* 31(5):649–662.

Luhmann, Niklas. 1982. *The Differentiation of Society.* New York: Columbia University.

Luhmann, Niklas. 1996. *Social Systems.* Stanford, CA: Stanford University Press.

Lyotard, Jean-François. 1984. *The Postmodern Condition: A Report on Knowledge.* Manchester: Manchester University Press.

Mannheim, Karl. 1951. *Man and Society in an Age of Reconstruction: Studies in Modern Social Structure.* New York: Harcourt Brace.

Marx, Karl.1973. *Grundrisse:* Foundations of the Critique of Political Economy, English version, London: pelican Marx Library.

Merton, K. Robert. 1996. *On Social Structure and Science.* Chicago: The University of Chicago Press.

Merton, K. Robert. 1973. *The Sociology of Science: Theoretical and Empirical Investigations.* Chicago: University of Chicago Press.

Mowery, C. David, Richard R. Nelson, Bhaven N. Sampat and Arvids A. Ziedonis. 2004. *Ivory Tower and Industrial Innovation: University-Industry Technology Transfer Before and After the Bayh-Dole Act.* Stanford: Stanford University Press.

Nevins, Allan. 1962. *The State Universities and Democracy.* Champaign, IL: University of Illinois Press.

Noble, David. 1976. *America by Design: Science, Technology, and the Rise of Corporate Capitalism.* New York: Knopf.

Nonaka, Ikujiro. 1991. "The knowledge creating company." *Harvard Business Review,* November—December, 69–104.

Nonaka, Ikujiro and Hirotaka Takeuchi. 1995. *The Knowledge-Creating Company: How Japanese Companies Create the Dynamics of Innovation.* New York: Oxford University Press.

Oliver, Christine. 1992. The antecedents of deinstitutionalization. *Organization Studies* 13: 563–588.

Polanyi, Karl. 2001[1944]. *The Great Transformation: The Political and Economic Origins of Our Time.* Boston: Beacon Press.

Powell, W. Walter and Paul J. DiMaggio, eds., 1991. *New institutionalism in Organizational Analysis.* Chicago: University of Chicago Press.

Powell, W. Walter and Kaisa Snellman. 2004. "The Knowledge Economy". *Annual Review of Sociology* 30:199–220.

Rossiter, Margaret. 1975. *The Emergence of Agricultural Science.* New Haven: Yale University Press.

Schmidt, Peter. 2002. "States Push Public Universities to Commercialize Research." *Chronicle of Higher Education* 48 (29): A26, March 29.

Scott, W. Richard. 2001. *Institutions and organizations* (2nd edition). Thousand Oaks, CA: Sage.

Scott, W. Richard and J. Meyer. 1991. The rise of training programs in firms and agencies: an institutional perspective." *Research in Organization Behavior* 13:297–326.

Selznick, Philip. 1996. "Institutionalism: Old and New". Administrative Science Quarterly 41 (2):270–277.

Selznick, Philip. 1948. "Foundations of the Theory of Organization". *American Sociological Review* 13(1):25–35.

Siegel, S. Donald, David Waldman and Albert Link. 2003. "Assessing the impact of organizational practices on the relative productivity of university technology transfer offices: an exploratory study." *Research Policy* 32(1): 27–48.

Simmel, G. 1950. *The Sociology of Georg Simmel.* Translated and edited by Kurt H. Wolff. New York: Free Press. [German original, 1908.]

Simpson, L. Richard & William H. Gulley. 1962. "Goals, environmental pressures, and organizational characteristics." *American Sociological Review* 27(3):344–351

Slaughter, Sheila and, and Larry L. Leslie. 1997. *Academic Capitalism: Politics, Policies, and the Entrepreneurial University.* Baltimore and London: The Johns Hopkins University Press.

Stehr, Nico.1994. Knowledge *Societies.* London: Sage.

Thursby, Jerry and Marie Thursby. 2002. "Who is Selling the Ivory Tower: Sources of Growth in University Licensing." *Management Science* 48 (1):90–104.

Touraine, Alain. 1971. *The Post-Industrial Society. Tomorrow's Social History: Classes, Conflicts and Culture in the Programmed Society.* New York: Random House.

von Hippel, Eric. 1988. *The Sources of Innovation.* Oxford: Oxford University Press.

144   JAMES DZISAH AND HENRY ETZKOWITZ

Washburn, Jennifer. 2005. *University Inc: The Corporate Corruption of Higher Education*. New York: Basic Books.

Warren, L. Roland. 1967. "The interorganizational field as a focus for investigation." *Administrative Science Quarterly* 12 (3):396–419.

Weber, Max. 1947. *Theory of Social and Economic Organization*. New York: Oxford University Press.

Weber, Max. 1958. *The Protestant Ethic and the Spirit of Capitalism*. New York: Scribners.

Wise, George.1980. A new role for professional scientists in industry: industrial research at General Electric, 1900–1916. *Technology and Culture* 21(3):408–429.

Znaniecki, Florian. 1940. *The social role of the man of knowledge*. New York: Columbia University Press.

CHAPTER EIGHT

CROSSING BOUNDARIES:
CREATING, TRANSFERRING & USING KNOWLEDGE

Harley D. Dickinson

Working out methods for using scientific and technical knowledge
in the cause of humanity is the great central problem of our time.

— Mott (1948) —

Creating, transferring and using knowledge for economic, political, and social purposes is a defining feature of contemporary societies. All human societies, of course, generate and use knowledge. Contemporary societies are distinguished in this regard by intentionally establishing specialized socio-technical knowledge systems designed for controlling nature and society. This characteristic warrants the label knowledge societies and explains why knowledge societies are "...to an unprecedented degree the product of [their] own action" (Böehme and Stehr 1986: 19). Knowledge societies, therefore, plan, develop, and manage socio-technical systems for creating, transferring, and using research knowledge and technology in manifold social and natural contexts (Holzner and Marx 1979: xix). Planning and managing differentiated socio-technical knowledge systems is part of an ongoing process of societal rationalization and structural differentiation associated with modernization (Habermas 1970, Holzner and Marx 1979, Palmer and Dunford 2002).

Human societies are complex and multifaceted (Urry 2006). This is reflected in efforts to describe and explain recent developments in contemporary societies. Several theories have been proposed for this task. Included, among these are post-industrial society (Touraine 1971, Bell 1973), post-modern society (Lyotard 1984), post-capitalist society (Drucker 1993), risk society (Beck 1992b), mode 2 society (Nowotny, Scott and Gibbons 2001), information society (Webster 2002), network society (Castells 1996, van Dijk 1999), and, of course, knowledge society (Böehme and Stehr 1986). Clearly, there is no obvious consensus on how best to characterize the nature and consequences of the changes taking place in contemporary societies. Despite different perspectives and emphasis, however, much of this literature, in various ways, explores the transformation of contemporary societies relative to changes in the relationships between science and society and the consequences of these changes for both.

As mentioned above, the emerging society—whatever one calls it—brings forth new socio-technical systems for generating, transferring and using research knowledge.[1] This occurs in both intra-organizational and inter-organizational, or societal, levels. Intra-organizational knowledge systems generally focus on identifying, managing, and using both explicit and tacit knowledge that exists already within an organization—either in its processes and procedures or as possessed by individuals (Alavi and Leidner 2001). This knowledge management literature pays little attention to the transfer and use of externally produced research knowledge. Inter-organizational approaches focus primarily on the production, transfer and use of research knowledge and technology between autonomous organizations (Weiss 1977). Both intra and inter-organizational knowledge systems have inherent within them new problems and potentials related to a variety of knowledge functions, including the production, organization, storage, transfer, retrieval, application, and evaluation of the effects of applying research knowledge.

In this chapter I focus on inter-organizational knowledge systems and particularly on networking across various boundaries as the chief procedure for addressing knowledge system functions (Castells 1996, Callon and Law 1982, Law and Williams 1982). To begin I set the context by briefly reviewing a selection of relevant literature on societal level transformation. Next, I focus on several boundaries—knowledge, spatial-temporal and socio-political—that need to be managed for effective knowledge transfer, translation or transformation to take place. Following this, I discuss boundary work and the role of boundary objects in establishing integrated knowledge production and utilization systems—a prerequisite for the transition to knowledge societies. The chapter ends with a brief conclusion.

---

[1] I refer to these as knowledge systems for convenience.

Knowledge and the New Society

In the period following World War II the most economically and technologically advanced societies, both capitalist and socialist, were
undergoing profound structural and cultural changes (Richta et al.
1969, Touraine 1971, Galbraith 1971, Bell 1973, Mandel 1975). Noting
this, social forecasters generally announced one of two things—either
we were witnessing the birth of a new type of society, or we were entering a new phase of development of existing society. Touraine (1971)
and Bell (1973), for example, both characterized the changes as indi-
cating the transition to a new post-industrial society. Mandel (1975),
on the other hand, from a Marxist perspective, argued the observed
changes indicated the full industrialization of capitalist societies and
the arrival of Late Capitalism, not a new post-industrial age.

In Touraine's (1971: 3) view the post-industrial age heralded the
emergence of what he termed programmed society. A concept that "...
most accurately indicates the nature of these societies' inner workings
and economic activity" (Touraine 1971: 3). In the post-industrial,
programmed society production methods and economic organization
were the epicenter of the new society. Moreover, in the programmed
society economic productivity and growth depended "...much more
directly than ever before on knowledge, and hence on the capacity of
society to call forth creativity" (Touraine 1971: 5). This was accom-
plished, according to Touraine (1971: 5–6) by intentionally transforming a wide range of social factors, including scientific and technical
research, directly into forces of production. Thus, Touraine (1971) saw
previously autonomous spheres of action being programmed to serve
the needs of increased productivity and economic expansion. In this
respect his view is similar to that of Galbraith (1971) who saw technology driven planning and the displacement of traditional market mechanisms as the hallmark of advanced post-War economies. This
especially was the case, according to Galbraith, in those sectors of the
economy based on new technologies and workforces with specialized
knowledge and skills.

Bell's (1973) view was similar, however, he preferred to use the term
post-industrial society because he felt it captured the interstitial character of societal development in the immediate post-War period, and
because he felt it was preferable to a number of other possible concepts,
including knowledge society, information society, or professional
society (Bell 1973: 37). But he too saw managed change and planned

innovation based on theoretical knowledge as defining features of the
new society (Bell 1973: 12). Bell's (1973) analysis of post-industrial
society focused on the transformation of three structural aspects of
industrial society; the social structure (comprising the economy, technology, and the occupational system), the polity, and culture. Set
within this analytical framework he identified five dimensions of post-
industrial society that distinguished it from industrial society: 1) the
centrality of theoretical knowledge as the source of innovation and
policy formation; 2) the creation of new "intellectual technologies"; 3)
the change from a goods producing to service economy; 4) the preeminence of the professional and technical class; and 5) the control of
technology and technological assessment (Bell 1973: 12). For my purposes, the first point is most relevant. Theoretical knowledge, according to Bell (1973: 26), "...increasingly becomes the strategic resource,
the axial principle" of post-industrial society, and the social institutions most directly responsible for producing new knowledge, including science and the universities, become its "axial institutions."

Science-Society Relations in the New Society

These broad socio-historical developments are the context for, and
focus of, a number of influential theories that focus more specifically
on the changing nature of science-society relations and the consequences of these for both society and science. Among the most well
known of these are the theories of Post-Normal Science (PNS), Mode
2 knowledge production, and the Triple Helix of science-industry-
government relations.

The theory of Post-Normal Science (PNS) maintains that Kuhn's
model of the self referential stages of cognitive development of science
is inadequate for understanding science-society relationships
(Funtowicz and Ravetz 1993: 740, Kuhn 1996). This is because a discipline-based normal science is oriented towards solving theoretical
puzzles raised by a dominant paradigm. This form of scientific knowledge production is well designed to build up bodies of disciplinary
knowledge, but it is less effective as a means of providing knowledge-
based solutions to contemporary social, economic and policy problems. Solving, or at least contributing to the solution of these problems,
however, is the task of a post-normal science standing at the "contested
interfaces of science and policy" (Ravetz 2004: 3).

According to the theory of PNS the "creation and implementation
of scientific knowledge in the public policy domain" (Hulme and

Ravetz 2009) is the result of a social contract between science and the public that democratizes science. In democratized PNS the public has two main roles: first, to be involved with validating scientific truth claims through a process of "extended peer review", and second, to participate in authorizing the use of scientific knowledge for formulating and implementing public policy (Hulme and Ravetz 2009). Despite these radical changes to the validation procedures characteristic of normal science, proponents of post-normal science maintain its processes of scientific knowledge production and validation is no different from those of normal science (Ravetz 2004: 3, Hulme and Ravetz 2009). This curious claim, of course, is vigorously contested as can be seen in the discursive storm raging in the blogosphere over the nature and consequences of the post-normal science of climate change (Hulme and Ravetz 2009).

The theory of Mode 2 knowledge production and the related theory of Mode 2 society both identify "institutional transgression" as the dominant transformative force at work in contemporary societies. Institutional transgression results in "the boundaries between state, market, culture and science ... becoming increasingly fuzzy" as "...the range of external factors that scientists must now take into account... inexorably and exponentially" increases (Nowotny, Scott and Gibbons 2001: 166). As a result, epistemological, institutional, and normative changes are occurring in the production and application of scientific knowledge (Gibbons et al. 1994: 2). Specifically, Mode 2 knowledge production is transdisciplinary, socially distributed, organizationally heterogeneous, reflexive, socially accountable, and characterized by "quality assurance" criteria that are distinct from the peer review procedures used to assess the knowledge claims of normal Mode 1 science. In Mode 1 science the production of knowledge is primarily motivated by efforts to solve discipline-based problems, to contribute to the development of disciplinary bodies of knowledge and methods, and it largely takes place in cognitive contexts, that is, in the minds of researchers.

The Triple Helix theory of industry-university-government relations addresses the commodification and capitalization of scientific knowledge, and the associated institutional and normative convergence between academia, industry, and government (Etzkowitz 2001, 2002, 2003, Etzkowitz and Leydesdorff 2000). It identifies three general patterns of relationship between science, industry, and government. In the first, government, industry, and science are separate institutions with strong boundaries and limited interaction. The second is characterized by institutional boundary crossing, integration and normative convergence. In the third, the state encompasses both industry and science thereby eliminating institutional boundaries and directly mandating relationships between these spheres of social action (Etzkowitz and Leydesdorff 1999: 138). The first pattern is historically dominant and characteristic of the institutional development of science in industrial capitalist societies. Since the Second World War the second pattern is increasingly prevalent in Western societies.

Despite differences, these theories all identify the crossing and redrawing of various boundaries as processes that are fundamentally changing both science and society. The boundaries being crossed include, but are not limited to, disciplinary boundaries as research increasingly takes place in interdisciplinary teams, knowledge, or epistemic, boundaries as new "quality assurance" criteria are introduced and applied, sectoral boundaries as it takes place in a variety of contexts of application, and socio-political boundaries as questions of interests raised by applying science and technology rise to prominence. Managing relations within and beyond these boundaries is an increasing challenge.

Types of Boundaries

In this section I briefly discuss three boundaries relevant to my present purposes; knowledge (epistemic) boundaries, socio-political boundaries, and spatial-temporal boundaries. I also discuss the types of boundary work associated with each. I argue that effectively crossing knowledge boundaries requires simultaneously crossing socio-political boundaries of interests, and spatial-temporal boundaries.

Knowledge Boundaries

Drawing on the work of early information theorists Carlile (2004) identifies three types of knowledge boundaries, namely, syntactic, semantic, and pragmatic. Syntactic boundaries result from quantitative differences in knowledge—as in the differences between expert and novice—relative to specialized domains of knowledge. Semantic knowledge boundaries are qualitative in the sense that they result from differences between the vocabularies—that is lexicons—of distinct bodies of specialized knowledge. The notion of pragmatic knowledge boundaries is derived from the work of American pragmatists such as William James, John Dewey and George Herbert Mead who maintained that "…all knowledge was grounded in practical experience and communication" (Calhoun et al. 2007: 6). From this perspective, pragmatic knowledge boundaries are seen to reflect contextual differences in the identities, power, interests and preferences of those possessing different types of specialized knowledge (Carlile 2004).

Knowledge transfer is the key to managing syntactic boundaries (Carlile 2004). This occurs when those with more knowledge help those with less to acquire and master it. Various types of apprenticeship training, including professional training, provide examples of knowledge transfer defined in this way (Lave and Wenger 1991). The knowledge being transferred between experts and novices, of course, includes the semantics—that is, the interpretive frameworks and systems of meaning—definitive for a discipline/profession. Managing knowledge across semantic boundaries entails knowledge translation (Carlile 2004).

Knowledge translation involves communicating with the goal of establishing new, and common interpretive frameworks and meanings, that is, a new and shared semantics (Carlile 2004). Like knowledge transfer, knowledge translation is a process of communicative action, the goal of which is mutual understanding and agreement on consequent courses of action within contexts delimited by commonly agreed upon horizons of relevance (Habermas 1984).

Pragmatic knowledge boundaries demarcate differences in the identities, power, motivations and interests of those who possess specialized knowledge. As such, and contrary to Carlile (2004), pragmatic boundaries probably are not best understood as knowledge boundaries at all. Rather, what he refers to as pragmatic knowledge boundaries are recognition that knowledge is contextual, embedded, and intimately connected with the identities, interests and preferences of those who possess it. For these reasons, I suggest pragmatic boundaries are primarily socio-political boundaries that reflect heterogeneous interests, including an interest in protecting and benefiting from the possession and use of specialized knowledge. It is for this reason that those who possess specialized knowledge often resist efforts to share it with others (Carlile 2004). These observations on what Carlile (2004) termed pragmatic knowledge boundaries point to the fact that there are other types of boundaries to knowledge transfer and translation rooted in the contextual and embedded nature of knowledge. Spatial-temporal and socio-political boundaries are two of these.

Spatial-Temporal Boundaries

Knowledge is socially constructed in concrete socio-political and spatial-temporal contexts. Time and space are often understood to be exclusively natural categories reflecting objective reality. Space and time are also socio-cultural constructs, however, with significant experiential effects and practical consequences (Beck 1992a, Thompson 1982). Experiences of time and space vary and the spatial-temporal boundaries characteristic of earlier phases of modernity is transformed with significant socio-cultural consequences.

Beck's notion of the *Risk Society*—what he also calls the second modernity—for example, posits that the deployment and use of modern science and technologies has altered both the predictability and manageability of the risks associated with its deployment and, consequently, socio-cultural concepts of time and space. In this regard, Lash (1993: 3) points out that the early modern concept of insurability that is "based on assumptions of foreseeability, compensatability, and limitations of hazards in space and time" is being superseded by a socio-cultural principle of risk that involves learning to live in a less knowable and controllable world. He continues

> the likes of Chernobyl and global warming were not foreseeable and their very scale makes them incompensatable. They transgress national boundaries so they are not limitable in space. And they contaminate future generations, so they are not limitable in time (Lash 1993: 3).

While I am sure some would argue about the predictability of nuclear accidents and perhaps, even the predictability of global warming, the point about limitability of consequences, however, seems less contentious.

Clearly some modern technologies do transgress boundaries of space and time and reduce our ability to control the consequences associated with their deployment and use. Others, however, can be seen to enhance control of time and space. New information and communication technologies (ICTs), for example, combined with the internet and the World Wide Web (the Web), have become important means of both breaching old and building new spatial and temporal boundaries. These technologies, combined with other communications media and new modes and systems of transportation, can be understood as decontextualizing technologies (McCarthy 1984) that enable both the creation of new spatial-temporal boundaries and new forms of social interaction in a new technology mediated cyberspace (Sterling 1992). Cyberspace is not a real space as we normally understand it, of course, but it is a 'place' where real things happen with real consequences. Sterling (1992) saw cyberspace as a new terrain, the latest globe spanning frontier where individuals are able to pioneer new identities, affiliations and interactions.

The Internet and the Web also facilitate the historically unique, nearly instantaneous, sharing of unprecedented quantities and varieties of information across both socio-political boundaries and the boundaries of time and space. Thus, the internet and the Web, like other de-contextualizing communications techniques and technologies, such as writing, the printing press, radio and television, "...make it possible to free communication from narrow spatio-temporal limitations and to employ it in multiple contexts" (McCarthy 1984: 406). Thus, the technology-enabled crossing of the boundaries of space and time inevitably creates new socio-political and epistemic frontiers of possibility and constraint.

The theory and practice of computer supported cooperative work (CSCW) illustrates this point. CSCW has been defined as the ways in which "collaborative activity can be supported by means of computer systems" (Carstensen and Schmidt 1999: 3). The CSCW matrix, introduced by Johansen (1988), arrays CSCW along two dimensions; spatially (work can be co-located or distributed), and temporally (work can be done synchronously or asynchronously). CSCW groupware enables the creation of new time and space boundaries within which new groups can cooperatively work. This capacity to work across spatial and temporal boundaries is a prevalent feature of innovation networks.

Socio-Political Boundaries

Knowledge and interests are two interrelated dimensions of organized social life—neither exist outside socio-political and spatio-temporal contexts, although as we have just seen, these boundaries can be either real or virtual and, in both cases, they are highly malleable and elastic. It is also a sociological truism that knowledge and interests are irreducibly heterogeneous in the sense that identities and interests are grounded in a variety of differences such as race, ethnicity, class, gender, sexual orientation, generation, nationality, and so on. It is also true that these identity differences entail diverse political, social, and economic interests that are themselves in constant flux. Thus, difference and change are constant. This has contradictory consequences. On one hand, heterogeneity (i.e., difference) results in conflict, coercion, domination, submission, resistance, withdrawal, or any of a wide range of non-cooperative and non-collaborative relationships. On the other hand, difference is also an incubator for collaboration, cooperation, creativity, and innovation. In the context of innovation, the challenge is to mobilize and manage the diversity of specialized knowledge and interests to achieve cooperation and creativity instead of stagnation and strife.

Intentionally crossing and redefining boundaries is associated with new boundary spanning roles and institutions. Knowledge brokers increasingly facilitate a number of boundary crossing processes (boundary-work), including crossing socio-political boundaries by forging new relationships and networks, thereby defining and redefining the needs, interests and identities of collaborators. Appropriately [re]defining the needs and interests of affected parties to planned change and enrolling them as collaborators in innovation is necessary for achieving desired outcomes (Callon and Law 1982, Law and Williams 1982, Star and Griesemer 1989, Akrich, Callon and Latour 2002*a*, 2002*b*).

Boundary-Work & Boundary Objects

Boundary-work is a unity of destructive, constructive and transformative processes. It involves breaching and repairing existing boundaries and fabricating new ones. Both individual learning and intentional social and technical change (innovation) involve boundary-work along the epistemic, socio-political, spatio-temporal boundaries discussed above. The notion of boundary-work originally was introduced by Thomas Gieryn to describe how, and to explain why, epistemic boundaries were constructed between science and non-science. Gieryn (1983: 782) argued that successful boundary-work helps define and realize the interests of scientists by rhetorically characterizing them, and their methods, knowledge, and values, as well as the consequences of their work, in positive terms while, at the same time, negatively characterizing alternative ways of knowing promulgated by competitors.

Thus, the motive underpinning boundary-work is to establish and protect interests including social interests (e.g., status and respect), economic interests (e.g., opportunities and rewards), and political interests (e.g., autonomy and authority). The styles and contents of the arguments used in the effort to achieve these outcomes vary depending on the interests and audiences being addressed. Gieryn (1983) shows, for example, that sometimes advocates for science emphasize its applied nature and practical value. At other times emphasis is placed on its contributions to more abstract goals such as refining the intellect and developing culture (MacCrae 1976: 41). Seen in this way, boundary-work is an embedded, contingent and rhetorical[2] process of communication intended to motivate its target audiences to desired action (Geertz 1973, Gieryn 1983, 1999, Mulkay 1995, Bloomfield and Vurdubakis 1995).

I agree in part with this analysis. Boundary-work is rhetorical in nature, but rhetoric is only one aspect of the art of persuasion. In this regard, rational argumentation based on challenging and defending truth, legitimacy and or truthfulness claims is at least as important as rhetoric (Habermas 1970, 1984, MacCrae 1976). This is because in contemporary use of the term, rhetoric need not have any relationship to truth, ethics or truthfulness. Indeed, rhetoric is often seen to be little more than self-serving lies and deception. It is for this reason that rhetoric and rhetoricians often are seen as prevaricating propagandists to be disbelieved and distrusted. If Gieryn's characterization of boundary-work as rhetoric is correct then success is unlikely to be sustainable. Boundary-work must also be attentive to truth, legitimacy and truthfulness claims, perhaps especially when it involves science. Challenging and defending truth, legitimacy and truthfulness claims, however, is the task of rational argumentation, not rhetoric (Habermas 1984). Therefore, rhetoric does not provide a comprehensive framework for understanding boundary-work.

Despite the limitation of his analytical approach, Gieryn's case studies demonstrate two interrelated types of boundary-work, what I will call offensive and defensive. Offensive boundary-work refers to the persuasive efforts of scientists "...to enlarge the material and symbolic resources" available to them. Defensive boundary-work refers to efforts to "...defend professional autonomy" (Gieryn 1983: 782). From this perspective it is clear both offensive and defensive boundary-work are motivated by socio-political interests.

---

[2] In classical thought the three rhetorical styles refer to appeals based on the character of the speaker (ethos); appeals based on logic and reason (logos); appeals based on emotion (pathos).

A third type of boundary-work needs to be recognized. I call this transformative boundary-work. Transformative boundary-work primarily is done at and across socio-political and epistemic boundaries. At epistemic boundaries it includes processes of knowledge transfer and translation and at socio-political boundaries it involves efforts to identify, redefine and harmonize heterogeneous interests. Identifying, redefining and harmonizing interests is another dimension and objective of the innovation process and a necessary dimension of effective knowledge translation and use (Callon and Law 1982, Law and Williams 1982, Akrich, Callon and Latour 2002*a*, 2002*b*). The communicative co-creation of boundary objects and intéressement devices are two aspects of boundary-work.

Boundary Objects & Intéressement

Innovation occurs in complex contexts involving various actors with heterogeneous interests (Star and Griesemer 1989, Akrich, Callon and Latour 2002*a*, 2002*b*). Consequently, successful innovation requires cooperative work across epistemic, socio-political and spatial-temporal boundaries. Creating boundary objects and intéressement devises are essential elements of this boundary-work.

In their seminal study Star and Griesemer (1989) introduced the concepts "boundary object" and "methods standardization" to describe and explain the translation of segregated (i.e., specialized) knowledge and its transformation into integrated knowledge in complex, socio-political environments characterized by a variety of actors with manifold interests. "Boundary objects" are defined by Star and Griesemer (1989: 393)

> as ...*scientific objects* which both inhabit several intersecting social worlds ... and satisfy the informational requirements of each of them. Boundary objects are objects which are both plastic enough to adapt to local needs and the constraints of the several parties employing them, yet robust enough to maintain a common identity across sites. They are weakly structured in common use, and become strongly structured in individual-site use. These objects may be abstract or concrete. They have different meanings in different social worlds but their structure is common enough to more than one world to make them recognizable, a means of translation. The creation and management of boundary objects is a key process in developing and maintaining coherence across intersecting social worlds (emphasis added).

This is a very abstract definition. To help clarify the nature of boundary objects, Star and Griesemer (1989) proposed a four element typology that included repositories, ideal types, coincident boundaries, and standardized forms. This typology was not intended to be comprehensive.

Working in an industrial as opposed to an academic context, Carlile and Rebentisch (2003) proposed an alternative, a three element typology of boundary objects consisting of technical specialists (people), mutually acceptable methods, and sharable artifacts. Clearly, Carlile and Rebentisch (2003) are not of the view that boundary objects must be scientific objects. The "anything or anyone can be a boundary object" approach is shared by Grey (2003) who states on his blog that boundary objects "...can be a set of information, conversations, interests, rules, plans, contracts, or even persons" (Grey 2003). There obviously is no agreement on how to define boundary objects. There is more agreement on what functions they serve.

The function of boundary objects is to facilitate the crossing of epistemic, socio-political, and spatial temporal boundaries. Relative to epistemic boundaries, boundary objects facilitate translating knowledge between multiple social worlds. Relative to socio-political boundaries the function of boundary objects is to maintain the autonomy of diverse collaborators while increasing communication and cooperative interaction between them (Star and Griesemer 1989: 404). Relative to spacial-temporal boundaries, boundary objects are a way to informationalize, disembody and decontextualize knowledge so that it is available for use across both time and space (Urry 2003: 64). Various types of repositories are examples of this type of boundary object.

The role of cooperatively co-produced boundary objects in helping to serve the interests of those on different sides of socio-political boundaries is commented on by Star and Griesemer (1989: 408): "As groups from different worlds work together, they create various sorts of boundary objects. The intersectional nature of the ... shared work creates objects which inhabit multiple worlds simultaneously, and which must meet the demands of each one." Thus, to be effective boundary objects must be co-produced (Star and Griesemer 1989). The effectiveness of their co-production is increased by assigning responsibility for this function within the collaborating organizations in a network (Cash et al. 2003). The collaborative and facilitated co-production of boundary objects is drawn upon by collaborators as they try to achieve mutual understanding and agreement (Cash et al. 2003).

In this way, boundary objects are a means of crossing and redrawing knowledge and other types of boundaries.

Interéssement is boundary-work at socio-political boundaries. It involves identifying one's own interests, imputing interests to others and structuring and transforming these to enrol others in the realization of one's own interests (Callon and Law 1982). Boundary objects facilitate intéressement. The identification and enrollment of allies (i.e., collaborators or partners) who support a course of action involves sharing specialized knowledge and developing common knowledge. Equally important, however, it also involves developing a mutual understanding of both shared and separate interests and an agreement on how best to realize both. The outcome of this "interest work" (Callon and Law 1982: 621) is always uncertain but it is essential to innovation, that is, both developing new knowledge and applying it.

Akrich, Callon and Latour (2002a: 205), for example, summarize the internal relationship between "interest work" and innovation: "Innovation is the art of interesting an increasing number of allies who will make you stronger and stronger." They also note:

> Since the outcome of [innovation] depends on the alliances which it allows for and the interests which it mobilises, no criteria, no algorithm, can ensure success a priori. Rather than speak of the rationality of decisions, we need to speak of the aggregation of interests which decisions are capable or incapable of producing (Akrich, Callon and Latour 2002a: 205).

This quotation clearly highlights the centrality and necessity of socio-political boundary work (i.e., interest work) in the innovation process. Akrich et al.'s (2002a, 2002b) emphasis on socio-political interest work was presented as a corrective to a one-sided and inadequate "build it and they will come" scientific-technical approach to innovation. Several factors determine the success or failure of innovation, including an organization's capacities to generate, diffuse, adopt, and adapt new knowledge and technology (Parent et al. 2007), but in the end, users have the final say: "The evaluation of the disadvantages and advantages of an innovation is entirely in the hands of the users: it depends on their expectations, their interests, on the problems which they raise" (Akrich et al. 2002a: 202). While this is true, those expectations and interests are not fixed.

Interest work and the creation of boundary objects is best understood as a process whereby all the interested parties attempt to identify their own interests, attribute interests to others, and, in many cases, to transform both in the effort to enroll allies for action (Star and Griesemer 1989, Callon and Law 1982). It is important that the interests of all partners are, and are seen to be, realized by this type of boundary-work. Initiating and managing this process is an increasing priority in the knowledge society. Innovation, like science, takes place primarily in loosely coupled networks of heterogeneous and autonomous partners. Command and control management practices cannot work in this context, nor do classical market mechanisms (Jones, Hesterly and Borgatti 1997). Thus, for the past couple of decades there has been a burgeoning literature on network management and network governance.

Dhaneraj and Parkhe (2006) provide a useful model of network management. They suggest the term "network orchestration" to describe the process of directing innovation in loosely coupled networks of self interested and autonomous organizations. Although it doesn't appear as if they mean to suggest the process is surreptitious as is usually implied by the word orchestrate, they clearly see orchestration as something done by a "hub firm" in innovation networks: "We define network orchestration as the set of deliberate, purposeful actions undertaken by the hub firm as it seeks to create value (expand the pie) and extract value (gain a larger slice of the pie) from the network" (Dhaneraj and Parkhe 2006: 659). Thinking of it like this looses the insight that the boundary work required for successful innovation is an "n-way" process where presumably everyone involved is attempting to create and extract additional value. Rather than this being the prerogative of one leader, Cash et al. (2003: 8089) suggest that responsibility for these leadership functions should be distributed and embedded in either brokering organizations or in the organizations of network members with clear lines of authority and accountability:

> Institutionalizing accountability of boundary managers to key actors on both sides of the knowledge-action boundary was crucial to building effective information flows. Such dual accountability arrangements forced boundary managers to address the interests, concerns, and perspectives of actors on both sides of the boundary.

Thus, whether responsibility for boundary work and boundary management is taken on by a hub organization, a brokering organization, or by network members themselves it has to be planned to be effective (Dhaneraj and Parkhe 2006). For Cash et al. (2003: 8088) it has to be planned and managed along three dimensions—communication, translation, and mediation.

In this regard, effective communication is "active, iterative, and inclusive" (Cash et al. 2003: 8088). One-way, sporadic, or non-inclusive communication is either ineffective or even counterproductive for managing knowledge and socio-political boundaries. Translating specialized, experiential and contextualized knowledge is required so that network members can understand each other (i.e., cross syntactic and semantic boundaries) and reach mutual understanding and agreed to actions. Mediation, as used by Cash et al. (2003), refers to the interest work required for managing socio-political boundaries. The effectiveness of mediation, considered as an aspect of interest work, was found to be improved in their research "…by enhancing the legitimacy of the process through increasing transparency, bringing all perspectives to the table, providing rules of conduct, and establishing criteria for decision making" (Cash et al. 2003: 8088).

Dhaneraj and Parkhe (2006), taking a related approach identified knowledge mobility, innovation appropriability, and network stability as necessary for effectively managing boundaries in innovation networks. Knowledge mobility is similar to Cash et al.'s (2003: 660) notion of communication. It is defined as "the ease with which knowledge is shared, acquired, and deployed within the network" (Dhaneraj and Parkhe 2006: 660). Orchestrating a suitable "appropriability regime" entails interest work intended "to ensure equitable distribution of value and mitigate appropriability concerns by focusing on the following processes: trust, procedural justice, and joint asset ownership" (Dhaneraj and Parkhe 2006: 663). Loosely coupled networks are inherently transient, impermanent and unstable, therefore, "…fostering a dynamic network stability" that "…aims for a nonnegative growth rate while allowing for entry and exit of network members" is important (Dhaneraj and Parkhe 2006: 661). Seen in this way, fostering network stability can be understood as additional dimensions of managing interests at socio-political boundaries.

Conclusion

It is widely accepted that in the context of post-industrial knowledge societies producing, transferring and using research knowledge and technology are interrelated processes that take place in loosely coupled networks of autonomous actors characterized by heterogeneous interests. The theories of PNS, Mode 2 knowledge production, and the Triple Helix of university, industry, government relations all address the nature and consequences of these interrelationships. We also have seen that effective collaboration for this purpose requires a variety of individuals and groups to work across the multiple boundaries of space and time, socio-political interests, and diverse knowledges.

In this chapter I have emphasized that these boundaries can be differentiated for analytical purposes, but actually they are inextricably intertwined such that changes to one effects changes to the others. Managing these boundaries for innovation is multidimensional and complex. The issue of managing multiple boundaries in loosely coupled systems like innovation networks is a topic that requires more examination. In particular, approaches integrating both epistemic and socio-political boundary work seem particularly timely and important.

Bibliography

Akrich, Madeline, Michel Callon and Bruno Latour. 2002a. "The Key to Success in Innovation, Part I: The Art of Intéressement." *International Journal of Innovation Management* 6(2): 187–206.

Akrich, Madeline, Michel Callon and Bruno Latour. 2002b. "The Key to Success in Innovation, Part II: The Art of Choosing Good Spokespersons." *International Journal of Innovation Management* 6(2): 207–225.

Alavi, Maryam and Dorothy E. Leidner. 2001. "Knowledge Management and Knowledge Management Systems: Conceptual Foundations and Research Issues." *Management Information Systems Quarterly* 25(1): 107–13.

Beck, Ulrich. 1992a. "From Industrial Society to Risk Society: Questions of Survival, Social Structure and Ecological Enlightenment." *Theory, Culture & Society* 9(1): 97–123.

Beck, Ulrich. 1992b. *Risk Society: Towards A New Modernity*. London: Sage.

Bell, Daniel. 1973. *The Coming of Post-industrial Society: A Venture in Social Forecasting*. New York: Basic Books.

Bloomfield, Brian P. and Theo Vurdubkis. 1995. "Disputed Boundaries: New Reproductive Technologies and the Language of Anxiety and Expectation." *Social Studies of Science* 25(3): 533–551.

Böehme, Gernot and Nico Stehr, eds. 1986. *The Knowledge Society: The Growing Impact of Scientific knowledge on Social Relations*. Dordrecht & Boston, Mass.: D. Reidel Publishing Company.

Calhoun, Craig, Joseph Gerteis, James Moody, Steven Pfaff, and Indermohan Virk, eds. 2007. *Contemporary Sociological Theory*, Second Edition. Malden, MA: Blackwell.

Callon, Michel. 1980. "Struggles and Negotiations to Define What is Problematic and What is Not: the Sociologic of Translation", in Karin Knorr, Roger Krohn and

Richard D. Whitley, eds., *The Social Process of Scientific Investigation, Sociology of the Sciences Yearbook*, Vol. 4. Dordrecht & Boston, Mass.: D. Reidel Publishing Company, pp. 197–219.

Callon, Michel and John Law. 1982. "On Interests and Their Transformation: Enrollment and Counter-Enrollment." *Social Studies of Science* 12: 615–25.

Carlile, R. Paul. 2004. "Transferring, Translating, and Transforming: An Integrated Framework for Managing Knowledge Across Boundaries." *Organization Studies* 15(5): 555–568.

Carlile, R. Paul and Eric S. Rebentisch. 2003. "Into the Blackbox: The Knowledge Transformation Cycle." *Management Science* 49(9): 1180–1195.

Carstensen, H. Peter and Kjeld Schmidt. 1999 (2003). "Computer Supported Cooperative Work: New Challenges to Systems Design", in K. Itoh, ed., *Handbook of Human Factors/Ergonomics,* Tokyo: Asakura Publishing, pp. 619–636 (in Japanese). English language version http://www.itu.dk/~schmidt/publ.html downloaded March 15, 2010.

Cash, David W., William C. Clark, Frank Alcock, Nancy M. Dickson, Noelle Eckley, David H. Guston, Jill Jäger, and Robert B. Mitchell. 2003. "Knowledge Systems for Sustainable Development." *Proceedings of the National Academy of Science* 100(14): 8086–8091.

Castells, Manuel. 1996. *The Rise of the Network Society*. Oxford: Blackwell.

Dhaneraj, Charles and Arvind Parkhe. 2006. "Orchestrating Innovation Networks." *Academy of Management Review* 31(3): 659–669.

Drucker, F. Peter. 1994. *Post-capitalist Society*. New York: Harper Business.

Edwards, Richard, Stewart Ranson and Michael Strain. 2002. "Reflexivity: Towards a Theory of Lifelong Learning." *International Journal of Lifelong Learning* 21(6): 525–536.

Etzkowitz, Henry. 2001. "The Second Academic Revolution and the Rise of Entrepreneurial Science." *IEEE Technology and Society Magazine* 20(2):18–29.

Etzkowitz, Henry. 2002. *MIT and the Rise of Entrepreneurial Science*. New York: Routledge.

Etzkowitz, Henry. 2003. "Innovation in Innovation: The Triple Helix of University-Industry-Government Relations." *Social Science Information* 42(3):293–337.

Etzkowitz, Henry and Loet Leydesdorff. 1999. "Whose Triple Helix?" *Science and Public Policy* 26(2):138–139.

Etzkowitz, Henry and Loet Leydesdorff. 2000. "Dynamics of Innovation: From National Systems and "Mode 2" to a Triple Helix of University-Industry-Government Relations to a Triple Helix of university-industry-government relations." *Research Policy* 29(2):109–123.

Funtowicz, Silvio and Jerome Ravetz. 1993. "Science for the Post-normal Age." *Futures* 25(7): 739–755.

Galbraith, John Kenneth. 1971. *The New Industrial State*, Second Edition. Boston: Houghton Mifflin.

Geertz, Clifford. 1973. *The Interpretation of Cultures*. New York: Basic.

Gibbons, Michael, C. Limoges, H. Nowotny, S. Schwartzmann, P. Scott, and M. Trow. 1994. *The New Production of Knowledge: The Dynamics of Science and Research in Contemporary Societies*. Thousand Oaks, Cal.: Sage.

Giddens, Anthony. 1990. *Consequences of Modernity*. Cambridge: Polity Press.

Giddens, Anthony. 1991. *Modernity and Self-Identity*. Cambridge: Polity Press.

Gieryn, F. Thomas. 1983. "Boundary-work and the Demarcation of Science from Non-science: Strains and Interests in Professional Ideologies of Scientists." *American Sociological Review* 48: 781–795.

Gieryn, F. Thomas. 1999. *Cultural Boundaries of Science: Credibility on the Line*. Chicago: University of Chicago Press.

Grey, Denham. 2003. "Boundary Objects and KM," Knowledge-at-Work blog site. (http://denham.typepad.com/km/2003/10/boundary_object.html. Accessed March 27, 2010).

Gross, R. Paul and Norman Levitt. 1998. *Higher Superstition: The Academic Left and Its Quarrels with Science*. Baltimore: The Johns Hopkins University Press.

Habermas, Jürgen. 1970. *Towards a Rational Society: Student Protest, Science and Politics*. Boston: Beacon Press.

Habermas, Jürgen. 1984. *The Theory of Communicative Action, Volume I, Reason and the Rationalization of Society*. Boston: Beacon Press.

Holzner, Burhart and John Marx. 1979. *Knowledge Application: The Knowledge System in Society*. Boston: Allyn and Bacon.

Hulme, Mike and Jerome Ravetz. 2009. "'Show Your Working': What 'Climategate' Means". (http://news.bbc.co.uk/2/hi/8388485.stm, (accessed February 18, 2010).

Jones, Candace, William S. Hesterly and Stephen P. Borgatti. 1997. "A General Theory of Network Governance: Exchange Conditions and Social Mechanisms." *The Academy of Management* Review 22(4): 911–945.

Johansen, Robert.1988. Groupware: *Computer Support for Business Teams*. New York and London: The Free Press.

Kuhn, Thomas. 1996. *The Structure of Scientific Revolutions*, Third Edition. Chicago: University of Chicago Press.

Lash, Scott. 1993. "Reflexive Modernization: The Aesthetic Dimension." *Theory, Culture & Society* 10: 1–23.

Lave, Jean and Etienne Wenger. 1991. *Situated Learning: Legitimate Peripheral Participation*. Cambridge University Press.

Law, John and Rob Williams. 1982. "Putting Facts Together: A Study of Scientific Persuasion." *Social Studies of Science* 12: 535–58.

Lyotard, Jean-François. 1984. The *Postmodern Condition: A Report on Knowledge*. Minneapolis: University of Minnesota Press.

MacCrae, Duncan. 1976. *The Social Function of Social Science*. New Haven and London: Yale University Press.

Mandel, Ernest. 1975. *Late Capitalism*. London: NLB.

McCarthy, Thomas. 1984. Translator's Introduction [to Jürgen Habermas Theory of Communicative Action, Volume I]. Boston: Beacon Press.

Mulkay, Michael. 1995. "Galileo and the Embryos: Religion and Science in the Parliamentary Debate on Human Embryos." *Social Studies of Science* 25 (3): 499–532.

Mott, D. Frederick. 1948. "Recent Developments in the Provision of Medical Services in Saskatchewan." *Canadian Medical Association Journal* 58: 195–200.

Nowotny, Helga, Peter Scott and Michael Gibbons. 2001. *Re-Thinking Science: Knowledge and the Public in an Age of Uncertainty*. London: Polity Press.

Palmer, Ian and Robert Dunford. 2002. "Who Says Change Can be Managed? Positions, perspectives and Problematics." *Strategic Change* 11(5): 243–251.

Parent, Robert, Mario Roy and Denis St-Jacques. 2007. "A Systems-based Dynamic Knowledge Transfer Capacity Model." *Journal of Knowledge Management* 11(6): 81–93.

Ravetz, Jerome. 2004. "The Post-normal Science of Persuasion." *Futures* 36(3): 347–357.

Richta, Radovan et al. 1969. *Civilization at the Crossroads: Social and Human Implications of the Scientific and Technological Revolution*. New York: International Arts and Science Press.

Star, Susan Leigh and James R. Griesemer. 1989. "Institutional Ecology, 'Translations' and Boundary Objects: Amateurs and Professionals in Berkeley's Museum of Vertebrate Zoology, 1907–1939." *Social Studies of Science* 19(3): 387–420.

Sterling, Bruce. 1992. *The Hacker Crackdown: Law and Disorder on the Electronic Frontier*. E-book. (http://www.gutenberg.org/files/101/101-h/101-h.htm).

Thompson, Edward Palmer. 1982. "Time, Work-Discipline, and Industrial Capitalism", in Anthony Giddens and David Held, eds., *Classes, Power, and Conflict: Classical and Contemporary Debates*. Berkeley and Los Angeles: University of California Press, pp. 299–309.

Touraine, Alain. 1971. *The Post-industrial Society: Tomorrow's Social History: Classes, Conflicts and Culture in the Programmed Society*. New York: Random House.

Urry, John. 2003. *Global Complexity*. Cambridge: Polity Press.

Urry, John. 2006. "Complexity." *Theory, Culture & Society* 23(2–3): 111–117.

van Dijk, Jan. 1999. The Network Society, Social Aspects of New Media. London: Thousand Oaks, New Delhi: Sage.

Webopedia.com. 2009. The Difference Between the Internet and the World Wide Web. Created 2002 last modified October 9, 2009, accessed February 17, 2010 (http://www.webopedia.com/DidYouKnow/Internet/2002/Web_vs_Internet.asp).

Webster, Frank. 2002. *Theories of the information Society*, Second Edition. New York: Routledge.

Weiss, Carol. 1977. *Using Social Science Research in Policy Making*. Lexington Books.

CHAPTER NINE

GOVERNING INNOVATION IN A KNOWLEDGE SOCIETY

Peter W.B. Phillips

Over the past generation the global economy has passed a critical threshold, transforming from a predominantly goods to services producing and consuming economy. Scholars and policy makers have struggled to understand and respond to the fundamental shift to one based on services in the global innovation system and the related governance challenges. Goods industries are unambiguously easier to control as the related production and marketing systems are mostly tied to specific locations and generally exhibit decreasing returns, which makes governing them tractable. Services production, in contrast, is increasingly disconnected from any single location and in some instances offers increasing returns to scale, such that the activities often transcend the reach of any existing governors.

Ultimately, one question underlies much of the angst in this post-industrial, knowledge-driven era dominated by globalization: who's in control? Given the ethereal nature of knowledge, one often gets the impression that no one is really in control. As production and consumption disengage from specific locations and into the ether and as more production and consumption are co-produced and co-consumed, it becomes harder to identify who is doing what when and where. Traditional systems that governed the industrial economy—particularly the nation state and profit-optimizing commercial firms—remain important, but are increasingly supported or undercut by new actors with new motivations and structures.

This chapter examines the fundamental challenges posed by the knowledge society, presents a conceptual framework for understanding the scope of governance of the system and offers an assessment of some implications for our economy and society.

The Context

Any discussion about innovation is ultimately about change. Although the rate, scale and scope of the change will vary depending on whether the technology involves small, iterative adjustments or poses large, transformative modifications, the challenge remains the same. Institutions need to respond and to adapt to the new circumstances. Although many institutions involved in governing a system are able to adapt to changing circumstances, inflexible institutions can block a change (for better or worse) or become increasingly irrelevant as new institutional pathways are developed to govern new circumstances. Existing institutions will end up either leading, following, or getting out of the way (either by design or by happenstance). The nature and process of making that fundamental choice about how to engage goes a long way to determining what, where, when, why, how and by whom new technologies are adapted, adopted and used, and whether that use generates social benefits. As Darwin suggests, it is not the strength of a system but rather the flexibility and adaptability of the system that will determine its lasting influence. If a system is perennially unresponsive or blocks fundamentally sound and advantageous change, it will face competitive pressures, either from within—for instance, society or some key actors may demand action—or from without—often resulting from declining economic or political influence.

The debate about who is controlling the rate, scale and scope of change pervades much of public discourse today. Discussions about the economy, our health and the environment, for example, are largely being driven or shaped by new opportunities or threats resulting from emerging technologies. As a result, analysis and discussion about the nature and scope of technological change is reaching ever increasing levels of hype, concern and angst.

The transcendent, expansive nature of transformative technological innovation poses some real challenges for governors. This is one of the more significant, identifiable underlying concerns about globalization. Increasing interconnectivity caused by transformative technologies is undercutting both our perceptions of and our capacity to isolate and specifically control new developments. Information technologies, combined with the many and varied advances in biological and materials processes, have linked previously disconnected parts of our world both physically and emotionally.

Although elite power relationships may be at the root of many of our systems, how they operate (that is, who has and uses power) has a major impact on the lot of the rest of us. Our futures are linked to how transformative innovations are handled. Individual and national welfare are a function of the long-term growth and development of our productive capacity. Both absolute and relative changes are important. In absolute terms, our ability to introduce new ways of doing things that either increases our socio-economic capacity or reduces the material costs of our consumption will be the basis for our collective prosperity. One might reasonably argue that people living in OECD countries have (or should have) enough resources to live comfortably but the majority of the rest of the world's population has very limited access to resources and suffers from the attendant risks and uncertainties of inadequate food, shelter, clothing, medical care, public security and environmental safety. New technologies and new institutions offer some hope that they can attain a higher level of prosperity and security without having to undergo all of the trials and failures experienced by OECD countries.

Furthermore, OECD countries are recognizing that their long term security and quality of life may be linked to the plight of the underdeveloped parts of the world. The global environment and public health have been shown to be great equalizers in recent years. Adverse weather and environmental change have punished both developed and developing countries in recent years and even though most of the new public health threats—such as AIDS, antibiotic resistant infections and various influenzas—have emerged from underdeveloped regions of the world they have had major economic and social impacts in many OECD nations.

Equally important for many is the fact that the relative ability of countries to benefit from new technological and productive opportunities determines a state's or society's economic, social and political status in the world. Countries that effectively and efficiently generate, gestate and commercialize new technologies and innovations tend to accumulate more wealth and power in the long run. Across time, one can see that countries that fail to adapt to change tend to ossify and lose status and power. The emergence, zenith and decline of past empires (e.g. the Greek, Roman, Ming, British, French, Spanish, Portuguese and Dutch) illustrate the opportunities and challenges of riding the waves of innovation. Each gained ascendancy through technological or institutional innovation and each ultimately failed to sustain dominance in the face of new, competing technological or organizational innovations. Currently, the member states of the OECD, led by the US, are arguably at a zenith (or at least local peak) of power and influence. Their future will in part be determined by how they respond to change. If they fail to adapt, other nation states that do may catch up and surpass them in terms of capacity and power.

Wright (2004:4) cautions us to remember that the 'idea of material progress is a very recent one—significant only in the past three hundred years or so—coinciding closely with the rise of science and industry and the corresponding decline of traditional beliefs.' Thus, our experience and understanding of change, especially our current exposure to overlapping, interlocking, inexorable technical, economic, social and cultural change, is a relatively recent circumstance. At the same time, many of the institutions we expect to govern the change process are products of an earlier and different period. It may be unrealistic to expect them to be able to respond easily or totally to the new pressures.

The Knowledge Society

The concept of a 'knowledge society' is one attempt to understand the fundamental economic and social transformation precipitated by the transition of the global economy into a knowledge and services-based system. Just as the earlier transformations from hunter-gatherer to agrarian societies and the agricultural and industrial revolutions were both precipitated by and contributed to new forms of governance, the transition into the knowledge society is challenging our systems of governance. Ironically, the industrial economy was waning even before it was fully diffused into the global economy. As early as the 1950s, services-generating employment and GDP contributed more than half of the activity in the economy in North America. By 2008, more than 64 percent of the world economy was generated in services-producing industries, with only 32 percent contributed by industrial production and four percent from farming. While a few countries, such as China, continue to generate more than half of their national income through goods production (60 percent in 2008), most countries had passed that point. The two leading economic regions, the EU and US, generated 71 percent and 79 percent respectively of their national income in 2008 through services producing activities while India, a leading developing nation, produced 54 percent of its income from services (CIA Factbook).

This transformation from goods to services production has both coincided with and been driven by a corresponding information revolution, where faster and cheaper communications, computation and data storage has generated a wave of new services and new demands. As far back as the 1930s, scholars have been writing about the role of information, knowledge, science and technology. The impact of those interrelated elements has been variously called the post-industrial society (Bell 1973), the service economy, the information and communications technology (ICT) revolution, and, increasingly the 'knowledge society' (Stehr 1984). UNESCO, in particular, has adopted the term 'knowledge society', or its variant, 'knowledge societies', within its institutional policies. Abdul Khan of UNESCO wrote 'the concept of "knowledge societies" includes a dimension of social, cultural, economical, political and institutional transformation, and a more pluralistic and developmental perspective' (UNESCO 2003).

Strange (1992: 121), a key scholar who defined the nature of international political economy, posited that the place to start analysis of what she called the knowledge structure is to 'determine... what knowledge is discovered, how it is stored, and who communicates it by what means to whom and on what terms... Power and authority are conferred on those occupying key decision-making positions in the knowledge structure.' Knowledge displays mercury-like properties—we can see it but it is hard to grab on to. The difficulty is that knowledge exhibits an array of dichotomies: it can be both explicit and implicit; it can be local or global; and it can be individual or collective (Jensen et al. 2004). This array of attributes means the functional space encompassed by the term is wide.

There have been various attempts through the millennia to parse the concept of knowledge into more tractable components. Aristotle, for example, offered three classes of knowledge: universal and theoretical knowledge; instrumental and practice-related knowledge; and normative, common sense-based knowledge. Alternatively, knowledge could be parsed based on its degree of codification and formalization (Polanyi 1962). Codified knowledge (similar to Aristotle's universal and theoretical knowledge) is systematic and reproducible whereas tacit knowledge (those skills and corresponding understandings that defy articulation or codification and correspond to Aristotle's instrumental and normative knowledge types) is considered intangible—residing in individuals or communities. Knowledge could also be categorized based on its primary purpose: 'propositional' knowledge relates to natural regularities and phenomena (also called 'knowledge what'); and 'prescriptive' knowledge consists of instructions that constitute techniques or routines (or 'knowledge how to') (Mokyr 2002).

There are at least four discernable types of knowledge: know-why, know-what, know-how and know-who (Lundvall and Johnson 1994, OECD 1996, Malecki 1997). One might conclude that the four possibilities emerge from combining the dyads of form (codified or tacit) and structure (whether residing in individuals or the collective). Know-why knowledge is codified and collective, know-what knowledge is codified and individual, know-how is tacit and individual and know-who is tacit and collective.

Each type of knowledge has specific features (OECD 1996). 'Know-why' refers to scientific knowledge of the principles and laws of nature, which for the most part is undertaken globally in publicly-funded universities and not-for-profit research institutes and is subsequently codified and published in academic or professional journals. 'Know-what' refers to knowledge about facts and techniques, which can usually be codified and transferred through the commercial marketplace. 'Know-how' refers to the combination of intellectual, educational and physical dexterity, skills and analytical capacity to design a hypothesis-driven protocol with a set of expected outcomes, which involves the ability of scientists to effectively combine the know-why and know-what to innovate. This capacity is often learned through education and technical training and perfected by doing, which in part generates a degree of difficulty for the uninitiated and makes it more difficult to transfer to others and, hence, more difficult to codify. Finally, 'know-who', which involves information about 'who knows what and who knows how to do what' is becoming increasingly important (OECD 1996). As the breadth of knowledge required to innovate expands, it has become absolutely necessary to collaborate. In today's context, know-who also requires knowledge of and access to private sector knowledge generators who at times may hold back the flow of crucial or enabling information, expertise and knowledge. Know-who knowledge is seldom codified but accumulates often within an organization or, at times, in communities where there is a cluster of public and private entities that are all engaged in the same type of research and development, often exchange technologies, research materials and resources and pursue common staff training or cross-training opportunities.

This categorization of knowledge goes part way to addressing Strange's challenge to find and focus on those who occupy key decision-making positions that determine what is discovered, how it is stored, and who communicates it by what means to whom and on what terms. In the first instance, the taxonomy reveals that there are both stocks and flows of knowledge, which would suggest that there will need to be correspondingly different actors responsible for governing their different functions. Furthermore, no one type of individual or institution can or will control all of the knowledge and its uses. Rather, there will be an array of individuals, public agencies, private enterprises and collective structures that will govern different types of knowledge, each potentially using a different set of processes and seeking a different set of objectives.

Knowledge—both the stocks and flows of new concepts and uses— is particularly important as it is the foundation of innovation in the knowledge society. As with much of the literature about technology and the economy, Joseph Schumpeter (1934) is credited with the first economic definition of innovation. He defined innovation as the introduction of a new good or a new quality of an existing good, a new method of production, the opening of a new market and the introduction of a new supply of inputs to a production system or a new organizational structure in an industry. Two points are clear from this definition. First, it explicitly separates invention from innovation, arguing that 'innovation is possible without anything we should identify as invention, and invention does not necessarily induce innovation' (Schumpeter 1939: 84). Second, Schumpeter is clearly talking about a process—'introduction'—by which something new is initiated or adopted. Ruttan (2003) concurs, suggesting the concept of innovation be extended to include the process by which new things emerge in science, technology and art. A variety of other researchers see creativity—defined as the production of novel and useful ideas in any domain—as the basis for innovation and so they define innovation as the successful implementation of creative ideas within an organization or social setting.

There is significant blurring of the lines between activities and actors, leading to difficulty in observing and assessing the efficacy of the differing modeling efforts. Some see innovation as fundamentally a firm or intra-firm event (e.g. Metcalfe 1995), others see innovation as an industrial event (e.g. Malbera and Orsenigo 1990), a community event (e.g. Freeman 1987, Lundvall 1992), a national event (e.g. Furman et al. 2002) or a collective event among a subset of specific institutions (e.g. Etzkowitz and Leydesdorff 1995). Innovation can thus involve more than the narrow innovation systems, but can encompass a wide range of actors who are geographically disbursed around the world.

A number of alternative models have been offered to explain how innovation actually happens. Etzkowitz and Leydesdorff (1995) characterize modern innovation systems as a triple helix of industry, government and university engaged in a collective effort to generate new science and technology. Gibbons et al. (1994) offer a complementary model, starting with the types of knowledge generated rather than with the institutions developing them. They posit that two modes of knowledge generation now exist: Mode 1, which they call traditional knowledge, is generated within disciplinary, primarily cognitive, contexts and governed by stable hierarchies and peer systems; and Mode 2 knowledge is created in broader, 'transdisciplinary' social/ economic networks by diverse, heterogeneous communities involving transient 'heterarchies'. They argue that Mode 2 knowledge tends to be more socially distributed knowledge production system and, hence, is both socially accountable and reflexive. This, they argue, makes Mode 2 knowledge a profound challenge to the traditional governing system because communication tends increasingly to take place across institutional boundaries and not only within established hierarchies.

Perri 6 (2001) suggests what we really are looking at are transformative technologies which represent fundamental changes. Transformative innovations are much more dynamic and expansive than technological iterations. This type of change involves disjointed, step adjustments in our productive and institutional capacity which displaces, destabilizes or overturns pre-existing systems. They are usually driven by new epistemologies, they offer significant complementarities (within and across sectors) and they tend to involve convergent, recombined or hybrid technologies. While they are often enthusiastically announced, they seldom remain under the control of any single sector, market or domain, as they tend to infiltrate and influence other activities over a long and variable timeline. The pervasive and expansive nature of transformative change creates uncertainty—it is seldom clear until well after a launch where, when, how, by whom and why the technology will spread to other uses—which tends to generate significant debate and controversy (Phillips 2007).

This inevitably leads to major gaps in the regulatory architecture for new transformative technologies and their products both domestically and internationally. These gaps may range from the absence of a common vocabulary that can be used to describe the technology's many facets, to customs classifications for the new goods created, to methods for assessing its risks and, ultimately, to methods of measuring its use value. Hence, in the period that follows the first commercial application of a fundamentally new technology there will be considerable national and international activity that attempts to complete the regulatory and governance architecture. As the architecture nears completion the major areas of disagreement become apparent. In the early period there may be considerable duplication of effort, jurisdictional confusion and conflicting outcomes as national and international organisations independently take the initiative to fill the void. There may also be private sector initiatives in international standard setting and trade facilitation (Phillips and Kerr 2000, Phillips 2007).

In the final analysis, the challenge of transformative technological change is not one of developing new information, knowledge, science or technology but a problem of organizing complex human relationships (Amabile et al. 1996).

Governing

The challenge is to examine ruling systems at all levels of human activity—from the family to international organization. In that context, governance encompasses both the activities of governments, and the many other channels through which commands flow in the form of 'goals framed, directives issues, and policies pursued' (Rosenau 1995: 15). Thus, global regulation involves geographic, social, cultural, economic and political processes that transcend boundaries. Once disaggregated, global governing, as political scientist James Rosenau asserts, is 'the sum of myriad—literally millions of—control mechanisms driven by different histories, goals, structures, and processes' (Rosenau 1995:16). In effect, we face new forms of distributed governing arrangements based on a more diffuse pattern of power and a set of 'meso-systems' (Paquet 2001). Distributed governing 'does not simply mean a process of dispersion of power toward localized decision making within each sector: it entails a dispersion of power over a wide variety of actors and groups' (Paquet 2001:190). A seemingly infinite array of distributions of power evolves in response to pressures to adjust to rapid change. 'The fabric of these new "worlds" is defined by the new dominant logic of subsidiarity in all dimensions: it welds together assets, skills and capabilities into complex temporary communities that are as much territories of the mind as anything that can be represented by a grid map' (Paquet 2001:190).

During periods of slow, iterative change the underlying, embedded governing structures of modern economies are not easily discerned. But during periods of major disruptive change, their role and function becomes clearer. The advent of knowledge-based economies has raised new concerns about who's in charge of governing the economy. In the knowledge economy, the key asset is the ability to innovate—the facility to develop, adopt and adapt new ideas, products, and organizational structures by combining existing ideas, products and structures in new ways. Ultimately, this process involves the identification, assembly and use of disparate types of information and knowledge through a wide range of social governing systems. Political scientist Lester Salamon (2002) suggests that finding the right tools to effectively govern in this environment will be difficult because these knowledge networks are plurifom (diverse), self-referential, asymmetrically interdependent and dynamic, and consequently do not share the same goals, operating styles, skills, worldviews, incentives and priorities.

Fundamentally, we are faced with a complex systems problem. There is no single approach to understanding the dimensions of the challenge of governing transformative technology. Economist Herbert Simon (2000:753) examined the concept of complexity in the context of regulation and similarly concluded that:

> the interest in recent years of many sciences in complexity and complex systems has drawn attention to the fact that most of the complex systems seen in the world are nearly decomposable systems. They are arranged in levels, the elements at each lower level being subdivisions of the elements at the level above. Molecules are composed of atoms, atoms of electrons and nuclei, electrons and nuclei of elementary particles. Multicelled organisms are composed of organs, organs of tissues, tissues of cells... Near decomposability is a means of securing the benefits of coordination while holding down its costs by an appropriate division of labour among subunits... nearly decomposable systems will adapt to the changing environment and gain in fitness more rapidly than systems without this property.

Simon (2000: 750) argues that although Adam Smith's invisible hand appears to secure coordination without obvious central planning, 'this invisibility of mutual dependence is deceptive. The usefulness of markets depends on a *shared* knowledge.' He notes that price information is often supplemented with extra-transactional information (such as quality reviews and product standards). As a result, we live in an organization economy, which exhibits a predominance of organizational over market activity (Simon 2000: 751). Given this, he posits that maintaining economic equilibrium cannot be left to the invisible hand of the market but rather requires government action (Simon 2000: 755). Albert Hirschman (1970), an institutional and development economist posited that loyalty, exit and voice form the foundational trilogy of institutional economics. He particularly saw voice as fundamentally a political or collective process whereas exit and loyalty are part of the economic exchange system. No system could survive without all three.

Hence, markets, except in very narrow static analysis, cannot be viewed as independent of other governing processes. Others have characterized the problem in the context of the underlying nature of goods or services: whether they are rivalrous or not; whether they can be made excludable; and whether voice is needed to deliver them (Mahoney 1992, Picciotti 1995). Different balances of these factors will lead to different costs for searching, negotiating and enforcing transactions through the marketplace. Particular institutions—the government sector, the private sector, the participatory sector, and hybrids of these 'pure' types—tend to be best suited to govern particular types of transactions (Mahoney 1992, Picciotti 1995). Each domain represents different individuals, involves different incentives and is effective in producing goods or attributes with specific characteristics.

Political scientists who look at state-to-state relationships in the context of globalization have increasingly been forced to consider new repositories and wielders of power. The traditional state-to-state framing of governance is based on two types of power: relational and structural power. Relational power, conventionally described by realists, is the power of 'A' to get 'B' to do something they would not otherwise do while structural power is the capacity to shape and determine the structures of the global political economy within which others have to operate. The difference is that structural power is not overtly coercive; rather it is the ability to determine how relationships and transactions shall be managed. New power systems facilitate more effective and efficient learning during times of rapid change—decentralized and flexible sub-routines are often based on 'moral contracts' and reciprocal obligations negotiated in the context of evolving partnerships.

This heterarchical system is a world without a pecking order. Instead, it displays 'strange loops' of authority, much like the game of paper, rock, scissors, where no one authority dominates in all circumstances, but rather dominates only under limited conditions (Paquet 2001). Economist Kenneth Boulding (1970) argues that human relationships can be classified as the compulsory, the contractual, and the familistic. The compulsory system involves threats (such as 'you do something for me or I'll do something nasty to you') which fundamentally depend on the credibility of the threat and the capability of the partners to effect their sides of the relationship. These types of arrangement could yield either zero-sum or negative-sum results. The contractual, exchange-based system involves voluntary bids, offers and contracting, which generally yield positive-sum outcomes for both parties. The familistic, integrative system involves status relationships (where one does something because they are a subject, parishioner, student, child ...). This yields three different methods of integration: coercive relations that distribute rights and obligations, led by the state; quid pro quo exchanges in the market governed by Marshallian supply and demand; and voluntary dealings, where cooperation, reciprocity and solidarity engage community and society (Paquet 2001). Boulding (1970:30) argues that society can be viewed as a triangle (his 'social triangle'), where all organizations—including the state, the market and civil authorities—are built on one or a balance of the three relationship systems.

This comprehensive triad of institutions—governments or states, the market and social or familial organizations—form the basis for all governing systems (Boulding, 1970, Paquet 2001, Benacek 2005). Each specific institutional structure tends to be more effective at producing particular types of goods (Picciotto 1995). The government sector is best at producing public goods—low excludability makes privatization infeasible and low voice makes it difficult for the collective sector to organize. The private sector tends to dominate whenever property rights can be assigned to make rival goods excludable. Exclusion allows private firms to sell at least at the marginal cost of production. The participatory sector is best at governing common pool goods—such as marketing services. The collective group will usually have more information that will enable them to more effectively manage the resource and capture the benefits.

Depending on the dominance or balance of these factors, public state, private market or collective authorities may offer the most effective loci for governance. This balancing act, however, does not happen in a vacuum. Rather, these institutions compete at the local or regional, national and international level. There are: discrete local, regional, national and international state-based structures; local and global liberal economic markets; and an array of communal associations, clubs or social action groups that span the range from local to global. We have seen that a number of social processes are producing increasingly greater complexity—competition and interdependence in the economy and society creates new roles for actors to fill; actors are at times being encouraged to add new subsystems and large systems are made up of smaller simpler subroutines. These complex systems inevitably involve variably coupled (from loosely to tightly), interdependent, multiple entities within a dense web of causal connections that is open to external events. The synergies within these open systems may both exhibit non-linear behaviors and generate synergies and feedback that stimulate learning. Canadian political scientist Thomas Homer-Dixon cautions us to avoid getting carried away with the sense of apparent chaos. He notes that although all human systems can exhibit some chaotic behavior,

> unlike natural systems, humans can learn, so they can change their behavior to avoid chaos. Although it is true that many social systems are extraordinarily complex and non-linear, they are not wholly disorganized systems; rather, they exhibit at least partial self-organization (Homer-Dixon 2001: 125).

The result is an ever changing pattern of new actors, playing new roles, often with less transparency of power, authority, accountability and responsibility.

It is important to keep in mind that in this relatively recent period of 'progress' we have done reasonably well. There are few glaring examples of significant, irreversible type I errors—that is, where we have either made errors of commission or have been unable to act to block, isolate and withdraw inherently unworthy or dangerous technologies once their adverse effects are known. In almost every case, new technologies have generated net social benefits, with the benefits far outweighing the costs. That is not to say that some technologies in some specific uses haven't caused harm to some (either anticipated or unanticipated) but, rather, is to say that those harms, though significant for individuals, have been relatively small and insignificant in the context of the use of the entire technology over time or space. More often one can point to circumstances where our inability to respond to a technology or innovation has led to it being delayed or abandoned, triggering a type II error, with the concomitant opportunity cost of not acting.

Implications

Our prevailing systems are challenged to remain efficient, effective and equitable in three significant ways. First, there is a serious question about the nature of the governing challenge—too little or too much control can be equally damaging to transformative change. Second, there would appear to be a greater degree of path dependence slipping into our economies and societies. Although that offers real hope for some, it presents serious challenges for others. Third, in the post-industrial, knowledge-based world we now live in, individuals and groups increasingly want, and probably need, to feel connected to the process of governing in ways that would have been unimaginable in past years.

First, it is unclear what the right amount of governance is. Rosenberg (1994) asserts that transformative technology requires the freedom to conduct experiments. Given the uncertainty about where, when and how new transformative technologies can be usefully adapted and adopted (and by extension our inability to identify who should be engaged), there is a fine balance between over-governing and under-governing the space for transformative innovation. Novelty and diversity, though honored in theory, are often looked on unfavourably or actively discouraged by those who hold power. There is a long history in most societies of the tyranny of the majority who benefit from legacy systems. In the context of innovation, scholars suggest that tolerance of a much larger range of diversity may be vital to attracting, retaining or motivating creative and talented individuals (Florida 2002).

Furthermore, regardless of any potential long term benefits of change, there are always likely to be more people and institutions that will prefer the status quo, because they value the certain, immediate or short-term gains more than the uncertain prospect of higher long-term benefits. Mancur Olson (1965) observed that it is hard to mobilize people to act positively in their own self interest when the benefits are widely distributed—the problem of mobilizing people in support of long-term change is compounded because of our strong preference for short-term results and the corresponding challenge of actually identifying who might have a stake in any change.

In addition, there is significant intolerance in many quarters to either major success or catastrophic failures. As incomes and welfare have risen, we have not always become more satisfied and content. There is evidence that consumers and citizens are increasingly influenced by their perceptions of their relative incomes and wealth rather than their absolute status. Extremes of wealth, though admired in the popular press and culture, elicit strong negative reactions from many individuals, states and civil societies. This sense of injustice at times leads governments to rebalance outcomes by recovering 'windfall' gains through taxation, legislation or policy. Similarly, there is significant unease in boardrooms, governments and civil authorities at losses sustained in the innovation process. As effort is increasingly networked in the inventive and gestation phases, more actors perceive they are acting as paymasters or partners in the process. There is a strong preference to win rather than lose. One result has been the rise of what one might characterize as a 'three stooges' syndrome, whereby actors who might individually have the capacity to work alone are willing to undertake risky or uncertain steps only with the support (real or perceived) of partners (Phillips 2007).

Thus, there is an increasing tendency for collaboration for the sake of risk management and not simply for knowledge generation. This form of strategy may make sense from an individual organization's perspective—as risks and losses are pooled and discounted while gains are often fully appropriated and counted by each partner—but involves significant costs. In many instances, an excess of layers of governing rules and structures is involved, with the corresponding loss of creative energy. Similarly, the emergence of transformative change has raised the perception of untenable losses resulting from the 'gales of creative destruction.' Although there may be some areas where the rate of capital investment and innovation are excessive, in most cases the concern is not that the investments are excessive but that the gains are distributed differently than any potential losses. Government monopolies and corporate oligopolies, in particular, are generally unenthusiastic about stranding capital that still has some economic value (such as schools in rural areas, medical equipment that is no longer cutting edge or existing versions of commercial products or services that may be useful but would be abandoned if new versions became available). By the same token, many citizens, consumers and civil authorities demand (if not practice) conservation of capital. One result is that governments and public regulatory processes are under continuous threat of being 'captured' by firms, innovators or civil authorities seeking either to make more room for innovation or to clamp down on the innovation space.

If the resulting governing systems are at root complex, distributed and interconnected networks of institutions that control the creation, evaluation and commercialization of new technologies, then finding how to create space for innovation is challenging. As with any complex system—with multiple levels of interdependent control, numerous subsystems and many subroutines involving a range of public, private and collective actors—there is a possibility that the system may generate small world effects, where small, discrete changes in any one part of the system may have little or no effect or, in some cases, may have profound, unanticipated consequences. Although policy-makers and industry could use this in a simplistic way to argue either that changes will have no effect or that any changes would be counterproductive, this approach does not need to lead to inaction. Rather, it should lead to a different approach to policy review and development. Thinking of governing as a complex system would suggest that reform should start first with an effort to determine the desired outcomes (including support for innovation, regulatory efficiency, distributional effects or ethical orientation) and then with an examination of the entire complex system as it relates to the desired outcomes. This would in many cases bring in other regulatory and market mechanisms as potential approaches to realize the policy outcome.

One final challenge in governing is that most complex systems ultimately face some diminishing returns. Although making a system more and more complex and interconnected may address problems as they arise, at some point the burden of maintaining such a system is likely to exceed any concurrent benefit. At that point, it often becomes more efficient, effective and equitable to discard the complex system and revert to some simpler form of governing (Wright 2004: 92). Hence, governing systems have to be flexible enough to both expand into areas requiring external management and to retreat when subsidiary capacity has caught up to the challenge.

Second, innovation and knowledge societies appear to exhibit a degree of path dependence that will shape our economies and societies. Neoclassical economic theory—involving the concepts of utility and profit optimization and David Ricardo's theory of comparative advantage—leads to the inexorable conclusion that the geographic distribution of production and consumption will be relatively deterministically defined. Theory posits that the working of the invisible hands of a multitude of optimizing actors and agents will align production and trade, such that regions or countries will produce and export goods and services with factor intensities that reflect their underlying relative factor endowments and will correspondingly import goods and services that have factor intensities that do not align with their factor endowments.

Hence, countries relatively endowed with land, will produce and export goods requiring relatively larger amounts of land (like food or forest products), those relatively endowed with labour will produce goods requiring relatively more workers than other factors (such as textiles) and those relatively endowed with capital will produce and export goods requiring intensive capital investments (such as advanced instrumentation and pharmaceuticals). Although production of a new technology, good or service might conceivably be undertaken in a country without the corresponding comparative advantage, the theory posits that the inexorable forces of the market would drive production towards the country with the appropriate factor endowments. In such a well-defined system, there is little role for the state (Irwin 1996). Whatever it tries would only have a limited term impact if the neoclassical theory holds.

Gilpin (2001) argues that several new theories of economic growth potentially create a new role for the state. The new theories of institutional economics (e.g. Coase 1937; Williamson, 1981), endogenous growth, (e.g. Lucas, 1988, Romer 1990; Grossman and Helpman 1991) and strategic trade (e.g. Spencer and Brander 1983 and Krugman 1996) combine to suggest that there may be localized increasing returns to scale caused by localized external economies of scope. The innovation systems or clusters literature (e.g. Lundvall 1992 and Porter 1990) makes an effort to examine what specific features of specific sectors or regions create this kind of geographic lock-in. Most, but not quite all, of this effort is directed to understanding the economic foundations for the apparent path dependency and observed economic agglomeration in sectors such as fashion, culture, biotechnology, computer programming, manufacturing and advanced instrumentation. Although there is undoubtedly economic agglomeration, it is not clear if it is a result of path dependency and, if there is any dependency, what causes it and whether it can be engineered or governed in a proactive way (David 1985, Arthur 1989).

One interpretation of the economic agglomerations seen around the world is that the nature of the innovation process generates strong localized, non-traded or location-specific externalities that attract highly innovative firms into clusters. Tacit know-how and know-who knowledge underpins much research and development related to transformative technologies and the innovation process often involves face-to-face interactions to function. Hence, those areas of innovation involving exploration, creativity and artifice tend to have a stronger incentive to agglomerate. The economic approach assumes that these linkages and effects exist in absence of any particular institutional or governing system. But governing institutions are clearly one significant variable that differs between sectors, technologies and regions. Some transformative technologies in specific areas are well served by comprehensive, enabling, flexible governing regimes, such that they are able to safely, expeditiously and economically develop and introduce a cascade of innovations. This often happens in economic agglomerations. Others face disjointed, inconsistent, cumbersome and expensive governing regimes, with the result that any technological candidates are ill prepared to enter the market successfully.

The evolution of those governing systems is far more likely to exhibit path dependency than arms-length transactions, if for no other reason than that most institutions are, by definition, a product of historical factors and tend to be located wholly or at least predominantly within a defined region or community (North 1991). Governments by definition are located in the region that elects and funds them, the vast majority of firms are locally-based (even most large multinational enterprises have a majority of their value added, markets and management in their country of origin) and the vast majority of interests and values-based civil authorities are primarily located or connected to a well delineated, geographically connected group of active supporters, adherents and members (Anon 2006). Hence, location still does matter, especially for institutions that claim a role in governing technological change.

This point has not gone unnoticed by others. There has been significant empirical research in recent years as people have attempted to determine the scope and impact of the relationship between the nature of governing systems and various economic outcomes. A range of empirical studies have been done: some have looked at correlations between social capital, state governing and economic outcomes (Putnam et al. 1993, Putnam 2000); some have looked at the relationship between government efficiency (such as corruption, rule of law, macroeconomic policies and trade policy orientation) and growth (World Bank 1997); and others have tested whether democracy is a determinant of growth (Helliwell 1994). Ultimately, path dependency will vary depending on the nature of the event being governed and who takes the lead. If the event fits in one of the pure domains where goods are unambiguously public, private or collective, then there may not be much path dependence. The competition between different institutions would drive the system towards the optimal public, private or collective institutional system. But if a transformative technology involves a good that fits in a hybrid world (where goods exhibit a mix of public, private and collective elements, including rivalry, excludability and voice), then which institution begins will matter a lot. Which governing structure takes the lead will in the end determine where decisions are made and in whose interest those decisions are made. These choices may ultimately determine the future of any transformative change (Phillips 2007).

Third, all governing systems, but especially distributed, nested systems of subroutines, involve hierarchies and these hierarchies inevitably create concerns about accountability (Rhodes 1995). As we become familiar with hierarchies, we tend to become more comfortable with their operation. But when faced with transformative change, governing systems are inevitably going to need to adapt and adopt new subroutines and new relationships to manage emerging risks and opportunities. This adaptation process raises three specific challenges: new structures inevitably require new management skills in governments and elsewhere that often are not fully identified or codified in training systems; new structures usually face questions about their accountability; and institutions that aspire to govern on behalf of others, whether old or new, are increasingly challenged to demonstrate their legitimacy (Salamon 2002). Any governing system needs to meet the prevailing standards of good governance, which involves standards of accountability, responsibility and transparency, what Black (2002) has called the 'ART' of governing.

There is extensive debate and analysis of how ART can be achieved. Although most states have moved to representative forms of government, where those chosen to lead and govern reflect the general interests of those they represent but use their own judgment to make decisions, many forms of delegated governing structures continue in the epistemic communities and industry associations. The ART of governing differs in each circumstance.

In representative systems operating in most nation-state governments and in many values-based civil authorities, there is often only a weak link between specific interests of the governed and decisions of the governors. In those circumstances, accountability is sustained by a balance of customs, rules and conventions that allow for open, transparent governing processes, procedural links between decisions, outcomes and decision makers and periodic opportunities to assess governors through elections. Although this process can work reasonably well in jurisdictions with clearly delimited elections and full and transparent procedures, it becomes particularly problematic when the power to govern is delegated to bureaucracies or to third parties. In these circumstances, transparency is often lost and questions arise about how responsible and accountable the system really is.

Complex governing systems in particular, are challenged to remain ARTful. Nested systems involving complex subroutines are always eyed suspiciously by the average citizen, particularly if the procedures are poorly defined and the decisions are difficult to understand in context. Many have called for our governing systems to become more 'reflexive.' At one level, this makes some sense, as the risks and benefits of any transformative technology are usually unknown, and probably unknowable, by any narrow set of governors. A wide number of actors from throughout the commercialization system, ranging from scholars and researchers in the epistemic community to ultimate consumers can and probably should have a chance to contribute to our assessments of transformative change.

Making our governing systems more reflexive, however, raises two potential problems. First, it will be vitally important for dialogue to be directed to areas where broader input is both valuable and valid. Upstream dialogue which addresses the 'what' of a technology (as in what do we need, what do we want, what will we tolerate) relates directly to values, interests and assumptions and would probably enhance the accountability, responsibility and transparency of our governing systems. The difficulty is that many dialogue processes are poorly structured, so that the debate often focuses on issues of 'how' rather than what. Values, interests and assumptions, though perhaps germane to the earlier stages of review, if engaged at this level often translate into special interests and contribute to regulatory capture. Second, reflexivity is likely not needed in every institution, but rather in the entire system. Thus, we need to find ways to engage in reflexive dialogue both up and downstream in the context of the entire governing system and not necessarily in each component of the system.

Finally, reflexivity is perhaps incompatible with the accountable and responsible state and the efficient market. Although civil authorities can articulate the views of groups in society—both for-profit groups that self-regulate and manage market functions such as pre-commercial, non-competitive research, standards setting and market development and not-for-profit social action groups that represent segments of society that cannot be adequately addressed by private or public actors—few are truly ARTful. Governments and industry have engaged a wide array of civil authorities in their systems designed to govern transformative technologies but there has been little thought directed to how one can ensure these organizations are truly voicing the views of a segment of society. Many are simply vehicles for special interests. Gilpin (2001) has suggested that at the extreme, there is a risk that we may end up with a neo-medieval system where we are over-governed by a complex web of vested interests, analogous to the guild structure of the middle ages. If we wish to avoid such an outcome, the public and private sectors will need to sort out what in their view constitutes a duly-constituted civil authority and then work with the various authorities to encourage them to develop appropriate governance models.

Although many civil authorities may adequately reflect the view of their members or adherents, the lack of transparency, formal accountability and procedures to ensure responsibility of their leadership undermines their long-term efficacy as vehicles for voice. Governing institutions need to aspire much more to be accountable, responsible and transparent in order to create and sustain the legitimacy of the overall governing system and its decisions. Our long-term economic and social future will depend on how we take up this challenge.

Bibliography

6, Perri. 2001. "Governing by technique: judgement and prospects for the governance of and With technology." In OECD, *Governance in the 21st Century*, Paris: OECD, accessed August 20, 2005 at <http://www.oecd.org/dataoecd/15/0/17394484.pdf, pp. 67–120>.

Amabile, M. Teresa, Regina Conti, Heather Coon, Jeffrey Lazenby and Michael Herron. 1996. "Assessing the work environment for creativity." *The Academy of Management Journal* 39(5): 1154–1184.

Anon. 2006. "Decoupled." *The Economist*, Feb 23.

Arthur, W. Brian. 1989, "Competing technologies, increasing returns and lock-in by historical events." *Economic Journal* 99(394): 116–31.

Bell, Daniel. 1973. *The Coming of Post-Industrial Society*. New York: Harper Colophon Books.

Benacek, Vladimir. 2005. "Three dimensions of modern social governance: Markets, hierarchies and kinships." *Pracovni Sesity Working Papers*, 1/2005.

Black, Julia. 2002. *"Critical reflections on regulation."* Australian Journal of Legal Philosophy 27:1–35.

Boulding, E. Kenneth, ed. 1970. *A Primer on Social Dynamics: History as Dialectics and Development*. London: Collier MacMillan Ltd.

Coase, Roland. 1937. "The nature of the firm." *Economica* 4(16): 386–405.

Darwin, Charles. 1859. *The Origin of Species by Means of Natural Selection: or, the Preservation of Favoured Races in the Struggle for Life*. London: J. Murray, 1906.

David, A. Paul. 1985. "Clio and the economics of QWERTY." *American Economic Review Papers and Proceedings* 75: 332–7.

Etzkowitz, Henry and Loet Leydesdorff. 1995. "The triple helix: university-industry government relations. A laboratory for knowledge based economic development." *European Society for the Study of Science and Technology Review* 14: 14–9.

Florida, Richard. 2002. *The Rise of the Creative Class and How It's Transforming Work, Leisure and Everyday Life*. New York: Basic Books.

Freeman, Christopher. 1987. *Technology Policy and Economic Performance: Lessons from Japan*. London/New York: SPRU/Pinter Publishers.

Furman, L. Jeffrey, Michael E. Porter and Scott Stern. 2002. "The determinants of national innovative capacity." *Research Policy* 31:899–933.

Gibbons, Michael, Camille Limoges, Helga Nowotny, Simon Schwartzman, Peter Scott and Martin Trow.1994. *The New Production of Knowledge*. London: Sage Publications.

Gilpin, Robert. 2001. *Global Political Economy: Understanding the International Economic Order*. Princeton: Princeton University Press.

Grossman, M. Gene and Elhanan Helpman. 1991. *Innovation and Growth in the Global Economy*. London: The MIT Press.

Helliwell, F. John. 1994. "Empirical linkages between democracy and economic growth." *British Journal of Political Science* 24(2): 225–48.

Hirschman, O. Albert. 1970. *Exit, Voice and Loyalty*. Cambridge, MA: Harvard University Press.

Homer-Dixon, Thomas. 2001. *The Ingenuity Gap*. Toronto: Vintage Canada.

Irwin, A. Douglas. 1996. *Against the Tide: An Intellectual History of Free Trade*. Princeton, NJ: Princeton University Press.

Jensen, Morten, Bjorn Johnson, Ned Lorenz and Bengt-Ake Lundvall. 2004. "Codification and modes of innovation." Paper presented at the DRUID Summer Conference, Elsinore, DK, June 14–16.

Krugman, Paul, ed. 1996. *Strategic Trade Policy and the New International Economy*. Cambridge: MIT Press.

Lucas, R. 1988. "On the mechanics of economic development." *Journal of Monetary Economics* 22: 30–42.

Lundvall, Bengt-Ake, ed. 1992. *National Systems of Innovation: Towards a Theory of Innovation and Interactive Learning.* New York: Pinter.

Lundvall, Bengt-Ake and Bjorn Johnson. 1994. "The Learning Economy." *Journal of Industry Studies* 1(2): 23–42.

Mahoney, T. Joseph. 1992. "The choice of organisational form: vertical financial ownership Versus other methods of vertical integration." *Strategic Management Journal* 13(8): 559–84.

Malbera, Franco and Luigi Orsenigo. 1990. "Technological regimes and patters of innovation: a theoretical and empirical investigation of the Italian case", in Arnol Heertje and Mark Perlman, eds., *Evolving technology and market structure: Studies in Schumpeterian Economics.* Anne Arbor: University of Michigan Press, pp. 283–305.

Malecki, J. Edward. 1997. *Technology and economic development: the dynamics of local, regional and national competitiveness.* Toronto: Longman.

Marshall, Alfred. 1890. *Principles of economics.* London: Macmillan.

Metcalfe, J. Stanley. 1995. "Technology systems and technology policy in an evolutionary framework." *Cambridge Journal of Economics* 19: 25–46.

Mokyr, Joel. 2002. "Innovation in an historical perspective: tales of technology and evolution." In Ben Steil, David G. Victor and Richard R. Nelson, eds., *Technological innovation and economic performance.* Princeton: Princeton University Press, pp. 23–46.

North, C. Douglas. 1991. "Institutions." *Journal of Economic Perspectives* 5(1): 97–112.

Olson, Mancur. 1965. *The logic of collective action: public goods and the theory of groups.* Cambridge, MA: Harvard University Press.

OECD. 1996. *The knowledge based economy.* Paris: OECD, accessed at <http://www .oecd.org/dsti/sti /s_t/inte/prod/kbe.htm>.

OECD. 2001. *Governance in the 21st century.* Paris: OECD, accessed August 20, 2005 at <http://www.oecd.org/dataoecd/15/0/17394484.pdf>.

Paquet, Gilles. 2001. "The new governance, subsidiarity and the strategic state", in OECD, *Governance in the 21st Century,* Paris: OECD, accessed on August 20, 2005 at http://www.oecd.org/dataoecd/15/0/17394484.pdf.

Phillips, Peter. 2007. *Governing transformative technological innovation: who's in charge?* Oxford: Edward Elgar.

Phillips, Peter and William A. Kerr. 2000. "Alternative paradigms: the WTO versus the Biosafety Protocol for trade in genetically modified organisms." *Journal of World Trade* 34(4): 63–75.

Picciotto, Roberto. 1995. "Putting institutional economics to work: from participation to governance." *World Bank Discussion Paper 304*, accessed August 15, 2005 at <http://www wds.worldbank.org/servlet/WDSContentServer/WDSP/ IB/1995/09/ 01/000009265_396 219115337/Rendered /PDF /multi_page.pdf>.

Polanyi, Michael. 1962. "The Republic of Science: Its Political and Economic Theory." *Minerva* 1: 54–74.

Putnam, Robert, Robert Leonardi and Rafaella Nanetti. 1993. *Making Democracy Work: Civic Traditions in Modern Italy*. Princeton: Princeton University Press.

Putnam, Robert. 2000. *Bowling Alone: The Collapse and Revival of American Community*. London: Simon & Schuster.

Porter, Michael. 1990. *The Comparative Advantage of Nations*. New York: Free Press.

Rhodes, Rod. 1995. *The new governance: governing without government*. The State of Britain Seminar II of a Joint ESRC/RSA seminar series, January 24.

Romer, Paul. 1990. "Endogenous technological change." *Journal of Political Economy* 98(5:2):S71–S102.

Rosenau, James. 1995. "Governance in the twenty-first century." *Global Governance* 1:13–43.

Rosenberg, N. 1994. *Exploring the Black Box: Technology, Economics and History*. Cambridge: Cambridge University Press.

Ruttan, W. Vernon. 2003. *Social Science Knowledge and Economic Development: An Institutional Design Perspective*. Ann Arbor: University of Michigan Press.

Salamon, M. Lester, ed., 2002. *The tools of government: a guide to new governance*, Oxford: Oxford University Press.

Schumpeter, Joseph. 1934. *The theory of economic development*. Cambridge, MA: Harvard University Press.

Schumpeter, Joseph. 1939. *Business cycles: a theoretical, historical and statistical analysis of the capitalist process*. New York: McGraw-Hill.

Simon, Herbert. 2000. "Public administration in today's world of organizations and markets." PS: *Political Science and Politics* 33(4): 749–56.

Spencer, Barbara and James Brander. 1983. "International R&D rivalry and industrial strategy." *Review of Economic Studies* 50: 707–22.

Stehr, Nico. 1994. *Knowledge Societies*. London: Sage.

Strange, Susan. 1988. *States and Markets*. London: Pinter.

UNESCO. 2003. *"Towards Knowledge Societies: An Interview with Abdul Waheed Khan."* At <http://portal.unesco.org/ci/en/ev.php-URL_ID=11958&URL_DO=DO _TOPIC&URL_SECTION=201.html>.

Williamson, E. Oliver. 1981. "The economics of organization: transaction cost approach." *American Journal of Sociology* 87(3): 548–577.

World Bank. 1997. *World Development Report 1997: The State in a Changing World.* Washington: The World Bank Group.

Wright, Ronald. 2004. *A short history of progress.* Toronto: Anansi.

CHAPTER TEN

PUBLIC POLICY ACTORS AND THE KNOWLEDGE-BASED SOCIAL ORDER

Michael W. Kpessa

Since the 1990s the discourse and the art of public policy making shifted from the state-centred bureaucratic and elite decision-making approaches to popular participation and citizenry consultation. This occurred within the context of what is generally perceived as 'good governance', broadly defined to include co-production of policy contents in a way that involves actors beyond bureaucrats and elected officials (Williams 2008). This shift is attributed to the following: (1) the emergence of knowledge economy as alternative to the state and market based approaches to ordering society (Drucker 1993, World Bank 1998, Nonka and Takeuchi 1995, Florida 1995, Drucker 1993); (2) the increasing recognition that bureaucrats and politicians do not have monopoly over policy, and that the public as policy beneficiaries must be actively consulted and involved in the policy processes (Bishop and Davis 2002, Clarke 2005, Needham 2007); (3) the rise of alternative yet additional centres of knowledge production (Etzkowitz 2003, Hessels and Lente 2008, Gibbons et al. 1994); and (4) the growing debates and ambiguities about the exact role of traditional institutions of higher learning in society (Osborne 2004, Dzisah 2007, Hargreaves 1999, Godin and Gingras 2000).

In the area of public policy making, this shift is reflected primarily in the rise and intensified activism of non-conventional policy actors in competing, cooperating, collaborating and challenging the position of the actors who hitherto exercise exclusive control over public policy processes. The new actors described collectively in this chapter as 'knowledge-based actors' have been variously depicted as epistemic community, policy networks, policy community, transnational actors, global policy actors, and policy entrepreneurs in the wider public policy literature. They are also defined by their strong emphasis on knowledge, and primarily differentiated from the conventional policy actors by their resort to the use of open and direct advocacy in promoting their pet policy ideas. The epistemological character of these types of policy actors is rooted in their role as quasi-centres of knowledge production and active disseminators of innovations.

This chapter analyzes the changing dynamics of the public policy making against the background of the emergence and active participation of new actors defined primarily by epistemology in what is now widely perceived as the knowledge society. It shows that although, existing analyses of the new policy actors in the emerging knowledge society remains fuzzy, the rise of such actors has resulted in a gradual shift from policy making based purely on cost benefit analysis to policy learning and knowledge transfer. Thus, acting as the mediators of learning and knowledge transfer, these actors adopt various strategies to diffuse new policy ideas across time and space. The chapter further discusses the changing patterns and complexities of modern public policy making in which the traditional boundaries between bureaucratic actors on one hand, and non-bureaucratic policy actors—the so called knowledge-based actors—and civil society groups on the other have diminished. A conceptual roadmap is provided for scholars interested in doing empirical study of knowledge-based actors or others involved in a policy domain in any specific national setting.

The chapter is divided in to six sections. While the first section provides an analysis of the intellectual context of public policy making in the knowledge society, the second section discusses the non-conventional policy actors engaged in various forms of ideational campaigns designed purposely to shape domestic policy processes. Section three focuses on the rise and emphasis on policy learning as an integral part of contemporary policy-making by arguing that it has enhanced the opportunity structures of knowledge-based actors to serve as diffusers of innovations. Three specific mechanisms through which knowledge and innovations are transferred from centres of knowledge production are examined in section four. The ways through which knowledge-based actors sought the attention of national policymakers, elected officials and citizens especially in relation to issue-framing and problem definition in the context of multiple actors are examined in section five while, the last section examines the possible implications of the changing patterns for overall policy governance.

The Intellectual Context of Contemporary Public Policy

One of the remarkable developments in the social sciences since the 1990s was the renewed interest in the relationship between knowledge, policy making and power. This new curiosity was couched in the form of evidence-based policy making with the added expectation that social scientists and other practitioners must arm national policy makers with evidence as to what works, why and what policy ideas have the greater propensity to generate expected outcomes (Parsons 2002). Although this concern was central to the emergence of the policy sciences (Lasswell 1951), the idea of grounding policy content on sound knowledge and solid evidence has until recently been consigned to the margins of both policy and academia (Fischer 1998, Lindblom 1990, De Loen 1997).

Until the renewed interest in knowledge and policy-making nexus, policy making has for the most part been about "muddling through rather than a process in which the social sciences or policy sciences have had an influential part to play" (Parsons 2002: 43). The notion that research in the social sciences does not influence policy-making in a substantive way is attributed to the fact that academics and policy makers mostly only interact after the policy processes have been exhausted. As noted by Jonathan Lomas, researchers often arrive at the tail end of the policy process, "brandishing their study after the issue has been framed within a particular context, after the various claimants for a voice have been adjudicated, the procedures for negotiation and exchange agreed upon, and often after the limits have been set around feasible options" (2000:140).

Similarly, national policy-makers often treat the research community like a retail store bringing in complicated questions and urgent deadlines that can hardly be met in the context of the requirements of conducting thorough research. Others argue that conducting research for the purpose of prescribing solutions for policy challenges could potentially undermine academic freedom and research as an art of curiosity (Findlay and Bidwell 2001). Against this background, emerged the evidence-based movement challenging the assumptions and the barriers that separate social scientific research and knowledge from being an integral part of modern policy-making. This movement, which started in health studies, has now spread to several policy areas including criminology, education, social work, economic, monetary, social security, labour market, and biotechnology policies (Trinder and Reynolds 2000, Thomas and Pring 2004).

The evidence-based movement argued that policy making should be based on solid and sound knowledge generated through rigorous research and presented in the form of systemic reviews or synthesis of findings from all important studies that meets specified and widely accepted methodological rigour (Hammersley 2001, Loughlin 2003). Thus, the fundamental role of evidence based on research knowledge in policy making is emphasized, while the reliability of experience and professional judgment as alternative sources of gathering oriented information is questioned. In the process, it was concluded that "because professionals sometimes do more harm than good when they intervene in the lives of people, their policies and practices should be informed by rigorous, transparent and up-to-date evaluations" (Chalmers 2003:22). A premise of the evidence-based movement is that research, whether it is done by governments, think tanks, academic institutions or any other group of individuals can offer knowledge about which policies and ideas have the higher probability of making the most positive impact. The expectation is that this can either be drawn from the experiences of other contexts, through focus group analysis or through other forms of feasibility studies.

The movement also argued that because the media as well as the public hardly pays attention to how policy information is generated, and individual scholars too have the tendency to overstate their research findings, knowledge-based evidence for policy-making must be in the form of reviews of the available literature and presented to lay audiences as well as to the national policy makers (Hammersley 2005, Chalmers 2003). In support of the movement's agenda, some governments especially in OECD countries challenged social scientists in academia and elsewhere to either make their research programs relevant to policy content or remain "largely irrelevant to the real debates that affect people's life chances" (Blunkett 2000:1). Similarly, transnational actors, especially the World Bank responded to criticisms of its trial and error cum one-size-fits all approach to structural adjustment in developing countries by highlighting knowledge as the essential component for development. The legacy of these developments was the (re)emergence of several different groups—knowledge-based actors—at both the domestic and international levels serving not only as mediators and carriers of innovative policy ideas from one jurisdiction to another, but also as quasi centers of knowledge production.

The Knowledge-Based Policy Actors

The proliferation of several non-traditional policy actors such as thinks tanks, individual experts, groups of individuals, transnational actors,

universities, and research institutes collectively referred to in the literature as epistemic community, coincided with a paradigmatic shift
towards citizenry engagement and participatory policy making. This
has opened the policy space beyond the scope of the corporatist and
pluralist theses on public policy making. The epistemic community
refers to a broader group of policy entrepreneurs with shared interest
in a policy area and a commitment to influencing the direction of
policy over time (Atkinson and Coleman 1992). They engaged in networking, that is, the mechanism through which contemporary policy
actors develop, discuss, share, spread and sustain a policy discourse
with government units and like-minded external policy actors. Policy
networking occurs at various levels and places especially through the
exchange of ideas at local and international seminars, workshops and
conferences (Mintrom and Vergari 1998).

Despite the growing involvement of policy entrepreneurs in policy
making process and the corresponding increased scholarly attention,
there is a lot of ambiguity and confusion about what exactly constitutes
policy epistemic community. Sutton (1999) for instance, argued that
an epistemic community refers to a closely-knit group of policy experts
from an array of institutions such as non-governmental organizations,
international organizations, research institutions who share and discuss similar beliefs and have access to privilege information to which
others have no access and are excluded. Thatcher (1998) on the other
hand, argued that epistemic community refers to civil servants located
in or within various units of government departments usually working
on policies, different from policy networks. For Thatcher, this represents a variety of issue-skilled individuals or policy activists coming
from various establishments such as the academia, circles of government, and others experts irrespective of professional training. Thatcher,
(1998) further indicated that the difference between the two concepts
is best understood when policy communities are seen as symbolizing
the divergence between policy insiders and outsiders, and policy
networks as the increasing shift towards open and inclusive policy
making.

In the last few decades, a great deal of scholarly attention has been
directed towards distinguishing the various concepts often used to
describe the new knowledge-based actors and what they do in contemporary policy making processes. Smith (1993) argued that policy networks are ubiquitous and all over the place but epistemic community
describes well-resourced social groupings that assist the state in making and implementing specific policies. Here, the concepts are used

almost exclusively in relation to the domestic policy environment. In another study, Atkinson and Coleman (1992), indicated that the relevance of policy networks and epistemic communities in policy-making goes beyond the level of the domestic settings to include interactions among policy actors at local, national and supranational levels. In their view, the growing interest in horizontal management meant that policy networking by epistemic communities has become the strategy for transmitting knowledge and ideas across time and space, and between the local and the global. This understanding of epistemic communities projects them as agents for policy learning and carriers of new policy ideas across time and space.

For the most part, the concepts employed in analyzing policy networks and/or epistemic communities do not lend themselves to easy operationalization and application in empirical research (Thatcher 1998). This problem is partially due to the inability of policy scholars to make a systematic distinction of new actors—a situation compounded by the use of different terminologies to describe similar actors and their activities. Boase (1996) noted that differences in the way scholars treat the concepts used in describing these new actors is a function of whether a scholar's analysis is located within corporatists or pluralist framework. Early studies in the United States employed the term 'network' to examine the role of a limited number of privileged groups (iron triangle) and their relationship with government (McConnell 1966, Heclo 1978). In addition, there is a distinction between Anglo-Saxon and a continental usage and application of policy network in contemporary research. March (1998) argued that Anglo-Saxon approach to network and epistemic community analysis is concerned with the actual and empirical presence of interest groups in policy-making process.

In continental Europe, however, network analysis is seen as a change in the reconfiguration of policy making. Arguably, the use and application of epistemic community and policy networks has been influenced not only by scholars' epistemological standpoint on the changes in policy-making, but also within the issue area, time and place in which their analysis is situated. For instance, several contemporary studies used different concepts but emphasize in one way or the other the following; transnational networks, international organizations, non-governmental organizations, state agencies, think tanks, pressure groups, transnational corporations and cross-national professional associations, academic experts, policy entrepreneurs, and bureaucrats as the main agents for the dissemination of innovations (Dolowitz

1998, Meseguer 2006, Newmark 2002; Orenstein 2003 and 2005, Rogers 1995, Simmons et al. 2006, Stone 1999 and 2001, Strange and Meyer 1993, Weyland 2005 and 2006, Orenstein 2005, Meseguer 2004). It is assumed that these policy actors are involved in providing alternative policy frameworks, critiquing existing policy models; exchanging information at conferences, workshops or seminars and symposia; advocating change; providing expert advice; and assisting with implementation of innovations (Newmark 2002, Stone 1999).

In an attempt to navigate the possibility of conceptual stretching and the analytical fuzziness that is associated with how contemporary knowledge-based policy actors are studied, other scholars introduced the term 'global policy' actors as an umbrella concept that provides a universe for existing and new actors involved in the processes of knowledge production and policy-oriented information sharing (Deacon 2007, Orenstein 2003, 2005, 2005 and 2008, Orenstein and Haas 2002). This categorization is illustrative but problematic since it lumps universities and all the various knowledge-based actors into the same universe without any analytical distinction. The use of multiple terminologies to describe the new actors in policy making renders them analytically fuzzy in the absence of institutional typology and consensus. However, categorizing them as new knowledge-based actors allows for realistic assessment and mapping of actors involved a policy making , as well as, the impact their interactions and relationships have on final policy decisions. It allows for analyzing the patterns of organized and unorganized relationships that shape policy agenda and decision-making processes in a given issue area (Parsons 1995).

Thus, the notion of other actors in public policy beyond the traditional bureaucrats provides a framework for understanding empirical observations that approximate critical changes in a given policy space and governance structures of modern societies (Kenis and Schneider 1991). In other words, analysis of epistemic community and policy networks or transnational actors helps to unravel the nature of interaction among different actors who share similar interests in a given policy area; and are willing to commit their financial, human and other resources for the purposes of achieving or harmonizing their interest (Borzel 1997).

The Shift Towards Policy Learning

Since the 1990s, labels such as, 'lesson-drawing' (Rose 1993), 'policy shopping' (Freeman 1999), 'policy brand-wagoning' (Ikenberry 1990), 'external inducement' (Ikenberry 1990), 'policy taking' (Carroll et al. 2003), 'direct coercive transfer'(Dolowitz and Marsh 1996) and 'systematically pinching ideas' (Schneider and Helen 1998) among others have been used in a attempt to capture the processes by which knowledge or new policy ideas are created and disseminated across different national jurisdictions. This illustrates not only the growing attention to policy learning as an integral part of contemporary policy making, but also an indicative of the influence of the new knowledge-based actors. Policy learning has been used extensively to explain both policy change and adoption of innovations in multiple national jurisdictions (Dolowitz and Marsh 2000, Dolowitz 1998, Evans and Davies 1999, Freeman 2007, Haas 1980, Rose 1993). Stone argues that policy learning denotes a "broader concept encompassing ideas of diffusion and coercion as well as the voluntaristic activity of lesson-drawing" (1999: 52). While the last two decades has witnessed a bourgeoning literature on policy learning, the act of policy learning itself is seen as being facilitated by the process of globalization (Evans 2006, Evans and Davies 1999, Freeman 2007, Levi-Faur and Vigoda-Gadot 2004, Rose 1993).

The significance of learning in this era is that, the focus is directed more at cross-national settings rather than domestic situations (Bissessar 2002, Dolowitz and Marsh 2000, Evans 2006, Hulme 2005, Levi-Faur and Vigoda-Gadot 2004, Wolman 1992). In addition, the scope of actors traditionally associated with policy learning has expanded to include non-governmental actors—epistemic communities, policy networks and experts (Greener 2002, Haas 1992, Hulme 2005, Stone 1999). Interest in the field has also shifted to the analysis of learning and transfer from developed to developing countries to include policy learning among developing countries (Larmour 2002). Evans observes that up "until recently, the study of policy transfer from developed to developing countries and, from developing countries to developing and developed countries [had] largely been ignored" (2006:12).

The emergence of knowledge-based actors, however, has dismantled this wall of policy learning making it possible for policy ideas to flow in all directions. According to Rose (1993) policy learning denotes "a programme for action based on a programme or programmes undertaken in another city, state, or national, or by the same organization in its own past" (p. 21). Some other scholars intimated that learning implies change in causal beliefs or policy choices based on lessons from the experience of others (Meseguer 2004, 2005 and 2006, Dobbin

et al. 2007, Simmons et al. 2006). Morrissey and Nelson (2003) identified two models of policy learning— decision-theoretical learning and
social learning. Decision-theoretical learning occurs when policy-
makers learn exclusively by doing. Policy-makers adopt a policy and
based on its outcomes after implementation, they evaluate the effectiveness of the policy against beliefs underlining existing alternatives.

Social learning is seen as the spread of new information that provides the basis for political elites to make new policy decisions. It is
a "process in which individuals apply new information and ideas to
policy decisions" (Busenberg 2001:173). According to Ikenberry
(1990:103), social learning is "the spread of new knowledge about the
way the world works." Hall defines it as "a deliberate attempt to adjust
the goals or techniques of policy in response to past experience and
new information" (1993:278). Morrissey and Nelson (2003) argue that
social learning occurs when policy-makers in a learning state observe
the choices made by policy-makers in other jurisdictions in a process
often but not always mediated by actors other than bureaucrats. Heclo
(1974) intimated that policy learning is engineered by social forces
who take advantage of socio-economic development and political
competition to influence policy change. Etheredge (1982) acknowl-
edges the role of social forces in policy learning, but argues that learning in policy circles can take place both at the individual or
organizational level. Bennett and Howlett (1992) posit that social
forces—policy networks, communities—and government institutions
are essential policy actors in the learning process.

Policy learning is thus, regarded as a horizontal activity that symbol-
izes how a "policy is passed or diffused from one nation to another"
(Meseguer 2005:72). In other words, policy is a demonstration of how
actions and activities of nations affect each other in a process mediated
by non-conventional actors. However, there is a general understanding
that policy-makers learn from experience with past policies and alter
their actions on the basis of their interpretation of how previous decision have fared in the past (Bennett and Howlett 1992). A search across
political spheres can provide an idea of what can be learned from
responses to a similar problem in another setting. But a key concern in
the policy learning literature is whether policy learning is a continuous, momentary, purposive, active or passive. For Heclo (1974), however, policy learning is a continuous change in government attitude in
response to external inducement. Hall (1993) also maintained that
policy learning is more a conscious effort on the part of policy makers

to alter policy objectives and mechanisms given the consequences of previous policies and the availability of new information. In the view of Etheredge (1982), policy learning is the process by which governments acquire and increase their knowledge base for the purposes of rendering their actions effective. Meseguer argues that policy learning, is not only voluntary and purposive, it is also based on a "better understanding of which policies may lead to particular outcomes" (2005:73).

Confronted with difficult policy decisions, policy-makers engage in 'policy shopping' for good practice by exploring results of particular policies from other national jurisdictions. Thus, the adoption of innovations is based on the notion that policy makers are convinced that such innovations are the best (Meseguer 2005). The assumption here is that policy makers have access to all the information required to do a cost-benefit analysis of a policy innovation before adopting it. The question is whether policy makers rely on perfect information or resort to shortcuts in the policymaking process. Analysts and scholars exploring this concern from rational learning perspective argue that policy learning is grounded on the assumption that policy makers are driven mainly by self-interest and have the capacity to "approximate principles of comprehensive rationality" (Weyland 2005:271). As a result, the emergence of a problem triggers a frantic search for solution through the scanning of relevant information within the international system. If in the process of analyzing the information obtained, any foreign ideas or practices demonstrate superiority over existing policies, such innovations are adopted (Weyland 2005).

Rational learning, therefore, is defined as the process of acquiring new and relevant information that allows policy makers to update their beliefs about the impact of a new policy (Meseguer 2005 and 2006). Policy makers are interested in relating new policies to their particular circumstances, and the experience of first or original movers becomes the basis for making cost-benefit calculations. Where the experience of first movers demonstrates remarkable success or meets efficiency goals, the innovation stands a better chance of being replicated by other countries. Rational learning is, therefore, seen as a process that leads to policy convergence (Meseguer 2006, Weyland 2005). From the perspective of bounded rationality, however, policy-makers are said to be limited in their ability to learn everything there is to know about a policy.

As a result, instead of pursuing the 'futile effort' of acquiring perfect information, they update their beliefs about a policy by relying on cognitive shortcuts (McDermott 2001). In other words, rather than "scanning all information" (Meseguer 2005:72), policy-makers reach out for what in their view are the most relevant and useful information. In such situations, policy makers simply turn attention to information that is geographically, culturally and historically close to the policy learning environment (Meseguer 2005). This means policy innovations attract dissimilar attention from neighbouring and other countries because policy-makers may only be interested in the basic principles of the innovation; and adopt those basic principles with adjustments to fit their specific circumstances (Weyland 2005). Huber (1991) noted that policy makers learn if, in the course of processing new information, their range of potential behaviours changes.

Whereas rational learning frameworks are used to analyze policy convergence among different countries, bounded rationality frameworks have guided analyses that seek to explain why different countries adopting a specific prevailing policy innovations diverge in the final institutional arrangements (Weyland 2006). James and Lodge (2003) argued that recent analyses of rational policy learning are nothing but re-packaged versions of the conventional model of rational decision-making. The traditional model postulates that when policy-makers are confronted with a policy problem, their search for solution most often explores four interrelated options. These options are setting goals to solve the problem, exploring all alternative options, examining the merits and demerits of all the options, and finally selecting the options that best resolves the problem or involves the least cost (Howlett and Ramesh 1995).

Similarly, bounded rational learning derives much of its premises from existing assumptions of the incremental decision-making model. This approach to policy making assumes that once confronted with problems, policy makers consider only limited options, combine values and goals in their analysis of policy challenges and become preoccupied with problems to be solved than searching for positive goals. They may also engage in trial and error by revising tried attitudes to the problem, do limited analysis of the consequences of chosen options even if the decision-making process involves many participants. Policy making is, here, seen as a process of political interaction—bargaining and compromise—among several self-interested actors. Hence, policy outcomes are perceived as the product of what is politically feasible rather than desirable (Howlett and Ramesh 1995).

However, Meseguer (2005) argued that both strands of policy learning—rational and bounded rationality—are united by the purposive acts of problem identification and search for solution. That is to say that the art of choosing solutions is based on observed experience and a better understanding of perceived outcomes. Though both rational and bounded rational policy learning pay attention to 'experience', they are divided by how experience is weighed based on innovations or new knowledge (Meseguer 2006). Both models are necessary for our understanding of policy change, policy convergence and policy divergence in different countries. There is nothing wrong with the availability of multiple learning processes. Besides, we must not expect uniformity in the processes of learning as the process is mediated by several institutional and contextual factors that impact the adoption of innovations.

In a nutshell, the increasing role of knowledge-based actors in policy making has positioned them as catalysts for international knowledge diffusion, providing new opportunities within and across national boundaries. Similarly, the rise of computer-mediated digital technologies, which permits the simultaneous manipulation and transmission of voice, video, and data, has created new opportunities for policy learning and knowledge exchange between and among domestic and global actors. This, in a way highlights the relevance of the new policy actors. The growth of policy learning in the increasingly knowledge-based social order, as an indispensable component of modern policy making, provides avenues for the policy actors to network and influence public policy-making within several jurisdictions.

Mechanisms for Mediating Policy Processes

The participation of new knowledge-based actors in policy-making, the emphasis on policy learning and transfer of ideas requires a thorough understanding of the mechanisms through which these actors influence or mediate the policy processes as carriers of knowledge from one location to another. There are three main mechanisms of knowledge transfer—coordination, inducement and interaction—used by the contemporary knowledge-based actors.

First, because most knowledge-based actors lack the necessary political legitimacy to directly make policies at the domestic level, they often utilize the instrument of policy coordination by deploying the legitimacy embedded in international or regional state organizations. Also, by simply evoking broader definitions of governance, which require active and open participation of multiple actors in the policy-making processes, these new policy actors find a route to the larger policy domain. In either case, the knowledge-based actors assigned themselves the role of setting a broader policy paradigm within which policies of countries must be aligned. For example, through its benchmarking and indicators program, the OECD has been successful in not only setting major educational policy agenda, but also coordinating the formulation and implementation of specific policy ideas pertaining to life-long learning in member countries (Dingeldey and Rothang 2009).

Second, knowledge transfer involves inducement of domestic actors especially by transnational actors acting in collaboration with national policy networks that share similar epistemological positions. Under the inducement strategy, powerful knowledge-based actors, especially international organisations and international non-governmental organizations set requirements that include the adoption of specific policy prescriptions or ideas by weaker nations or members of an international institution as a basis for aid, loan, and/or technical assistance (Dobbin et al. 2007). Such requirements often compel aid-recipient countries to adopt specific policy ideas espoused or supported by the donor institutions and countries. This compulsive strategy serves as a means by which donor countries promote their policy ideas and exerts influence over aid-dependent countries. For instance, the move towards private social security as a contemporary policy innova-tion in different national settings can best be explained through an analysis and understanding of a vertical imposition and coercive trans-·fer of knowledge emanating, especially, from the World Bank and the International Monetary Fund (IMF) (Dietmar and Gilardi 2006).

The force associated with policy imposition is exercised by interna-tional organizations, governments and nongovernmental actors by means of sanctions and threats (Owen 2002), information or expertise monopolization, and manipulation of economic cost and benefit strategies (Dobbin et al. 2007). Stated differently, influential knowl-edge-based actors encourage knowledge transfer and the adoption of innovations, especially, in developing countries by utilizing the "car-rots and sticks" instruments (Weyland 2005) not only because of their unmatched pecuniary resources and research infrastructure, but also because of the desperate circumstances of governments in the least developed nations. As such, Brooks (2002) argued that policy innovations developed or supported by powerful knowledge-based actors such as the World Bank and the IMF are more likely to be easily transferred to countries that benefit from loans and development assis-tance provided by these transnational actors.

A significant number of recent studies generally concur that the major explanatory variable for the transfer of neo-liberal policy ideas across many countries in the world since the 1980s can be traced to the strategy of inducement adopted by the transnational actors acting in collaboration with domestic policy networks with whom they share common policy positions (Brooks 2002 and 2006, Stallings 1992, Orenstein 2005 and 2008). In fact, the transfer and spread of innovative practices, especially, in the area of social protection in many countries could not have taken place without the influence of norms and ideas spread by the leading transnational actors and epistemic communities of the day (Orenstein 2003). Thus, inducement as a policy transfer strategy enables knowledge-based actors to exploit the weakness of national policy makers due to the embedded power asymmetries. Huber and Stephens (2000), noted that the conditions attached to aid and assistance were the main instruments for inducing policy diffusion and knowledge transfer.

The third mechanism through which knowledge-based actors mediate transfer of innovative ideas across different national jurisdiction is based on a broader sociologically informed view of these actors as agents of persuasion (Chwieroth 2007: 7). The premise of this interaction-based explanation is that when actors agree to dialogue, with time they consciously or unconsciously develop collective identities that affect how they perceive and pursue their interests (Risse 2004). Thus, communication between national policy makers and knowledge-based actors promoting specific innovations allows both categories of actors to develop new meaning of themselves and their role in pursuit of policy change through a process of self-reflexive interaction.

Interaction provides the platform for exercising 'influence' through persuasion, argument, and exchange of ideas. Influence as used in this context is the ability to persuade or convince others to accept one's preference or policy choices or to desire the same objective. From an ideational perspective, bureaucrats and elected officials yield to ideas promoted by knowledge-based actors if the former felt validity claims in their own policy preferences have been challenged by alternatives offered by the latter (Risse 2004). In the knowledge-based economy, the non-conventional actors often resort to the use of influence by appealing to (a) the *intellect* (persuading people that a particular course of action is intrinsically the best); (b) *passion* (changing peoples' mind by appealing directly to their emotions and sentiments); *(c) self-interest* (convincing people to support a course of action because of the inherent or potential benefits they will get); and (d) *group solidarity*—persuading people to act or follow a particular course of action because it is in collective interest—(Dickerson and Flanagan 1998).

Often influential knowledge-based actors exploit the power of language, diction and 'repetitiveness' to compel behavioural changes in the domestic policy making circles. In this sense, apart from the reasonableness of an influencing actors' policy argument in the interaction process, the ability of national policy makers, especially, in developing countries to provide alternative arguments or resist external influence is weakened for a number of reasons.

First, the lack of resources to conduct research and provide counter policy arguments, fear of losing support (financial etc) from major knowledge-based actors in a policy process compels national actors to assimilate the arguments of new actors and, thus, mediating the diffusion of ideas. Interaction, therefore, enables the exercise of influence through language especially in a situation of 'politics of choicelessness' conditioned largely by the creation of 'no exit' for the target actor. The premises of 'politics of choicelessness' does not mean the absence of policy alternatives for the bureaucrats or national policy-makers to choose from as an 'exit strategy'. Rather, it denotes that their ability to resist ideas offered by dominant knowledge-based actors is often weakened in the interactive process by the former's careful selection of words designed purposely to alter the ideational disposition of national policy makers. Thus, though the national actors have a 'voice' in the interaction process, the expression of that voice occurs largely within the frame or boundaries of policy ideas of the knowledge-based actors. This, therefore, creates an environment of ideational dependency.

Interaction as a channel of knowledge transfer treats ideas as causal mechanisms or ideational preferences of national policy actors. However, it is the content of interaction and how that content is packaged and presented to national policy makers and their domestic audiences that determines whether innovations promoted by knowledge-based actors are adopted within national settings. Thus, interaction as a strategy depends on the availability of knowledge resources, intelligence, and research to construct persuasive arguments, as well as, backup pecuniary resources. This explains why most knowledge-based actors—domestic and transnational—have become actively involved in the business of research and knowledge creation (Gibbons et al. 1994). The notion of interaction, in the form of debates, idea exchanges, and mutual discussions also suggest that national policy makers and knowledge-based policy actors with whom they interact have the opportunity to challenge the validity claims underlining any causal or normative presumptions. It is through these processes, that the search for a consensus about the "understanding of a situation as well as justifications for the principles and norms guiding their action" (Risse 2004:294) is conducted.

When national policy makers and knowledge-based policy actors are engaged in an interaction, they by that very act, also agree to be persuaded by the best argument. Thus, their goal is not to necessarily achieve one's fixed preference or options but to find a reasoned and justifiable consensus. As Risse (2004) notes, in the process of interaction, within the context of national policy, those who find the ideas being promoted by mediating knowledge-based actors reasonable, would abandon their quest to attain or justify their fixed preferences and interests by transforming their worldview or interests under the circumstances of better arguments. One of the primary assumptions underlying the utility of interaction as a mechanism for knowledge transfer is the fact that it allows actors in the policy domain to explore the process of truth seeking rather than satisfaction maximization, deliberation rather than persuasion, and problem-solving rather than compromise. In spite of their fixed policy preferences, this strategic reasoning enables them to keep an open-mind about arguments challenging the validity claims of their policy preferences (Risse 2004). Similarly, the openness of interaction in a policy deliberation energizes actors to act beyond what are perceived as historically constructed or rule-guided modes of operation, thereby, enhancing openness and learning from each other's perspective.

Interaction, therefore, constitutes a learning process or mechanism through which actors acquire new information, assess their preferences, interests and perceptions "in the light of new empirical and moral knowledge, and—most importantly—can reflexively and collectively assess the validity claims of norms and standards of appropriate behaviour" (Risse 2004: 288). Cowan et al. (2000) argued that information is a set of structured signals that go into human consciousness through the senses; it is a 'memo' containing ordered data. When an actor processes or finds the information acquired meaningfully, that information constitutes or becomes knowledge (Fleck 1997). However, the reliance on interaction, inducement and coordination in multi-actor policy environments promotes competing and often conflicting policy ideas in issues areas. This requires the promoters of new policy innovations must not only be persuasive, and resourceful, but also find ways to communicate these ideas in ways that outpace those of their competitors while, at the same time, appealing to national policy-makers. This has elevated issue-framing as a strategy through which knowledge-based actors market their ideas to national policy-makers and domestic audiences.

Issue-Framing as Knowledge Marketing Strategy

In the market place of multiple policy ideas and actors competing for attention of bureaucrats and elected officials, issue-framing is the currency of exchange. Issue framing in a policy-making context refers to the art of presenting ideas, innovations, and social research findings in a way that appeals to one's intended audience. It involves the ability of intelligently exploiting language, diction and phrases to produce a desirable effect on an actor's audience. Issue-framing is not only a communication tool, it is also a device for measuring the way and manner in which knowledge-based actors desirous to exert influence on the policy process in a given issue area, present their defined policy problems and pet solution. Although issue-framing is widely used and studied, there is no definitive model or universally accepted definition (Entman 1993). As such, few scholars have attempted to narrow its conceptual field by creating a common understanding. The origins of issue-framing theory are traceable to studies in sociology and cognitive psychology.

The first recognized work in this area emerged in sociology in the mid-1970s with Erving Goffman's groundbreaking study *Frame Analysis: An Essay on the Organization of Experience*. In this work, Goffman (1974) examined how our basic perceptions of the world around us are unconsciously guided by cognitive frames. Over time the use of framing in sociology and psychology became more critical in its application. However, some scholars began to ask whether frames arose out of norms, and were truly adopted, or whether those in power chose and pushed specific frames in a conscious and persuasive manner.

In addition, some social constructivists analyzing issue-framing began to look at how shared knowledge within a given society could be used to create a legitimate social purpose (Payne 2001). Their argument is that actors used and constructed ideas and symbols to manipulate and ultimately change how the public thought about an issue in order to push through certain agendas (Ross 2000). The shift in the focus of study from individual cognitive behaviour to broader understandings of ideational persuasion and power were significant, and allowed for greater utilization of framing in communicating policy ideas.

Thus, outside of sociology and cognitive psychology, framing theory has been extensively used in the public policy literature. Here, the focus is not on the traditional government agencies and institutions, but rather how non-state actors, especially the knowledge-based actors, structured their ideas and streamlined their messages in order to incite action and challenge dominant social discourses (Keck and Sikkink 1998). The objective is to understand the political struggles that knowledge-based actors face, and their ability to challenge existing policies and influence the construction of new norms based on their ideas and knowledge. Snow and Benford (1988) noted that framing allows knowledge-based actors to identify problems, suggest solutions, or mobilize the general public against bureaucrats and others interested in maintaining and protecting the status-quo. In their view, a well constructed frame has a higher probability of leading to changes in existing policy.

Policy changes in this context therefore involves the altering of dominant ideas by what Klandermans (1997) referred to as consensus mobilization—the process through which various knowledge-based actors promoting different ideas compete with each other by spreading their ideas among the general public. However, existing research on issue-framing shows that the process through which knowledge or innovative ideas are created and packaged to challenge existing paradigms is complex especially for actors whose aim is to alter the status quo (Tarrow 1998). The competition for influence and struggle over policy ideas through issue-framing also occurs between knowledge-based actors and national policy makers. This is because they are actively engaged in a constant struggle to gain dominance to pursue their own political agenda.

As such, scholars interested in political behaviour often investigate how policy issues are partially framed to understand how governments alter, manipulate and foster the creation of meaning through the manipulation of language in speeches, policies, and documents (Brewer and Gross 2005; Gross and Brewer 2007). Similarly, some feminists investigated how the framing of issues by various policy actors worked to structure public policy and ultimately reproduce gender inequalities (Fraser 1989; Armstrong 1998).

The focus on issue-framing is particularly useful for understanding a society that is imbued with multiple knowledge-based actors. The importance stems from the fact that it enables us to speak directly to how ideas and knowledge are generally manipulated by actors in a competitive policy environment. It is based on this assessment that Stone, (2001) intimated that issue-framing entails causal ideas which have a moral component whereby actors use language in such a way as to project blame or cause. As Entman noted "to frame is to select some aspects of a perceived reality and make them more salient in a communicating text…to promote a particular problem definition, causal interpretation, moral evaluation, and/or treatment recommendation for the item described" (1993:52) Thus, knowledge-based actors use issue-framing to highlight their particular pet policy ideas, innovations or solution in opposition to ideas and solutions promoted by other actors in a specific policy environment.

In fact, from the standpoint of any actor in a policy domain, issue-framing presents an overly simplified viewpoint by excluding all others. Thus, the framing of policy challenges and ideas critical to their resolution is an active process that incorporates cultural understandings, structural barriers, and societal problems. In other words, issue framing is critical if dominant discourses in public policy making are to be shaped (Ross 2000). This implies that the process of issue-framing is not neutral, but purposively selective and representative of the biases and disposition of the knowledge-based actors (Stone 1989).

Overall, analysis of issue-framing as a knowledge marketing device makes it possible to understand how specific policy ideas, such as neo-liberalism, came to be dominant, which actors promoted them, what alternative frames existed, how accepted norms were challenged, and how actors used discourse and symbols to manipulate outcomes. The importance of framing in the context of this analysis is that knowledge-based actors design frames for their policy ideas in a way that simplifies, prioritizes and structures the flow of public discourse in a given policy area. In so doing, knowledge-based actors bundle key concepts, stock phrases and stereotyped images to reinforce their preferred ways of interpreting policy challenges and solutions. They regularly search for innovative ways to attract the attention of national policy makers and the support of ordinary citizens by framing old policy challenges in new ways or by intelligently moving political relevant information quickly to locations where it has a greater potential to make the desired impact. Consequently, some scholars view knowledge-based actors as sites of ideational and political negotiation as well as mediators of contemporary public processes (Keck and Sikkink 1998).

Conclusion

The shift toward knowledge society has transformed public policy-making by expanding the number of actors involved in the policy decision making. Consequently, policy-making is, increasingly now more than before, a matter of context of ideas. Public policy making has also become a process of direct application of knowledge for the purposes of increased growth and welfare, as well as a means for pushing back the boundaries of knowledge and exploiting it for practical uses. The increased involvement of knowledge-based actors challenges conventional explanations based on pluralist, corporatist and other theoretical frameworks.

Beyond this, the phenomenon in which bureaucrats and knowledge-based actors are implicated in policy making and implementation at all levels challenges the core assumptions of classical realist theory. These assumptions are: (a) that states are the basic units of analysis in the international system because they are the only governing actors in that realm; (b) that states act in their national self-interest which overrides all other interests; and (c) that the international system is anarchical—conflicts and wars are inevitable—because the world lacked global governing structures higher than sovereign national states (Smith 1999).

Empirically, these assumptions are far removed from the real world. The modern state is sandwiched between transnational actors like the World Bank, International Monetary Fund (IMF), and the International Labor Organization (ILO) among others from above and domestic policy networks in various countries from below. Carroll et al (2003) argue that the influence of knowledge-based actors is a pervasive palpable phenomenon in both the developed and the developing world. Thus, realists' perspective on the state as a unitary policy actor is oblivious of the fact that several actors—both state and non-state—are involved in policy negotiations or defining best practice that is, shaping each other's interest and preferences.

Also, the power of national policy-makers over public policy is both lessened and further legitimized by a complex interactive process of policy-making. Apart from these theoretical concerns, the fact that transnational actors are able to liaise with domestic policy communities to exert influence in domestic political settings is yet another manifestation that integration and increased interdependence is a defining character of the knowledge society. The active participation of knowledge-based actors in setting and shaping policy at the domestic levels, however, raises concerns about democratic deficits. The involvement of multiple non-conventional policy actors in the domestic policy space means competition among different groups, both transnational and national.

A major concern with this development has to do with exactly who knowledge-based actors represent. These raise several questions: (1) whose interests are they promoting with their policy ideas? (2) Whom are they accountable to? and, (3) how internally democratic are they? Dahl (1999) noted that by their nature, most knowledge-based policy actors, especially the transitional ones, are not democratic in their deliberative and decision-making processes. They often lack the necessary institutions and participatory mechanism for direct electoral, accountability and transparency required of bureaucrats in national policy environments (Moravcsik 2004). Acting as mediators and conveyors of policy ideas from one jurisdiction to another and from centers of knowledge production to points of direct usage, knowledge-based actors have been instrumental in the cross-fertilization of policy ideas, and in the process legitimized the shift to a knowledge-based social order.

Policy making in the knowledge society, thus, requires new conceptualization and fresh theoretical insight. Transformations in the making and perception of public policy open up the possibility for investigating several interrelated issues and queries. The first has to do with the relationship between bureaucrats and knowledge-based actors. Secondly, how this relationship differs across policy domains and national political systems and what strategies used by various actors to navigate institutional rules of policy making. Thirdly, what are the main internal decision-making processes utilized by knowledge-based actors and what constitute their relations to others within the policy community? Also what are the implications of different patterns of interactions among bureaucrats and knowledge-based actors, and to what extent issue-framing impact or affect policy choices and outcomes?

Bibliography

Armstrong, Patricia. 1998. "Missing Women: A Feminist Perspective on the Vertical Mosaic", in Richard C. Helmes-Hayes and James E. Curtis, eds. *The Vertical Mosaic Revisited*. Toronto: University of Toronto Press, pp.116–144.

Atkinson, Michael and William Coleman. 1992. "Policy Networks, Policy communities and the Problem of Governance." *Governance* 5 (2):154–80.

Bennett, Colin, and Michael Howlett. 1992. "The Lessons of Learning: Reconciling Theories of Policy Learning and Policy Change." *Policy Science* 25:275–294.

Bishop, Patrick, and Glyn Davis. 2002. "Mapping Public participation in Policy Choices." *Australian Journal of Public administration* 61 (1):14–29.

Bissessar, Ann Marie, ed. 2002. *Policy Transfer, New Public Management and Globalization: Mexico and the Caribbean*, edited by. Lanham: University of America.

Blunkett, D. 2000. *Influence or Irrelevance: can Social Science Improve Government?* Swindon: ESRC, and Department for Education and Employment.

Boase, Joan Price. 1996. "Institutions, Institutionalized Networks and Policy Choices." *Governance* 9:287–310.

Borzel, Tanja A. 1997. "What's So Special About Policy Networks? – An Exploration of the Concept and Its Usefulness in Studying European Governance." *European Integration Papers (EIoP)* 1 (16).

Brewer, Paul R., and Kimberly Gross. 2005. "Values, Framing, and Citizens' Thoughts about Policy Issues: Effects on Content and Quantity." *Political Pyschology* 26 (6): 929–948.

Brooks, Sarah. 2002. "Social Protection and Economic Integration: The Policies of Pension Reform in an Era of Capital Mobility." *Comparative Political Studies* 35 (5):491–523.

Brooks, Sarah. 2006. *Competitive Diffusion: Understanding the Spread of Structural Pension Reforms across Nations*. New York: World Bank Institute.

Busenberg, George J. 2001. "Learning in Organizations and Public Policy." *Public Policy* 22 (3):173–189.

Carroll, Barbara, Terrance Carroll, and Frank Ohemeng. 2003. "Is there a Distinctive 'Third World' Policy Proccess? Evidence from Botswana, Ghana and Mauritius," in *Canadian Political Science Association Conference*. Halifax, Nova Scotia.

Chalmers, Iain. 2003. "Trying to do More Good than harm in Policy and Practice: The Role of Rigorous, Transperent and Up-to-date Evaluations." *Annals of the American Academy of Political and Social sciences* 589:22–40.

Chwieroth, Jefferey. 2007. "Neoliberal Economists and Capital Account Liberalization in Emerging Markets." *International Organization* 61:443–463.

Clarke, John. 2005. "New Labor's Citizens: Activated, Empowered, Reponsibilized and Abandoned?" *Critical Social Policy* 25 (4):447–467.

Cowan, Robin, Paul David and Dominique Foray. 2000. "The Explicit Economics of Knowledge Codification and Tacitness." *Industrial and Corporate Change* 9:211–253.

Dahl, Robert. 1999. "Can International Organizations Be Democratic? A Skeptic's View," in Democracy's Edges", in Ian Shapiro and Casiano Hacker-Cordon, eds. *Democracy's Edges*. Cambridge: Cambridge University Press, pp.19–36.

De Loen, Peter. 1997. *Democracy and the Policy Sciences*. New York: State University of New York Press.

Deacon, Bob. 2007. *Global Social Policy and Governance*. Los Angeles. London. New Delhi. Singapore: Sage Publications.

Dickerson, Mark, and Thomas Flanagan. 1998. *An Introduction to Government and Politics: A Conceptual Approach*. Fifth Edition ed. Toronto: Nelson: Internaional Publishing Company.

Dietmar, Braun, and Fabrizio Gilardi. 2006. Taking 'Galton Problem' Seriously: Towards a Theory of Policy Diffusion. *Journal of Theoretical Politics* 18(3): 298–322.

Dingeldey, Irene, and Heinz Rothang, eds. 2009. *Governance of Welfare State Reform: A Cross National and Cross-Sectoral Comparison of Policy and Politics*. Cheltenham: UK: Northampton: M.A., USA: Edward Elgar.

Dobbin, Frank, Beth Simmons, and Geoffrey Garrett. 2007. "The Global Diffusion of Publi Policies: Social Construction, Coercion, Competition or Learning?" *Annual Review of Sociology* 33 (21):1–23.

Dolowitz, David, and David Marsh. 1996. "Who Learns from Whom: A Review of Policy Transfer Literature." *Political Studies* 44 (2):343–57.

Dolowitz, David, and David Marsh. 2000. "Learning from Abroad: The Role of Policy Transfer in Contemporary Policy Making." *Governance* 13 (1):5–25.

Dolowitz, David P. 1998. *Learning From America: Policy Transfer and the Development of British Workforce State*. Sussex: Sussex Academic Press.

Drucker, Peter. 1993. *Post-Capitalist Society* New York: Harper Business.

Dzisah, James. 2007. "Institutional Transformations in the Regime of Knowledge Production: The University as a Catalyst for the Science-based Knowledge Economy." *Asian Journal of Social Sciences* 35 (1):126–140.

Entman, Robert. 1993. "Framing: Toward Clarification of a Fractured Paradigm." *Journal of Communication* 43:51–58.

Etheredge, Lloyd 1982. "Government learning: An Overview", in Samuel L. Long, ed. *The Hand Book of Political Behaviour*. New York: Pergamon, pp. 73–161.

Etzkowitz, Henry. 2003. "Research Groups as Quasi-Firms: The invention of the Entrepreneurial University." *Research Policy* 32:109–121.

Evans, Mark. 2006. "At the Interface between Theory and Practice-Policy Transfer and Lesson-Drawing." *Public Administration* 84 (2):479–489.

Evans, Mark, and Jonathan Davies. 1999. "Understanding Policy Transfer: A Multi-Level, Multi-Disciplinary Perspective." *Public Administration* 77 (2):361–385.

Findlay, Len M., and Paul M. Bidwell, eds. 2001. *Pursuing Academic Freedom: Free and Fearless?* Saskatoon: Purich Publishing Ltd.

Fischer, Frank. 1998. "Beyond Empiricism: Policy Inquiry in a Postpositivist Perspective." *Policy Studies Journal* 26 (1):129–146.

Fleck, James. 1997. "Contingent Knowledge and Technology development". *Technology Analysis and Strategic Management* 9(4):383–397.

Florida, Richard. 1995. Towards Learning Region. *Futures* 27 (5):527–36.

Fraser, Nancy. 1989. *Unruly Practices: Power, Discourse, and Gender in Contemporary Social Theory.* New York: Polity Press.

Freeman, Richard. 1999. Policy Transfer in Health Sector. Working Paper (http://www.pol.ed.ac.uk/research/working_paper.html).

Freeman, Richard. 2007. Epistemological Bricolage: How Practitioners Make Sense of. *Administration and Society* 39:476–498.

Gibbons, Michael, Camille Limoges, Helga Nowotny, Simon Schwartzman, Peter Scott, and Martin Trow. 1994. *The New Production of knowledge: The Dyamnics of Science and Research in contemporary Societies.* London; Thousand; New Delhi: Sage Publications.

Godin, Benoit, and Yves Gingras. 2000. "The Place of Universities in the System of Knowledge Production." *Research Policy* 29:273–278.

Greener, Ian. 2002. "Understanding NHS Reform: The Policy-Transfer, Social Learning, and Path Dependency Perspective." *Governance* 15 (2):161–183.

Gross, Kimberly, and Paul R. Brewer. 2007. S"ore Losers: News Frames, Policy Debates, and Emotions." *The Harvard International Journal of Press/Politics* 12:122–133.

Haas, E. 1980. "Why Collaborate? Issue Linking and International Regimes." *World Politics* 32:357–405.

Haas, Peter M. 1992. "Epistemic Communities and International Policy Coordination: An Introduction." *International Organization* 46(1):377–404.

Hall, Peter A. 1993. "Policy Paradigms, Social Learning, and the State: The Case of Economic Policymaking in Britain." *Comparative Politics* 25 (3):275–296.

Hammersley, Martyn. 2001. "On Systemic Reviews of Research Literatures : A Narrative Response to Evans and Benefield." *British Educational Research Journal* 27 (5):543–54.

Hammersley, Martyn. 2005. "Is Evidence-Based Practice Movement Doing More Good than Harm? Reflections on IAIN Chalmer's Case for Research-Based Policy Making and Practice." *Evidence and Policy* 1 (1):85–100.

Hargreaves, David H. 1999. "The knowledge-Creating School." *British Journal of Educational Studies* 47 (2):122–144.

Heclo, Hugh. 1974. *Modern Social Politics in Britain and Sweden: From Relief to Income Maintenance.* New Haven: : Yale University Press.

Heclo, Hugh. 1978. Issue Network and the Executive Establishment. In *The New American Political System*, edited by A. King. Washington DC AEI.

Hessels, Laurens K., and Harro van Lente. 2008. "Re-thinking New Knowledge Production: A Literature Review and a Research Agenda." *Research Policy* 37 (4):740–760.

Howlett, Michael, and M. Ramesh. 1995. *Studing Public Policy: Policy Cycles and Policy Subsystems.* Toronto. New York. Oxford: Oxford University Press.

Huber, Eevelyn and John D. Stephens. 2000. "The Political Economy of Pension Reform: Latin America in Comparative Perspective." In *Occasional Paper*. Geneva: United Nations Research Institute for Social Development.

Huber, George P. 1991. "Organizational learning: the contributing processes and the literatures." *Organization Science* 2 89–115.

Hulme, Rob. 2005. "Policy Transfer and the Internationalization of Social Policy." *Social Policy and Society* 4 (4):417–42.

Ikenberry, John G. 1990. "The international spread of privatization policies: inducements, learning and policy 'bandwagoning'", in Ezra Suleiman and John Waterbury, eds. *The Political Economy of Public Sector Reform and Privatization*. Westview: Oxford, pp. 88–110.

James, Liver, and Martin Lodge. 2003. "Limitations of Policy Transfer and Lesson Drawing." *Political Studies Review* 1(2):179–193.

Keck, Margaret E. and Kathryn Sikkink. 1998. *Activist beyond Borders: Advocacy Networks In International Politics*. Ithaca and London: Cornell University Press.

Kenis, Patrick, and Volker Schneider. 1991. "Policy Networks and Policy Analysis: Scrutinizing a New Analytical Toolbox," B. Marin and R. Mayntz, eds. *Policy Networks. Empirical Evidence and Theoretical Considerations.* Boulder/Colorado, Frankfurt: Campus Verlag: Westview Press, pp. 25–59.

Klandermans, Bert. 1997. *The Social Psychology of Protest.* Cambridge, MA Blackwell.

Larmour, Peter. 2002. "Conditionality, Coercion and Other Forms of 'Power': International Financial Institutions in the Pacific." *Public Administration and Development* 22 (3):249 260.

Lasswell, D. Harrold. 1951. "The Policy Orientation," in Sandra Braman, ed. *Communication Researchers and Policy-Making.* Cambridge. Mass: MIT Press, pp. 85–104.

Levi-Faur, David and Eran Vigoda-Gadot, eds. 2004. *International Public Policy and Management: Policy Learning Beyond Regional, Cultural, and Political Boundaries.* New York: Mercel Dekker.

Lindblom, Charles A. 1990. *Inquiry and Change*. New Haven: Yale University Press.

Lomas, Jonathan. 2000. "Connecting Research and Policy." *Canadian Journal of Policy Research* (spring):140–144.

Loughlin, M. 2003. "Review of Goodman, K., Ethics and evidence-based medicine: fallibility and responsibility in clinical science." *Journal of Evaluation in Clinical Practice* 9:141–144.

Marsh, David, ed. 1998. *Comparing Policy Networks*. Buckingham: Open University Press.

McConnell, Grant. 1966. *Private Power and American Democracy*. New York: Knopf.

McDermott, Rose. 2001. "The Psychological Ideas of Amos Tversky and their Relevance for Political Science." *Theoretical Politics* 13 (1):15–33.

Meseguer, Cavadonga. 2004. "What Role for Learning? The diffusion of Privatization in OECD and Latin American Countries." *Journal of Public Policy* 24 (3):299–325.

Meseguer, Cavadonga. 2005. Policy Learning, Policy Diffusion, and the Making of the New Order. *The Annals of the American Academy of Political and Social Sciences* 598(1):67–82.

Meseguer, Cavadonga. 2006. "Rational Learning and Bounded Learning in Diffusion of Policy Innovations." *Rationality and Society* 18(1):35–66.

Mintrom, Michael and Sandra Vergari. 1998. "Policy Networks and Innovation Diffusion: The Case of State Education Reform." *Politcs* 60 (1): 26–48.

Moravcsik, Andrew. 2004. "Is there a 'Democratic Deficit' in World Politics? A Framework for Analysis." *Government and Opposition* 39 (2): 336–363.

Morrissey, Oliver, and Doug Nelson. 2003. "Characterizing International Policy Learning." Paper presented at the *Joint Leverhulme Centre for Research on Globalization and Economic Policy/Murphy Institute Conference on the Political Economy of Policy Transfer, Learning and Convergence*. Tulane University, April 12.

Needham, Catherine. 2007. "Realising the Potential of Co-production: Negotiating Improvments in Public Services." *Social Policy and society* 7(2):221–231.

Newmark, Adam J. 2002. "An Integrated Approach to Policy Transfer and Diffusion." *Review of Policy Research* 19 (2):151–178.

Nonaka, Ikujuro, and Hirotaka Takeuchi. 1995. *The Knowledge-Creating Company*. New York: Oxford University Press.

Orenstein, Mitchell A. 2003. "Mapping the Diffusion of Pension Innovation," in Robert Holzmann, Mitchell Orenstein and Michal Rutkowski, eds. *Pension Reform in Europe: Process and Progress*. Washington, DC: The World Bank, pp. 171–194.

Orenstein, Mitchell. 2005. The New Pension Reform as Global Policy. *Global Social Policy* 5 (2):175–202.

Orenstein, Mitchell. 2008. *Privatizing Pensions: The Transnational Campaigns for Social Security Reforms*. Princeton, NJ: Princeton University Press.

Mitchell A Orenstein, Martine R. Haas. 2002. "Globalization and the Development of Welfare States in Post-communist Europe." BCSIA Discussion Paper 2002–02, Kennedy School of Government, Harvard University, February 2002.

Osborne, Thomas. 2004. "On Mediators: Intellectuals and the Ideas trade in the Knowledge Society." *Economy and Society* 33 (4):430–447.

Owen, John M. 2002. "Foreign Imposition of Domestic Institutions." *International Organization* 56(2):317–407.

Parsons, Wayne. 2002. "From Muddling Through Up- Evidence Based Policy Making and the Modernization of British Government." *Public Policy and Adminstration* 17 (43):42–60.

Parsons, Wayne 1995. *Public Policy: An Introduction to the Theory and Practice of Policy Analysis*. Chetenham, UK, Lyme US: Edward Elgar.

Payne, Rodger A. 2001. "Persuasion, Frames, and Norm Construction." *European Journal of International Relations* 7(1):37–61.

Risse, Thomas. 2004. "Global Governance and Communicative Action." *Government and Opposition* 39 (2):288–313.

Rogers, Everett M. 1995. *Diffusion of Innovations*. 4th ed. New York: The Free Press.

Rose, Richard. 1993. *Lesson-Drawing in Public Policy: A Guide to Learning Across Time and Space*. Chatham. New Jersey: Chatham House.

Ross, Fiona. 2000. "Framing Welfare Reform in Affluent Societies: Rendering Restructuring More Palatable?" *Public Policy* 20 (2):169–193.

Schneider, Anne, and Ingram Helen. 1998. "Systematically Pinching Ideas: A Comparative Approach to Policy Design." *Public Policy* 8 (1):61–80.

Simmons, Beth, Frank Dobbin, and Garrett Geoffrey. 2006. "Introduction: International Diffusion of Liberalism." *International Organization* 60(4):781–810.

Smith, Malinda. 1999. "Globalization and International Relations Theory," in Janine M. Brodie and Sandra Rein, eds. *Critical Concepts: An Introduction to Politics*. Scarbrough, Ontario: Prentice Hall Allyn & Bacon.

Smith, Martin J. 1993. *Pressure, Power and Policy: State Autonomy and Policy Networks in Britain and the United States*. Hervester Wheatsheaf, Hemel: Hempstead, Herts.

Snow, David A. and Robert D. Benford. 1988. "Ideology, Frame Resonance and Participant Mobilization." *International Social Movement Research* 1:197–219.

Stallings, Barbara. 1992. "International Influence on Economic Policy," in Stephan Haggard and Robert R. Kaufman, eds. *The Politics of Economic Adjustment*. Princeton: Princeton University Press, pp. 41–88.

Stone, Deborah. 1989. "Causal Stories and the Formation of Policy Agendas." *Political Science Quarterly*. 104:281–300.

Stone, Deborah. 2001. *Policy Paradox: The Art of Political Decision-Making*. 2nd ed. New York: W.W. Norton & Company.

Stone, Diane. 1999. "Learning Lessons and Transferring Policy Across Time, Space and Disciplines." *Politics* 19(1):51–59.

Stone, Diane. 2001. "Learning Lessons, Policy Transfer and the International Diffusion of Policy Ideas." University of Warwick: Center for Study of Globalization and Regionalization.

Strange, David, and John W. Meyer. 1993. "Institutional Condition for Diffusion." *Theory and Society* 22 (4):487–511.

Sutton, Rebecca. 1999. "The Policy Process: An Overview." Portland House, London: Overseas Development Institute.

Tarrow, Sid. 1998. *Power in Movement: Social Movement, Collective Action and Politics*. Cambridge MA: Cambridge University Press.

Thatcher, Mark. 1998. "Development of Policy Network Analysis: From Modest Origins to Overarching Frameworks." *Journal of Theoretical Politics* 10 (4):389–416.

Thomas, Gary and Richard Pring. 2004. *Evidence-Based Practice in Education*. Maidenhead: Open University Press.

Trinder, Liz and Shirley Reynolds. 2000. *Evidence-Based Pratice: A critical Appraisal*. Oxford: Blackewell Science.

Weyland, Kurt. 2005. "Theories of Policy Diffusion: Lesson from Latin American Pension Reform." *World Politics* 57(2):262–295.

Weyland, Kurt. 2006. Bounded Rationality and Policy Diffusion: Social Sector Reform in Latin America. Princeton, NJ: Princeton University Press.

Williams, David. 2008. *The World Bank and Social Transformation in International Politics: Liberalism, Governance and Sovereignty* London and New York: Routledge.

Wolman, Harold. 1992. "Understanding Cross National Policy Transfers: The Case of Britain and the US." *Governance* 5 (1):27–45.

World Bank. 1998. *Knowledge for Development, World Development Report*. Washington D.C: The world Bank.

CHAPTER ELEVEN

REGIONALIZED HEALTH CARE SYSTEM IN CANADA: TOWARDS A KNOWLEDGE MANAGEMENT STRATEGY

William Boateng

Decision-making is a complex activity, and often difficult, if not impossible to attribute any particular decision to the use of a specific form of knowledge. Although effective decision-making in an information age implies the use of scientific knowledge, the relationship between scientific knowledge and decision-making is often indirect and varied (Weiss 1979). Typically, scientific knowledge must compete with other forms of tacit knowledge—e.g. popular understandings, value based judgments, political imperatives—and the attraction of the status quo. This is no less true for health care decision making, and the extent to which scientific evidence combines with other forms of knowledge in this context needs to be examined. Effective decision-making in organizations arguably should be based on the extent to which explicit and tacit forms of knowledge are marshalled and managed, with emphasis being placed on the dominant form of knowledge informing the decision-making processes. Understanding the knowledge that underlies health care decision-making, and how that knowledge is acquired, stored, validated, shared and applied is an important first step in ensuring effective knowledge management.

Ensuring effective knowledge management in support of health care decision-making requires that organizations adopt a knowledge management strategy to guide the various knowledge processes. There are many approaches to the development of knowledge management strategies in organizations as there are "no one size fits all". The key is for organizations to align their knowledge management strategies with overall organizational strategies and goals. A clear knowledge management strategy is, therefore, important for achieving organizational goals and objectives. This is increasingly apparent in contemporary knowledge-based society, where knowledge is not only important organizational resource, but its management is critical to long-term organizational success (Leonard 1999, Hansen et al. 1999, Smith 2001).

However, while leaders in the business sector have long recognized the value of managing knowledge, other sectors like health care have lagged behind in doing so. There is, therefore, the need for knowledge management to be applied to other areas of social life, including the health care industry (Metaxiotis et al. 2005).

The health care sector is one area that knowledge management has failed to feature prominently in strategies geared towards organizational success in spite of the wealth of knowledge at the disposal of health care decision-makers. Knowledge availability in itself, though positive, can become an effective organizational resource depending on how such knowledge is managed. Therefore, examining the knowledge management strategies and practices, particularly at the macro levels of health care decision-making is critical. Macro level health care decision-making in Canada is the prerogative of Regional Health Authorities (RHAs). They are mandated to make decisions that promote a more evidence-based social determinants approach to restructuring the health care delivery system (Tomblin 2003).

Since preferred strategy for managing knowledge should be designed in a manner that enhances the goals and objectives of the organization, there is the need for organizations to critically examine the knowledge forms—explicit and tacit—underlying their decision-making and how that knowledge is marshalled and managed, with emphasis on the dominant form of knowledge informing the decision-making processes. As a result, this chapter examines the forms of knowledge available to regional health care decision-makers in order to identify strategies relating to such knowledge forms. This is an important step towards improving overall health care delivery in Canada and our understanding of the role of knowledge management in regionalized health care decision-making.

Levels of Health Care Decision-Making

Modern health care systems are confronted with the task of effectively managing the resources necessary for improving the health and well-being of those they are committed to serving. Fulfilling this task successfully implies sound and effective decision making throughout the entire system. Contemporary health care systems can be divided into macro, meso and micro levels of decision-making. Each level has a distinct mandate, but all are linked to contribute to overall health care system performance (National Advisory Council on Aging 2005, Wilson et al. 1995).

Macro-level decisions involve the overall planning, organizing, delivery and evaluation of health services within the health regions. The decisions making body at this level within the Canadian health care system are the Regional Health Authorities (RHAs). They are appointed by provincial governments to oversee the functions and operations of the health regions. RHAs are mandated to render the following responsibilities; (1) assess the health needs of the persons to whom the RHAs provide health services, (2) prepare and regularly update an operational plan for the provision of health services, (3) provide the health services that the sector minister determines the RHAs to provide, (4) co-ordinate the health services the RHAs provide with those provided by other providers of health services, (5) evaluate the health services that the RHAs provide, (6) ensure that the RHAs promote and encourage health and wellness, and (7) do any other things that the sector minister may direct. To perform these responsibilities, the RHAs rely on the technical expertise of their chief executive officers, the administrative chairs and senior technocrats of the health regions.

Administrative decisions and priorities made by the chief executive officers and senior management working in collaboration with health care professionals and local stakeholder groups take place at the meso-level of the health care decision-making process. Decisions made at this level have to be endorsed at the macro-level by the RHAs. The fact that RHAs normally do not initiate but rather endorse administrative decisions has given a dual connotation of their role. On the one hand, they are perceived as advisors. On the other hand, they come across as decision-makers. Officially, RHAs have the mandate to validate all decisions made within a health region, thus making them important players in the overall health care decision-making process. The micro-level health care decision-making involves individual medical practitioners, clinicians and/or teams. They are generally based on clinical information, and affect directly the treatment of patients. These are decisions made by frontline staff of the health regions.

Decisions made at each level can and do influence all levels. Micro level decisions, for example, are influenced broadly by the macro level, though this is often restricted to budget-based resource allocation. While there is no direct relationship between decision-makers at the macro and the micro levels, the meso-level health care decision-makers, however, exercise tremendous influence on decisions made at the micro level. Health targets to be attained by clinicians and resources to be used for that purpose are determined by the meso-level decision-makers upon approval from the macro-level decision-makers. In Canada, RHAs in 10 of the 13 provinces and territories make decisions at all the three levels in their respective health regions. This chapter focuses only on the RHAs as macro-level decision-makers within the Canadian health care system.

Regionalization and Health Care Decision-Making in Canada

Regionalization as an approach to the provision of health care services in Canada is defined variously in the literature. The Canadian Centre for Analysis of Regionalization and Health (CCARH 2004) defines regionalization as the processes involved in the creation of autonomous organizations responsible for the administration of health care services within a defined geographic region in a province or territory. Frankish et al. (2001) define health regions as bodies responsible for health care-related decisions and policies affecting the population of defined geographical areas through public participation. Dickinson (2002) develops a more comprehensive view, defining health regions as system(s) of health governance designed to increase local citizen involvement in health care planning and service delivery, to facilitate greater integration and coordination of the health care system, and to increase the efficiency and effectiveness of the health care system.

The effectiveness of regionalization as a policy instrument depends largely on the effectiveness of the decisions made by the various RHA members. Such decisions are invariably based on RHA members' ability to manage the knowledge at their disposal. Although regionalization is referred to as a single policy innovation, there are variations in its structure and implementation, and regionalization structures within provinces in Canada have grown and changed over the years (CCARH 2003), there are still common features. CCARH (2004) identified four main features of regionalization in Canada: (1) the definition of regions by geography; they occupy specific territory, (2) the existence and authority of the health regions are at the discretion of the provincial government, (3) the consolidation of authority at the regional level, as opposed to its previous distribution among many programs and communities, and (4) the responsibility of the regions cover considerable health services, spanning at minimum community, long-term, residential and acute care services, and often extending to mental health, addictions, public health, and health promotion services.

Regionalization, therefore, becomes an important policy initiative, and RHA members are now central to the making of critical health care decisions. RHA members, thus, face pressures from governments, citizens and health professionals to not only represent their health regions but also to ensure cost-effective and efficient health services delivery in a timely and transparent fashion (Frankish et al. 2002). Measuring up to these expectations implies that individuals appointed to serve as RHA members meet some qualification criteria. The appointment of RHA members—most of whom are mainly lay people—has received mixed feelings from the public. Some believe that lay individuals cannot properly make the technical, medical or clinical decisions usually made by health professionals (Sullivan and Scattolon 1995). Others counter that since RHA members are not required to make clinical or medical decisions, they certainly can be comprised of lay people or non-health professionals (Frankish et al. 2002). This, however, does not relegate to the background the need for qualifications in the appointment of RHA members. Requisite qualifications for RHA members may include relevant experience (health care involvement, experience in education and/or social services, etc.) and specific knowledge, skills or abilities related to public relations, law, finance, strategic planning, evaluation, or health impact analysis. The range of such qualifications works to ensure a mix of expertise on a given RHA membership (Dolan 1996, Walker 1999).

Knowledge Forms and Management

Though 'knowledge', 'data' and 'information' are often used interchangeably, they are yet distinct. The fundamental difference between these concepts is that while data are conceived of as unorganized facts and observations, information goes beyond by virtue of it being contextualized. Information, therefore, is data placed in context. Knowledge is also information, but such information can be judged to ascertain its truthfulness. Knowledge could be said to be formal when it is based on scientific evidence, whose validity and reliability can be tested over a reasonable period of time. Informal knowledge, differently, is experiential in nature and is acquired after an exemplary practice has been put to use over a period of time. Informal knowledge, unlike formal knowledge, is difficult to replicate since the means for its acquisition are difficult to share (Connell et al. 2003).

Polanyi (1964) identifies explicit and tacit forms of knowledge as the two forms of knowledge used in organizations. These two forms of knowledge are currently recognized as the *de facto* knowledge categorization informing decision-making in almost all organizations. Polanyi believes that a large part of human knowledge is tacit. Knowledge of this type is action-oriented and has a personal quality that makes it difficult to communicate. Accessing tacit knowledge, therefore, presents a number of challenges, due to factors such as the absence of explicit scientifically repeatable process for eliciting such forms of knowledge. Explicit knowledge, however, can be communicated across time and space. Conceptually, there is a clear distinction between these two forms of knowledge. Nevertheless, they are not discrete or independent in the practical sense. These forms of knowledge are not dichotomous, but mutually dependent and reinforcing (Alavi and Leidner 2001, Lam 2002). Fostering a dynamic interaction between tacit and explicit knowledge, therefore, generates new forms of knowledge vital for organizations (Nonaka and Tekeuchi 1995, Lam 2002). Individuals in organizations learn by actively participating in the processes involved in knowledge creation. Through these processes, knowledge is transformed within and between forms usable by people in organizations.

The literature thus emphasizes two major and complementary forms of knowledge, tacit and explicit. An unresolved issue remains, however, it is not clear which form of knowledge is prerequisite for the other. Two lines of arguments emerge here. Lam (2002), and Nonaka and Tekeuchi (1995) argue that tacit knowledge serves as a prerequisite for explicit knowledge. A contrary view argues that explicit knowledge precedes tacit knowledge (Polanyi 1967, Dreyfus and Dreyfus 1988). Resolving this issue is important, but not essential to enriching knowledge management in organizations. What is essential is an organization's ability to mobilize and integrate the tacit-explicit knowledge forms into a productive knowledge management strategy. Both knowledge forms play a decisive role in the development and management of knowledge in organizations. In the context of health care macro level decision-making, however, the literature is relatively mute on the main knowledge form as well as various knowledge management strategies used in health care decision-making. This needs to be understood in order to identify the conditions that facilitate and/or impede the decision making processes. Again, an understanding of the knowledge management processes in health care decision-making will assist in creating the enabling organizational culture to sustain effective management of knowledge.

Knowledge management in the context of regionalized health care decision-making remains under explored. The literature has little to say about the main knowledge forms as well as the knowledge management strategies used in regionalized health care decision-making. This needs to be understood in order to identify the conditions that facilitate and/or impede the decision-making processes. Knowledge management is defined as "the process, by which an organization creates, captures, acquires and uses knowledge to support and improve the performance of the organization" (Kinney 1998: 2). It can also be understood as the exploitation and development of the knowledge assets within an organization, aimed at furthering the goals and objectives of the organization (Metaxiotis et al. 2005). Knowledge management, therefore, can be said to involve a conscious effort to incorporate strategies and practices that ensure maximum use of knowledge in organizations with the aim of advancing the goals and objectives of the organization. It is presently recognized that successful organizations are those that create new knowledge, disseminate it widely throughout the organization, and represent it into new technologies and products (Metaxiotis et al. 2005, Hansen et al. 1999, Leonard 1999). Perceiving knowledge management as a condition of organizational success makes it imperative for organizations to embrace and engage in it.

Since knowledge management involves a number of interconnected processes, the best way of understanding it is through the knowledge system perspective. The knowledge system concept refers to the institutionalization of knowledge processes in modern societies (Holzner and Marx 1979). Knowledge processes include those activities related to the production, organization, distribution, application and mandating of knowledge. The knowledge system is, therefore, related to the entire learning capacity of society (Holzner and Marx 1979). It is conceptualized as a holistic approach in understanding knowledge-based processes in modern societies, and implies that knowledge processes should be perceived as interdependent processes. Such interdependency is enhanced when all of the knowledge processes are well managed. The knowledge system is thus strengthened through knowledge management.

Since knowledge management is comprised of many different processes from knowledge creation to utilization, organizations can best maximize knowledge use by ensuring proficiency in coordinating all

the activities involved in the processes. Deliberately managing knowledge in organizations, therefore, becomes one of the critical activities
and practices, as organizations aim to maximize the use of knowledge
at its disposal. Effective knowledge management for organizations
should, therefore, be approached from the knowledge system perspective. Placing any aspect of the knowledge management above the others may diminish its value within organizations. An understanding of
knowledge management from a knowledge system perspective makes
it a strong analytical tool for understanding the organizational use of
knowledge. The ways in which knowledge is acquired, created, stored,
retrieved, and applied, therefore, constitute the main parameters or
dimensions of knowledge management.

In order for RHA members to take full advantage of knowledge
management in making decisions, policies must be related to the management of the knowledge they used to inform their decisions. RHA
members encounter many challenges in making health care decisions
aimed at managing and improving the health care system. These
include (1) the integration and coordination of the administration and
delivery of services, (2) the consolidation of funding, (3) the development of an information infrastructure and measurement indicators
that allow for outcome-based evaluation, (4) the creation of mechanisms
that provide for citizen participation while at the same time limiting
the tendency toward domination by purely local and/or professional
interests, and (5) the provision of more long-term stability and authority commensurate with accountability to RHAs (Lewis et al. 2004).

A particular challenge of interest to this study is the development
of an information infrastructure in aid of RHA members' decision-
making. Recall that knowledge management is central to organizational success (Hansen et al. 1999). Unfortunately, the current health
care system, particularly the macro level, often lacks the adequate
mechanisms for managing the type of information that can effectively
inform health care decision-making (Lewis et al. 2004, Frankish et al.
2002, Abidi 2001). Modern health care systems generate massive
amounts of knowledge and information (Abidi 2001). While this is one
of its great strengths, at the same time, this resource is not yet fully
leveraged for improving the management and delivery of health care
services. Currently, health care administrators are expected to manage
and disseminate information and data to mostly lay RHA members,
in a timely, useable form that supports their decision-making.
Regrettably, some health care administrators dismiss or reject this
"knowledge providing" role as a demotion rather than as an important

role in the overall making of decisions (Frankish et al. 2002). The reluctance on the part of health care administrators to make valuable knowledge, information, and data available to RHA members may be one of the factors responsible for RHAs general inability to take advantage of knowledge management.

There is, therefore, the need to step up knowledge management at the macro level health care decision making. This is particularly critical in light of studies that portray knowledge utilization among RHA members in Canada as somewhat lacking (Frankish et al. 2002). Research evidence, however, is not the only source of information informing RHA members' decisions. Lavis et al. (2002) found that most health policies draw on a variety of information other than citable research, including (1) what people outside the health department do, (2) what people outside the health department think or want, and (3) what people inside the health department think or want. Information from other sectors, including what people outside the health department say they do, was the most frequently used type of information in health care decision-making. Information from policy documents from previous or related policies was also frequently used in policy-making. These types of inputs were typically obtained from peers and/or stakeholders mainly in the form of tacit knowledge. HEALNet (1997) further found out that majority of RHA members in Saskatchewan were more influenced by their own experience and knowledge than by statistical data when making decisions.

Clearly, both tacit and explicit forms of knowledge inform regionalized health care decision-making. These two knowledge forms, when collected and managed effectively, may serve as important resources in health care decision-making. As indicated earlier, an essential factor for the success of regionalization in contemporary knowledge-based society is the embrace of and engagement in a more rigorous management of available knowledge in informing health care decision-making. As such, a critical understanding of the existing knowledge management strategies and practices in relation to the forms of knowledge used in health care decision-making are critical.

Knowledge Management Strategies

A knowledge management strategy is simply a plan that describes how an organization intends to better direct its knowledge for the benefit of that organization and its stakeholders. A good knowledge management strategy is closely aligned with the organization's overall strategy and objectives. Selecting the right knowledge management strategy is, therefore, an important prerequisite for attaining organizational objectives. Hansen et al. (1999) point at two contrasting strategies for knowledge management: codification and personalization. They believe that the best knowledge management strategy is always a combination of the two, but with a stronger emphasis on one. While a codification strategy is appropriate for explicit knowledge to thrive, the personalized knowledge management strategy better supports the use of tacit knowledge in organizations (Jasimuddin et al. 2005). Since tacit and explicit knowledge forms are complementary, an organization's efforts towards knowledge management should be focused on instituting the most appropriate strategy. These knowledge management strategies have distinctive features.

The codification management strategy ensures the re-use of explicit knowledge by capturing, codifying, classifying and making available knowledge to support routine problem solving. Uniformity in action is ensured since knowledge is recycled to guide decision-making. Questions regarding organizational problems and the usual response to them serve as the primary questions guiding codification strategies in organizations. For such questions to be resolved, libraries of procedures, policy documents, guidelines, data collection forms, typical cases and outcomes, and risk assessment tools derived from all parts of the organization must be developed and made available to all individuals in the organization. The codification knowledge management strategy also thrives on the availability of incentives to encourage staff to use the system. This implies that organizations adopting the codification knowledge management strategy should reward the use of, and contributions to, document databases as recognition of staff adherence to policies.

The codification strategy, in general, involves intensive investment justified by multiple knowledge re-use. At the same time, the codification strategy seems to overemphasize internally generated explicit knowledge re-use, without any reference to the use of external explicit knowledge in the form of research evidence. This is a flaw that is not addressed in the strategies of knowledge management presented by Hansen et al. (1999). Since explicit knowledge comes from both internal and external sources, attempts at its management should be comprehensive enough to reflect this duality. This notwithstanding, the codification knowledge management strategy based mainly on internal explicit knowledge can complement the evidence-based decision-making paradigm, which also seems to be tilted towards externally generated explicit knowledge to the neglect of explicit knowledge generated internally in an organization. Harmonizing the codification knowledge management strategy and the evidence-based decision-making paradigm has the potential to provide a more comprehensive perspective on explicit knowledge management in health care decision-making.

The personalization knowledge management strategy, on the other hand, is suitable for a one-off, medium to long-term high risk, strategic problem with no precedent solution. This strategy shares tacit knowledge by helping staff to identify experts and enhance conversations to create novel solutions. The forms that solutions to problems might take—and who in the organization might know about the solution— are the primary user questions guiding the personalization knowledge management strategy. Online resumes, list of skills and publications for staff and external experts, e-mail discussion lists, regular case meetings, workshops, video-conferencing, co-located staff, the provision of a coffee area, and staff secondment assist in identifying individuals who might have solutions to problems on hand (Wyatt 2001).

Since communication is the bedrock of the personalization strategy, organizations adopting this strategy must reward direct communication with others, as well as recognizing experts and original solutions. This strategy of managing knowledge entails a modest investment, justified by improved frequency and quality of communications (Hansen et al. 1999, Wyatt 2001). As both the codification and personalization knowledge management strategies exhibit contrasting features, they should be commensurate with the dominant knowledge form of any given organization. The features of the two knowledge management strategies indicate clearly that organizations embedded with routine and non-routine tasks lend themselves largely to codification and personalization knowledge management respectively. The two knowledge management strategies have their unique advantages and disadvantages.

In the case of the personalization strategy, it is recommended for its sustainable advantages, especially for its immobility and inimitability (Spencer 1995, Ambrosini and Bowman 2001), its contribution to innovation (Alversson 2001), and its low investment in information technology (Johannessen et al. 2001). Disadvantages associated with the personalization strategy include an organization's inability to store knowledge beyond the minds of individuals without some process of articulation. In other words, personalized knowledge is difficult to be communicated to others (Connell et al. 2005). There is also a reluctance to share tacit knowledge when pursuing personalization strategy because of fear of losing power and status associated with an individual's possession of knowledge (Szulanski 1996). The most serious difficulty associated with personalization strategy is the risk of losing knowledge due to loss of employees (Jasimuddin et al. 2005), thus making organizations "internally vulnerable" (Hall and Andriani 2003).

The codification strategy protects the loss of knowledge associated with the exit of employees because such knowledge is taken from individuals and codified for general organizational use. The fact that knowledge is codified, however, makes organizations "externally vulnerable" since knowledge can easily be leaked out of the organization. It is also costly pursuing a codification strategy as it is based heavily on information and computer technologies. The choice of knowledge management strategy should also be based on the organization's knowledge and objectives. Business and profit-oriented organizations are more likely to embrace the personalization strategy to insulate themselves against knowledge leakage to "business rivals" (Jasimuddin et al. 2005). All other things being equal, health care decision-makers, like most decision-makers in non-profit oriented organizations, may not necessarily be afraid of knowledge leakage. In this case, they are likely to be better off if they codify knowledge and share it with others in the industry for quality service outcomes.

In spite of the benefits associated with the codification of health care knowledge, Wyatt (2001) called for the development of personalization strategy for knowledge management in health care decision-making. Since RHA members' decisions are based both on tacit and explicit knowledge, an understanding of how members manage both explicit and tacit knowledge in their decision-making is necessary. The adoption of a knowledge management strategy helps pave the way to overall organizational success. Consequently, achieving effective and functional knowledge management in health care decision-making, as a step towards improved health care system requires that relevant organizations adopt a knowledge management strategy. There are many approaches since there is "no one size fits all". Hansen et al. (1999) identify the codification and the personalization knowledge management strategies as the two main strategies for managing knowledge within organizations. Since the main purpose of knowledge management is to assist organizations in achieving their goals, the choice of knowledge management strategy should be specifically tailored to, and aligned with, overall organization strategy and goals.

The codification and the personalization knowledge management strategies support explicit and tacit knowledge forms respectively. Attempts at adopting knowledge management strategies should, therefore, be based on a thorough understanding of the primary type of knowledge informing decision-making in the organization. It is clear from the literature that both forms of knowledge inform decisions made in organizations, with a greater emphasis on one than the other. Effective decision-making is, therefore based on the extent, to which these two complementary forms of knowledge are both organized and managed, with emphasis on the dominant form of knowledge informing the health care decision-making process. Examining the knowledge underlying health care decision-making and how that knowledge is acquired, stored, validated, shared and applied, is essential in ensuring effective knowledge management. An essential factor for the success of regionalization in health care delivery in contemporary information age is the embrace of and engagement in a more rigorous evidence-based decision-making process.

Unfortunately, however, a recognized problem within the current health care system is the lack of adequate mechanisms for the managing of information informing health care decision-making (Lewis et al. 2004, Frankish et al. 2002, Abidi 2001). Addressing these problems demands effective management of knowledge. Such an intervention is critical in identifying the facilitators of, and barriers to, knowledge management in regionalized health care decision-making process in Canada. A critical review of the documentations available to RHA members showed that members' decisions are informed more by explicit, rather than tacit, knowledge. In other words, they rely mainly on professional reports received from management as part of the regular RHA members' package to guide board discussions. Such professional reports include management research, extracts from subscribed journals of management, RHA members' discussions at formal meetings, and detail of other activities of the health region. The knowledge management practices evident in the literature and those adopted by the RHA members in support of codification and personalization knowledge management strategies are presented in tables 11.1 and 11.2 respectively.

Table 11.1. – Knowledge management practices* in support of RHAs codification knowledge management strategies

Knowledge management practices – (identified in the literature)	Knowledge management practices – RHAs
• Libraries of procedures • Policy documents • Guidelines • Data collection forms • Typical cases and outcomes • Risk assessment tools	• No libraries of procedures • Professional and annual reports • No guidelines • No data collection forms • Minutes, and conference reports • No risk assessment tools

* Knowledge management practices entail the actions as well as the facilitators of codification strategies.

Table 11.2. – Knowledge management practices* in support of RHAs personalization knowledge management strategies

Knowledge management practices – (identified in the literature)	Knowledge management practices – RHAs
• Online resumes • List of skills • Publications for staff and external experts • E-mail discussion list • Telephone discussions • Regular case meetings • Workshops • Video conferencing • Co-located staff • The provision of a coffee area • Staff secondment	• No online resumes • No list of skills • No publications for staff and external experts • Email discussions • Telephone discussions • No regular case meetings • Workshops • No video conferencing • Members dispersed in health region • No coffee area • No staff secondment

* Knowledge management practices entail the actions as well as the facilitators of personalization strategies.

It must also be noted that achieving effective knowledge management in health care decision-making involves a combination of many varia- bles such as the organizational-based structure and culture, and the extent of individuals' interactions in organizations (Lesser and Prusak 1999, Donoghue et al. 1999). Important here is the observation that individual's neither work in isolation, nor are they (usually) able to make wholly autonomous decisions. They work in organizations embedded with routines and established cultures, which influence their actions regarding knowledge use in decision-making. Individuals' examples of knowledge utilization, therefore, are greatly shaped by the extent to which they have been socialized into their "communities of practice" through membership in a subculture, and as part of its ongoing learning process. Such informal networks have tremendous impact on worker cognition and behaviour (Wenger 1998, Brown and Duguid 1991). Communities of practice manifest themselves in organizational cultures, which serve as major motivation or impediment to knowledge sharing (Alavi and Leidner, 2001).

Though, RHA members may not qualify completely as communities of practice, they may well be said to exhibit some features similar to communities of practice. Such features include the positive relationship that exists among the members, the engagement in team activities, ability to engage in informal tacit knowledge sharing through the use of telephone and emails, and the inter-organizational search for knowledge. These features can be perceived as critical prerequisites for the formation of communities of practice. At best, RHA members may be described as possessing almost all the fundamental features for the formation of communities of practice. This opportunity, however, has not been exploited to support the management of tacit knowledge by the RHA members.

The Way Forward

The following recommendations are worth considering in ensuring improved knowledge management in health care decision-making process. For these recommendations to work, they should be supported by the organization's culture particularly with regards to knowledge management.

1. There is the need for RHA members to have explicit or official policy on knowledge management. The absence of explicit policy guiding knowledge management negates the benefits associated with these practices. Knowledge management policy is critical in spelling out in clear terms the overall objectives of the

RHAs, the knowledge management strategies and practices to be adopted by its members, and systematically designing ways of ensuring that knowledge management strategies and practices adopted by RHA members are commensurate with, and lend credence to the objectives of the organization.

2. Following the analysis of the knowledge management practices depicted in the literature on regionalized health care system, it is evident that RHA members are adopting codification knowledge management strategies more than personalization knowledge management strategies. Since codification knowledge management strategies ensure re-use of explicit knowledge by capturing, codifying, classifying and making available knowledge to support routine problem solving, the availability of RHA members' incentives enshrined in the official knowledge management policy of the organization becomes paramount. This is important because codification knowledge management strategies, unlike personalization strategies, need to be carefully and tactically nurtured to maximize its impact in organizations.

3. Efforts at enhancing the use of codified knowledge in regionalized health care decision-making should be directed at broadening the explicit knowledge base of RHA members to include externally-based relevant research. This will complement the internally-based inputs provided by senior management of the health regions. The internally-based evidence placed at the disposal of RHA members may not be enough evidence in making evidence-based decisions. RHAs stand to gain a lot from external evidence by learning from experiences of other health care researchers. Such an attempt will advance significantly RHA members' efforts in embracing evidence-based decision-making.

4. RHA members should also be very cautious and tactful in relying mainly on senior management of health regions for inputs to inform their decisions. This is important because over-reliance on senior management by RHA members will amount to erosion of their power base as independent advisory body in the health care decision-making process, as enshrined in the act underlying regionalization. Again, senior management will be more empowered and unaccountable if given the opportunity to fully steer the directions of RHA members' activities.

RHA members should be encouraged and motivated to informally have discussions on management inputs, have them evaluated well in advance of formal RHA members' meetings, so they become fully represented in decisions made by the RHAs.

5. Furthermore, RHAs should have personnel specifically responsible for knowledge management at the board level. Another option for the health regions is to re-train and resource the administrative staff specifically working with the board members to play the role of knowledge managers in addition to their administrative duties.

6. Since RHA members also use tacit knowledge in informing their decisions, it is expected that they engage in some knowledge management practices that support personalization strategies. It is a fact that, not everything individuals or a group of people know can be codified as documents or tools for "universal" use.

7. Supporting personalization knowledge management strategies means that an intervention is put in place to facilitate the management of tacit knowledge. One such intervention is the community of practice approach. Even though communities of practice generally emanate voluntarily, they can be deliberately introduced and nurtured in organizations (Wenger et al. 2002). Cultivating communities of practice among health board members means arrangements such as: formal physical, virtual spaces to facilitate free flow of information among members, and organizational motivation for members to belong to such communities are provided.

8. Through the communities of practice approach, RHA members can engage in informal discussions to facilitate tacit knowledge sharing to enrich members' decisions. The online rather than face-to-face communities of practice seem to be the best fit for the RHA members. Though computer-based online communities of practice can be costly, they can support RHA members' interaction despite their dispersed geographical destinations.

9. Furthermore, since communities of practice can go beyond an organization, online communities for RHA members can be broadened to incorporate other individuals from related health organizations to share knowledge on health care.

10. Finally, the public will also have the opportunity to be part of RHA members' discussions by participating in such online communities. Such a move will indeed make regionalization a true democratic intervention in health care decision-making process in Canada.

Bibliography

Abidi, Syed Sibte Raza. 2001. "Knowledge management in health care: Towards "knowledge driven" decision support services." *International Journal of Medical Informatics* 63(12):518.

Alavi, Maryam and Dorothy E. Leidner. 2001. "Review: knowledge management and knowledge systems: Conceptual foundations and research issues." *MIS Quarterly* 25 (1):107–136.

Alversson, Mats. 2001. "Knowledge work: Ambiguity, image and identity." *Human Relations* 54 (7):863–886.

Brown, John S. and Paul Duguid. 1991. "Organizational learning and communities-of-practice: Toward a unified view of working, learning, and innovation." *Organization Science* 2(1):40–57.

Brown, John S. and Paul Duguid. 2001. "Knowledge and organization: A social-practice perspective." *Organization Science* 12 (2):198–213.

Canadian Centre for Analysis of Regionalization and Health. 2003. "Regionalization: where has all the power gone to?" Newsletter, January 2003.

Canadian Centre for Analysis of Regionalization and Health. 2004. http://www .regionalization.org/Regionalization/Regionalization.html. Last visited September 30, 2010.

Connell, N. A. D. Con, Jonathan H. Klein, and Powell, P. L. 2003. "Its tacit knowledge but not as we know it: Redirecting the search for knowledge." *Journal of the Operational Research Society* 54(1):140–152.

Dickinson, Harley. 2004. "A sociological perspective on the transfer and utilization of social scientific knowledge for policy-making", in Louis Lemieux-Charles and Francois Champagne, eds., *Using knowledge and evidence in health care: Multidisciplinary perspectives*. Toronto: University of Toronto Press, pp. 41–69.

Dickinson, Harley. 2002. "Health care, health promotion, and health reforms," in Singh Bolaria, and Harley Dickinson, eds., *Health, illness, and health care in Canada*. Third Edition. Toronto: Nelson Thomson Learning, pp. 351–371.

Dreyfus, Hubert L. and Stuart E. Dreyfus. 1988. "Why computers may never think like people." *Technology Review* 89(1):42–62.

Frankish, C. James, Elan C. Paluck, Deanna L. Williamson and Dawne C. Milligan. 2001. "The use of population health and health promotion research by health regions in Canada." *Canadian Journal of Public Health* 92 (1):19–23.

Hansen, Morten T., Nohria, N., and Tierney, T. 1999. "What's your strategy for managing knowledge?" *Harvard Business Review* 77(2):106–116.

Hansen, Morten T. 1999. "The Search-transfer problem: The role of weak ties in sharing knowledge across organizational subunits." *Administrative Science Quarterly* 44(1):82–111.

HEALNet. 2002. http://healnet.mcmaster.ca/nce/. Retrieved September 30, 2010.

Holzner, Burkart and Matthew Harmon. 1998. "Intellectual and organizational challenges for international education in the United States: A knowledge system perspective," in John N. Hawkins, Carlos Manuel Haro, Miriam A. Kazanjian, Gilbert W. Merkx and David Wiley, eds., *International Education in the New Global Era: Proceedings of a National Policy Conference on the Higher Education Act, Title VI, and Fulbright-Hays Programs*. Los Angeles: International Studies and Overseas Programs University of California.

Holzner, Burkart and John H. Marx. 1979. *Knowledge application: The knowledge system in society*. Boston, Mass. Allyn and Bacon.

Jasimuddin, Sajjad M., Jonathan H. Klein, and Con Connell. 2005. "The paradox of using tacit and explicit knowledge strategies to face dilemmas." *Management Decision* 43(1):102–112.

Lam, Alice. 2002. "Alternative societal models of learning and innovation in the knowledge economy." *International Social Science Journal* 54(1):67–82.

Lavis, John N., Susan E. Ross and Jeremiah E. Hurley. 2002. Examining the role of health services research in public policymaking. *Milbank Quarterly* 80 (1):125–154.

Leonard, Dorothy. 1999. *Wellsprings of knowledge: Building and sustaining the sources of innovation*. Boston, Mass: Harvard Business School Press.

Lewis, Steven and Denise Kouri. 2004. "Regionalization: making sense of the Canadian experience." *HealthcarePapers* 5(1):12–31.

Metaxiotis, Kostas, Kostas Ergazakis and John Psarras. 2005. "Exploring the world of knowledge management: Agreements and disagreements in the academic/practitioner community." *Journal of Knowledge Management* 9(2):16–18.

Nonaka, Ikujuro, and Hirotaka Takeuchi. 1995. *The Knowledge-Creating Company*. New York: Oxford University Press.

Polanyi, Michael. 1964. *The study of man*. Chicago: University of Chicago Press.

Polanyi, Michael. 1967. *The tacit dimension*. London: Routledge and Kegan Paul.

Szulanski, Gabriel. 1996. "Exploring internal stickiness: Impediments to the transfer of best practice within the firm." *Strategic Management Journal* 17: 27–43.

Tomblin, Stephen. 2003. "Ability to manage change through regionalization: Theory versus practice." Paper presented at the *Australasian Political Studies Association Conference,* University of Tasmania, Hobart, September 29.

Wenger, Etienne. 1998. *Communities of practice: Learning, meaning, and identity.* Cambridge: Cambridge University Press.

Wenger, Etienne, Richard McDermott and William M. Snyder. 2002. *Cultivating communities of practice: A guide to managing knowledge.* Boston: Harvard Business School Press.

Wilson, Ruth, Margo S. Rowan and Jennifer Henderson. 1995. "Core and comprehensive health care services: Introduction to the Canadian Medical Association's decision-making framework." *Canadian Medical Association Journal* 152(7):1063–1066.

Wyatt, Jeremy C. 2001. "Management of explicit and tacit knowledge." *Journal of the Royal Society of Medicine* 94:6–9.

PART III

UNIVERSITIES, INTERMEDIATE ACTORS AND
THE KNOWLEDGE ECONOMY

CHAPTER TWELVE

FACILITATING KNOWLEDGE TRANSFER: THE ROLE OF INTERMEDIATING ORGANIZATIONS[1]

Amy Scott Metcalfe

For over a decade the non-profit sector has grown in size and has increased its sphere of influence in civil society. Indeed, the rise of voluntary organizations worldwide has been described as an "association revolution" (Salamon 1994). Recently, Domhoff has written about the political diversity of non-profit organizations and their relationship to the "power elite" and the corporate sector (Domhoff 2009). However, in the field of higher education there is a dearth of research concerning the role of organizations beyond the scope of the state, the market, and higher education institutions. Enders noted that there are "many international organizations, like professional organizations, interest organizations, and scientific organizations" that should be considered part of the higher education policy process (2004: 377). Thus, despite the idea that academic institutions are "learning organizations" (Dill 1999) and part of a complex system of policy-making, there has been little scholarly attention paid to the inter-organizational networks surrounding the academy that influence and participate in the exchange of knowledge.

This chapter is concerned with the role of "intermediating" organizations and knowledge transfer within university-industry-government (UIG) relations. The discussion begins with a review of literature on inter-organizational ties and boundary-spanning behaviors, followed by a critique of several leading models of higher education governance with regard to their recognition of external organizations. The chapter then includes a definition and discussion of "intermediating"

---

[1] This chapter is an expansion of an article titled, "Examining the trilateral networks of the triple helix: Intermediating organizations and academy-industry-government relations" that appeared in a special edition of *Critical Sociology* 36(4):503–519. The author is grateful to the publisher (Sage) for permission to revise the piece for inclusion in this book.

organizations, those organizations that intentionally and actively facilitate UIG relationships. Finally, a case study of an intermediating organization in Canada is presented, with a discussion of its role in regional development and innovation processes.

Inter-Organizational Ties and the Non-Profit Sector

In his work on inter-organizational relations in Britain and the United States, Ware (1989) situated his discussion within the context of capitalist democracies, and as such his conceptualization of these interactions was both economic and political. He used the term "intermediate organization" to refer to "organizations which in law are private institutions but which take a legal status that prevents the distribution of any profits they might make," and which "lie between the state and the profit-making sector" (1989: 1). Intermediate organizations, in Ware's definition, include "churches, non-profit-making hospitals and social welfare agencies, famine relief agencies, 'private' universities, consumer cooperatives, credit unions, and social clubs" (1989: 1). He added that some organizations are "semi-private," in that they have legal status as charities but are awarded most of their operational funds by the state. Ware challenged the concept of non-profits as isolated from the public and private sectors, and stated that their "relations with the market and the state are far more complex, and far less 'independent' than the 'third sector' image suggests" (1989: 6). He recognized the tension that exists between intermediate organizations and commercial enterprises, a theme that has been popularized in the business press under the heading of unfair competition.

Ware described organizations as being one of the following, along a public/private continuum: state-owned agencies, un-owned private organizations, non-profit distributing privately-owned organizations, or privately owned profit-distributing organizations. In terms of revenue source, he placed organizations within the earning categories of: taxes or transfers from tax-originating income; donations, subscriptions, and other non-tax, non-commercial income; or sales of goods and services (Ware 1989: 11). The distinctions between public and private entities in Ware's organizational typology are useful to narrow the field of study, but are too rigid for use in the current era of non-profit commercialization. For example, many non-profit organizations participate in the sale of goods and services, albeit usually related to their mission and community charter. Another reason for caution in the application of Ware's typology of public and private entities is that these distinctions will necessarily vary from country to country depending on the legal boundaries between the commercial sector and the state. In this era of governmental outsourcing and privatization, the "public sector" has become a quasi-marketplace. As well, the sources of income for many non-profit organizations that are discrete from the state are diverse, consisting of income from government in the form of membership dues paid by state agencies on behalf of public-sector employees, philanthropic donations, corporate sponsorships, federal grants, and the sale of goods and services.

In addition to Ware's concept of the organizational boundaries between the public and private sectors, it is important to note Weisbrod's recognition of competition and commercialization within the non-profit sector (Weisbrod 1998). In *To Profit or Not to Profit: The Commercial Transformation of the Nonprofit Sector* (1989), Weisbrod argued that two simultaneous changes are occurring within the non-profit world, particularly in the United States: the rapid growth of non-profit organizations and an increasing commercialization of these "third sector" entities; points that were echoed by Domhoff (2009). While Weisbrod's analysis covered several types of non-profit organizations, his findings are particularly relevant to higher education, especially as for-profit educational institutions become more visible in the inter-organizational landscape. The blurring of boundaries between public and private organizations is a key component of Weisbrod's research, and he stated that "the competition between nonprofits and private firms is made even more complex by the fact that at the same time that nonprofits are moving into activities that have previously been the domain of for-profit firms, private firms are expanding into traditionally nonprofit areas" (1998: 5). Weisbrod noted, however, that in some sectors, such as higher education, competition between non-profits and private firms is not as common as strategic alliances and partnerships. He cited as examples the research alliances between pharmaceutical companies and universities and partnerships between athletic apparel companies and university teams. Significant to this discussion is the notion that non-profit organizations are seeking external resources through the development of commercial products and services, which may or may not be ancillary to the knowledge-centric missions of these organizations.

Academic Boundary-Spanners

Aldrich and Herker (1977) were some of the first researchers to discuss boundary-spanners and their behaviour of crossing between an organization and its environment. They explained that membership defines the organizational boundary, and that power within the organization often revolves around who governs the rules for membership status. They saw two functions of boundary-spanning roles: information processing and external representation. Aldrich and Herker hypothesized that the number and intensity of boundary-spanning roles within an organization is in part influenced by the size of the organization, and they relied upon Thompson's (1967) categories of organizational technology when they linked boundary-spanning behavior with the type of processes used to achieve organizational goals. While boundary-spanners are naturally those at the top-level of the organization where there is extensive contact with the external environment, those individuals close to the technical core are also likely to have boundary-spanning roles and concomitant organizational influence, particularly when they have social networks that extend beyond their normal work requirements.

Aldrich and Herker also noted that power within an organization can be concentrated within these boundary-spanning roles to the extent that these individuals are "gatekeepers" of information necessary for organizational survival. Although research on boundary-spanning was explored throughout the 1980s and early 1990s, the co-evolving empirical strands of networked organizations, learning organizations, and strategic alliances have eclipsed research on boundary-spanners. Indeed, within practitioner-oriented business literature, the concept of "boundary-less" organizations is prevalent as managers attempt to achieve efficiency by flattening bureaucratic hierarchies and removing physical and cultural barriers to organizational success.

Intermediary Organizations and Knowledge Transfer

In a review of literature associated with knowledge transfer and university-industry relations, Agrawal (2001) categorized recent scholarship as being concerned with (i) firm characteristics, (ii) university characteristics, (iii) geography in terms of localized spillover, and (iv) channels of knowledge transfer. Interestingly, none of the

categories included literature that focused on inter-organizational relations beyond the university-industry dynamic. Of particular relevance
to this discussion, Agrawal's essay did not mention intermediary
organizations or the role of non-university, non-firm actors within the
knowledge transfer process.

In contrast, the role of intermediaries was explicitly the topic of
Smedlund's work on knowledge systems (2005). Expanding from the
definition that intermediary organizations are those that function "in
the midst of the users and producers of knowledge" (2005: 210),
Smedlund argued that the innovation function of intermediaries is
broad and includes direct and indirect aspects of knowledge transfer.
Smedlund also noted that organizations could serve intermediary roles
at the macro, meso, and micro levels, to different ends. For example, at
the regional (meso) level, intermediary organizations could:

> improve the image and identity of the region, leverage the social capital
> and encourage communities of practice in the region, create appealing
> environments to creative individuals, and generate local, regional,
> national and international links and relationships of knowledge creation,
> knowledge transfer and knowledge implementing (Smedlund 2005: 218).

This type of activity was empirically investigated by Kodama (2008),
who studied the membership-driven Technology Advanced Metropolitan Area (TAMA) Industrial Vitalization Association Inc., in
Japan. The TAMA Association is an autonomous organization with
membership from the industrial, academic and governmental sectors.
Kodama found that in regions where there were sufficient numbers of
organizations involved in the knowledge transfer process, intermediary organizations like the TAMA Association could help connect entities and foster partnerships, depending on the absorptive capacities of
the participating organizations.

Higher Education Governance Models and External Organizations

The Triangle of Coordination

One of the most enduring conceptual frameworks in comparative
higher education is Burton Clark's 'triangle of coordination' described
in his book titled, *The Higher Education System: Academic Organization
in a Cross-national Perspective* (1983). Clark's identification of "three
ideal types—state system, market system and professional system..."
(1983: 136) arose from his interest in inter-organizational analysis and

the social, economic, and political forces that affect education (Clark 1965). Clark utilized his triangle to compare the governance tensions among eight national higher education systems (the former USSR, Sweden, France, Italy, Britain, Canada, Japan, and the United States). Each of these national systems was placed within the triangle near the point of strongest governing influence (state authority, market, or academic oligarchy), providing a visual and relational comparison.

At the time of Clark's writing in the early 1980s, he correctly perceived that the impact of the market was strongest in the United States, whose higher education system was soon to become a model (for better or for worse) for entrepreneurial behaviour in postsecondary education worldwide. He wrote, "in this triangular conception of types of integration, most of the overt action in most national systems is located to the left of the midpoint: the open battle is between state officials and professors" (1983: 145). While the predominance of state and faculty control may have been true in the 1980s, Clark's triangle presciently was the tip of an arrow pointed directly toward the market. Yet, as he was informed by a pre-Bayh-Dole era, before entrepreneurial policy-making in higher education had become widespread (at least in North America), Clark expressed market coordination in terms of internal competition for the traditional forms of academic exchange (i.e., tuition, tenure, and prestige) and not as a driver of national and global economic development strategies.

Indeed, the word "industry" is not indexed in *The Higher Education System*, and Clark's definition of "corporatism" in postsecondary systems as the co-optation of government by special interest groups is very different from the "commercialization" that is implied by the same term today (see Bok 2003: 3). While Clark's model has been utilized to understand the tensions that exist between academe, the state, and the market (see Bracco et al. 1999), the past two decades have been marked by a social shift that views higher education as more of a private good than a public good. This shift has impacted the applicability of the triangle model to contemporary postsecondary institutions and their inter-organizational relationships. The triangle of coordination is limited in five important ways.

First, the category of "academic oligarchy" is rooted in the presumption of faculty preeminence, and does not fit with the trend of administrative accretion (Leslie and Rhoades 1995) and the rise of support professions within the academy (Rhoades 1998). Faculty senates and peer-review are still viable forces within academic governance, but the cadre of "academic professionals" is now larger than tenured and tenure-accruing professors. Second, the triangular construct of the model emphasizes the oppositional pulls of academe, the market, and the state, but does not allow for the representation of partnerships and alliances among them, even though the intent of the triangle is to understand coordination and integration of academic governance. When higher education institutions are leveraged by state governments as vehicles of economic development, which includes participation within the market through patented inventions, licensing, and spin-off companies, the relations between academe, the state, and the market are much more recursive than a triangle can convey. Third, as organizations are becoming more understood as being embedded within complex inter-organizational networks, a tripartite analysis is no longer sufficient to describe the forces at work within and without higher education institutions. Many types of organizations participate in the arena of higher education coordination, including nongovernmental organizations and special interest groups, whose place on the triangle is not apparent. The fourth limitation of Clark's triangle of coordination is that it is unable to capture the increasing diversity of higher education's institutional forms. As for-profit schools of higher learning emerge (such as the University of Phoenix) and as two-year community colleges continue to evolve into baccalaureate-granting institutions (particularly in the US), the presumption of a monolithic "university" type is no longer valid. Further, e-learning campuses, many of which use the title "university," stretch the conventional notions of "academic oligarchy" and shared governance.

The triangle model does not permit us to ask, "How do the state and the market interact with these new institutional types?" In addition, it is not clear how the changing role of faculty in these evolving institutional types can be better understood using the triangle model. For example, do contract faculty who teach primarily undergraduates interact with the state and market in the same way as research faculty who are also CEO's of start-up companies? Finally, in a global economy it is more difficult to pinpoint an entire country's higher education system within Clark's triangle of coordination. Individual institutions within national postsecondary systems are interacting with the market and industry with marked difference. E-learning programs in particular fields, for example, connect institutions (or particular academic units within institutions) with foreign markets in ways that the triangle cannot depict. A business college, for example, may be closely tied to market influences both domestic and international, yet the university as a whole may have a more nationalistic or local focus. In addition, international research programs can involve several governments and higher education systems, creating networks of innovation and market participation schemas that cannot be likened to flat triangles of single-state governance.

The Triple Helix

While Burton Clark's model of higher education coordination has been widely utilized, the triple helix model also pertains to the relations between universities, the market, and government. Since the publication of Clark's triangle of coordination in the 1980s, higher education governance has experienced significant changes, many of which are addressed in the triple helix model (Tuunainen 2005). In *Universities and the Global Knowledge Economy* (1997), Etzkowitz and Leydesdorff presented the 'triple helix' of academy-industry-government relations. A visual metaphor of the intertwining nature of universities, industry, and government, the triple-helix is not surprisingly based upon the organic DNA structure so important to the burgeoning investment field of biotechnology.

Like Clark's triangle of coordination, the triple helix is concerned with the representation of the academy, the state, and the market, but Etzkowitz and Leydesdorff conceptualized their model during a period of emerging academic entrepreneurship and innovation-centered policy-making in the 1990s. As university research became more responsive to the interests of industry by shifting away from basic science toward applied science and technoscience (Gibbons et al. 1994), the triple helix model was co-opted from these research and development pursuits to describe the reflexive and recombinant nature of industry, universities, and government. The triple helix implies an evolutionary process in contrast to Clark's static triangle shape, within which the three strands form inter-organizational bonds. Between the strands are 'trilateral networks' of cooperative interaction, which strengthen the ties between the three strands and provide multiple paths for inter-agency collaboration.

Etzkowitz (2003) further articulated the evolutionary aspects of the triple helix in describing four stages of its formation: (i) internal transformation in each of the helices, (ii) influence of one helix upon another, (iii) creation of a new overlay of trilateral networks and organizations from the interaction among the three helices, and (iv) a recursive effect of the triple helix networks both on the spirals from which they emerged and on the larger society (2003: 301). Of these stages, the third is the most relevant to this discussion. Although Etzkowitz describes organizations that 'typically form to fill gaps in an innovation system' (2003: 301) such as Joint Venture in Silicon Valley, Knowledge Circle of Amsterdam, and the New England Council, this type of organization has not been widely examined in the triple helix literature. In addition, these organizations on the trilateral networks should not be confused with the 'hybrid organizations' that Etzkowitz described as also being situated within the trilateral networks, as these are more commonly known as the entrepreneurial university or other Mode 2 institutions (Nowotny et al. 2001).

While the trilateral networks of the triple-helix permit an understanding of the interactions between research universities and government–industry innovation systems, the model exhibits several limitations for scholars of university-industry-government relations. One limitation of the trilateral network approach is a structural reliance on three organizational types or sectors (university, industry, government), which inhibits researchers of innovation cycles, economic development, and academic entrepreneurialism from understanding or examining the influences of organizations that are not higher education institutions, industrial firms, or government entities. Yet, organizations whose very mission is the fostering of these cross-sector relationships do exist. While the interstitial location of these organizations is important as the name 'trilateral networks' suggests, their function might go unrecognized without a more process-oriented model.

The Glonacal Agency Heuristic

The need for a more expansive governance model was addressed by Marginson and Rhoades, as they stated, "we need to study how local actors and institutions extend their activities to the international stage" (2002: 286). Marginson and Rhoades developed a 'glonacal agency heuristic' to describe the various influences on higher education governance and policy-making. Their model focuses on these dimensions to emphasize "the intersections, interactions, mutual determinations of these levels—global, national, and local—and domains—organizational agencies and the agency of collectivities"—(2002: 289). Their model goes beyond Clark's triangle of coordination and Etzkowitz and Leydesdorff's triple helix to create "crystals" of "interconnected hexagons" located in three-dimensional space. Significant contributions of the model include the ability to discuss inter-organizational reciprocity, the magnitude of ties, organizational historicity and social embeddedness, and spheres of influence (geographical and functional).

Although their glonacal agency heuristic is a positive step toward re-conceptualizing the tripartite structure of academic governance, their model is too complex for practical application. Yet, they correctly state that if the inter-organizational field around higher education can be considered, a larger variety of organizational actors can be contemplated.

The Model of Intermediating Organizations

The concept of intermediating organizations is tied to a theoretical tradition that has addressed the changes brought to higher education by the 'new economy' and globalization (Slaughter and Rhoades 2004). The widespread use of information technologies has stretched the boundaries of time and place, has introduced new commodities of exchange, and has emphasized resource stress within organizations (Castells, 2000). Further, in the 'new economy' the external organizational environment is characterized by intense competition, innovation, flexibility, and risk (Carnoy 2000, Carnoy et al. 1993). Globalization, as described by Levin (2001), manifests itself in organizations such as higher education institutions through production processes, technological innovation, and dependence upon these innovations.

The terms 'mediating,' 'intermediary,' and 'intermediate' have been used to describe interstitial organizations in higher education and public policy (Berger and Neuhaus 1977; Harkavy and Puckett 1991, El-Khawas 1997, Ware 1989). Continuing the use of terminology common to organizational studies to describe the mediating nature of some organizations (Braun 1993, Burch 2002, Honig 2004, Pavetti et al. 2000, Wynn 2000), *intermediating organizations* are here defined as those organizations that are intentionally situated between the state, industry, and higher education. Intermediating organizations may be foundations, associations, consortia, independent research centers (including research parks), or special interest groups. It is hypothesized that each type of intermediating organization mentioned above will have unique characteristics, and therefore should be explored independently (Metcalfe 2004, Slaughter and Rhoades 2004).

Intermediating organizations are situated within a vast inter-organizational field concerned with higher education and the role of universities in society (Cook 1998). In an early work that set out to describe the inter-organizational space of American higher education, Murray (1976) described higher education associations as being core lobbies, satellite lobbies, or peripheral lobbies. In his system, core lobbies are the "central cluster of large associations representing the principal institutional constituencies in higher education" (1976: 82) such as the American Council on Education (ACE) and the American Association of Universities (AAU). Satellite lobbies are "the associated cluster of organizations which represent a specialized constituency within the context of the more comprehensive associations," and are further divided into research and non-research university categories. An example of a satellite lobby is the Council of Graduate Schools (CGS). Peripheral lobbies are those that represent "(i) individual institutions or systems; (ii) small associations; (iii) functional, discipline organizations; (iv) occupational groups, and (v) special task organizations" (1976: 84).

While Murray's typology is spatially organized around a focal entity (the US federal government), intermediating organizations can be better understood and organized by their central characteristics.

Table 12.1. Typology of intermediating organizations

Type	Description	Examples
Associations	Institutional Consortia Disciplinary/Scholarly Professional/Managerial Trade/Industrial	Internet2 Association of University Technology Managers (AUTM)
Foundations	Educational Philanthropic Research	Canada Foundation for Innovation (CFI)
Centres and Institutes	Identity-based Issue-based Research-based Think Tanks/Institutes	Conference Board of Canada Glion Colloquium

Like many of the organizations described by Murray, intermediating organizations intentionally operate as liaisons between higher education, the market, and the state. Thus, the types of intermediating organizations can be organized as in Table 12.1, but not all organizations matching the descriptions above should be classified as intermediating in nature.

In creating a model of intermediating organizations, the limitations of Clark's triangle of coordination and the structural challenges of the triple-helix and glonacal agency heuristic were considered. Therefore, the model is a networked structure that regards the nature of the ties between organizations as a potential unit of analysis with as much significance as the organizations themselves. Flows between the trilateral networks are of particular relevance to the model of intermediating organizations. In addition to these concepts, these organizations are often between the public and private sectors (Ware 1989) and increasingly involved in the commercialization of the nonprofit sector (Weisbrod 1998). Further, professional accretion, professionalization, and the potential impact of professional associations can be addressed with the model (Metcalfe 2004; Greenwood et al. 2002, Wilensky 1964).

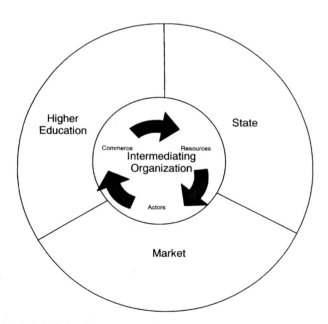

Figure 12.1. Model of an intermediating organization.

The model situates the Intermediating Organization at the center of the diagram. This is conceptual as well as practical, as from this perspective the Intermediating Organization is the primary organizational unit of analysis and the focus of inquiry. Surrounding the Intermediating Organization are sections representing the market, higher education, and the state. These are described as 'sets' because each is far more complex than can be described in a model or diagram. The state, for example, as noted above, can be local, national, regional, or global in scope and governance (Marginson and Rhoades 2002). The market may be divided into different industrial sectors and types of businesses. Higher Education can be further sub-categorized by control (public/private), geographic region, size, and institutional ranking. Thus, while the model is fairly simple at first glance, it is intended to have wide applicability.

The model shows three 'flows' of exchange that occur between the organizational sets, which are central to the influence of intermediating organizations: the Flow of Actors, the Flow of Resources, and the Flow of Commerce. The flows connect the state, industry, and higher education to the intermediating organization, and to some extent the flows intersect each organizational set. Each of these flows is described in more detail below, but it is significant to note that each of these flows can be a source of income for the intermediating organization (through membership dues, special contracts, and sales of goods and services). These flows express the transactions that take place between and among formally defined organizational entities. These flows also highlight the perceived and real transparencies and opacities of organizational boundaries. A fundamental tenet of the model is that an organizational border is a boundary-object, socially-constructed, which is utilized by actors to serve the interests of themselves and their affiliated groups (Guston 2001, Lynn 2005, Sapsed and Salter 2004, Star 1989).

The three flows are grounded in the literature of higher education research and the scholarship of organizations. The Flow of Actors, for example, was developed to recognize the role of individuals within organizations, specifically those that can be described as 'boundary-spanners' (Aldrich and Herker 1977). The Flow of Actors also encompasses concepts of networks (Scott 2000, Thompson 2003) and changes in academic labor (Rhoades 1998, Rhoades and Sporn 2002). At the most basic level, organizations are dependent upon the Flow of Actors because without people, organizations do not exist. People move between the public and private sectors as employees, consultants, customers, volunteers, etc. In contrast to typical organizational research, the model of intermediating organizations assumes that individuals have a variety of affiliations, be they formal or informal, temporary or static. Within most organizations people hold several affiliations simultaneously; their identities are shaped by these organizations as they shape the organizations themselves.

There are three types of exchange within the Flow of Resources: knowledge, financial, and emblematic (prestige). The Flow of Resources has been conceptualized with the consideration of resource dependency theory (Pfeiffer and Salancik [1978] 2003) and its limitations, as described by Slaughter and Rhoades (2004). The Flow of Resources is based upon the concepts of knowledge exchange (Castells 2000, Delanty 2001, Gibbons et al. 1994, Godin and Gingras, 2000), financial exchange (McChesney et al. 1998, Rifkin 2000, Smith 2000), and emblematic exchange (Gulati 1995, King and Slaughter 2004). Knowledge exchange is an important function of organizations, and it is critical to the value of an intermediating organization. Without efficient methods for knowledge exchange an intermediating organization will not be utilized by other organizations in the UIG sectors because the Flows of Actors, Resources, and Commerce depend upon reliable information.

Financial exchange is the 'bread and butter' aspect of an intermediating organization, where revenues and expenditures are examined. As nonprofit organizations, many intermediating organizations are subject to open records laws and as such financial data are often publicly available. Emblematic exchange is also a publicly visible form of affiliation. Tokens of exchange are used, such as organizational logos, partnership programs, and naming opportunities. Other aspects of affiliation that are considered emblematic exchanges are strategic alliances and sponsorships that involve visible name recognition. Emblematic exchanges confer legitimacy and they advertise affiliation to organization members and non-members.

Finally, the Flow of Commerce was conceptually informed by research on the corporatization of the non-profit sector (Weisbrod 1998) and examinations of higher education institutions as commercial sites (Barrow 1990, Bok 2003, Gould 2003, Kirp 2003, Schiller 1999, White and Hauck 2000). The Flow of Commerce is the trade of goods and services that flows through intermediating organizations.

Intermediating organizations can participate in a 'micro-market' that they help shape by selling goods and/or services to their members and to non-members. Intermediating organizations also create opportunities for competition and collaboration between public and private entities, which may or may not be members of the organization.

The Flow of Commerce differs from the Flow of Resources in that the latter includes grants and sponsorships while the former is concerned solely with commercial activity. Management of the Flow of Commerce is an entrepreneurial endeavor for intermediating organizations. Structures such as corporate partner programs stratify vendors and corporate members in such a way as to capitalize on existing competition between companies while creating incentives for increased revenues through corporate sponsorships and vendor services (Metcalfe 2004). Intermediating organizations do not just broker merchant relationships; they also provide members with legitimated vendor lists and product endorsements, either directly or indirectly.

Polodny (1994) discussed inter-organizational linkages within an environment marked by uncertainty as functions of trust and prestige. Polodny stated, "the greater the market uncertainty, the more that organizations engage in exchange relations with those whom they have transacted in the past" (1994: 458). Furthermore, "the greater the uncertainty, the more that organizations engage in transactions with those of similar status." For this reason intermediating organizations are hypothesized to strengthen ties between the public and private sector, as membership status within the intermediating organization helps to confer legitimacy and status upon the potential partners. Further, emblems of the intermediating organization serve to remind members of their common affiliation.

The Intermediating Organization model is intended to aid in the understanding of the ways in which public/private networks form, specifically the ties between higher education, government, and industry. Intermediating organizations are a type of 'go-between' that advance the progress of relationships between the respective boundary-spanners of public and private groups, relations that might lead to direct ties across sectors and increased knowledge transfer. In contrast with other organizations, intermediating organizations are strongly directed toward external constituents and opportunities, but it would be wrong to say that these organizations are solely 'dependent' upon these external resources.

Case Study of the Ottawa Centre for Research and Innovation (OCRI)

To better understand how the theory of intermediating organizations might be applied to real-world university-industry-government relationships, a case study of the Ottawa Centre for Research and Innovation (OCRI) is described below. The centre can be defined as an intermediating organization that functions as a liaison between the public and private sectors. Founded in 1983, the Ottawa Centre for Research and Innovation, (originally named the Ottawa-Carleton Research Institute, with the same initials), is a nonprofit, membership-based organization, with over 625 organizational members from the public and private sectors. The OCRI has described itself as a "rallying point for business, education and government to advance Ottawa's globally competitive knowledge-based economy" (OCRI 2009). In this succinct summary of its mission, the OCRI's leadership clearly considers the organization to be ideally situated between the academy, industry, and government. As a 'rallying point,' the OCRI serves an intermediating function by brokering an inter-organizational space where individuals from public and private entities can meet, discuss mutually supportive goals, and strategize ways to achieve those goals. In turn, the public and private sectors fund the organization through membership dues, sponsorships, and grants.

When analyzed through the framework of intermediating organizations, the impact of the OCRI on university-industry-government relations is seen through a Flow of Actors, a Flow of Resources, and a Flow of Commerce. With over 45 staff members and 28 people on the Board of Directors who sit on various committees, the Flow of Actors within OCRI is complex. Within this group, the interplay between actors in the public and private sector can be observed. For example, the Board of Directors for OCRI is composed of individuals from over a dozen business ventures, companies and trade associations (including the prominent Canadian firms Nortel and Research in Motion), government officials (the Mayor and the Councilor of the City of Ottawa), and representatives from colleges and universities (such as Carleton University and the University of Ottawa). The Board of the OCRI provides an opportunity for Ottawa's leadership from business, academe, and government to convene on matters of regional economic development.

Participation on the OCRI board is a shared experience that allows each actor to make contacts across the public-private divide and among the three areas of university-industry-government relations. OCRI's Flow of Resources entails the money, information, and prestige that are exchanged between public and private members of the organization. Membership dues, particularly from corporate members, are an important transaction for OCRI. Annual dues range from 300 Canadian dollars for an individual membership to $10,000 Canadian dollars for companies with more than 1,000 employees. With about 625 members (individuals and organizations), the dues are a significant revenue source for OCRI. Other funds come from private foundations and government grants for specific programs and services. About 20 percent of the OCRI operating budget comes from an annual grant from the City of Ottawa ($1.592 million in 2005). In addition, OCRI sells space for banner advertisements on the search results pages of its web site, at the top of the home page, and in email communications to members.

Perhaps the greatest Flow of Resources within and around OCRI is the transaction of knowledge. OCRI hosts a variety of programs for small businesses, educators, and community members that help to support the infrastructure of the region. For example, the OCRI was an inaugural partner of Ottawa's Software Process Improvement Network (SPIN), which they had described as "a forum for the free and open exchange of software process improvement expertise, experiences and ideas" (OCRI 2009). The objective was to "promote process improvement, increased process maturity and high quality software-based products in the Ottawa region, through an active program of networking, presentations, publications/discussion groups, as well as liaise with other similar groups" (OCRI 2009). As SPIN members came from academe, industry, and government, the Ottawa SPIN is just one example of the many programs that OCRI offers to increase the technical knowledge-base of the region and UIG relations.

In addition, OCRI partners with other regional groups to offer specialized conferences. In 2008, OCRI partnered with the National Research Council Canada and Carleton University to offer an Executive Symposium on Photonics Commercialization. The event was described as bringing "senior executives from leading photonics corporations together with high ranking government officials to present their perspective on the commercialization of photonics" (OCRI 2009). As the conference was co-sponsored by a federal-level research council and a local university with a specialization in the field of Photonics, the event demonstrates OCRI's interest in bridging the public and private sectors by fostering opportunities for the commercialization of public research.

One of the more direct intermediating roles that OCRI plays is the co-sponsorship of a set of university research chairs in high tech fields. The chairs are funded through a partnership between the OCRI, Communications and Information Technology Ontario (CITO), and the Natural Sciences and Engineering Research Council of Canada (NSERC), representing the interests of the university-industry-government triad. Known as the OCRI/CITO/NSERC Industrial Research Chair (IRC) program, the chairs are meant to be awarded to individuals who conduct research that "presents unique industrial opportunities and that responds to industrial needs" (OCRI 2009). At present, there are three chairs in the following areas: Real-Time Multimedia Distributed Database Systems (University of Ottawa), Performance Engineering of Real-time Software (Carleton University), and User-Centred Product Design (Carleton University). Each chair is selected for a renewable five-year term.

Prestige exchange between OCRI and other organizations is noted through their strategic alliances. The OCRI web site lists these ties, preceded by the statement, "Partnerships and alliances have been the enablers of success for OCRI. Partnerships with local, provincial and national organizations allow OCRI to broaden their efforts to advance Ottawa's technology community" (OCRI 2009). The web site then lists the local, provincial, and national alliances in research and development (Table 12.2). These strategic alliances are spread between trade organizations and government research centers, with academic involvement occurring in both. As such, the strategic alliances built between OCRI and the organizations listed above create ties between universities, industry, and government.

The third flow that occurs between OCRI and public/private entities is the Flow of Commerce. OCRI, like many intermediating organizations, hosts various conferences that showcase the goods and services of their membership. For example, the OCRI hosts an annual Ottawa Venture and Technology Summit. The event is hosted under the direction of OCRI's Ottawa Capital Network, which forms connections between investors and business ventures in the region. The Summit provides a forum for angel investors to hear presentations from several companies seeking capital, which are hand-picked by the Ottawa Capital Network on the basis of management strength, connections to Ottawa, and uniqueness of products or services. To be included in the Summit, companies have to be "Canadian-owned, privately held, Ottawa based".

Table 12.2.   R&D alliances between OCRI, universities, industry, and government, 2009

Local (City of Ottawa)	National Capital Institute of Telecommunications
Provincial	Ottawa Photonics Cluster
	Ottawa Photonics Research Alliance
	Ontario Centres of Excellence:
	• Communications and Information Technology Ontario
	• Materials and Manufacturing Ontario
	• Photonics Research Ontario
	• Centre for Research in Earth and Space Technology
	Ontario Ministry of Economic Development and Trade
National	National Research Council
	Natural Sciences and Engineering Council
	Industry Canada
	Canada Research Chairs

Through the Summit and other events, OCRI directly supports the Flow of Commerce in Ottawa. As much of the commercial activity supported by these events is high-tech in nature, OCRI is directly tied to the knowledge-spillovers that occur between educational institutions, government research centers, and industry. Indeed it could be stated that OCRI helps the private sector to capture knowledge-spillovers and to make academic science part of Ottawa's knowledge economy.

Conclusion

This chapter presents a new model for higher education research and the investigation of innovation networks. The model of inter-mediating organizations presented here is intended to aid future research regarding the role of external organizations in the university-industry-government relationship, leading to a new consideration of inter-organizational behavior and external influence. Intermediating organizations, which may be foundations, associations, consortia, independent research centers, or special interest groups, are hypothesized to actively position themselves between the state, industry, and higher education in order to fulfill their missions and increase organizational legitimacy, power, and revenue. Three inter-organizational 'flows' have been conceptualized to connect the organizational sets. These transactional processes are: the Flow of Actors, the Flow of Resources, and the Flow of Commerce. The three flows are grounded in the literature of higher education research and the sociology of organizations.

A focus on intermediating organizations is essential to our understanding of the ways in which public/private networks form, specifically the ties between higher education, industry, and government. These of 'go-between' organizations foster relationship building between the respective boundary-spanners of public and private groups, relations that might lead to direct ties across sectors in the form of strategic alliances and organizational partnerships. In contrast with other organizations, intermediating organizations are strongly directed toward external constituents and opportunities, but as stated above, it would be wrong to say that these organizations are solely 'dependent' upon these external resources. The Ottawa Centre for Research and Innovation (OCRI) is a good example, as it is both driven to support its partner organizations and to grow as an independent organization with its own agenda.

However, much like higher education institutions are theorized to be potentially moved toward the needs of external resource providers (Slaughter and Rhoades 2004), the entrepreneurial behaviors of the OCRI may influence its organizational mission of over time, aligning it more closely with the needs of universities, industry, and government.

Bibliography

Aldrich, Howard and Diane Herker. 1977. "Boundary Spanning Roles and Organization Structure." *Academy of Management Review* 2: 217–30.

Agrawal, Ajay. 2001. "Univeristy-to-Industry Knowledge Transfer: Literature Review and Unanswered Questions." *International Journal of Management Reviews* 3(4): 285–302.

Barrow, Clyde W. 1990. *Universities and the Capitalist State: Corporate Liberalism and the Reconstruction of American Higher Education, 1894–1928.* Madison, WI: The University of Wisconsin Press.

Berger, Peter L. and Richard John Neuhaus. 1977. *To Empower People: The Role of Mediating Structures in Public Policy*. American Enterprise Institute for Public Policy Research: Washington, DC.

Bok, Derek. 2003. *Universities in the Marketplace: The Commercialization of Higher Education*. Princeton University Press: Princeton, NJ.

Bracco, Kathy Reeves, Richard C. Richardson, Patrick M. Callan, and Joni E. Finney. 1999 "Policy Environments and System Design: Understanding State Governance Structures." *Review of Higher Education* 23(1): 23–44.

Braun, Dietmar. 1993. "Who Governs Intermediary Agencies? Principle-agent Relations in Research Policy-making." *Journal of Public Policy* 13(2): 135–62.

Burch, Patricia. 2002. "Constraints and Opportunities in Changing Policy Environments: Intermediary Organizations' Response to Complex District Context", in Amy M. Hightower, Michael S. Knapp, Julie A. Marsh, and Milbrey W. McLaughlin, eds., *School Districts and Instructional Renewal*. New York: Teachers College Press, pp. 111–26.

Carnoy, Martin. 2000. *Sustaining the New Economy: Work, Family, and the Community in the Information Age*. New York: Russell Sage Foundation.

Carnoy, Martin, Manuel Castells, Stephen S. Cohen, and Fernando Henrique Cardoso. 1993 *The New Global Economy in the Information Age: Reflections on our Changing World* University Park, PA: Pennsylvania State University Press.

Castells, Manuel. 2000. *The Rise of the Network Society, Second Edition*. Oxford: Blackwell Publishers.

Clark, Burton R. 1965. "Interorganizational Patterns in Education." *Administrative Science Quarterly* 10(2): 224–237.

Clark, Burton R. 1983. *The Higher Education System: Academic Organization in Cross National Perspective*. Los Angeles, CA: University of California Press.

Cook, Constance. E. 1998. *Lobbying for Higher Education: How Colleges and Universities Influence Federal Policy*. Nashville, TN: Vanderbilt University Press.

Delanty, Gerard. 2001. *Challenging Knowledge: The University in the Knowledge Society*. Buckingham, UK: Society for Research into Higher Education and Open University Press.

Dill, David D. 1999. "Academic Accountability and University Adaptation: The Architecture of an Academic Learning Organization." *Higher Education* 38: 127–154.

Domhoff, William G. 2009. "The Power Elite and Their Challengers: The Role of Nonprofits in American Social Conflict." *American Behavioral Scientist* 52(7): 955–973.

El-Khawas, Elaine. 1997. "The Role of Intermediary Organizations" in Marvin W. Peterson, David D. Dill, and Lisa A. Mets, eds., *Planning and Management for a Changing Environment: A Handbook on Redesigning Postsecondary Institutions*. San Francisco: Jossey-Bass Publishers, pp. 66–87.

Enders, Jürgen. 2004. "Higher Education, Internationalisation, and the Nation-State: Recent Developments and Challenges to Governance Theory." *Higher Education* 47(3): 361–382.

Etzkowitz, Henry. 2003. "Innovation in Innovation: The Triple Helix of University-Industry Government Relations." *Social Science Information* 42(3): 293–337.

Etzkowitz, Henry and Leydesdorff, Loet, eds. 1997. *Universities and the Global Knowledge Economy: A Triple-Helix of University-Industry-Government Relations.* London: Continuum.

Gibbons, Michael, Camille Limoges, Helga Nowotny, Simon Schwartzman, Peter Scott, and Martin Trow. 1994. *The New Production of Knowledge: The Dynamics of Science and Research in Contemporary Societies.* London, Thousand Oaks, CA: Sage Publications.

Godin, Benoit and Gingras, Yves. 2000. "The Place of Universities in the System of Knowledge Production." *Research Policy* 29: 273–78.

Gould, Eric. 2003. *The University in a Corporate Culture.* New Haven, CT: Yale University Press.

Greenwood, Royston, Roy Suddaby, and C. R. Hinings. 2002. "Theorizing Change: The Role of Professional Associations in the Transformation of Institutionalized Fields." *Academy of Management Review* 45(1): 58–80.

Gulati, Ranjay. 1995. "Familiarity Breeds Trust? The Implications of Repeated Ties on Contractual Choice in Alliances." *Academy of Management Journal* 38: 85–112.

Guston, David H. 2001. "Boundary Organizations in Environmental Policy and Science: An Introduction." *Science, Technology, and Human Values* 26(4): 399–408.

Harkavy, Ira and John L. Puckett. 1991. "The Role of Mediating Structures in University and Community Revitalization: The University of Pennsylvania and West Philadelphia as a Case Study." *Journal of Research and Development in Education* 25(1): 10–25.

Honig, Meredith I. 2004. "The New Middle Management: Intermediary Organizations in Education Policy Implementation." *Educational Evaluation and Policy Analysis* 26(1): 65–87.

King, Samantha J. and Sheila Slaughter. 2004. "Commodifying University Identity: Logos, Trademarks, and Sports R Us", in Sheila Slaughter and Gary Rhoades, *Academic Capitalism in the New Economy.* Baltimore: Johns Hopkins University Press, pp. 256–78.

Kirp, David L. 2003. *Shakespeare, Einstein, and the Bottom Line: The Marketing of Higher Education.* Cambridge, MA: Harvard University Press.

Kodama, Toshihiro. 2008. The Role of Intermediation and Absorptive Capacity in Facilitating University-Industry Linkages: An Empirical Study of TAMA in Japan. *Research Policy* 37: 1124–1240.

Lynn, Monty L. 2005. "Organizational Buffering: Managing Boundaries and Cores." *Organization Studies* 26(1): 37–61.

Marginson, Simon and Gary Rhoades. 2002. "Beyond National States, Markets, and Systems of Higher Education: A Glonacal Agency Heuristic." *Higher Education* 43: 281–309.

McChesney, Robert W., Ellen Meiksins Wood, and John Bellamy Foster. 1998. *Capitalism and the Information Age: The Political Economy of the Global Communication Revolution.* New York: Monthly Review Press.

Metcalfe, Amy S. 2004. *Intermediating Associations and the University-Industry Relationship.* Unpublished doctoral dissertation, Center for the Study of Higher Education, University of Arizona.

Murray, Michael. 1976. "Defining the Higher Education Lobby." *The Journal of Higher Education* 47(1): 79–92. Nowotny, Helga, Peter Scott, and Michael Gibbons. 2001. *Re-Thinking Science: Knowledge and the Public in an Age of Uncertainty.* Cambridge, MA: Polity Press.

Ottawa Centre for Research and Innovation (OCRI) 2009. Organization website. Retrieved from http://www.ocri.ca.

Pavetti, LaDonna, Michelle Derr, Jacquelyn Anderson, Carole Trippe, and Sidnee Paschal. 2000. *The Role of Intermediary Organizations Linking TANF Recipients with Jobs* (MPR Reference No: 8543–400). Washington, DC: Mathematica Policy Research, Inc.

Pfeffer, Jeffrey and Gerald Salancik. 2003. *The External Control of Organizations: A Resource Dependence Perspective.* Stanford, CA: Stanford University Press. (Original work published 1978).

Polodny, Joel. M 1994. "Market Uncertainty and the Social Characteristics of Economic Exchange." *Administrative Science Quarterly* 39: 458–483.

Rhoades, Gary. 1998. *Managed Professionals: Unionized Faculty and Restructuring Academic Labor.* Albany, NY: State University of New York Press.

Rhoades, Gary and Barbara Sporn. 2002. "New Models of Management and Shifting Modes and Costs of Production: Europe and the United States." *Tertiary Education and Management* 8(1): 3–28.

Rifkin, Jeremy. 2000. *The Age of Access: The New Culture of Hypercapitalism Where All of Life is a Paid-for Experience.* New York: Jeremy P. Tarcher/Putnam.

Salamon, Lester M. 1994. "The Rise of the Nonprofit Sector." *Foreign Affairs* 73(4): 109–122. Sapsed, Jonathan and Ammon Salter. 2004. "Postcards from the Edge: Local Communities, Global Programs and Boundary Objects." *Organizational Studies* 25(9): 1515–1534.

Schiller, Dan. 1999. *Digital Capitalism: Networking the Global Market System.* Cambridge, MA: MIT Press.

Scott, John P. 2000. *Social Network Analysis: A Handbook, Second Edition.* London and Thousand Oaks, CA: Sage Publications.

Slaughter, Sheila and Gary Rhoades. 2004. *Academic Capitalism in the New Economy: Markets, State, and Higher Education.* Baltimore, MD: Johns Hopkins University Press.

Smedlund, Anssi. 2005. "The Roles of Intermediaries in Regional Knowledge Systems." *Journal of Intellectual Capital* 7(2): 204–220.

Smith, Tony. 2000. *Technology and Capital in the Age of Lean Production: A Marxian Critique of the "New Economy"*. Albany, NY: State University of New York Press.

Star, Susan. L. 1989. "The Structure of Ill-structured Solutions: Boundary Objects and Heterogeneous Distributed Problem Solving" in L. Gasser and M. N. Huhns, eds., *Distributed Artificial Intelligence, Vol. 2*. London: Pitman, pp. 37–54.

Thompson, James. 1967. *Organizations in Action*. New York: McGraw-Hill.

Thompson, Grahame F. 2003. *Between Hierarchies and Markets: The Logic and Limits of Network Forms of Organization*. Oxford: Oxford University Press.

Tuunainen, Juha. 2005. "Hybrid Practices? Contributions to the Debate on the Mutation of Science and University." *Higher Education* 50(2): 275–98.

Ware, Alan. 1989. *Between Profit and State: Intermediate Organizations in Britain and the United States*. Cambridge: Polity Press.

Weisbrod, Burton A. ed. 1998. *To Profit or Not to Profit: The Commercial Transformation of the Nonprofit Sector*. Cambridge: Cambridge University Press.

White, Geoffrey D. and Flannery C. Hauck. eds. 2000. *Campus, Inc.: Corporate Power in the Ivory Tower*. Amherst, NY: Prometheus Books.

Wilensky, Harold L. 1964. "The Professionalization of Everyone?" *American Journal of Sociology* 70(2): 137–58.

Wynn, Joan R. 2000. *The Role of Local Intermediary Organizations in the Youth Development Field*. Chicago, IL: Chapin Hall Center for Children.

CHAPTER THIRTEEN

IDEALS AND CONTRADICTIONS IN KNOWLEDGE CAPITALIZATION

James Dzisah

Universities as institutions of knowledge are undergoing significant changes that are linked to such factors as the globalization of the economy, the rise of technologies based on generic forms of knowledge, the erosion of universities grant economy, the ability of universities to hold and exploit patents, the gradual breakdown of boundaries between basic and applied research, and the shift toward a knowledge-based economy (Baber 2001, Etzkowitz et al. 1995). In both scale and intensity, these alterations have led to critical reflections on how scientific and technological innovations should be enhanced by policy decisions so as to bridge the gap between discovery and application. However, since theory occupies such an essential place in academic scholarship, different authors have devoted considerable time and effort in detailing, albeit from varying theoretical outlooks the essential elements and inferences. For Marx, the function of theory was to guide men in changing the world. For Mannheim, theory was to provide scientific guidance for action directed towards 'planning for freedom' (Zeitlin 1997:383–4). For Manuel Castells theory is "a tool to understand the world, not an end for intellectual self-enjoyment" (1997:3). In the burgeoning scholarship on university-industry-government interactions, one can equally discern two, albeit, similar but competing theoretical explications: the 'Mode 1-Mode 2' thesis (Gibbons et al. 1994) and the 'triple helix' of university-industry-government relations (Etzkowitz and Leydesdorff 1997) model.

These models detailed the contours of the rise of knowledge and its effects on intellectual property regimes and the capitalization of knowledge. In the 'Mode 1-Mode 2' model, Gibbons and his collaborators saw a move away from the traditional knowledge practices that delinked academia from society, perpetuating in the process, the so-called 'ivory tower' ideals. In the context of 'Mode 1', the scene of knowledge production is institutionally differentiated from the site of application (Gibbons et al. 1994). The recognition that individuals from both public and private realms, inside and outside the confines of the university have penetrated "conventional organizations to which their continuing attachment to an 'external' knowledge-based community represents a valuable asset" (David and Foray 2002:9) is a testament that, a new political economy of knowledge is unfolding. This, in effect, gives credence to the argument that in a 'Mode 2' era knowledge production has become part of a larger process in which scientific, technological, and industrial knowledge productions have all become closely intertwined (Gibbons et al. 1994).

As analytic and normative model, the triple helix theory is derived from the changing role of government in different societies in relation to academia and industry (Etzkowitz and Leydesdorff 1997). Its basis is the recognition that the relations among relatively independent but interdependent institutional spheres are critical to improving the conditions for innovation in a knowledge-based society (Etzkowitz 2008). The triple helix model comprises three basic elements: (1) a more prominent role for the university in innovation, on a par with industry and government in a knowledge-based society; (2) a movement towards collaborative relationships among the three major institutional spheres in which innovation policy is increasingly an outcome of interaction rather than a prescription from government; (3) in addition to fulfilling their traditional functions, each institutional sphere 'takes the role of the other' in some regards, such as a university taking government's role of initiating development projects or industry's role of firm formation. The institutional spheres still perform their traditional functions, but increasingly assume the tasks of advancing innovation (Etzkowitz 2008).

This new dynamism notwithstanding, there is an ongoing debate as to why universities—institutions dedicated to the preservation, transmission, and production of knowledge with distinctive culture— should be persuaded by policy-makers to adopt industrial traits that are contrary to the very existence of universities as undefiled instruments of society (Axelrod 2002, Brooks 1993, Cohen 2000, Pelikan 1992, Slaughter and Leslie 1997, Washburn 2005). The general orientation, to paint in broad strokes, is that academic integrity is being undermined by the lure of corporate research dollars (Washburn 2005, Axelrod 2002, Turk 2000, Slaughter and Leslie 1997). In other words, there are potential deleterious effects in allowing industry to fund university research. With this debate in mind, the chapter utilizes survey data to explore some of the core issues raised in this segment of the academic literature. It is argued that the perception of pervasive influence is not imaginary. There is a real or perceived conviction that the receipt or non-receipt of research funds from industry affects the idea of knowledge as a commodity. This reflects the broader debate on universities as instruments of knowledge and society (Habermas 1970, Delanty 2001a, Pelikan 1992).

Globalization and Knowledge Capitalization

The process of globalization, traceable to the advances in information and communication technologies, has drastically reconfigured the notion of time and space (Giddens 1990, Harvey 1989, Castells 1996). Globalization has brought, along with its pervasiveness, a structural reorganization of societies, which in many ways is realistically different from those of the last quarter century (Bell 1973). It manifests itself in different spheres and fields. In terms of knowledge, the transformation is felt around institutions of higher education as they increasingly come under the twirl of academic capitalism. These changes have occurred almost simultaneously with increasing recognition of the dual theoretical and practical impetuses of scientific research (Etzkowitz et al. 2000). Whilst the process of the capitalization of academic scientific knowledge is not benign across the academic landscape, recent acceleration of the process has generated much debate in many circles. The dominance of these debates is understandable from the perspective that the study of the nature and causes of the transformation of universities is a relatively new area of interest.

In spite of this, the fact remains that scientific research and economic activity are no strange correlates. In terms of university, industry, and government relations, the linkage is exemplified by various attempts to develop science and technology parks, centres of excellence, and other university-based research innovators (Castells and Hall 1994, Etzkowitz and Leydesdorff 1997). While the explicit nature, the sheer size of the practice, and the manner in which "policies encouraging the university to become a driver of knowledge-based economy" (Etzkowitz 2002:1) are being pursued are novel in many ways, the transformation of academic science into economic outcome is as old as modern universities (Jacob and Stewart 2004). The reality, however, is that modern universities are established to aid the socio-economic development of their respective locales, regions and nations. In essence, universities are to help quicken the production of human and social capital with the expectation that both will in the long run be combined to produce economic capital.

However, the nature, substance, and structure of these economic development tasks are often ambiguously left to the discretion of various stakeholders—university faculty and administration, private sector industries, local, regional, and national governments. This is why until recently, attempts were made to distinctively separate university and industrial research (Kleinman 1995). This distinction in a way makes for a superficial policing of boundaries by drawing an imaginary line between scholarly and industrial research. In spite of this barriers, basic and applied research interact in a variety of ways, particularly through consultancy work done for industry by some academic faculty (Etzkowitz 2002). However, in the rigorous sense of the distinction between basic and applied science, "academe was perceived as doing the necessary fundamental science that often preceded application and industrial development" (Croissant et al. 2001:108—109). The outcome of this separation was that it left "control of commercial opportunities of academic research in the hands of industry whereas control over the direction of research and the choice of research topics was left to academic scientists" (Etzkowitz 2002:13).

The boundary crossing has not abated but, continues to gradually increase. In spite of this, it will be naive to overly simplify the emerging political economy of knowledge. The rising socio-economic agenda is complex as it combined elements of previous economic activities into new modes: agricultural, industrial and knowledge. As Paul Krugman notes, while the "rise of new technologies makes old advantages irrelevant and offers new opportunities…the past is not completely irrelevant" (2000:271). Since the structures, growth and trajectories of science and knowledge production are influenced by their specific social contexts, we must equally explore the underlying constitutive social structures, depending on classical analysis if necessary, to understand current transformations. In this regard, the writings of Marx, Durkheim, Weber, Mannheim and the rest often revealed more than passive acquiescence of the implications of the social in the emerging transformations.

By integrating, albeit from different theoretical viewpoints comprehensive reflections on the intricate interaction between science and society (Baber 2000), the aforementioned classical sociologists provided us with the basic tools to examine contemporary transforma-tions in both the regime and institutions of knowledge. For instance, Karl Marx's framework for analyzing the dynamics of social change is embedded within the constant interaction between an objective natu-ral world and human agency. In parallel, new forms of knowledge capi-talization are shaped by the evolving social, economic and cultural factors operating at different levels, space and time. Marx in some of his writings went beyond the idea that the "institutionalization and growth of science and technology is moulded and shaped by the chang-ing social and political context" (Baber 2000:140). In fact, Boris Hessen (1971 [1931]), also located the roots of Newton's *Principia* in the emer-gent social and economic context of the period in which Newton worked. Hessen's analysis unpacked the fact that Newton's laws of motion were formulated partly in order to grapple with the "problem of delineating the optimal conditions for projectile motion on the bat-tlefield" (Baber 2000:140).

This communal nature of science while cherished is not by any stretch of imagination formalized into law that requires contemporary scientists, who are working in different socio-economic, political and cultural environments to desist from pursuing knowledge beyond their initial curiosities. However, significant chunk of early research into university-industry relations was full of moral lamentations about the perceived erosion of the normative structure of science (Kleinman and Vallas 2001). In large part, this was a reflection of the seminal work of Robert Merton (1973:240), in which he detailed the ethos of science: universalism, disinterestedness, organized skepticism and communalism. The ethos of 'universalism' is understood to mean that "truth claims, whatever their source, are to be subjected to pre-estab-lished impersonal criteria: consonant with previously confirmed knowledge' (Merton 1973:270). Since "objectivity precluded particu-larism" (Merton 1973:270), knowledge claims in the scientific realm must be rooted in some impersonal and universalistic criteria.

The ethos of 'disinterestedness' is meant to guarantee impartiality in the appraisal of knowledge claims. In the same breath 'organized skepticism' ensures that knowledge claims are accepted not on the basis of the rank or stature of a particular scientist but on the basis of scrutiny through established standards and measures. This is meant to guarantee that logical regularity and empirical precision are the only criteria for accepting what counts as scientific knowledge. The ethos of 'communalism' refers to the exchange of knowledge within a scientific community. This is crucial because without it, other scientists cannot subject knowledge claims to critical scrutiny. Merton was, in fact, aware that in practice, the ethos of science may not be adhered to by all scientists. He, therefore, fashioned them along the lines of a Weberian ideal-type in order to set up the normative features that are critical for the development of scientific knowledge.

It is also likely that the breakdown of the norms of science into a state of anomie is the first stage of transition to a new set of norms. Indeed, such normative change is a social process in which a significant number of persons go through the same experience and express similar but new conclusions. When a controversy arises and values such as academic research are threatened, it may be interpreted as the replacement of the norm of disinterestedness. This normative change has arisen not only from the practices of industrial science and the emergence of entrepreneurial dynamics within academia but, also from the external pervasive influences on the university, in the form of government policies such as the changes in the disposition of intellectual property arising from federally funded research in the US and the establishment of business-led centres of excellence in Canada. This normative change explains the reconstruction process of the renewal of social roles and institutions (see Etzkowitz, chapter one this volume for a more detailed discussion).

Ideals and Contradictions

The idea of the neutrality of knowledge has been at the centre of knowledge capitalization debates. For Habermas (1972), knowledge is formed only on the basis of interest and as such, academic science and knowledge, in the physical, natural, social or critical theoretical domains are socially constructed and inherently interest-laden. This is a call to recognize the ideals and contradictions within the academia itself and those that come with the university's visible presence in the global economy (Kleinman 2003). In spite of this, in some quarters, academic scientists who engaged in collaborative research with industry are not only seen as inherently skewing research and scholarship in favour of industrial patrons (see Turk 2000), but are also construed as infringing upon the very idea of scientific neutrality (Croissant and Restivo 2001). The ultimate measuring rod as alluded to in the preceding section is the ideal-typical Mertonian norms of science.

However, Jencks and Riesman (1969) have, in a much broader context, catalogued the contradictory nature of the university landscape. As they note, some of the ideals and contradictions emanated from the rewards that came with academic scientists' effort in successfully prosecuting World War II. The instant return in the US, for instance, was a remarkable increase in external support for academic research. This support soon became accessible to scholars outside the pioneering physical, biological, and social science research domains, with incomes flowing into the humanities as well (Jencks and Riesman 1969:14–15). Deviating from the way research support was extended to universities in the past, these new federal grants and contracts were, for all intents and purposes, given to individuals or groups of scholars rather than to their institutions. As such, when academic scientists moved from one university to another, their federal grants moved with them. In addition, these grants were made largely on the basis of individual's professional competence, which further enhanced the stature of academic scientists as institutional fundraisers (Jencks and Riesman 1969:14–15).

Similarly, there were debates about the place of vocational skills in a liberal arts education. The idea of simultaneously engaging theory and practice was a bridge too far for many as they contended that universities must be free from labour market demands. In this regard, critics were quick to argue that universities were corrupted by vocationalism (Jencks and Riesman 1969:199). The nostalgia and moral lamentations embedded in this line of thinking induced compassion and succeeded in obscuring critical analysis of what universities should and must do. As purists argue "universities were pure and undefiled seats of learning where students came to get a liberal education" (Jencks and Riesman 1969:199). More so, professors were viewed as interested only in broadening minds with no interest whatsoever in advancing themselves through government contracts and business consulting (Jencks and Riesman 1969).

While these arguments served all sorts of polemical purposes, the fact of the matter really is that the so-called 'golden age' was overly exaggerated as all past university students were apprehensive about their future careers as are the present generation (Jencks and Riesman 1969). In fact, while unique changes have taken root, the point of departure is that earlier generation of university students have job orientations that were slightly different from contemporary students as the economy becomes increasingly knowledge-driven. Admittedly, there is an element of cost associated with any progress and, as such, ideals always come with contradictions. One persisting contradiction has to do with the fact that academic scientists and, to an extent, industries are sustained primarily from the same sources and resources— taxpayers (Slaughter and Leslie 1997) as happened with the global financial crisis resulting in banks and Wall Street bailouts in 2008.

In spite of this, there has always been the desire from various stakeholders of higher education to attach an instrumental goal to academic research (Carroll 2004, Noble 2001). This is a consequence of the ideals and contradictions that comes with the university's unique position as a citadel of knowledge. It is, probably, based on similar lines of reasoning that David Noble (2001) argued that the interest in information technology for distance learning is entirely commercially driven. For him, since neither technology nor learning drove the mania for correspondence courses, contemporary drive to deliver courses on the internet, in parallel, is nothing but a pretext to commodify higher education. There is a genuine fear that in university-industry collaborative circumstances, academic capitalists will gain power as middle managers and professors will lose power as education is commodified and the university becomes no different from any other business venture (Delanty 2001a).

The realization is that while universities have proved to be imperfect instruments of economic development, the very efforts they have devoted to tackling the labour market demands of students compromised their fundamental role as islands of culture and critical thought in a materialistic society (Axelrod 2000 and 2002). In spite of this, as Axelrod (1982) notes, university-industry relations seem to have been more a matter of cultural leadership than an overt attempt on the part of corporations to control research and teaching. The problem, as he sees it stems from the stated goals of liberal education, which sometimes are so "all-encompassing that everything, including job training and applied research appear to fall within its domain" (Axelrod 2002:5).

This aside, Axelrod (2002) brought out yet another contradiction in the university's role when he indicated that the "liberal arts and the professors employed to teach them have benefited from a prevailing popular belief in the job-training function of higher education." It will, as he indicated, be naïve for academics to "assume that universities would be supported or enrolled at current levels if the institutions were stripped of their economic role in favour of an exclusively cultural one" (Axelrod 2002:31). However, one must add that there are differential outcomes in knowledge capitalization by universities. In most instances, these differences are steeped in distinctive institutional contexts. This shapes the transfer of knowledge from public sources to private firms. In the process, the institutional prestige of research universities is defined in terms of both academic and industry science. Consequently, both the process and the success rate for transferring promising basic science into industry varies significantly across research universities (Owen-Smith and Powell 2001).

Research Technique

The chapter is based on a survey research conducted among academic scientists drawn from the agriculture, biomedical, computer, engineering and physical sciences at the University of Saskatchewan, Canada. The research utilized a stratified sampling method which involves the process of grouping members of a population into relatively homogenous category before sampling (Babbie 2001). As a data-collection instrument, stratified sampling is highly regarded for obtaining a greater degree of representativeness. The departments—agriculture, biomedical, computer, engineering and physical sciences—were surveyed as they were judged to contain academic scientists whose research activities interact directly or indirectly with industrial partners and are typically at the intersection of knowledge capitalization activities.

The selected academic scientists were sent a four-page questionnaire through the university's internal mailing system. If the questionnaire was not return within four weeks an email reminder was sent asking whether a second mailing was required. Out of the hundred questionnaires sent, sixty-one was completed and returned. While, this is a very high return rate for a survey, for a comprehensive analysis of instantiations of pervasive influences within the academia the sample is small and, therefore, the findings must be cautiously discussed without undue and unnecessary over generalization. The analysis discussed in this chapter is gleaned from Chi-square values of bi-variate cross-tabs.

The Knowledge Society

With the increasing shift in the economy to the organization and management of scientific innovations (Drucker 1993, Porter 1990),

knowledge embodied by creativity and enterprise has become arguably, the driver of the global economy. Scholars from diverse perspectives and theoretical linings have devoted quite considerable amount
of time and effort to surveying the centrality of knowledge and its relationship with the industrial structure (Bell 1973, Drucker 1993, Florida
1995, Castells 1996). The way and manner this relationship is explored
differs but has largely been captured by giving knowledge a prominent
role in the social organization of the economy and larger society. For
Daniel Bell (1973), knowledge had become the axial principle of the
post-industrial society. Peter Drucker (1993) and Ikujiro Nonaka
(1991) pointed out that capitalism is entering into a new age of knowledge creation and continuous learning.

Drawing on Bell's framework, Nico Stehr (1994), detailed the shift to
ever-greater dependence of the economy on knowledge production.
Gibbons and his collaborators (1994) argued that the contexts of
knowledge production and use have increasingly become matted.
For Richard Florida, the human mind has become the main "source of
value and economic growth in knowledge-intensive capitalism"
(1995:528). Castells (1996) intimated that apart from the distinct
nature of its productivity growth, the economy also work as a unit in
real time and on a planetary scale. Accordingly, there is an "eventual
realization of the productivity potential contained in the mature industrial economy because of the shift toward a technological paradigm
based on information technologies" (Castells, 1996:91). However, for
Delanty, if we take a much broader view of "knowledge as entail-
ing more than science but also cultural knowledge, the university
can be seen as the space where the project of modernity unfolded
through cognitive struggles, in particular between science and culture"
(2001b:150).

While, the differences exhibited within the literature indicate
the lack of consensus within the community of scholars, the lack of
clarity rather emboldened the search for an overriding innovation
policy niche. This effort has produced numerous initiatives based on
university—community partnerships and diverse knowledge production schemes.

Implications of Industrial Funding for the Academia

There is the perception that the capitalization of knowledge affects the
inward calling of science and the material condition of scientists.

While the debate about the ethical implications of university-industry relationships transcends academic boundaries, the media hype of assorted university-industry intimations in the biotechnology-related fields in the 1980s were based on "assumptions about the correctness or reality of these traditional notions of scientist-autonomy" (Kleinman and Vallas 2001: 457). In some circles the spread of market values into the academia is seen as constraining the conduct of academic science (Washburn 2005). Critical assessments are required to understand the extent of the impact of the boundary transgressions on academic science.

However, the substance of the debate in most instances is vague and to a degree misconstrues the sources of the institutional impediments on the university. As Gibbons and his collaborators reminded us "science has always both shaped and been shaped by society" (1994:22). In spite of this, the recurrent issue in the debate on the increasing university-industry partnership, nevertheless, has been that industry funding of university research has deleterious effects on academic science. The relevance of this debate stems from the underlying linkage to six factors that are explored in this chapter: (i) the impact of industrial power on academic scientists; (ii) the place of basic research in the modern university; (iii) the impact of economic criteria in allocation of institutional resources; (iv) the impact of economic criteria in determining faculty recruitment; (v) the quest by industry to commodified knowledge; and the (vi) surrender of intellectual autonomy by academic scientists.

The Impact of Industrial Power on Academic Scientists

The data from the survey showed that those who received funding from industry have relatively positive views about university-industry relations compared to those who do not receive industrial funds. For instance, while about 62 percent of industry funding recipients are likely to perceive corporate influence to be the 'right amount', about 50 percent of non-recipients are likely to be of the same opinion (P<0.004). However, about 22 percent of non-industry funding recipients are likely to indicate that private companies have 'too much power' to influence the academic research agenda. Similarly, corporate influence is perceived as being 'too little' by recipients of industry funds compared to non-recipients of industry funds. This showed that the receipt/non-receipt of industry funds influenced how academic

scientists surveyed perceived university-industry relations to be transforming the university.

In addition, when the relationship between the rank of academic
faculty and corporate influence was explored, it was realized that about
75 percent of 'professors' and 44 percent of 'associate professors' indicated that industry have the 'right amount of influence.' Among the
professoriate, about 33 percent of 'associate professors', and 19 percent
of 'professors' are likely to state that industry have 'too little power'.
It is possible that the high percentage of 'professors' who view private industry companies as having the 'right amount of power' have
cultivated mutual working relationships with industry, and also their
academic and administrative experiences over the years may have
helped in tempering sentiments with reality. However, among the non-
industry funding recipients, about 73 percent of 'professors', 44 percent
of 'associate professors' and 33 percent of 'assistant professors' indicated that private industry have the 'right amount' of influence. The
most significant result has to do with the response to 'whether private industry companies have too much influence.' Here, among the
non-industry funding recipients, about 25 percent of 'assistant professors', 22 percent of 'associate professors' and 18 percent of 'professors'
perceived industry to have 'too much influence' and are setting the
academic research agenda.

It is quite interesting that in percentage terms, perception tends to
move downwards as one move up the academic ladder. As such, there
is the likelihood that academic scientists who have not received industry funding but perceived industry as having 'too much influence' are
likely to be 'assistant professors', followed by 'associate professors' and
then full 'professors'. The indication is that as one moved up the professorial ladder, there is an attitudinal transformation. Consequently,
'professors' at the higher end of the professorial ladder and recipients
of industry funding tend to perceive corporate influence to be minimal. The indication from the survey is that academic scientists believed
they have control over their research activities even when these
research activities are financed by industrial partners.

The Place of Basic Science in Knowledge Capitalization

There is the hint that the receipt or non-receipt of funds from industry
influence how academic scientist perceived the place of basic science
in contemporary academic transformations. In fact, while 67 percent

of academic scientists who received industrial funds 'disagree' with the assertion that university-industry linkage relegate basic research into the background; the parallel response among non-industrial funding recipients was about 44 percent. However, the survey did reveal that non-corporate funding recipients—22 percent—are more likely than those who received industrial support—19 percent—to agree that basic research is being relegated to the background. It is clear that industry funding influences perception when it comes to the question of whether basic research is being relegated to the background or not. This finding is not different from what Blumenthal et al. (1986) found in their study of biotechnology faculty.

One must, however, emphasizes that the 22 percent of non-industry funding recipients who think that basic research is being relegated to the background deserve to be taken seriously. Their perceptions lend credence to the assertion made by Turk (2000) to the effect that basic research is getting diminishing thought for lack of short-term commercial return. They also furthered the observation that it will be naïve for "academics today to assume that universities would be supported or enrolled at current levels if the institutions were stripped of their economic role in favour of an exclusively cultural one" (Axelrod 2002:31). As such, the importance of basic science to the academic enterprise cannot be overemphasized. It is critical that steps are taken by stakeholders to ensure an enduring confidence in the relevance of basic science to the whole academic system. As elaborately detailed by Vannevar Bush (1995[1945]) in his widely cited report, *Science: the endless frontier*:

> Basic research leads to new knowledge. It provides scientific capital. It creates the fund from which the practical applications of knowledge must be drawn...Today, it is truer than ever that basic research is the pacemaker of technological progress...A nation which depends upon others for its new basic scientific knowledge will be slow in its industrial progress and weak in its competitive position in world trade, regardless of its mechanical skills (1995: viii).

The Impact of Economic Criteria in Institutional Resource Allocation

Apart from the issue of the relegation of basic science into the background, there is also the idea that university-industry relations are gradually replacing academic scholarship with monetary/economic considerations. In other words, ability to garner corporate research dollars has become more important in the decision-making process in terms of how institutional resources are allocated to different academic units. The term 'economic criteria' is used here to denote a professor's ability to bring in external funds mainly from industrial sources. The argument is that the resources departments get is dependent upon the ability of their departmentalized academic faculty in securing external research grants. To explore this debate, the relationship between the 'rank' of academic scientists and the criteria for institutional resource allocation was examined.

The survey data showed that junior professors are more likely than their senior colleagues to assert that economic rather than academic criterion is the dominant factor in institutional resource allocation (P<0.004). In fact, about 77 percent of 'assistant professors', 61 percent of 'associate professors' and 30 percent of 'professors' indicated that 'economic criterion' is much more prominent in the allocation of institutional resources. Furthermore, among industrial funding recipients, about 29 percent of those who are professors and 67 percent of associate professors perceived the allocation of institutional resources as determined by economic rather than academic criteria. In addition, while about 41 percent of 'professors' 'disagree' with the assertion that 'economic criteria' is more relevant when it comes to the allocation of institutional resources, only about 11 percent of 'associate professors' perceived the issue in a similar manner.

The data further revealed that junior professors are more likely than senior professors to perceive 'economic criteria' as influencing the allocation of institutional resources. Among non-industry funding recipients, about 25 percent of 'professors', 57 percent of 'associate professors' and 83 percent of 'assistant professors' perceived economic criteria as having a greater impact on the allocation of institutional resources compared to academic criteria. However, there is a decline in the influence of 'economic criteria' in institutional resource allocation as one moved upwards from the level of assistant professor. In terms of the category 'disagree', about 22 percent of 'associate professors' compared to about 58 percent of 'professors' do not view 'economic criteria' as playing significant role in institutional resources allocation. A critical analysis of the responses revealed that, to some extent, academic scientists who received industry funding are more likely to perceive 'economic criteria' as determining the institutional allocation of resources compared to colleagues who do not receive funding from industry.

The Impact of Economic Criteria in Recruitment of Faculty

The extent to which economic criterion determines the recruitment of faculty seems not to be a major influence as it was in terms of allocation of institutional resources discussed in the previous section. Academic scientists were asked whether the recruitment of academic faculty is based on the ability to attract corporate research dollars. This question was analyzed using the age-cohorts of academic scientists during the time of the survey in 2005. Among academic scientists who received industry funding, 50 percent of those within the 30–40 age category, 22 percent of those within the 41–50 age category and about 22 percent of academic scientists within 51–65 age category perceived 'economic criteria' as holding sway when it comes to the academic faculty recruitment. On the other hand, about 67 percent of those within 51–65 age range and 56 percent of those within 41–50 age bracket 'disagree' that 'economic criterion' is the overriding factor when it comes to faculty recruitment. This shows a strong level of perception among relatively younger professors compared to senior professors.

In the case of the academic scientists who did not receive industrial funds, about 30 percent of those within the 30–40 age group, six per cent of those in the 41–50 age bracket, and 20 percent of those within the 51–65 age range indicated that 'economic criterion' is a major factor in faculty recruitment. The majority of non-industrial funding recipients do not perceive 'economic criteria' to be relevant in faculty recruitment. In this regard, about 30 percent of those within 30–40 age group, 65 percent of those within 41–50 age categories and 60 percent of those within 51–65 age brackets do not think that economic criterion is the major factor in faculty recruitment. Thus, among the academic scientists who received funds from industry, this incidence is explained by 43 percent while it accounted for about 57 percent among non-industrial funding recipients. Comparatively, industry funding recipients have slightly higher perception, albeit positive one, of the influence of economic factors compared to colleagues who are non-recipients of industrial research funds.

Industrial Quest to Privatize Knowledge

Another contentious issue in the university-industry relations debate is the perception that industry is implicitly seeking to privatize academic knowledge. This issue is explored in the survey through the impact that academic scientist felt the increasing use of university facilities by industrial partners for market-driven research is having on the autonomy of the university. The results revealed that the receipt or non-receipt of funding from industry has a considerable effect on perception (P<0.003). In fact, among academic scientists who received industry funding, 62 percent 'disagree' that the use of university facilities by industry is leading to the 'privatization' of the university. The corresponding figure among non-industry funding recipients is about 53 percent. However, eight percent of those surveyed who received industry funding and 34 percent of non-industrial funding recipients perceived the use of university facilities by industry as leading to the 'privatization' of the university. It is clear that the perception of academic scientists of the industrial use of university facilities is moderated by the receipt or non-receipt of industry funding.

However, if the issue of industrial use of university facilities results to 'privatization' is explored based on professorial ranks, there are marked differences. For instance, among full 'professors', about six percent of recipients of industry funding and 17 percent of non-industry funds recipients 'agreed' that the usage of university facilities by industry leads to the privatization of the university. In addition, about 67 percent of industry funding recipients and 75 percent of non-recipients 'disagree' that the industry's use of facilities leads to the 'privatization' of the university. In terms of 'associate professors', 11 percent of industry funding recipients and 33 percent of non-industry funding recipients perceived the use of university facilities by industry as leading to the 'privatization' of the university. Again, 44 percent of industry funding recipients compared to 57 percent of non-recipients 'disagree' that use of university facilities by industry leads to the 'privatization' of the university. Among 'assistant professors', however, about 55 percent of non-industry funding recipients were of the view that the use of university facilities by industry leads to the privatization of the university.

In fact, the data showed that the receipt or non-receipt of industry funding affects the way the use of university facilities by industry is perceived to be leading, either to the 'privatization' of the university or not. But, a critical analysis of the different professorial ranks indicates an underlying attitudinal transformation. Thus, the perception of industrial use of university facilities is affected by the receipt or non receipt of industry funding. This incidence is about 48 percent among 'professors', 31 percent among 'associate professors' and 21 percent among 'assistant professors'.

The Surrender of Intellectual Autonomy

In terms of intellectual autonomy, the debate tends to take on a life of its own with much broader implications. This is because the question of autonomy is usually linked to the issues of academic freedom. The argument is that academic freedom is endangered by the demands that universities become more market-driven (Horne 2001). In the survey, 65 percent of academic scientists who received industry funding and 33 percent of non-industry funding recipients 'disagreed' with the assertion that academic scientists working on industrially funded projects are surrendering their intellectual autonomy. However, about 12 percent of industry funding recipients and 24 percent of non-industry funding recipients 'agreed' that those academic scientists who conduct industrial sponsored research are surrendering their intellectual autonomy to industrial partners. It is apparent that the receipt or non-receipt of industry funding has a considerable impact on the way academic scientists perceived whether intellectual autonomy is either compromised or not.

It is clear that industrial funding impacts the perception that there is a loss of intellectual autonomy in university-industry interactions. However, there is not enough evidence to conclude that intellectual autonomy is being surrendered to industrial partners. In spite of this, William Graham argued that "bias of money steers research topics as well as methods, and since university teaching is so closely tied to research, it steers teaching programs and course contents as well" (2000:26). Also, Slaughter and Rhoades (1990) declared that industry-university relations have undermined the autonomy of knowledge, academic freedom, and have as a consequence, reinforced the hierarchical structure of universities by giving control to central administrations. However, the argument that university-industry partnerships are harming the core functions of the university cannot be fully ascertained since the available data is not very comprehensive to argue that traditional academic functions such as teaching and basic research are being compromised. Consequently, there is the need to look at multiple factors in order to unpack the seemingly multifaceted variables at work before such arguments can be empirically validated.

Conclusion

The chapter explored ideals and contradictions in knowledge capitalization through a survey data. It shows that the receipt or non-receipt of industry funding affects the perception of academic scientists. It was revealed that academic scientists who received industrial funding have relatively more positive views about university-industry relations than those who do not receive such funds. However, one cannot conclusively indicate that entrepreneurial activities of academic scientists are deleterious to the functioning of the university. For instance, while it was noted that industry funding impacts the perception of the surrender of intellectual autonomy, it is not at all clear that intellectual autonomy is being surrendered to industrial partners. Consequently, in an increasingly knowledge-based economy, the desire to identify and add new innovative methods to economic development have brought to the fore the contested nature of knowledge and its producing institutions.

The landscape of academic knowledge production continues to change significantly. However, the changes are not radically new. There is continuity in the sense that each new task is evolving out of an effort to meet a previous goal. As such, the most distinctive change lies in the fact that research funding sources are now more diversified. Immediately after World War II, almost all research funding came from government and philanthropic sources. While the desire to translate academic research into economic activity has collided with nostalgia, we must equally acknowledge that the resistance and agitations are not the rumblings of isolated individuals, but an indication that changes are taking place as the old order gives way to new: the emerging age of knowledge. There are negative as well as positive consequences in the drive to encourage universities to embrace the global bazaar. As public institutions, universities engagement with industrial partners and the ensuing capitalization of knowledge must continually be dissected and debated. This will safeguard the ideals while minimizing the contradictions.

Bibliography

Axelrod, Paul. 2002. *Values in Conflict: The University, the Marketplace, and the Trials of Liberal Education.* Montreal and Kingston: McGill-Queens University Press.

Axelrod, Paul. 2000. "What is to be done? Envisioning the University's Future," in James L. Turk, ed., *The Corporate Campus: Industrialization and the Dangers to Canada's Colleges and Universities.* Toronto: James Lorimer, pp. 201–208.

Axelrod, Paul. 1982. *Scholars and Dollars: Politics, Economics and the Universities of Ontario 1945–1980*. Toronto: University of Toronto Press.

Babbie, R. Earl. 2001. *The Practice of Social Research*. Belmont, CA: Wadsworth Thomson Learning.

Baber, Zaheer. 2008. "Global DNA: Genomics, the Nation-State and Globalisation." *Asian Journal of Social Science* 36 (1), 104–119.

Baber, Zaheer. 2001. "Globalization and Scientific Research: The Emerging Triple Helix of State-Industry-University Relations in Japan and Singapore." *Bulletin of Science, Technology and Society* 21 (1): 401–408.

Baber, Zaheer. 2000. "An ambiguous Legacy: The Social Construction of the Kuhnian Revolution and Its Consequences for the Sociology of Science." *Bulletin of Science, Technology and Society* 20 (2):139–155.

Bell, Daniel. 1973. *The Coming of Post-Industrial Society*. London: Heinemann.

Brooks, Harvey. 1993. "Research universities and the social contract for science," in Lewis M. Bramscomb, ed., *Empowering Technology*. Cambridge: MIT Press, pp. 202–234.

Blumenthal, David, Michael Gluck, Karen Seashore, Michael A. Stoto, and David Wise. 1986. "University-Industry Research Relationships in Biotechnology: Implications for the University. *Science* 232 (4756): 1361–1366.

Bush, Vannevar. 1995 [1945]. Science: The Endless Frontier (Reprint edition of 1995). Stratford, N.H.: Ayer Company Publishers.

Castells, Manuel. 1997. *The Power of Identity*. Oxford: Blackwell.

Castells, Manuel. 1996. *The Rise of the Network Society*. Oxford: Blackwell.

Castells, Manuel and Peter Hall. 1994. *Technopoles of the World: The Making of 21st Century Industrial Complexes*. New York: Routledge.

Carroll, K. William. 2004. *Corporate Power in a Globalizing World: A study in Elite Social Organization*. Toronto: Oxford University Press.

Cohen, Marjorie Griffin. 2000. "Trading Away the Public System: The WTO and Post Secondary Education," in James L. Turk, ed., *The Corporate Campus: Commercialization and The Dangers to Canada's Colleges and Universities*, edited by. Toronto: James Lorimer and Company Ltd, pp. 123–14.

Croissant, Jennifer and Sal Restivo, eds. 2001. *Degrees of compromise: Industrial Interests and Academic Values*. New York: SUNY Press.

Croissant, Jennifer L., Gary Rhoades and Sheila Slaughter. 2001. "Universities in the Information Age: Changing Work, Organization, and Values in Academic Science and Engineering." *Bulletin of Science, Technology and Society* 21(2):108–118.

David, A. Paul and Dominique Foray. 2002. "An introduction to the economy of the knowledge society." *International Social Science Journal* 171:9–23.

Delanty, Gerard. 2001a. *Challenging knowledge: The University in Knowledge Society*. Ballmoor: Open University Press.

Delanty, Gerard. 2001b. "The University in the Knowledge Society." *Organization* 8(2):149–153.

Drucker, Peter. 1993. *The Post-Capitalist Society*. Oxford: Butterworth-Heinemann.

Etzkowitz, Henry. 2008. *The Triple Helix: University-Industry-Government Innovation in Action*. Routledge: London.

Etzkowitz, Henry. 2002. *MIT and the Rise of Entrepreneurial Science*. London and New York. Routledge.

Etzkowitz, Henry, Eugene Jnr. Schuler and Magnus Gulbrandsen. 2000. "The Evolution of Entrepreneurial University," in Merle Jacob and Tomas Hellstrom, eds., *The Future of Knowledge Production in the Academy*. Ballmoor, Buckingham: Open University Press, pp. 40 60.

Etzkowitz, Henry, Andrew Webster Peter Healey, eds.1998. *Capitalizing Knowledge: New Intersections of Industry and Academia*. New York: The State University of New York Press.

Etzkowitz, Henry and Loet Leydesdorff, eds. 1997. *Universities in the Global Knowledge Economy: A Triple Helix of Academic-Industry-Government Relations*. London: Cassell.

Florida, Richard.1995. "Toward the learning region." *Futures* 27 (5):527–536.

Gibbons, Michael, Camille Limoges, Helga Nowotny, Simon Schwartzman, Peter Scott, and Martin Trow. 1994. *The New Production of Knowledge: The Dynamics of Science and Research in Contemporary Societies*. London, Thousand Oaks, CA: Sage Publications.

Graham, William. 2000. "Academic Freedom or Commercial License?," in James L. Turk, ed., *The Corporate Campus: Commercialization and the Dangers to Canada's Colleges and Universities*. Toronto: James Lorimer, pp. 23–30.

Habermas, Jürgen. 1972. *Knowledge and Human Interests*. Boston: Beacon Press.

Habermas, Jürgen. 1970. *Toward a Rational Society*. Boston: Beacon Press.

Hessen, Boris. 1971 [1931]. "The social and economic roots of Newton's *Principia*", in Nicolai I. Bukharin, ed., *Science at the crossroads*. London/New York: Frank Cass, pp. 151–212.

Horne, Michael. (2001) "Academic Freedom in Canada: Past, Present, and Future," in Len M. Findlay and Paul M. Bidwell, eds., *Pursuing Academic Freedom: "Free and Fearless"?* Saskatoon: Purich Publishing Ltd, pp. 21–36.

Jacob, Margaret C., and Larry Stewart. 2004. *Practical Matter: Newton's Science in the Service of Industry and Empire, 1687–1851*. London: Harvard University Press.

Jencks, Christopher and David Riesman. 1969. *The Academic Revolution*. New York: Doubleday.

Kleinman, Daniel Lee. 2003. *Impure Cultures: University Biology and the World of Commerce*. Madison, Wisconsin: The University of Wisconsin Press.

Kleinman, Daniel Lee. 1995. *Politics on the endless frontier: Postwar Research Policy in the United States*. Durham, NC: Duke University Press.

Kleinman, Daniel Lee and Steven P. Vallas. 2001. "Science, Capitalism, and the Rise of the "Knowledge Worker": The Changing Structure of Knowledge Production in the United States." *Theory and Society* 30(4):451–492.

Krugman, Paul. (2000) "The future of New England," in Peter Temin, ed., *Engines of Enterprise: An Economic History of New England*. Cambridge, MA: Harvard University Press, pp. 261–276.

Merton, Robert K. 1973. *The Sociology of Science: Theoretical and Empirical Investigations*. Chicago: University of Chicago Press.

Noble, David F. (2002) *Digital Diploma Mills: The Automation of Higher Education*. Toronto: Between the Lines.

Nonaka, Ikujiro. 1991. "The knowledge creating company." *Harvard Business Review*, November—December, 69–104.

Owen-Smith, Jason and Walter W. Powell. 2001. "To Patent or Not: Faculty Decisions and Institutional Success at Technology Transfer." *Journal of Technology Transfer* 26(1–2): 99–114.

Pelikan, Jaroslav. 1992. *The Idea of the University: A Re-examination*. New Haven: Yale University Press.

Porter, E. Michael. 1990. *The Competitive Advantage of Nations*. New York: Free Press.

Slaughter, Sheila and Larry L. Leslie. 1997. *Academic Capitalism: Politics, Policies, and the Entrepreneurial University*. Baltimore and London: The Johns Hopkins University Press.

Slaughter, Leslie, and Gary Rhoades. 1990. "Renorming the Social Relations of Academic Science: Technology Transfer." *Educational Policy* 4(4):341–361.

Stehr, Nico.1994. *Knowledge Societies*. London: Sage Publications.

Turk, James L., ed. 2000. *The Corporate Campus: Industrialization and the Dangers to Canada's Colleges and Universities* Toronto: James Lorimer.

Washburn, Jennifer. 2005. University Inc: The Corporate Corruption of Higher Education. New York: Basic Books.

Zeitlin, Irving M. 1997. *Ideology and the Development of Sociological Theory*. Upper Saddle River, New Jersey: Simon & Schuster.

CHAPTER FOURTEEN

IN THE GREY AREA:
UNIVERSITY RESEARCH AND COMMERCIAL ACTIVITY – THE CASE OF LANGUAGE TECHNOLOGY

Tarja Knuuttila

Universities are facing multiple and partly contradictory challenges. In order to fulfill the emerging "third mission", they have become complex organizations offering multiple societal services, such as, contract research, education, consulting and the commercialization of research. Simultaneously, they suffer from the severe shortage of resources while the pace of demands requiring them to deploy extra resources continues to mount. As these developments coincided with the call for increasing accountability, transparency and effectiveness, the university system seems certainly to be on the edge of a crisis (for a detailed analysis of the seeming university crisis, see Toby Huff, this volume). Moreover, as a response to the intensifying impact of the globalization of economy, policy makers are increasingly urging universities to take on the task of fostering economic prosperity through scientific research and innovation (Nieminen 2005, Slaughter and Leslie 1997).

Consequently, it seems that the apparent contradictions confronting universities today are a testament to the fact that as critical institutions of society, universities must undergo internal changes reflecting those of the larger society. Thus, the intense discussion in the literature relating to the 'Mode 2' knowledge production and knowledge capitalization seeks to come to terms with the aforementioned changes and contradictions (Gibbons et al. 1994, Etzkowitz and Leydesdorff 1997, Slaughter and Leslie 1997). In some circles, the tenor of the argument is ratcheted up a notch with the claim that in a knowledge-based century, universities must subsume, if not supersede many functions of the industrial spheres (Etzkowitz and Dzisah 2010). This claim is based on the observation that an increasing number of academics who have taken on the entrepreneurial mantle, by taking advantage of national innovation policies, did so successfully while remaining within the confines of the university (Gulbrandsen 2005, Tuunainen 2005, Shinn and Lamy 2006, Tuunainen and Knuuttila 2008).

The chapter focuses on the challenges that such a hybridization of academic work and business activity faces through a case study on the commercialization of language technology via spin-off firms. University spin-offs provide a strategic site to study the possible contradictions of commercialized science since they operate at the interface of both university and business sectors like patenting and licensing offices, business incubators, venture capitalists and public research institutes. The spin-offs often provide the most immediate contact between academic research and business activity. The chapter traces the developmental trajectory of one research group, which operated at a comprehensive public university in Finland, the University of Helsinki. It details the micro level practical management of academic spin-offs concentrating on the possibilities and problems that emerged, how the problems were solved, and which perspectives informed various academic and entrepreneurial actors. It contends that there are certain inherent ideals and norms that the university has come to embody that cannot easily be reconciled with entrepreneurial principles. Yet, some of the problems faced by the research group could have been avoided had appropriate regulations and procedures concerning the commercial activity in the universities been in place.

Universities in Knowledge Economy

The pivotal position of universities in the knowledge economy as well as in technology transfer has been conceptualized through the use of such terminologies as the 'Mode 2' knowledge production (Gibbons et al. 1994) and the 'Triple Helix' of University-Industry-Government relations (Etzkowitz and Leydesdorff 1997). Gibbons et al. (1994), the proponents of the 'Mode 2' knowledge production thesis, claimed that we have in fact entered a new mode of knowledge production starting in the 1980s.[1] The transition between 'Mode 1' and 'Mode 2' represents a break from the alleged theory-driven basic science to an

---

[1] For critical discussion of the so-called epochal break, see Nordmann Alfred, Hans Radder and Gregor Schiemann, eds. 2011. *Science Transformed? Debating Claims of an Epochal Break*. Pittsburgh: University of Pittsburgh Press.

interventionist science produced within the context of application (Gibbons et al. 1994). Accordingly, in 'Mode 2', and in contrast to 'Mode 1', the problems of various societal groups and organizations are set as the starting points of research, instead of the previous focus on purely scientific questions (Nowotny et al. 2001: 65). While the 'Mode 2' thesis is presented at a general level, the triple helix argument has more plausible empirical footing (Etzkowitz 2003).

However, it must be noted that the triple helix thesis contains also a speculative claim concerning the emergence of the entrepreneurial university, which is asserted to be embedded within triple helix relations (Etzkowitz 2003). This development is purported to usher in a 'Third Academic Revolution', which results from "an 'inner logic' of academic development that previously expanded the academic enterprise from a focus on teaching to research" (Etzkowitz 2004:69).[2] Entrepreneurial universities develop as the traditional university incorporates private business activities into its activities hybridizing them with public academic work. Though the final form of the so-called 'Mode 2' and/or entrepreneurial university is not discernible at this stage, the fact remains that universities are undergoing substantial changes as a result of the commodification of academic research.

Commodification, narrowly defined, refers to the commercialization of university research. However, commodification is in fact a more all-pervasive phenomenon where "all kinds of scientific activities and results are predominantly interpreted and assessed on the basis of economic criteria" (Radder 2010: 3). These activities are exemplified by such incidents as the increasing practice of cost-based accounting among sub-units in a university organization (Radder 2010) and the way academics have become increasingly affected by the profit motive and market-like behaviour in their efforts to secure external grants (Slaughter and Leslie 1997). In addition to these quasi-market activities, university scientists have also taken on direct entrepreneurial roles as founders of university spin-off companies. This has, for decades, been a salient feature in biotechnology and information technology programmes at major universities (Kenney 1986).

Although earlier studies on university-industry research relationships have paid attention to the effects of commercialization on the

---

[2] For a different kind of analysis of an entrepreneurial university see Clark, 1998; Marginson and Considine, 2000.

university practices, they have more often than not generalized from a few macro-level instances without a proper attention to the micro level realities, in which actors face challenges of commodification in their daily routines. These studies have either used cross-sectional quantitative data (e.g. Blumenthal et al. 1986) or portrayed in broad strokes the changing landscape of the academy (e.g., Krimsky 2003, Tuunainen 2005). However, there is also a growing body of studies that seek to find out how the actors in university-industry interactions conceive of the 'Mode-2' policies adopted by most research funding agencies and, more generally, the commodification of academic knowledge (see Kleinman and Vallas 2006, Vallas and Kleinman 2007, Wald 2007). In other words, though academic scientists form an integral part of the nascent transformations in the capitalization of knowledge, their perspectives are more often than not ignored and relegated to the periphery (for exceptions, see Dzisah 2010, Göktepe-Húlten 2010). As such, this chapter brings a new perspective to the debate by engaging the different actors involved in knowledge capitalization by exploring the long-term developmental trajectory of a research group and its spin-off companies.

Overview of Research Technique

The data utilized in this chapter detail the practical imperatives faced by the language technology research group at the University of Helsinki. It is gleaned from documents over a time-span of nearly twenty years, including research proposals and reports, publications and external evaluations. Moreover, twenty-four interviews were conducted in 2000 and 2004. The interviews were semi-structured and lasted typically from one to three hours and involved members of the language technology research group, and employees as well as owners of spin-off companies. In fact, most of those interviewed performed multiple roles in these organizations. The analysis is also informed by research field notes on the informal discussions with various actors in these institutions. From the interviews, informal discussions and documents of all kinds emerged a narrative of the language technology research group, a group that saw its academic path erode as it became commercially successful.

Consequently, what follows is a story of how the boundaries between academic and commercial activity became blurred, redefined and finally reconstituted. It is, also, a story of the multiple roles assumed by the actors, who in the process tried their best to figure out where exactly their commitments lied. It is also a narrative about how the contradictions of commercialization found their way into the very heart of the daily interaction of a research group. While the proponents of the entrepreneurial university tend to take the perceived contradictions and conflicts of interests as indicators that the transition from one academic mode of production to another is underway (Etzkowitz 2008), a closer look at these conflicts provides a clue as to which roles require adequate procedures and regulations and which simply become tolerated and negotiated daily.

The Case of the Language Technology Research Group

> Commercialization disturbs the theoretical work here, and then it starts to be one of the most challenging dilemmas: on the other hand, you are a professor trying to promote free science, and on the other you have a firm with private commercial interest. Things went pretty well for a long time but then the younger colleagues started to consider this interaction odd—this is a sort of *grey area* that we have talked very little about in our research group (The leader of the language technology research group).

By the end of 1999, the co-leader of the language technology research group was contacted by the author in order to study this research group, which had become very successful in both academic and commercial terms. The group had done cutting edge research in the field of language technology for nearly twenty years, spinning out of its research three different firms. Two of the three spin-offs were still in business and doing relatively well. The professors in charge of the group were (and still are) ardent spokespersons for language technology not only in Finland, but across the entire Nordic region.

This is not surprising since before the late 1990s, practically all language technology companies founded in the Nordic countries were of Finnish origin. Their origins can in most cases be traced back to individual researchers or research groups at Finnish universities (Arppe 2005). Thus, the language technology research group was supposed to provide a prime example of entrepreneurial science combining an ambitious academic research mandate with commercial success. However, the author soon learned that the group had only recently broken up, as many of its major researchers had left the academia. Therefore, instead of trying to uncover the recipe for the previous success of the language technology research group, this chapter rather details the reasons for its consequent demise.

The Beginning of Commercialization

The language technology research group started commercializing its research from its initial infancy in the 1980s. This development was largely a direct consequence of its research agenda. The empirically based approach of the group towards developing language independent theories and tools to manage and analyze unprocessed text produced important early applications. These breakthroughs, particularly in computational morphological disambiguation, propelled the group into instant prominence, with orders from large Finnish companies and government offices which needed new language-technology applications, especially word processing tools. These orders were managed through the department's administration and written in the form of formal research contracts. With the inflow of revenue, the department bought computers, which were very expensive in those early days: for instance one Mikro-Mikko computer that was bought as a part of one contract with a large Finnish publishing house cost more than the yearly budget of the department. The resulting money and equipment were more than welcome by the department, which had, like many other small departments in the humanities, constant problems in generating funding for its activities.

Nonetheless, the department had some difficulty in incorporating the extra income attained from such contracts into its yearly budget, as no clear procedures existed for chargeable service and research at the university. In trying to solve such problems, the leaders of the group, i.e., the professor of the department and the principal researcher of the group approached the university administration. In the mid-1980s, the attitude of the administration towards commercialization was negative: the university did not want to have anything to do with it. Similarly, the professor who led both the group and the department argued that the commercial orders received had nearly nothing to do with scientific research. In his opinion, the personnel at the university were expected to do research instead of engaging in commercial activities. As the professor stated:

> It was sort of selling. Those contracts were not genuine research contracts in the sense that we would have needed to do research to execute

what stood in them. In fact, we just sold programmes that were already made here...Of course, some configuring work was done.

Eventually, in 1987, the professor and the principal researcher of the group decided to go ahead with the commercialization idea and established a company into which all commercial activities were transferred. In the beginning, the activities were on a small scale, with the principal researcher working part-time for the company. As he also obtained a professorship in the department in question, the company hired its first full-time employee to replace him. The company grew rather slowly in the beginning, relying on projects of diverse kinds for which it hired researchers from the department typically for a few months at a time. In the mid 1990s the company started to grow faster due to large contracts with a big international information technology company.

However, in spite of this development there were lingering problems due to the fact that the two professors owned a company that was commercializing research done in their academic department. The department was criticized by some faculty members for overly concentrating on language technology. In their view, the department should have had a wider research orientation as it was expected to be responsible for the entire discipline of general linguistics. Later, the quality of the research done in the department was questioned. However, even before these criticisms were levelled, internal tensions grew within the group due to disagreements about the ownership of intellectual property and the allocation of academic credits.

Balancing Academic Credits with Intellectual Property Rights

One of the ways in which the tension between the two institutional orders broke out in the case of the language technology research group was related to the characteristic ways academia as opposed to business categorize their achievements and 'ownership'. Whereas the origin or 'ownership' of ideas in science has traditionally been indicated by credits given to colleagues, the more formally defined intellectual property rights indicate ownership in business. Property ownerships convey to the owner both the exclusionary right, that is, the right to exclude others from using his/her property, and the right to appropriate economic returns (Owen-Smith 2006). The situation is different in science where scientific articles do not have such exclusivity and others can use

findings to further their own research. Moreover, there is no monetary cost involved in giving others credit. However, in the case of the
language technology research group, the relationship changed because
of commercialization: the disagreements concerning the economic
rewards unleashed also a latent struggle within the group concerning
academic priorities and credits.[3]

The language technology research group proved over the years to be
highly successful in both academic and economic terms. Apart from
some big international research projects, it succeeded in acquiring, on
constant basis, significant amounts of other external research grants.
As a result, the group hired more scientists who continued the tradition of merging academic research with business. The new and mostly
younger researchers licensed the programs they developed to the company owned by the professors. Soon the younger generation began
to think that their contribution to the economic activities of the professors' company should have been institutionalized. In other words,
they expected to be given shares in the company. Despite some preliminary negotiations, the professors did not consider accepting the
younger researchers as shareholders. This created a poisoned research
atmosphere within the group. The younger generation attributed the
reluctance of the professors to accept them as shareholders to the
professors' inability to recognize that despite their pioneering work,
the technology was not the fruit of the professors' research only.

The implicit boundary between the 'original innovators' and the
'subsequent developers' that was created into the research group was
contested by the younger generation also in their research articles.
They questioned the professors' assumed priority on two fronts: firstly,
they singled out predecessors for the professors' own innovations and,
secondly, they delineated some other forerunners than their professors
to their own work. These disagreements relating to academic credits
worsened as the company started to market the licensed programs as if
they were developed in the company. In the field of language technology a cornucopia of researchers from the university and the commercial world exist. Apart from new ideas, innovative and critical tools are
all highly appreciated and traded within this instrumental community

---

[3] For a case in which commercialization terminated a long-term scientific collaboration between two research groups, see Saari, E. 1999. "Dynamics of collaboration:
The case of Finnish and American aerosol research groups." *Science Studies* 12(1):
21–43.

(cf. Mody 2006). Consequently, as the company sold the programs as if they were developed by the firm and not by the researchers of the department, the researchers never received the academic credit they needed to advance their academic careers. The roles of younger faculty in developing the technology remained partly unrecognized, even in the academic context. The situation was described by one of the researchers:

> We travelled abroad a lot in those days and nearly every time when we presented our work, we were asked how our work was related to that of the professors' company, that is, didn't the company do it much better... we were thus not given the credit we deserved.

The managers of the firm (who were not the professors who were only the major shareholders of the company at that time) saw the situation differently. As the former sales manager described the situation:

> When you start to negotiate a real commercial utilization with international IT companies, you need to have full intellectual property rights to the programs and to their codes. In this kind of a situation you really do not want to highlight the fact that you did not develop the program in the firm, since the next question would be whether you have the code and whether you can support its application.

To this the former managing director of the firm added that in his opinion it was totally correct to market a licensed program as a product of the firm, since the firm took the responsibility for the further development and the technical support of the product. These disagreements about intellectual property rights and academic credits originated largely because the two professors[4] set up the company originally to manage the commercial contracts received by the department without paying too much attention to the intellectual property and academic credit issues. This also raised the question of who has the right to benefit from publicly funded collective research work. The members of the group faced a rather fundamental question: how should the economic rewards of collective research be distributed among diverse contributors? As there were no clear answers to this question, the disagreements escalated to involve the academic priority and credits as well.

Interestingly, the two professors also thought that their company should have made it clear that the technology it was promoting was

---

[4] Later, the principal researcher was also appointed to the position of a full professor. See above.

developed by the researchers working at the academic department. However, the professors did not think that they were to be blamed for the inflamed situation since they had externalized the business activity from the university. They accused the managing director of their own company for the misunderstanding about the origins of the commercialized technology. From the perspective of the younger researchers, the professors should have done something about the company's policy since they were on its executive board. The employees of the company held a similar view. They thought that the professors—the principal owners and board members of the firm— should have assumed a stronger leadership of the commercial activities of the company, especially in the middle of the IT crash that took place in Finland at the turn of 2000s. One of the managers of the firm who was also a post-graduate student at the home department of the spin-off company explained:

> I think that [the professors] took the company seriously enough, for instance they took always part to its strategy meetings. But since their primary occupation was in the university, they always prioritized it, and the company became secondary.

Thus both the researchers in the university and the employees of the company were of the view that the professors should have been more interested in the activities of their company. Some employees were also confused by the way the professors acted as spokespersons for the entire Finnish language technology branch in international circles. In their opinion the professors should have highlighted the strengths of their company instead of heaping praise on the entire Finnish language technology industry. It, therefore, seems that despite their efforts, the professors were not very successful in managing their multiple roles as academics, principal owners of a company, and representatives of Finnish language technology. They tried to manage their multiple duties by keeping their academic work separated from their business activities but the fine line they tried to draw between the two activities was contested from both sides. By holding important positions in both academe and business they were supposed to assume equal commitment to both.

The Openness of Communication and the Quality of Research

Apart from the strife on intellectual property rights and academic credits, difficulties were also brewing in other fronts. After a long period of academic and commercial success, the department received, in the late 1990s, a very disappointing research assessment evaluation. The evaluation report stated that:

> Given the high degree of excellence that the department achieved in the eighties and early nineties, the results for the period covered by this evaluation are disappointing. Considering the level of support and the number of people involved one would expect to see more interesting results and more scientific output.

The evaluators were worried about the impact the commercial ties were having on the kinds of research being conducted and the overall research focus of the department. In their opinion, there was a real danger that the group's initial success in commercialization was shifting the research focus from "scientifically interesting but 'difficult' issues to problems whose solutions might be more financially rewarding." Also, though the evaluators admitted that the commercial success of the methods developed "validate the value of scientific work", they were worried that the "presence of competing commercial interests in the same department gets in the way of a free exchange of ideas." Indeed, the exclusiveness of commercial property rights and the related secrecy do not fit well with the academic norm of open communication. Apart from this situation the problem facing the research group was further complicated. Frustrated with their exclusion from the professors' company the younger generation set up a company of their own in 1997. This created a secretive atmosphere within the group. In the words of the other professor:

> For some years already we have had the problem that the whole truth has not been laid out on the table either in our internal discussions or in our publications…It is a big ethical problem, indeed. How much you can hide—and still act as a credible academic researcher—when you know that you have something that is commercially relevant as well?

A disagreement concerning one doctoral dissertation provides an apt example of the contradictions the researchers of the group encountered while simultaneously trying to fulfil the requirements of both academia and business. The doctoral candidate in question belonged to the group of younger researchers who had established their own company. He was accused of being intentionally vague in describing a new *parser* he had been developing. The university grading committee made the following remark concerning the thesis:

> XX…has in some important points, especially when it comes to algorithmic descriptions and design principles, refrained from the scientifically

detailed descriptions that would have been desirable. This is contrary to the principle of openness that is central to science.

In the opinion of the doctoral candidate he had only acted in a way that had become a departmental convention. Moreover, he referred to the new policy of the University of Helsinki concerning innovations and academic research:

> When we were starting our company I went to a couple of functions organized by the University of Helsinki. At one of them the Rector of the university was speaking…and his message was that there was no sense in telling everything to the Japanese and Americans and letting them collect the money from our innovations. The university needs publications but it does not mean that all things should be revealed.

As for the other worry of the evaluators—the apparent turning from the 'difficult' issues to the easier but financially more rewarding problems—the professors themselves started to consider that their success in gaining external funding also contributed to the very erosion of the successful scientific research program. They argued that external grant requirements exert strong pressure on researchers to meet grant objectives, and the numbers of projects that the researchers are simultaneously involved in prevent fresh and innovative initiatives. As the other professor noted:

> I am a bit worried about this development [towards commercially motivated projects]: money pours in of course, and the students get funding, but these projects have usually rather short time spans and concrete problems, which need to be solved in one way or another. One danger is that theses do not get ready but that what is being done is usually beneficial for somebody, but does not really add to the academic competence of the younger researchers.

Last but not the least, the evaluators also shared some of the fears of the faculty who had since the early 1990s been complaining about the narrow focus of the Department of General Linguistics, where the language technological research took place (see above).

Convergent Cultures

Studies on the university-industry interactions have highlighted the increasing institutional convergence (Vallas and Kleinman 2007, Owen-Smith 2006, Kleinman and Vallas 2006). As Steven Vallas and Daniel Kleinman pointed out, this convergence is asymmetrical in that

"the market pressures and entrepreneurial practices increasingly per-
vade academia, even as university-like codes and practices are adopted
by science-intensive firms" (2007:7). It is not surprising then that the
spin-off companies started by the members of the language technology
research group followed a similar trajectory. Both firms were science-
intensive in the sense that they sought to capitalize the cutting edge
research done by the group. However, the drive to conduct research
necessary to sustain the growth of the companies and the flow of scientific ideas within the department became a double-edged sword.

In a much broader context, there is an inherent assumption among
the staunch advocates of the entrepreneurial university that innovative
academic research spawns good commercial products. In terms of the
entire language technology branch in Finland, the stark reality was
that the commercialization of language technology research proved to
be complex activity with several barriers to maneuver. Turning academic research into viable commercial products is both time and
resource consuming, and there is the likelihood that advanced technology might not necessarily be a unique selling point because of five
interrelated issues. Firstly, language technology has its unique problems in that it provides no such fantastic grandiose visions to lure venture capitalists as, for instance, biotechnology does. Secondly, it is an
embedded technology that is not visible to most of the end-users.
Thirdly, the market for the language technology tools is dominated
worldwide by one big company. Fourthly, the products are easily reproduced and copied. Lastly, the small size of the companies within the
Finnish language technology sector and the fact that the entire industry was based on spin-offs from university research caused problems.

Consequently, the inability to attract venture capital coupled with
the failure to raise enough funds from other sources negatively
impacted the ability of the spin-offs to continue on their initial innovative growth path. In fact, most of the academic owners and employees
of these spin-off firms admitted that they had a more rosy vision of
how to sell their programs than what turned out to be the case. The
younger researchers who set up the new firm indicated that their intention was to continue academic research in tandem with managing the
company. However, they found out that this was practically impossible. They reflected upon the lessons learnt:

> Innovation is just a tiny piece of a certain product, and that again is just
> a tiny bit of the whole process of getting the product into the interna-
> tional market and to be able to also sell it there. The programs made by

the university researchers are not ready to say the very least. We were more optimistic about that in the beginning. But the needs of the users are so different. It is absolutely not enough that the output of the program is correct. It has to be produced in a manner that it is easy to introduce, and it has to be adequately supported...Because of this it is not conceivable that—making saleable products—would be done as a secondary occupation in the academic world.

In addition to the small size and the inadequate financial support of the companies, their academic company culture proved to be commercially unproductive. When in the 1990s the company owned by the professors was expanding heavily, the managers that were recruited from the business sector found out that the culture of the spin-off company was too heavily bound to the values of academia. While academics eulogize theoretical ideas and original solutions, in the commercial world emphasis is placed on usability, supplementary services and existing demand. One of the former chief executives of the professors' company complained about the perfectionist attitude of the employees—most of whom were recruited from academia—as well as about their "slight contempt" for simple commercial tasks. A former sales manager of the professors' company summed up the situation in the following way:

> When the company started to grow out of its earlier research group in the 1990s, we found out that the interests of the research and those of the company were not necessarily congruent...Those things that were 'hot' in the academia, like speech technology, were still far off from anything that could be commercialized, and things that would have been easily converted into saleable tools, such as terminology extraction and spell check, were not at all considered as interesting in the research side...

These differences in aims became apparent when the company started facing commercial problems during the 'dot-com bubble'. It had invested too heavily on developing speech technology, which in retrospect turned out to be overly optimistic. Moreover, the professors, who still sat on the executive board, were reluctant to dismiss personnel, who were largely their former students. Thus, the company became financially strained and was eventually sold to a larger corporation.

Boundaries Blurred, Redefined and Closed

The story of the language technology research group can easily be cast in terms of boundary work (Gieryn 1999, Kinchy and Kleinman 2003,

Tuunainen 2005). The commercial activity it engaged in gave rise to conflict-ridden work of drawing boundaries (Tuunainen and Knuuttila 2009). At the different stages in the development of the language technology research group and its spin-offs, the actors had to redefine the relationship between scientific research and commercial activity. The boundaries of the two activities were blurred to begin with, but as the commercial activity grew in volume, a separate company was established. Though the professors thought they had established a boundary between their academic and commercial activities by externalizing the task of 'marketing' to the company, neither the researchers nor the employees found the erected boundary justified.

The disagreements revolving around the drawing of an artificial boundary between the research group's academic and commercial activities were further complicated by the exclusion of the younger generation of researchers from the participation on equal basis in commercial activities. The professors, too, began to feel increasingly disquiet about the situation, as one of them explained:

> we were no longer credible professors once we had a firm that applied the research done in the department...I understand more than well that the other researchers were worried about, or at least secretly wondered in their minds what was going on...

When the younger generation of the language technology research group established their own company the situation became even more complicated. In the early days, the participants could act as if the commercial activity and its responsibilities were relegated primarily to the business side of the boundary. However, with the breakaway group establishing a rival company within the department, the business interests and boundary-work had now found their way into the very heart of the department's research activities. Eventually, at the end of the 1990s, the key younger researchers gave up their academic careers and moved to work for their newly formed company. This practically meant the end of the language technology research group. The professors, however, chose to remain within the academia; withdrawing themselves from business activity by selling off their company to a larger corporation.

Consequently, the conflicts ensuing from hybridizing academic work with business were resolved by separating the two activities from each other. As a result, the business activity and its dedicated actors moved away from academia that from the perspective of the university was not a satisfying resolution, as many competent researchers were lost and a successful research program terminated.

In the Grey Area?

The visions of hybridizing and transforming academic research, which are encapsulated in such models as the 'Mode 2' and the 'triple helix' of university-industry-government relations assume typically in a constructivist fashion that the existing organizations may willingly be moulded into new formats. However, as the case of the language technology research group shows, there are certain inherent ideals that the university has come to embody that cannot readily be reconciled with the dictates of entrepreneurial activity. Even though the language technology research group seemed to provide a prime example of the entrepreneurial science, its development ran oddly against the tide of the official research policy. The group began its commercialization process long before the widespread notion of academic capitalism gained common currency in Finnish academia. However, the group dissolved in an entirely different institutional context in which the outspoken science policy was to enhance the commercial application of the academic research.

A closer analysis of the reasons for this development revealed several problems and contradictions, some of which seem easier to solve than others. This applies especially to those problems that were due to the lack of institutional setting. When the language technology research group started its commercialization, rules and regulations that could have governed the process and pre-empt many teething problems were absent. The institutional landscape in Finland has since then changed and such problems as the establishment of two competing spin-offs in the same department are highly unlikely to occur. According to relatively recent legislation in Finland, universities rather than individual researchers have the rights to innovations born out of externally funded projects.

Moreover, the language technology research group had tried to license their programs through the former technology transfer office of the University of Helsinki only to find out, as the one of the professors put it, "[this TTO] could not do it: they did not, in fact, either market or sell". On this front there has also been considerable improvement as a new larger and more resourceful technology transfer office was established in 2001, owned by the University of Helsinki and the State of Finland through VTT Technical Research Centre of Finland, which is the biggest research organization in Scandinavia.

The issues of the openness of scientific discussion, the one-sidedness of research and the possible deterioration of its quality are much more difficult to resolve because of the direct impact they have on teaching and research. Time will tell whether these potential side-effects of knowledge capitalization will be tolerated by the academia. Commercialization is also potentially harmful to scientific collaboration as research is an informal, cooperative and relatively anti-hierarchical endeavour. It is plausible that commercialization may obstruct these cooperative and collegial relationships. Although one must add that also academic status competition hinders cooperation and the free exchange of ideas (Vallas and Kleinman 2007).

From the commercial point of view, one of the most solid doubts concerning the prospects of the entrepreneurial university is the commercial viability of university start-ups. The question that must be asked is whether academics can be considered the right actors for business activities given their characteristic interests and motivations. As Göktepe-Húlten (2010) indicates, patenting is often regarded as a part of a scientific research programme rather than an end in itself. Giuri et al. (2007) and Gulbrandsen (2005) point out, in turn, that solving interesting research puzzles, gaining recognition, and getting personal satisfaction are important factors pushing forward the desire to commercialize. This explains why in spite of the available expert knowledge base, the incursions of academics into the realm of business have produced only little success. This assessment applies also to the case of the language technology research group. The professors derived little dividends from their companies and the strategic direction of the company was largely based on the academic interests of the professors. As such, many important decisions were not made on sound commercial basis but rather with academic motives, leading to several complaints by the managers recruited from the world of business.

Also the manner in which the question of intellectual property rights escalated in relation to the issue of academic credits showed how difficult it is to bridge the diverging academic and business practices. The commitment to the traditional university values might also explain the uneasiness the two professors felt about their multiple roles as academics, entrepreneurs and major actors in the Finnish language technology scene.[5] This led them to choose to leave the commercial activity altogether for which the company merger gave a convenient opportunity. Another reason for their prioritizing the university even at the expense of their own firm was most probably due to the constraints of taking care of too many things—teaching and supervising, doing research and leading a research group and a company that is commercializing its research. There are good reasons to ask whether academic personnel are able to manage all the different tasks that have recently been assigned to them.

Conclusion

The case of the language technology research group provides a good example of the gap between discovery and application. Innovations can take long time to mature and the crucial inventions are often made well before the technical, not to mention the commercial, possibilities of utilizing them even exist. For instance, the two-level morphology, on which a big part of the commercial activities of the language technology research group was founded, can be traced back to the generative model of the phonological structure of the English language developed by Chomsky and Halle (1968). Their seminal work inspired discussions on general modelling of phonetic or phonological structure (Jakobson et al. 1952).

Also the role of technology was critical: whole branch of language technology would not have existed without computers. Moreover, when the language technology research group was established at the beginning of 1980s, personal computers were a rarity. Thus, it took ten years from the research group to turn the two-level model into a substantial commercial income. This was because the technology was developed using multi-programming operating systems with virtual memory in a university setting. However, the operating system that allowed for running multiple applications with genuinely flexible and sufficient virtual memory spread broadly to the consumer market only after the introduction of the *Windows 95*. Already this example from

---

[5] The two professors were remarkably active and visible also in other fronts. The other professor functioned also as a Dean of the Faculty of Arts at the University of Helsinki and the other one in turn was the central actor in the successful initiatives to get more external and public funding to the language technology sector in Finland and even in Nordic countries.

such a practically geared and instrumental field as language technology shows that the idea of a new mode of research done in 'the context of application' may—if taken too short-sightedly as the major criterion for funding—actually impede innovation.

Last but not the least, due to the free and open source software the domain of language technology appears to be on the verge of already moving again beyond the entrepreneurial mode. To be sure, the availability of free program code was a norm among the academic researchers even before the dawn of commercialization. For instance, the second flagship innovation of the language technology research group, the constraint grammar, never got the international recognition it deserved due to its early commercialization. Though the professors' company distributed it free of charge to research institutes, it never spread widely as researchers were not given access to the code. The practices of free and open software development seem to fit the academia better than the imperatives of business activity. It will be interesting to see whether, and on which conditions, anything like that could happen in such more investment-heavy fields as biotechnology, nanotechnology and materials science.

Acknowledgment

I would like to thank the Academy of Finland for supporting this research.

Bibliography

Arppe, Antti. 2005. "The Very Long Way from Basic Linguistic Research to Commercially Successful Language Business: the Case of Two-Level Morphology", in Arppe, Antti, Lauri Carlson, Krister Lindén, Jussi Piitulainen, Mickael Suominen, Martti Vainio, Hanna Westerlund, Yli-Jyrä, Anssi, eds., *Inquiries into Words, Constraints and Contexts*, CSLI Studies in Computational Linguistics ONLINE, 2–16.

Blumenthal, David, Michael Gluck, Karen Seashore, Michael A. Stoto, and David Wise. 1986. "University-Industry Research Relationships in Biotechnology: Implications for the University. *Science* 232 (4756): 1361–1366.

Boon, Mieke and Tarja Knuuttila. 2011. "Breaking up with the Epochal Break: The Case of Engineering Sciences", in Nordmann Alfred, Hans Radder and Gregor Schiemann, eds. *Science Transformed? Debating Claims of an Epochal Break*. Pittsburgh: University of Pittsburgh Press.

Clark, Burton R. 1998. *Creating entrepreneurial universities: Organizational pathways of transformation*. Oxford: International Association of Universities Press.

Chomsky, Noam and Morris Halle. 1968. *The Sound Patterns of English*. New York: Harper and Row.

Dzisah, James. 2010. "Capitalizing knowledge: the mind-set of academic scientists."*Critical Sociology* 36(4):555–573.

Etzkowitz, Henry. 2003a. "Innovation in innovation: The triple helix of university-industry government relations." *Social Science Information* 42(3):293–337.

Etzkowitz., Henry. 2003b. "Research groups as 'quasi-firms': The invention of the entrepreneurial university." *Research Policy* 32(1): 109–21.

Etzkowitz, Henry. 2004. "The triple helix and the rise of the entrepreneurial university", in Grandin Karl, Nina Wormbs and Sven Widhalm, eds., *The science-industry nexus: history, policy, implications*. Sagamora Beach, MA: Science History Publications, pp. 69–91.

Etzkowitz, Henry.2008. *The Triple helix: University-Industry-Government Innovation in Action*. London and New York: Routledge.

Etzkowitz, Henry and James Dzisah. 2010. "Who Influences Whom? The Transformation of University-Industry-Government Relations." *Critical Sociology* 36(4):491–501.

Gibbons, Michael, Camille Limoges, Helga Nowotny, Simon Schwartzman, Peter Scott, and Martin Trow. 1994. *The new production of knowledge*. London: Sage Publications.

Gieryn, Thomas F. 1999. *Cultural boundaries of science: Credibility on the line*. Chicago: The University of Chicago Press.

Giuri, Paola, Myriam Mariani, Stefano Brusoni, Gustavo Crespi, Dominique Francoz, Alfonso Gambardella, Walter Garcia-Fontes, Aldo Geuna, Raul Gonzales, Dietmar Harhoff, Karin Hoisl, Christian Le Bas, Alessandra Luzzi, Laura Magazzini, Lionel Nesta, Önder Nomaler, Neus Palomeras, Pari Patel, Marzia Romanelli and Bart Verspagen. 2007. "Inventors and invention processes in Europe: Results from the PatVal-EU survey." Research Policy 36 (8):1107–1127.

Gulbrandsen, Magnus. 2005. "But Peter's in it for the money"–The liminality of entrepreneurial scientists." *VEST* Journal for Science and Technology Studies 18(1–2):49–75

Göktepe-Hultén, Devrim. 2010. "A Balancing Act: Factors behind the Formation of Academic Entrepreneurship." *Critical Sociology* 36(4):521–535.

Jakobson, Roman, Gunnar Fant and Morris Halle. 1952. *Preliminaries to speech analysis: the distinctive features and their correlates*. MIT Acoustics Laboratory Technical Report 13. Cambridge, MA: MIT Press.

Kenney, Martin. 1986. *Biotechnology: The university-industrial complex*. New Haven: Yale University Press.

Kinchy, Abby J. and Daniel L. Kleinman. 2003. "Organizing Credibility: Discursive and Organizational Orthodoxy on the Borders of Ecology and Politics." *Social Studies of Science* 33(6): 869–96.

Kleinman, Daniel Lee and Steven P. Vallas. 2006. "Contradiction in convergence: Universities and industry in the biotechnology field," in Frickel Scott and Kelly Moore, eds., *The new political sociology of science: Institutions, networks, and power*. Madison: The University of Wisconsin Press, pp. 35–62

Krimsky, Sheldon. 2003. *Science in the private interest: Has the lure of profits corrupted biomedical research?* Lanham: Rowman & Littlefield Publishers.

Marginson, Simon and Mark Considine. 2000. *The Enterprise University: Power, Governance and Reinvention in Australia*. Cambridge: Cambridge University Press.

Mody, Cyrus. 2006. "Corporations, universities, and instrumental communities: Commercializing probe microscopy, 1981–1996." *Technology and Culture* 47(1): 56–80.

Nieminen, Marko. 2005. *Academic research in change. Transformation of finnish university policies and university research during the 1990s*. Saarijärvi: The Finnish Society of Sciences and Letters.

Nowotny, Helga, Peter Scott and Michael Gibbons. 2001. *Re-Thinking Science: Knowledge and the Public in an Age of Uncertainty*. Cambridge: Polity Press.

Nordmann Alfred, Hans Radder and Gregor Schiemann, eds. 2011. *Science Transformed? Debating Claims of an Epochal Break*. Pittsburgh: University of Pittsburgh Press.

Owen-Smith, Jason. 2006. "Commercial imbroglios: Proprietary science and the contemporary university", in Frickel Scott and Kelly Moore, eds., *The new political sociology of science: Institutions, networks, and power*. Madison: The University of Wisconsin Press, pp. 63–90.

Radder, Hans, ed. 2010. *The Commodification of Academic Research: Analyses, Assessments, Alternatives*. Pittsburgh: University of Pittsburgh Press.

Saari, Eveliina. 1999. "Dynamics of collaboration: The case of Finnish and American aerosol research groups." *Science Studies* 12(1): 21–43.

Shinn, Terry and Erwan Lamy. 2006. "Paths of commercial knowledge: Forms and consequences of university-enterprise synergy in scientist-sponsored firms." *Research Policy* 35(1)0: 1465–1476.

Slaughter, Sheila and Leslie L. Leslie. 1997. *Academic capitalism: Politics, policies, and the entrepreneurial university*. Baltimore: The Johns Hopkins University Press.

Tuunainen, Juha. 2004. *Hybrid Practices: The Dynamics of University Research and Emergence of a Biotechnology Company*. Doctoral Dissertation, Department of Sociology, Research Reports No. 244. Helsinki: University of Helsinki.

Tuunainen, Juha. 2005. "Contesting a hybrid firm at a traditional university." *Social Studies of Science* 35(2): 173–210.

Tuunainen, Juha and Tarja Knuuttila. 2008. "Determining the norms of science: From epistemological criteria to local struggle on organizational rules?" in Välimaa, Jussi and Oili-Helena Ylijoki, eds., *Cultural Perspectives on Higher Education*. Verlag: Springer, pp.138–153.

Tuunainen, Juha and Tarja Knuuttila. 2009. "Intermingling Academic and Business Activities – A New Direction for Science and Universities?" *Science, Technology & Human Values* 34(6):684–704.

Vallas, Steven P. and Daniel L. Kleinman. 2007. "Contradiction, convergence and the Knowledge economy: The confluence of academic and commercial biotechnology." *Socio-Economic Review* 6(2): 283–311.

Wald, Andreas. 2007. "The Effect of 'Mode 2'-Related Policy on the Research Process: The Case of Publicly Funded German Nanotechnology." *Science Studies* 20(1): 26–50.

CHAPTER FIFTEEN

PUBLIC UNIVERSITIES AND EMERGING FUEL CELL TECHNOLOGY: INSIGHTS FROM SINGAPORE AND MALAYSIA

Zeeda Fatimah Mohamad

The idea behind the call for universities in developing countries to embrace entrepreneurial mandate is derived from the notion that to compete, developing countries must enter new and emerging technology areas in their initial stages. The UN Millennium Project Task Forces on Science, Technology and Innovation (Juma and Lee 2005), emphasized that these new roles by universities in the developing world would allow the countries to take an active part in the prevailing and challenging trends of global knowledge economy. With this policy interest in mind, the chapter explores the extent to which universities in latecomer countries are contributing to the development of new emerging technologies. It examines this issue from the perspective of innovation and technological systems approaches focusing on the contributions of universities in Malaysia and Singapore to the development of fuel cell technology. Fuel cell technology is a new and emerging technology associated with the provision of cleaner and distributed sources of energy. According to the technological systems framework, the role of universities in the development of new emerging technologies is based on their contribution on a number of system level functions: knowledge development, knowledge diffusion, and entrepreneurial experimentation, direction of search, legitimation and resource mobilization.

Universities and New Technology Development

Carlota Perez and Luc Soete (1988) proposed that it is possible to leap-frog technological trajectories through the process of catching-up[1]

---

[1] Catching-up is the term used to describe how developing countries (i.e. those that arrive late on the industrial scene) manage to narrow the productivity and income gap with the advanced countries (Fagerberg and Srholec 2005: 2)

if latecomer countries take advantage of the windows of opportunity[2] temporarily created by the transition to new technologies. In other words, the process of *early entry*[3] could be used to enhance the catching-up process (Perez and Soete 1988). They saw early entry strategy as based on acquiring the capacity for participating in the generation and improvement of technologies, as opposed to the simple use of them (Perez and Soete 1988: 458). This means entering the development of new technologies as early imitators. That is to say jumping quickly into the innovation bandwagon once the market and the technology is opened up by initial innovators. In other words, entering the technology's development during the introduction or emerging phase of the technology life cycle. The idea of early entry was motivated by concerns that most developing countries continue to face enormous difficulties in the drive to industrialize, and that the infrastructural gap between the industrialized West and developing societies remains wide (Perez and Soete 1988: 458).

As a result, they believe that firms in developing countries should exploit the windows of opportunity such as free flow of technological knowledge, reduced competition due to lock-in of leaders in past technologies and lower investment in expensive and standardized capital goods, which are available during the early phase of the technology's life cycle to increase the pace of the catching up process. They argue that universities could act as a set of actors to overcome barriers associated with scientific and technical knowledge during the so called introduction phase because of their free access to knowledge in the early stages of technological development (Perez and Soete 1988).

The biggest problem for early entry, in their opinion, is not because developing countries lack necessary actors, like universities, which are able to exploit and develop the science and technical part of the technology. Rather, the question as to whether endogenous generation can be sustained as the system evolve through constant technological development and continuous flow of investment. While Perez and Soete's proposition on the role of universities in early entry and its supporting arguments were in most part theoretical, their assessment has,

---

[2] This refers to specific periods where the conditions are favourable to the latecomer countries to participate in the development of a new technology.

[3] Catching up strategy is simply referred to as 'early entry' in this chapter. The author believed that 'early entry' can be considered as one of three broad alternative of catching-up strategies.

however, opened up an avenue for public discourse on the role of universities in the development of emerging technologies. This detailed research agenda is attractive for developing countries eager to transform their innovation weak link—universities to jump start the commercialization of new technologies.

The Triple Helix of Innovation

Universities' role in technological innovation has mostly been emphasized as direct relationships with firms (Mansfield and Lee 1996). Logically, existing research on the role of universities in economic development tend to emphasize their work in terms of technological innovation as a two way flow involving university—industry linkages rather than a system wide phenomenon. Treating the university's role as a system-wide issue, however, might be more pressing for latecomer countries that lack local innovative firms. In this context, local universities are usually seen as a beacon for anything related to new scientific discovery and advanced technological development. Recently, efforts have been directed at analyzing the role of universities within the context of innovation systems, the complex organizational and institutional landscapes that influence the creation, development and dissemination of innovation (Mowery and Sampat 2005).

This stems from the realization that though universities fulfil broadly similar functions in the innovation systems, the importance placed on these roles varies considerably, and is influenced by the local industry, the size and structure of publicly funded R&D performers and other actors. Hence, a move towards an innovation systems approach is recommended, especially in areas where the university's role is rather vague and not adequately understood (Mowery and Sampat 2005). The triple helix model has partially adopted this approach as a result of its extensive focus on the overlay of communication and expectations that reshaped the institutional arrangements among three different actors: universities, industries and government agencies. These three institutional spheres—public, private and academic—which formerly operated at arms' length, are now seen as independent, yet intertwined in the drive to further innovation in an increasingly knowledge-based society (Etzkowitz and Leydesdorff 1988 and 2000). In this regard, university and government actors are assumed to be symbolically able to take on the roles of each other. In other words, universities and governments must be placed on equal functional footing as firms.

In spite of this, a closer reading of the literature, however, suggests that while the triple helix demonstrates that the university's role is very much interlinked with other parts of the innovation system, the fact of the matter is that the model is more concerned with looking at how universities are affected by the co-evolution of the three organizational spheres into accepting and performing a more prominent role in the entrepreneurial process. As such, attention is placed on the significance of incubators (Etzkowitz 2002a, Etzkowitz et al 2005), the entrepreneurial university (Etzkowitz, 2002b; Etzkowitz et al. 2000) and the increasingly pseudo-firm like character of university actors (Etzkowitz 2003) in fostering wider economic development. Consequently, the triple helix is based on the role of universities in technological innovation is embodied in university-industry-government linkages and attempts to position universities—the concept of entrepreneurial university—as knowledge-based actors along the lines of firms.

The National Systems of Innovation

Similar to the triple helix of university-industry-government relations, another approach that recognizes the role of universities in the innovation process is the systems of innovation (SI) approach. However, there is less specific analysis of the role of universities in the SI literature, mainly because the systems of innovation literature emphasizes firms as learning organizations embedded within a broader organizational and institutional context, with other organizations, such as universities, typically considered to be the sources of firms' learning process. Thus, the analysis of the roles of universities was largely ignored (for an exception, see Jacobsson, 2002).

However, Jacobsson utilizes the 'functional analysis' approach to explore the role of universities in industrial transformation within the innovation system framework. He provides examples of how universities as a set of actors that can contribute to the development of functions that are essential for the overall development of an innovation system. He indicated that the role of universities in the process of industrial transformation (or development of new emerging technologies) could be conceptualized in terms of their contribution to a range of system level functions. While Jacobsson did not elaborate on how the framework might be operationalized, his intention was clear. He was only interested in providing "a selective and interpretive review of the literature on university-industry relations, to identify questions for further research" (Jacobsson 2002: 345).

The set of ideas proposed by Jacobsson have the potential to analyze the full impact of universities in other important areas in the innovation process outside publications, conferences, consulting, patents, licensing, prototypes and start-ups that have, until now, been the focus of academic research (Mowery and Sampat 2005). It is perhaps based on this promise that Rosenberg (1992) suggested that there are paths of influence and causation within the universities' role in technological innovation which have not been systematically identified or examined, much less measured. In this case, the attempt by Jacobsson (2002) through the use of a much broader systems framework may be a useful step to exploring the role of universities, which, as suggested by Rosenberg (1992), intentionally or unintentionally, have been overlooked.

Consequently, inspired by the initial idea by Jacobsson, this the chapter employed the technological system framework and its functional analysis (Carlsson and Stankiewicz 1991) as its analytical framework. This approach allows for the exploration of multiple cases in this instance, the role of four local public universities—the University Kebangsaan Malaysia (UKM), Universiti Teknologi Malaysia (UTM), Nanyang Technological University (NTU) and National University of Singapore (NUS)—in the development of fuel cell technology within two Southeast Asian developing countries. The data used in the chapter is collected from interviews, documentation, archival records, direct observation and physical artifacts. These five sources are amongst the most common methods that are usually employed in a case study research (Yin 2003). The data is mainly qualitative, though some quantitative data was used in contextualizing the global emergence of fuel cell technology.

Fuel Cell Technology as a Complex Technology System

Fuel cell technology[4] is based on the electrochemical process in which hydrogen and oxygen are combined to produce electricity, heat and water. Several types of fuel cell technology are currently being developed and are classified according to the types of electrolytes, and

---

[4] Biological fuel cells and metal fuel cells can also be considered as fuel cells, but not within the definition used in this chapter.

grouped according to their operating temperature. The low temperature group includes proton exchange membrane fuel cells (PEMFC), direct methanol fuel cells (DMFC), alkaline fuel cells (AFC) and phosphoric acid fuel cells (PAFC). The high temperature group includes molten carbonate fuel cells (MCFC) and solid oxide fuel cells (SOFC), which operate at temperatures of over 600°C. The core and most novel part of the technology is the fuel cell stack. However, the fuel cell stack needs to be supported by other technologies, collectively referred to as the balance of system (BOS). The BOS includes the fuel system, fuel delivery system, air system, cooling system, humidification system, electrical system, hydraulic system, control system, etc. The combination of fuel cell stack and BOS comprises the entire 'fuel cell technology'. The extent to which the BOS is required may change for different types of fuel cells and their eventual application. The BOS frequently constitutes a large proportion of the engineering within a fuel cell system (Larminie and Dicks 2003:19–21).

It is important to note that a fully operational fuel cell technology includes the fuel cell stack and the BOS, and also its connection to its final application and hydrogen source. As an energy conversion technology, fuel cell technology has the potential to provide a cleaner and quieter ways of producing electricity for a broad range of applications. There are currently three main commercial application areas for fuel cells: stationary power,[5] transport,[6] and portable equipment.[7] Applications for the space and military sector represent much smaller and very specialized markets (Fuel Cell Today 2004b). However, in spite of its promising advances, the hydrogen source remains a major barrier to the deployment of fuel cell technology worldwide. As at now, there is no infrastructure capable of supporting the supply of hydrogen required for the mass introduction of fuel cells (Pilkington 2004). As such, most of the actors involved in developing the technology are

---

[5] This includes power for residential and non-residential applications (such as schools, office blocks, banking facilities, factories) for different power ranges from small (1-10kW), medium (10-300kW) and large (250kW-10MW) (Cacciola, 2001: 68).

[6] This includes cars, buses, trains and various niche vehicles (e.g. aircraft, scooters, forklifts, motorcycles, wheelchairs, human transporters).

[7] Fuel cell technology is seen as an important source for mobile electronic devices. It has several advantages over conventional batteries, such as increased operating times, reduced weight and ease of recharging (Fuel Today, 2004b).

sourcing hydrogen by reforming hydrogen rich fossil fuels, such as gasoline and natural gas (Fuel Cell Today 2004c).

By preserving the dependence on fossil fuel, this 'reforming technology' has the advantage of sourcing hydrogen without the need to radically transform existing infrastructures and industrial networks. It has been argued that this provides little or no benefit in terms of reducing emissions and may result in 'lock-in' to an inferior technology, which could prevent a radical transition towards a low carbon economy (Hart 2000). There is an ongoing attempt directed at producing more sustainable forms of hydrogen through electrolysis of water by using renewable energy sources, such as, solar, geothermal, biofuel and wind energy, and biological processes. Compared to the reform of fossil fuel, the development of more sustainable forms of hydrogen sources are still at the experimental stage and prospects are uncertain.

At this stage, fuel cell technology is not a clear-cut emerging technology, especially when it is viewed within the perspective of a functional and workable technical system. It is very important to note that the most novel parts of the fuel cell system are the fuel cell stacks and the use of pure hydrogen from sustainable sources. Other parts of the fuel cell system, such as the BOS, fuel cell applications and the use of hydrogen from fossil fuel, are relatively much more established, and innovation in these more conventional areas are closely associated with developments in the more novel parts of the technology. In this case, as emphasized by Mytelka (2003 and 2004) capabilities in system integration and a broad science knowledge base is very important in advancing this technology. This is why the development of this technology is replete with partnerships between new and old actors with combinations of different expertise, resources and experiences.

Emerging Phase of Fuel Cell Technology

The history of fuel cells goes back to 1839, when a British judge and scientist, Sir William Robert Grove, discovered that he could generate electricity by combining oxygen and hydrogen. Sir Grove built a device called a 'gas battery' using sulphuric acid as the electrolyte and platinum as the catalyst. His invention was enhanced fifty years later by the scientists Ludwig Mond and Charles Langer, who used Grove's invention for the development of a practical device they called a 'fuel cell'. Commercial development of Mond and Langer's device was hindered by the exorbitant cost of platinum. In 1932 another British scientist, Sir Francis Bacon, managed to construct a cell that used an alkaline electrolyte (now known as the AFC), which utilized nickel as the catalyst (Koppel 1999 cited in Hall and Kerr 2003: 464). Several modifications have been made to these original inventions. This includes basic research fundamental to the design of various types of fuel cell currently being developed: SOFC, MCFC, DMFC, PAFC and PEMFC (Crawley 2006a, 2006b, 2007a, 2007b, and 2007c).

However since its invention more than hundred years ago, fuel cell technology is still at the emerging phase of development and deep uncertainties about whether it will gain wide-scale market acceptance continues (Hellman and Van den Hoed 2007: 306). As pointed out by Hart, "the fuel cell is one of the oldest energy technologies known to man, yet its development has lagged behind that of its less elegant and often less efficient cousins, such as the internal combustion engine and the gas turbine" (2000: 2). Currently, the fuel cell market is dominated by prototypes and demonstrations in niche applications, with the total number of installed fuel cell units reaching less than 25,000 in 2006. While the question remains as to whether the technology will progress beyond this stage, the fuel cell market has experienced an impressive rate of growth since the end of the 1990s (Adamson and Crawley 2007).

However, the fact that fuel cell technology has experience fluctuating periods of success and failure since its emergence must not be lost in debates about future viability. The most obvious fluctuations involve the shift from AFC/PEMFC and military/space applications in the early periods to PAFC/MCFC and large stationary application in the middle period and finally to PEMFC/DMFC/SOFC and portable/medium-small stationary/transport application in the current period. Also during this long introduction phase of its development, the various actors in particular the US, UK, Germany and Japan gave high-level support to private sector R&D activities. As a result, much of the technology has been appropriated by large companies and public organizations in the industrialized world (Schaeffer 1998).

In spite of this, fuel cell technology is still characterized by intense R&D and demonstration activities, with only minimal success in full scale commercialization. This is because as an energy technology, the development of fuel cells is very costly and complicated by the high level of system integration, and the broadness of the scientific and technological knowledge base required. As a result, public-private partnerships have been used rather extensively as a mechanism to deal with this challenge. These partnerships have not been limited to the local or national level, but also at the regional and international levels. Examples of these broad public-private partnership includes programmes such as the European Union Framework Fuel Cell Programme, the PACo network in France, the Hydrogen and Fuel Cell Committee in Canada, the Freedom Car Programme in the US, the Transport Energy Strategy in Germany and various fuel cell specific projects in Japan[8] (OECD 2006).

Furthermore, fuel cell technology is highly influenced by three associated policy domains: environmental, energy and industrial (OECD 2006). Environmental policy is associated with the issue of global climate change and trans-boundary air pollution, while energy policy is associated with dwindling global sources of fossil fuel. At present, industrial policy is perceived as less of a global issue, but some policy-makers are expressing concerns about how growth in emerging energy technology like fuel cells can increase the industrial gap between developed and developing countries (Mytelka and Boyle 2006). Even though some of the leading latecomer countries like Korea, China, India, Taiwan, Thailand, Malaysia and Singapore are actively participating in the development of this technology, the involvement of other developing countries is less evident. In fact, most latecomer countries are still unprepared to deal with the rapid advances in this technology (Mytelka and Boyle 2006).

Insights from Singapore and Malaysia

Shaping the Contribution of Universities

The extent of the significance of universities' contribution to the development of fuel cell technology is directly related to the intensity of non-university actors within the larger national innovation system. In Singapore, for example, the contribution of universities to fuel cell innovation is significant and reasonably comprehensive. There is an equivalent if not more, active involvement by non-university actors as

---

[8] This includes the Project for Development of Platform Technologies for Highly Efficient Fuel Cell Systems and the Project for Development of Technologies for the Commercialization of Highly Efficient Fuel Cell Systems within the Japanese government's 2000 Millennium Project.

well. Correspondingly, in Malaysia, the overall development of system functions remains weak and unbalanced. There is limited involvement from non-university actors. This is an indication that the initiation of a fuel cell innovation system, even in the emerging phase, cannot depend on the universities' activities alone, but requires strategic support and systematic interaction with other relevant actors.

The Role of Government Agencies

There are clear differences in the roles played by the governments of Malaysia and Singapore, with the latter appearing to be more hands-on than the former. The Singaporean government, particularly through the role of three of its agencies, Economic Development Board (EDB)[9], *STAR[10] and Ministry of Environment and Water Resources (MEWR)[11] have provided extensive administrative, infrastructural and political support for various actors in almost all areas of system function. However, in Malaysia, the government's role has been confined mainly to supporting university activities. The differences in governmental support and role have a significant impact on the overall development of system functions in these countries. Singapore's technology foresight programme, in which the idea of the development of fuel cell technology is proposed, was specifically designed by EDB and A*STAR to incorporate the views of different actors, both local and foreign interested in the economic value of developing new energy technologies.

The high political autonomy of government agencies in Singapore and the clear economic implication of this exercise for its actors make certain the full participation of various stakeholders. This made the foresight initiative to be grounded in the political and economic reality

---

[9] EDB is Singapore's lead agency responsible for planning and executing strategies to sustain Singapore's position as a global hub for business and investment (EDB 2007).

[10] A*STAR was established in 1991 to foster world-class scientific research and talent for a knowledge-based Singapore. It is organised into two research councils: the Biomedical Research Council and the Science and Engineering Research Council. The two research councils fund and oversee 12 public research institutes in the Life and Materials Sciences areas. It also actively supports and is the owner of the largest pool of made-in-Singapore technologies that are available for licensing to industry (A*STAR 2007).

[11] MEWR is the agency responsible for delivering and sustaining a clean and healthy environment and water resources in Singapore. MEWR started as the Ministry of Environment in 1972. In 2004, it was renamed to reflect the ministry's expanded role in managing water as a strategic national resource (MEWR 2007).

of the country as the policy framework was based on serious negotiation and agreement among diverse set of local and foreign stakeholders. Even the country's Fuel Cell R&D Programme was under the
management of A*STAR and EDB, and this required the universities,
local PRIs and Rolls Royce to align their activities with each other.

The Malaysian government, on the other hand, took a more hands-off
approach by relying on researchers in UTM and UKM to lead the planning, execution and administration of the country's fuel cell foresight
iniative. Compared to Singapore, the Malaysian foresight initiative was
much more experimental, with a less unifying aim and little political
influence. Furthermore, UKM and UTM had little capacity to attract
serious participation and inputs from various stakeholders. The outcome
of the foresight exercise ended up reflecting the research interests of
the universities and elicited very little interest from other stakeholders.

Furthermore, the types of government agencies that are actively
involved in the development of fuel cells in Singapore are more diverse
than in Malaysia. This includes agencies that are in-charge of industrial
development (EDB), energy efficiency and environmental protection
(MEWR), development of science and technology (A*STAR), housing
(Housing Development Board or EDB) and defence (Ministry of
Defence or MOD). The close cooperation between A*STAR and EDB
has been very important in integrating the activities of different actors
in almost all areas of system function. The close integration between
different government agencies under the newly established Clean
Energy Programme led by the influential ex-prime minister of
Singapore, has the potential to further enhance this coordination.
In Malaysia, the Ministry of Energy, Water and Communication
(MEWC)[12] and and its R&D division, Pusat Tenaga Malaysia (PTM)[13]
were the only agencies involved. This provided few points of contact
for actors to obtain administrative and political support from the
government. Unlike A*STAR in Singapore, the Ministry of Science,

---

[12] MEWC (formerly – before 2004 – the Ministry of Energy, Communications and
Multimedia) was established in 1978 to "facilitate and regulate the growth of industries
in the energy, water and communication sectors to ensure the availability of high quality, efficient and safe services at a reasonable price to consumers throughout the country" (MEWC, 2007).

[13] PTM was registered in 1998 as a not-for-profit company under MEWC to fulfill
the need for a national energy research centre and to co-ordinate various activities in
the energy sector due to the long lead times for energy projects. PTM's aim was to
become a one-stop focal point for linkages with universities, research institutions,
industries and international energy partners (PTM 2007).

Technology and Innovation (MOSTI)[14] only plays its role in funding university research but was not actively interacting with other actors in the development of the technology.

In addition to their broad position in the development of system functions, government agencies have also played an important role in enabling the universities to contribute to the development of fuel cells. In several instances, particularly in Singapore, the universities were given direct mandates by government agencies to undertake specific functions. This top-down tendency is connected to the fact that researchers in public universities within Malaysia and Singapore are considered public servants (Wong 2007). Hence, if the need arises, it is not unusual for researchers in these public universities to be appointed or asked by government to provide expertise in the name of 'national service'. This is the result of the continuation of Malaysia's and Singapore's post-independence economic and social development policy, where the activities of public universities are still under the rigid control of government, and universities are expected to actively participate in the country's development strategies.

In Malaysia and more especially in Singapore, top-down relationships with government have been fundamental in pushing forward university activities in various areas of the overall system. For instance, in Malaysia, UTM and UKM used the appointment of their research leaders on the National Steering Committee on Solar, Hydrogen and Fuel Cells as a platform to legitimize the technology, which in turn gave them the leverage to convince the government to develop a national roadmap for local actors. In Singapore, NTU researchers used existing advisory committees and specific projects already established by the government to guide their contribution. Even NTU's contribution to entrepreneurial experimentation was based mainly on government instructions rather than university initiative.

It must, however, be noted that these government directed contributions would not have taken place without the universities ability to build strong foundations in the technology. Important examples in this case are the universities' proactive efforts in R&D. It was only when the universities had built strong scientific capability and a reputation in various aspects of fuel cell R&D that the political demands for their directed contribution in functional development started. This was particularly evident in the significant role played by Professor Chan of

---

[14] MOSTI was created by the Malaysian government in 1976 to promote R&D, awareness and appreciation in the field of science and technology (MOSTI 2007).

the NTU in Singapore. He managed to enhance his reputation in govenrmnet circles by first building a reputable international research profile at the NTU. This eventually captured the attention and interest of Rolls Royce, followed by A*STAR and EDB.

Table 15.1. List of system functions and associated activities with clear direction from the government

System Functions	University's activities with clear direction from the government
Knowledge development	• Selected by a public-private consortia to provide scientific and technical support for a demonstration project [NTU] • Requested by the government to collaborate with the local PRIs and Rolls Royce to develop new fuel products in the Science and Engineering Research Council (SERC) Fuel Cell Programme [NTU, NUS]
Knowledge diffusion	• Acted as government representative in disseminating updated information about the country's progress in developing policies to support the development of the technology to local and international community [NTU]
Direction of search	• Acting on behalf of the government to coordinate the whole process of national level direction of search, from choosing methods of consultation, selecting the list of stakeholders, leading the consultation process, producing relevant outputs and conducting follow up to the process [UKM, UTM] • Selected by the government's to provide direction of search by participating in government coordinated platforms in foresight, techscan and research programme [NTU]
Legitimation	• Acted on behalf of the government to plan and develop national level committee that can be used to legitimise the development of the technology [UKM, UTM]

(Continued)

Table 15.1. (*Cont.*)

System Functions	University's activities with clear direction from the government
	• Supported efforts by the government to legitimise the development of the technology [NTU]
Enterpreneurial experimentation	• Selected by the government to showcase research expertise in order to attract entrepreneurial activities by foreign actors [NTU] • Appointed by government to provide expert advice to foreign firms [NTU]
Human Resource mobilization	• Requested by government to support human resource training for the development of a particular type of fuel cell product within the SERC fuel cell programme [NTU, NUS]

Source: Author

The Role of Large Firms

Firms, particularly large energy-related firms, have made an important contribution to functional development in both countries, but their roles have developed in different ways. In Malaysia, government-linked firms like Petronas and Tenaga Nasional Berhad (TNB) have been particularly important in creating initial attention to the fuel cell technology, through their business networks. This network was then used to encourage fuel cell research in the universities. In UKM, even before any specific government funding, TNB had provided small private funding for fuel cell related research. In UTM, the former chief executive officer of the research unit of Petronas was fundamental in promoting interest in and providing practical exposure to fuel cells among UTM researchers. However, as the interest of TNB and Petronas declined, the contribution of the universities was significcnatly affected.

As at now, both firms have mixed views about the role of the universities in the development of the technology. While they agree that government should support university fuel cell research as a creative academic activity, they nevertheless, think that fuel cell is not an issue of national importance and thus must not be accorded any preferential status. The firms and the key government agency involved, that is, the Ministry of Energy, Water and Communication, are of the opinion that the development of other technologies, such as biofuel and nuclear, is more viable. As a result, though the universities continue to receive support, the support of these key actors in policy related functions such as legitimation, direction of search and market formation are declining. In addition, the low involvement in fuel cells by large firms is an indication that they will not be hiring trained graduates in fuel cells anytime soon.

However, in Singapore, the sitution is quite the opposite. The early involvement in fuel cell technology by the universities was not induced by firms, but largely depended on the activities of the university researchers. In fact, to begin with, interest from firms and government agencies in the activities of the universities was lacking. But NTU managed to conduct its earliest research on fuel cells based on indirect financial support from a British multinational firm (British Gas) in a research project aimed at producing hydrogen by reforming fuel. The situation changed dramatically when the research leader from NTU managed to induce the interest of another British multinational firm, Rolls Royce, to establish its fuel cell manufacturing and R&D centre in Singapore. The presence of Rolls Royce strengthened the universities' role in the direction of search, human resources mobilization, knowledge development, knowledge diffusion, and the establishment of a national level Fuel Cell Programme. The significant role played by the Economic Development Board (EDB), a government agency, in supporting universities in Singapore resulted indirectly from the desire to support the firms involved rather than a direct policy of supporting the universities.

The EDB, Singapore's lead agency responsible for sustaining its position as a global hub for business and investment has a core mission to develop promising industries for the country. This requires them to build linkages between firms, especially foreign multinationals, and relevant actors in the local innovation system. In the case of Rolls Royce, this is relatively easy as a result of nearly 50 years of partnership, particularly in the marine and aerospace industries. Thus, while it was through the intitiative and the the early interest in fuel cell technology development of one of the uiversities that led to the request for partnership with Rolls Royce, the company's eventual decision to invest in Singapore was very much influenced by their established business relationship with the Singaporean government via EDB.

This was particularly apparent when Rolls Royce, with the assistance of EDB, iniatiated discussions with Temasek Holdings, the investment arm of the Singaporean government, on the possibility of a fuel cells development joint-venture.

Public Research Institutes

Another important difference between the Malaysian and Singaporean cases is the level of involvement by local public research institutes (PRIs) in the development of system functions. In Singapore, four PRIs were active in fuel cells activities: Institute of Materials Research and Engineering (IMRE)[15] in the area of membrane development; Institute of High Performance Computing (IHPC)[16] in computational modeling; Singapore Institute of Manufacturing Technology (SIMTech)[17] in industrial manufacturing and Institute of Chemical and Engineering Sciences (ICES)[18] in the area of catalyst. These institutes are not only conducting research in fuel cell technology, but were also producing publications, patents, conducting research and providing industrial assistance. Such active involvement in the sector has allowed the PRIs to develop active research collaboration with the universities by providing active technical expertise and support to the universities. This was evident when NTU sought the assistance from IHPC in order to conduct complex simulations for its fuel cell system.

In Malaysia only the Malaysian Institute of Nuclear Technology (MINT)[19] and PTM, have had a limited role in developing the technology. This is primarily because in both institutes, involvement in fuel cell technology, are mostly oriented towards supporting university

---

[15] IMRE was established in 1996 to create knowledge, develop human capital and transform technology through innovative research in materials science and engineering. It has a well recognised research group in membrane development for polymer electrolyte membrane fuel cells—PEMFC (IMRE 2007).

[16] IHPC was established in 1998 to develop and promote the application of high performance computing technologies, particularly for analysing and solving complex and challenging computational problems such as fuel cell modelling (IHPC 2007).

[17] SIMTech was established in 1993 to enhance the competitiveness of the local manufacturing industry, i.e. through the generation and application of advanced manufacturing technology and development of associated human capital (SIMTech 2007).

[18] ICES was established in 2002 and its establishment is strategically aligned with Singapore's growing emphasis on the importance of developing small molecule development, new chemical synthesis routes and process analytical technologies (ICES 2007).

[19] MINT is local Malaysian PRI specialising in nuclear technology.

research. They are not interested in conducting research activities for the wider innovation system. However, this limited role has been essential. UTM's core research in fuel cell membrane would have been more challenging to develop without the technical and infrastructural assistance from MINT, while the administrative assistance by PTM was essential for supporting UKM's and UTM's initiative in building the fuel cell roadmap and promoting fuel cell technology to actors and stakeholders in the energy sector.

The management of R&D is also an important area of difference between Malaysia and Singapore. In Singapore, fuel cell R&D within NTU, NUS, IMRE, IHPC, SIMTech and ICES is under the management of A*STAR, a government agency. In the area of physical sciences, A*STAR has a specific role in supporting public sector R&D in fields essential to Singapore's manufacturing industry with specific focus on four industrial clusters: electronics, chemical, infocomms and engineering (A*STAR 2007). Under this strategic direction, activities among the universities and PRIs is closely coordinated to prevent unnecessary duplication. In fact, it can be seen that the four clusters are actually in line with the research areas that are critical for fuel cells technology, that is, electronics—application for DMFC and PEMFC, chemical—development of membrane and catalyst, infocomms— complex modeling, and engineering—systems integration. Not surprisingly, these areas eventually have become the key elements of the government's SERC Fuel Cell Programme. In Malaysia, however, MINT and PTM belong to two different agencies with different strategic orientations: MINT is under MOSTI and PTM is under MEWC. Though MOSTI does support R&D activities that are essential for other ministries, its orientation is much more general, that is, development of energy or environmental technologies. As such, it is not able to actively coordinate fuel cells related activities.

Again, apart from the structure of management, the PRIs influence on the contributions of universities to the development of fuel cell technology is attributed to history. Most PRIs in Singapore have had close working relationships with the country's two public universities since their inceptions. The older research institutes, such as IMRE, SIMTech and ICES, are spin-offs of the universities and the first two are still located within the universities. As a result, co-supervision and staff exchanges are institutionalized. This relationship provides a strong foundation for the two types of actors to increase their research links in fuel cells. It is also not surprising that some university researchers in

Singapore also hold positions in the PRIs. For instance Prof. Lee Jim Yang, an active fuel cells researcher, is a professor in NUS and an adjunct principal scientist in IMRE. Similarly, Professor Birgersson of NUS used to be an active researcher in fuel cell modeling in IHPC.

In Malaysia, research institutes and universities that are involved in fuel cell research do not enjoy a similar historical and locational relationships. In fact, the links between the universities, MINT and PTM in the area of fuel cells is an *ad-hoc* one. For instance, the relationship between UTM and MINT is based on a friendship between their respective lead researchers, while that of UKM-UTM and PTM is based on the proactive moves of university researchers in convincing PTM to initiate a policy related project on fuel cells.

Policy Environment and Its Impact

The policy environment shaped the contribution of both universities non-university actors. Synergy between energy, environmental and industrial policy, the openness to internationalization, and responsiveness to demand side policy was instrumental in influencing fuel cell development initiatives. In Singapore the stronger coordination of the three policy areas had a positive influence on the contributions made by the universities and other actors to functional development. In contrast, the weak explication of these policy features have contributed to the unbalanced development of system functions in Malaysia.

Synergy between Energy, Environment and Industrial Policies

In Malaysia, the development of system functions in fuel cells was very much influenced by the renewable energy policy, while in Singapore, industrial development and environmental protection policies were much more significant. In addition, both countries have different resource endowments: Malaysia is medium-sized country, with rich natural resources, while Singapore is a small city-state with extremely limited natural resources. This has provided a challenge and opportunity for the universities and other actors to be innovative in different policy areas. As such, one can state that the broad policy conditions in Singapore were more conducive for Singapore's universities to enhance their contribution to the development of fuel cell technology compared to their counterparts in Malaysia.

In fact, Singapore, has managed to establish itself as an efficient headquarters for global business, with the interest of key industrial policy actors to transform the country into a business hub for clean energy technologies, while the environmental policy community led by MEWR is tasked to increase the country's image as a clean city in terms of increasing urban air quality and energy efficiency. Indeed this policy convergence is not due to similar interests in supporting projects for clean energy technologies, but is derived also from the heightened global commitment to the mitigation of climate change. Thus, climate change issues have provided the necessary platforms for both policy communities to use the environmental and economic merits of fuels cells to align global environmental concerns with the country's interests in marketing Singapore as a hub for clean energy technologies. With the powerful presence of Rolls Royce, the policy environment has dramatically increased the synergy and interest of various actors to support the development of fuel cells in the country.

The interests of the Malaysian energy policy community in promoting the development of renewable energy have been slow and continue to lag behind the dominance of natural gas. Also, popular alternative energy options in Malaysia, such as biomass, nuclear and hydroelectric power, are the technology options that could be used directly without the need for a conversion technology such as fuel cells. As a result, although the community's interest in fuel cell technology has been encouraging, actual policy commitment to support the specific development of the technology has been rather general at best, and has actually decreased overtime. This is evident in the declining interest of key players within the Malaysian renewable energy arena such as MEWC, TNB and Petronas. However, even with decreasing commitment from the renewable energy policy community, renewable energy policy has been the sole policy driver for the technology in Malaysia.

It is clear that the policy environment in Malaysia is relatively weaker compared to that of Singapore. The policy areas within which the universities in Malaysia are embedded leave little space for the universities to wiggle and grow. This is clear if we examine the geographical and historical contexts of Malaysia and Singapore. In Malaysia, from the beginning, the interest in cleaner energy technologies, such as fuel cells, was closely embedded within the country's interest in increasing the use of renewable energy in natural resource domains such as hydropower, solar energy and biomass. In Singapore, interest in clean energy technology is associated with the acute needs of efficiency for a

small country, with one of the highest rates of energy consumption in
the world.

Openness to Internationalization Policies

The level of internationalization is another critical policy difference between the Malaysian and Singaporean universities. Singapore
unlike Malaysia had an extremely open policy for encouraging active
foreign participation in the development of its economy. The high level
of internationalization affects policies and practices of the universities
such that the Academic Research Fund used to fund the research activities of universities in Singapore is managed by a special committee
chaired by renowned researchers from internationally recognized universities and research institutes such as, Oxford, MIT, Max Planck
Institute and the National Natural Science Foundation of China. Also,
nearly half of the researchers in Singapore's universities and research
institutes are foreigners who receive high salaries with sufficient freedom to make active contributions to the development country's innovation system. In Malaysia, while the internationalization is considered
important by universities, its implementation has been more cautious
as a result of the overarching social priority in ensuring the welfare of
'Bumiputra' staff and students in higher education. Thus, foreign
researchers receive fewer incentives and opportunities to extend themselves in Malaysia. This explains why their contributions are smaller
compared to Singapore.

In addition to the international composition of their staff, students
and advisors in Singapore universities are expected and explicitly
instructed by the government to undertake various types of collaborative activities with international actors. This strong pressure to interna-
tionalize research is not apparent in Malaysian universities. This is
especially evident in relation to the universities' fuel cell research programme. Since the beginning, activities of Malaysian universities were
oriented towards developing indigenous technologies, exploiting local
markets and encouraging local firms to participate. The activities of
the universities in Singapore on the other hand, were international in
nature with much more outward priority. The development of links
with Rolls Royce to develop cell fuel technology, the exploitation of
export markets and the attraction of foreign investment and firms is
a testament to the international rather than nationalistic orientation of

the universities. In fact, the nationalistic orientation towards developing a made-in Singapore fuel cell product has only been encouraged by the government after the country's main objective of exploiting international opportunities was achieved.

Responsiveness to Demand-side Policies

One of the key strategies of the industrial and environmental policy communities in Singapore has been to support the development of test bedding projects for clean energy technology. Demonstration projects play an interesting part in the development of fuel cell technology. They are essential in showcasing the workings of the technology, how it can be effectively diffused and used in a particular locality. Therefore, demonstration projects bring multiple benefits to system function development, both in the obvious area of knowledge development and diffusion, legitimation, attraction of venture capitalists and market formation. Demonstration projects are essential for enhancing both the supply and demand sides of the innovation process. Based on these benefits, the relevant government agencies in Singapore, have played an active role in bringing foreign firms, such as, Daimler Chrysler, Segway and Idatech to conduct demonstration projects in Singapore in different types of transport application and a stationary application. In fact, all the local universities, local firms and polytechnics were involved in these activities.

In addition, the demonstration projects were also extended to British Petroleum (BP) to test fuel cell applications with a hydrogen refuelling system. It is important to note that the higher responsiveness to conducting demonstration projects in Singapore is also related to the policy to brand Singapore as a global clean energy business. The government of Singapore uses energy, environmental and technological rationale to attract foreign players to invest and establish their operations in this city-state. Singapore has institutionalized this process through the establishment of the multi-agency Clean Energy Programme Office or CEPO, with the mandate to make Singapore a global test-bed for early adoption of clean energy products and solutions. On the other hand, there are no clear demand side policies for fuel cells in Malaysia. Demonstration projects are scarce, and mostly implemented by the universities with little support from other actors. Furthermore, unlike Singapore, the development of fuel cells in

Malaysia has been much more related to R&D policy with no clear connection to industrial policy. Even the involvement of its Ministry of Energy, Water and Communications has been focused more on encouraging R&D rather than on the diffusion or adoption of the technology. As a result, the development of fuel cells in Malaysia is unbalanced. There are lots of activities on the supply side, but with no sufficient demand to push the innovation process forward.

Conclusion

It is clear that the technological system framework based on the national systems of innovation approach provides useful insights in understanding the role of universities in the development of fuel cell technology, as an emerging technology. This is because the extent to which the universities in Malaysia and Singapore were able to contribute to the development of fuel cell technology is not only related to their own activities, but critically linked to the much broader interaction with different sets of actors and functions. As such, universities contribution is dependent on the ability and decisions of other actors to make use of what universities have to offer. In other words, though the universities in Singapore and Malaysia conduct various activities in the development of an emerging technology, their actual contribution is limited to the competencies, needs and perceptions of other actors in the system, at both local and international levels.

Since the interactions among policy decisions must be analyzed for a comprehensive understanding of the role of the universities, efforts directed at promoting the role of universities' in the development of an emerging technology like fuel cells need to be complemented by proper understanding and appreciation of the whole system or policy environment. In fact, in the industrialized world, this systemic aspect may be downplayed for the obvious reason that the innovation system is much more developed. As such, there is little policy intervention within the higher education system. In the developing world where the innovation system is underdeveloped, it may be risky to adopt such a 'hands-off' approach in dealing with the impact of the policy environment that generally shaped the contributions of universities.

The proactive system level consideration can considerably enhanced the contribution of the universities in two major ways. First, recognizing and acknowledging the synergistic role of particular actors, that is, government agencies, large firms and PRIs, to shape the activities of universities and the ways in which this can be capitalized upon. Secondly, recognizing the influence of broader policy environment and how this can affect the space within which the universities maneuver. It is imperative for policy makers in developing to consider the specific circumstances of their innovations systems, their strengths and weaknesses and how they complement the activities of their universities before embarking on policy borrowing or copying. This will help in making an informed decision concerning how feasible it is to support universities role in the development of emerging technologies. Such considerations would enable policymaking to be more realistic and dynamic.

Acknowledgement

While ambiguities, mistakes and factual errors are my sole responsibility, I will like to acknowledge the debt and gratitude the chapter owes to my PhD dissertation supervisors at the Science and Technology Policy Research (SPRU), University of Sussex, UK, Prof. Martin Bell and Dr. Jim Watson. The discussions with the examiners, Prof. Staffan Jacobsson and Dr. Adrian Smith, and colleagues: Miss Rocio Alvarez Tinoco, Andrea Campos, Ki-Seok Kwon and Robert Bryne and a number of researchers at SPRU were invaluable.

Bibliography

A*STAR. 2007. About A*STAR [Online] Singapore, A*STAR. Available from: http://www.a star.edu.sg/a_star/2-About-A-STAR [Accessed 1 September 30, 2010.

Adamson, M., & Crawley, G. 2007. *2006 World Survey-Geographical: Research Report.* London: Fuel Cell Today.

Adner, Ron and Daniel A. Levinthal. 2002. "The emergence of emerging technologies." *Management Review* 45(1):50–66.

Agrawal, Ajay. 2001. "University to industry knowledge transfer: Literature review and unanswered questions." *International Journal of Management Review* 3(4):285–302.

Akamatsu, Kaname. 1962. "Historical pattern of economic growth in developing." *The Developing Economies* 1:3–25.

Albuquerque, Eduardo D. M. 1999. "National systems of innovation and non-OECD countries: Notes about a rudimentary and tentative "typology"." *Brazilian Journal of Political Economy* 19(4):35–52.

Amsden, Alice H. 2001. *The rise of "the rest": Challenges to the west from late industrializing economies*. New York: Oxford University Press.

Anderson, Philip and Michael L. Tushman. 1990. "Technological discontinuities and dominant designs: A cyclical models of technological change." *Administrative Science Quarterly* 35(4):604–633.

Bance, P., Nigel P. Brandon, Girvana, B., Holbeche, P., O'Dea, S. & Steele, B. C. H. 2004. "Spinning-out a fuel cell company from a UK University—2 years of progress at Ceres Power." *Journal of Power Sources* 131(1–2): 86–90.

Benneworth, Paul and Gert-Jan Hospers. 2007. "Urban competitiveness in the knowledge economy: Universities as new planning animateurs." *Progress in Planning* 67: 105–197.

Bergek, Anna and Staffan Jacobsson. 2004. "The Emergence of a growth industry: A comparative analysis of the German, Dutch and Swedish Wind Turbine Industries", in Metcalfe, John Stan and Uwe Cantner, eds., *Change, Transformation and Development*. Heidelberg: Physica-Verlag, pp. 197–228.

Bergek, Anna, Staffan Jacobsson, Bo Carlsson, Sven Lindmarkii and Annika Rickne. 2005. "Analyzing the dynamics and functionality of sectoral innovation system-a manual." Paper presented at the DRUID Tenth Anniversary Summer Conference 2005, Copenhagen, Denmark.

Bergek, Anna, Staffan Jacobsson, Bo Carlsson, Sven Lindmarkii and Annika Rickne. 2008. "Analyzing the functional dynamics of technological innovation systems: A scheme of analysis." *Research Policy* 37(3):407–429.

Berkhout, Frans, Adrian Smith and Andy Stirling. 2004. "Sociotechnical regimes and transition contexts", in Boelie Elzen, Frank W. Geels and Ken Green, eds., *System Innovation and the Transition to Sustainability: Theory, Evidence and Policy*. Camberley: Edward Elgar, pp. 48–75.

Cacciola, G., V. Antonucci and S. Freni. 2001. "Technology up date and new strategies on fuel cells." *Journal of Power Sources* 100(1–2):67–79.

Carlsson, Bo and Staffan Jacobsson. 1991. "What makes the automation industry strategic?" *Economics of Innovation and New Technology* 1:257–118.

Carlsson, Bo, Staffan Jacobsson, Magnus Holmén and Annika Rickne. 2002. "Innovation systems: analytical and methodological issues." *Research Policy* 31(2):233–245.

Carlsson, Bo and Rikard Stankiewicz. 1991. "On the nature, function and composition of technological systems." *Journal of Evolutionary Economics* 1(2):193–118.

Crawley, Gemma. 2006a. *Alkaline Fuel Cells (AFC): Research Report*. London: Fuel Cell Today.

Crawley, Gemma. 2006b. *Polymer Electrolyte Membrane Fuel Cells (PEMFC): Research Report*. London: Fuel Cell Today.

Crawley, Gemma. 2007a. *Direct Methanol Fuel Cells (DMFC): Research Report*. London: Fuel Cell Today.

Crawley, Gemma. 2007*b*. *Solid Oxide Fuel Cells (SOFC): Research Report*. London: Fuel Cell Today.

Crawley, Gemma. 2007*c*. *Molten Carbonate Fuel Cells (MCFC): Research Report*. London, Fuel Cell Today.

De Campos, Andre. 2006. *University-industry links in late-industrialising countries: A study of Unilever Brazil*. Unpublished PhD Thesis, Brighton: University of Sussex.

Economic Development Board. 2007. "About Us: Singapore."Available from: http://www.edb.gov.sg [Accessed 4 May 2007]. Last visited September 30, 2020.

Etzkowitz, Henry. 2002*a*. "Incubation of incubators: innovation as a triple helix of university–industry–government networks." *Research Policy* 29(2):115–128.

Etzkowitz, Henry. 2002*b*. *MIT and the rise of Entrepreneurial Science*. New York: Routledge.

Etzkowitz, Henry. 2003. "Research groups as 'quasi-firms': the invention of the entrepreneurial university." *Research Policy* 32: 109–121.

Etzkowitz, Henry, Jose de Mello and Mariza Almeida. 2005. "Towards "meta-innovation" in Brazil: The Evolution of the Incubator and the Emergence of Triple Helix." *Research Policy* 34:411–424.

Etzkowitz, Henry and Loet Leydesdorff. 1988. "The endless transition: A "triple helix" of university-industry-government relations." *Minerva* 36:203–208.

Etzkowitz, Henry and Loet Leydesdorff. 2000. "The dynamics of innovation: from National Systems and "Mode 2" to a Triple Helix of university–industry–government relations." *Research Policy* 29:109–123.

Fagerberg, Jan E. and Martin Srholec. 2005. "Catching-up: What are the critical factors for success?" Background paper for the UNIDO World Industrial Development Report 2005 (Preliminary version). Oslo: Centre for Technology, Innovation and Culture, University of Oslo.

Freeman, Christopher and Carlota Peréz. 1988. "Structural crisis of adjustment, business cycles and investment behaviour," in Giovanni Dosi, Christopher Freeman, Richard R. Nelson, Gerald Silverberg and Luc L. Soete, eds., *Technical Change and Economic Theory*. London: Pinter Publishers, pp. 38–66.

Fuel Cell Today. 2004*a*. "Education Kit 2: The Technology." [Online] UK, Fuel Cell Today. Available from: http://www.fuelcelltoday.com/media/pdf/education-kit/The-Technology.pdf [Accessed 29 May 2007]. Last visited September 30, 2010.

Fuel Cell Today. 2004*b*. "Education Kit 3: The Application." [Online] UK, Fuel Cell Today. Available from: http://www.fuelcelltoday.com/media/pdf/education-kit/The-Technology.pdf [Accessed 29 May 2007]. Last visited September 30, 2010.

Fuel Cell Today. 2004*c*. "Education Kit 5: Fuel Reforming." [Online] UK, Fuel Cell Today. Available from: http://www.fuelcelltoday.com/media/pdf/education-kit/Fuel-Reforming.pdf [Accessed on 29 May 2007]. Last visited September 30, 2010.

Geels, Frank W. 2004. "From sectoral systems of innovation to sociotechnical systems. Insights about dynamics and change from sociology and institutional theory." *Research Policy* 33(7–8):897–920.

Gunasekara, Chrys. 2006. "Universities and associative regional governance: Australian evidence in non-core metropolitan regions." *Regional Studies* 40(7):727–741.

Hall, J. and R. Kerr. 2003. "Innovation dynamics and environmental technologies: the emergence of fuel cell technology." *Journal of Cleaner Production* 11(4): 459–471.

Hart, D. 2000. "Sustainable energy conversion: Fuel cells - the competitive option?" *Journal of Power Sources* 86:23–27.

Hellman, Hanna L. and Robert van den Hoed. 2007. "Characterising fuel cell technology: Challenges of the commercialisation process." *International Journal of Hydrogen Energy* 32(3): 305–315.

Hekkert, Marko P., R. A. A. Suurs, Hans van Lente, & Kuhlmann, S. 2007. "Functions of innovation systems: A new approach for analysing technological change." *Technological Forecasting & Social Change* 74(4):413–432.

Hobday, Mike. 1994. "Technological learning in Singapore: A test case of leapfrogging." *Journal of Development Studies* 30(3):831–858.

Jacobsson, Staffan. 2002. Universities and industrial transformation: an interpretative and selective literature study with special emphasis on Sweden. *Science and Public Policy* 29(5):345 365.

Jacobsson, Staffan and Anna Bergek. 2004. "Transforming the energy sector: the evolution of technological systems in renewable energy technology." *Industrial and Corporate Change* 13(5):815–849.

Johnson, Anna. 2001. "Functions in Innovation System Approaches." DRUID's Nelson Winter Conference, Aalborg, Denmark. June 2001

Juma, Calestous and Yee-Cheong Lee. 2001. *UN Millennium Project Report: Task Force on Science, Technology and Innovation.* New York: United Nations.

Kemp, Rene, Johan Schot and Remco Hoogma. 1998. "Regime shift to sustainability through process of niche formation: The approach of strategic niche management." *Technological Analysis and Strategic Management* 10(2):175–195.

Kim, Linsu. 1997. *Imitation to innovation: The dynamic of Korea's technological learning.* Boston: Harvard Business School Press.

Larminie, James and Andrew Dicks. 2003. *Fuel cell systems explained.* Second Edition. Chichester: John Wiley & Sons Ltd.

Mansfield, Edwin and Jeong-Yeon Lee 1996. "The modern university: contributor to industrial innovation and recipient of industrial R&D support." *Research Policy* 25(7):1047–1058.

Ministry of Environment and Water Resources. 2007. "About MEWR." [Online] Http://mewr.gov.sg/sgp2012/about.htm [Accessed 25 April 2007]. Last Visited September 30, 2010.

Mohamad, Zeeda F. (2003). *An exploratory study on direct participation in new technologies by developing countries: Lesson to be learned from the development of solar photovoltaics technology in the United Kingdom.* Unpublished MSc Thesis, Science and Technology Policy Research (SPRU), University of Sussex, Falmer, UK.

Mohamad, Zeeda F. 2009. *The role of universities in national catching-up strategies: Fuel cell technology in Malaysia and Singapore.* Unpublished PhD Thesis, Brighton: University of Sussex.

Ministry of Science, Technology and Innovation. 2007. "*About Us: Introduction.*" [Online] MOSTI, Malaysia. Available from: http://www.mosti.gov.my [Accessed 31 March 2007]. Last Visited September 30, 2010.

Mowery, David C. and Bhaven N. Sampat. 2005. "Universities in national innovation systems", in Jan Fagerberg, David C. Mowery and Richard R. Nelson, eds., *The Oxford handbook of innovation.* Oxford and New York: Oxford University Press, pp. 209–239.

Mytelka, Lynn Krieger. 2003. "New wave technologies: Their emergence, diffusion and impact. The case of hydrogen fuel cell technology and the developing world." UNU/ INTECH Discussion (Paper DP 2003–3)

Mytelka, Lynn Krieger. 2004. "Catching up in new wave technologies." *Oxford Development Studies* 32 389–405.

Mytelka, Lynn and Grant Boyle. 2006. *Hydrogen fuel cells and transport alternatives: Issues for developing countries. Policy Brief 3.* New York: United Nations University Press.

Mytelka, Lynn and Grant Boyle, eds. 2008. *Making Choices about Hydrogen: Transport Issues for Developing Countries.* New York: United Nations University Press.

Organization for Economic Co-operation and Development (OECD). 2006. *Innovation in Energy Technology: Comparing National Innovation Systems at the Sectoral Level: A Research Report.* Paris: OECD.

Peréz, Carlota. 1988. "New technologies and development," in Christopher Freeman and Bengt-Ake Lundvall, eds., *Small countries facing the technological revolution.* London: Frances Pinter, pp. 85–97.

Pérez, Carlota, and Luc Soete. 1988. "Catching-up in technology: entry barriers and windows of opportunity," in Giovanni Dosi, Christopher Freeman, Richard R. Nelson, Gerald Silverberg and Luc L. Soete, eds., *Technical Change and Economic Theory.* London: Pinter Publishers, pp. 458–479.

Pilkington, Alan. 2004. "Technology portfolio alignment as an indicator of commercialisation: An investigation of fuel cell patenting." *Technovation* 24(10): 761–771.

Pusat Tenaga Malaysia (PTM). 2007. "About Us" [Online] PTM, Malaysia. Available from: http://www.ptm.org.my [Accessed 10 April 2007]. Last Visited September 30, 2010.

Rosenberg, Nathan and Richard R. Nelson. 1994. "American universities and technical advance in industry." *Research Policy* 23(3):323–348.

Rothaermel, Frank T., Shanti D. Agung and Lin Jiang. 2007. "University entrepreneurship: a taxonomy of the literature." *Industrial and Corporate Change* 12(7):921–941.

Schaeffer, Gerrit Jan. 1998. *Fuel Cells for the future: A contribution to technology forecasting from a technology dynamics perspective.* Unpublished PhD Thesis, University of Twente, Netherlands.

Utterback, James M. 1994. *Mastering the dynamics of innovation.* Boston, MA: Harvard Business School Press.

Vernon, Raymond. 1966. "International investment and international trade in product life cycle". *The Quarterly Journal of Economics* 80:190–207.

Wong, Poh-Kam. 2007. "Towards an entrepreneurial university model to support knowledge-based economic development: The case of the National University of Singapore." *World Development* 17(7–8): 523–527.

INDEX